EVERYDAY JUSTICE IN MYANMAR

NIAS–Nordic Institute of Asian Studies
NIAS Studies in Asian Topics

58 Reinventing Social Democratic Development: Insights from Indian and Scandinavian Comparisons ✤ *Olle Törnquist and John Harriss (eds)*

59 Fieldwork in Timor-Leste: Understanding Social Change through Practice ✤ *Maj Nygaard-Christensen and Angie Bexley (eds)*

60 Debating the East Asian Peace: What it is. How it came about. Will it last? ✤ *Elin Bjarnegård and Joakim Kreutz (eds)*

61 Khaki Capital: The Political Economy of the Military in Southeast Asia ✤ *Paul Chambers and Napisa Waitoolkiat (eds)*

62 Warring Societies of Pre-colonial Southeast Asia: Local Cultures of Conflict Within a Regional Context ✤ *Michael W. Charney and Kathryn Wellen (eds)*

63 Breast Cancer Meanings: Journeys Across Asia ✤ *Cynthia Chou and Miriam Koktvedgaard Zeitzen (eds)*

64 Empire and Environment in the Making of Manchuria ✤ *Norman Smith (ed.)*

65 Mythbusting Vietnam: Facts, Fictions, Fantasies ✤ *Catherine Earl (ed.)*

66 Departing from Java: Javanese Labour, Migration and Diaspora ✤ *Rosemarijn Hoefte and Peter Meel (eds)*

67 Engaging Asia: Essays on Laos and Beyond in Honour of Martin Stuart-Fox ✤ *Desley Goldston (ed.)*

68 Performing the Arts of Indonesia: Malay Identity and Politics in the Music, Dance and Theatre of the Riau Islands ✤ *Margaret Kartomi (ed.)*

69 Hearing Southeast Asia: Sounds of Hierarchy and Power in Context ✤ *Nathan Porath (ed.)*

70 Asia Through Nordic Eyes: Fifty Years of Nordic Scholarship on Asia ✤ *Geir Helgesen and Gerald Jackson (eds)*

71 Everyday Justice in Myanmar: Informal Resolutions and State Evasion in a Time of Contested Transition ✤ *Helene Maria Kyed (ed.)*

72 States and Societies in Motion: Essays in Honour of Takashi Shiraishi ✤ *Khoo Boo Teik and Jafar Suryomenggolo (eds)*

NIAS Press is the autonomous publishing arm of NIAS – Nordic Institute of Asian Studies, a research institute located at the University of Copenhagen. NIAS is partially funded by the governments of Denmark, Finland, Iceland, Norway and Sweden via the Nordic Council of Ministers, and works to encourage and support Asian studies in the Nordic countries. In so doing, NIAS has been publishing books since 1969, with more than two hundred titles produced in the past few years.

UNIVERSITY OF COPENHAGEN

norden
NORDIC COUNCIL OF MINISTERS

EVERYDAY JUSTICE IN MYANMAR

Informal Resolutions and State Evasion in a Time of Contested Transition

edited by
Helene Maria Kyed

NIAS PRESS

Everyday Justice in Myanmar
Informal Resolutions and State Evasion
in a Time of Contested Transition
Edited by Helene Maria Kyed

Nordic Institute of Asian Studies
Studies in Asian Topics, no. 71

First published in 2020 by NIAS Press
NIAS – Nordic Institute of Asian Studies
Øster Farimagsgade 5, 1353 Copenhagen K, Denmark
Tel: +45 3532 9501 • Fax: +45 3532 9549
E-mail: books@nias.ku.dk • Online: www.niaspress.dk

A CIP catalogue record for this book is available from the British Library

ISBN: 978-87-7694-281-6 (hbk)

Typeset in Minion Pro 11/14
Typesetting by Donald B. Wagner
Cover design by by NIAS Press

Cover illustration: Detail from a painting by Eikaza Cho. Reproduced with the kind permission of the Pansodan Gallery, Yangon.

Printed and bound in the United States
by Maple Press, York, PA

Contents

Figures

Foreword

Myanmar is undergoing an exciting, but also an unpredictable, time of transition to democracy. Many challenges to justice remain an everyday concern for a large proportion of the people in the country, not least the poor and those belonging to the many minorities. Myanmar is a multi-ethnic country, where a plethora of groups practise their own culture, traditions and customs and where different religions co-exist and intersect – Buddhism, Christianity, Hinduism, Islam, Animism and others. This book takes stock of this diversity by exploring the multitude of ways in which people seek and think about justice. The empirically rich studies that the book contains have been driven by an openness and a deep engagement which aims to understand local people's own perspectives on challenges to justice and how they would like to see these addressed. A major finding is that Myanmar is a country with a high degree of legal pluralism. At the same time, the majority of people in the country would prefer to have disputes and crimes which affect them settled as locally as possible. This raises important questions about the functioning of local justice systems and the role of the state.

This book is the result of five years of intensive and fruitful research collaboration between Myanmar and Danish researchers. It was in 2013 that Mikael Gravers from Aarhus University first came to our Anthropology Department at the University of Yangon and asked me if we would be interested in doing collaborative research on everyday justice and security in Myanmar. At that time the university was just beginning to open for international collaboration. We eagerly agreed and this led to our first project with Danish researchers, who were from the Danish Institute for International Studies and from Aarhus University. The project also led us into collaboration with the research NGO Enlightened Myanmar Research Foundation (EMReF), which has strengthened our outreach and exchanges with researchers within Myanmar. Our research has always been based on in-depth anthropological studies at the most local level, carried out in many different places in Myanmar. Individually and in teams we have conducted fieldwork in Karen and mixed wards in Yangon city and in villages and towns in Kayin/Karen State, Mon State, Kachin State and in the self-administered zones of the Naga, the Pa-O and the Danu. Among us we have researchers with different backgrounds and belonging to different ethnic groups: Burmese, Shan, Naga, Mon, Karen and Danish. Many but not all of our studies are included in this book. Other publications are on the way, and some have already been published in the Independent Journal of Burmese Scholarship. Our project has also benefited students and teachers more broadly at the Department of Anthropology, University of Yangon: we have shared our academic knowledge and provided teaching in methodology and theory, and the project has also sponsored a library containing both some of the newest and some of the most classical works of anthropology. At international conferences we have shared our findings, including in Japan, the UK, the USA, Australia and in Denmark. It is our hope that our joint research efforts and outcomes will contribute meaningful and new knowledge on everyday justice practices that will be of importance for the development of democracy in Myanmar within the wider globalised world.

Professor Mya Mya Khin, Head of Department
of Anthropology, University of Yangon

Acknowledgements

This book is the result of a little more than five years of intensive research collaboration between Myanmar and Danish researchers – from the Anthropology Department of the University of Yangon, the Enlightened Myanmar Research Foundation (EMReF), the Danish Institute for International Studies (DIIS) and Aarhus University. We came together around 'Everjust', the short name for the 'Everyday Justice and Security in the Myanmar Transition' project, which began in early 2015 and which is set to end in March 2021. Our joint research has been driven by a shared passion and commitment to better understanding and communicating the justice needs, practices and perceptions of ordinary people in Myanmar during a time of challenging political transition. Together we developed our research questions and analytical framework; and together we conducted ethnographic fieldwork across different regions of Myanmar. It has been a fruitful and compassionate journey that will produce long-lasting friendships and professional interchanges within the Everjust 'family'.

Along the way we have benefited from the support and assistance of many people, without which this book would not have been published. Our biggest debt of gratitude goes to all the many residents of our fieldwork sites who were willing to share their stories and concerns with us. This book is dedicated to them. Although we will never be able to repay them fully, it is our hope that communication of our research findings will provide insights and raise questions that may be able, in the long run, to help improve their access to justice and security. At the very least we hope to have given them a voice within current debates about justice in Myanmar. We are also grateful to all the local authority representatives who had enough trust in us to give us access, for our fieldwork, to villages and wards that often had no prior experience with researchers. Our gratitude also goes to all those people working for NGOs and ethnic minority organisations who helped us during fieldwork in Mon, Karen, Naga, Pa-O and Danu areas and in Yangon.

The project is also deeply indebted to Professor Ardeth Thawnghmung, who has been a great source of support throughout our work. She connected our institutions at the very beginning, and has given us regular feedback, constructive criticism and encouragement during our field research and the preparation of publications. Mikael Gravers, who led the Everjust research at Aarhus University and who has been involved in work in Myanmar for several decades, also deserves a special acknowledgment. His in-depth knowledge and dedication have been invaluable.

In Myanmar the Anthropology Department of the University of Yangon and the EMReF have provided the necessary homes for EverJust. It took several months and quite a bit of persistence to arrange an MoU with the University of Yangon, the first ever between Danish and Myanmar research institutions. Had it not been for the dedication to the project of Professor Mya Mya Khin (the head of the Anthropology Department), this would have been impossible. We also extend our sincere gratitude to the then Rector of the University of Yangon, Professor U Pho Kaung, who facilitated the MoU.

At the beginning of the project the EMReF was a young research NGO with an incredible team of researchers, vibrant and dedicated, led by its founders, Myat The Thitsar and Myat Thet Thitsar. Their commitment, courage and willingness to move into a new area of research around issues of justice and security has been absolutely invaluable for the project and has contributed to an excellent level of academic research outside the university sector as well as within it. A special thank you is due to Thi Thi Win from EMReF, who diligently managed all the finances together with Lai Yin Myint, and we are also thankful to Kyaw So Win, who helped with travel arrangements and other logistical matters.

A number of translators, interns and research assistants helped us along the way in the different field sites and we wish to extend our gratitude to them – to Saw Hay Htoo, Saw Eh Htoo, Naw San San Myint, Ma Khine War Tun, Saw Say Wah, Saw Eh Dah, Nan Myint Myint Kyi, Khain Zar Lin, Saw Lay Kapaw, Saw Htoo Wha Paung Paung, Aye Mon, Nyan Tun Aung, Ko SP, Khun Win Naing, Khine Mar Oo, La Min Tun, Nay Yee, Mehm Myo Htet Oo, Mi San San Htwe, and Myint Myat Thu.

At the Danish Institute for International Studies (DIIS) in Copenhagen the project benefited from the support of Annette Holm, who diligently managed our budgets and accounts, and from Lars Kristian Mathiesen, the head of the library at DIIS, whose team assisted with literature. Nellie Vase and Olivia Hammershøy, our student assistants in the Peace and Violence Research Unit at DIIS, also deserve special thanks for assisting in setting up the chapters, looking over the references and checking for errors in the book manuscript. Last but not least, DIIS senior researcher Louise Riis Andersen (DIIS) lent her critical editorial eye to a number of the chapters in this book and raised important and constructive questions that helped us to analyze our material beyond the local context in which we have been working.

Throughout the project we have also benefited from constructive dialogue with numerous other researchers who are not members of our research project, but whom we consider our 'EverJust friends'. We especially wish to extend our gratitude, in no particular order of importance, to: James C. Scott, Justine Chambers, Gerard McCarthy, Ashley South, Michael Lidauer, Mark Duffield, Matthew Walton, Judith Beyer, Morten Pedersen, Susanne Kempel, Nick Cheesman, Chosein Yamahata, Melissa Crouch and not least Kirsten McConnachie and Elizabeth Rhoads, who contributed chapters to this book. We have been fortunate to have Anders Baltzer Jørgensen on our team as an affiliated researcher and contributor to this volume. We are also very grateful to Mike Griffin, who has supported the project through his teaching of academic writing skills at the University of Yangon.

We have benefited from regular dialogue with various consultants, NGO and INGO workers who have been deeply involved in matters related to justice, security, and governance in Myanmar. Many people might be mentioned in this regard, but we want to extend our special gratitude to Caitlin Rieger who, first in her role as justice advisor in the UNDP and later as head of the British Council's MyJustice project funded by the EU, supported our project right from the beginning and has helped push the policy agenda forward in relation to informal justice in Myanmar. Her team at MyJustice have always been a valuable support, and we have held workshops with them in which we shared our research findings on community-based justice with NGOs, government justice actors, ethnic organisations and international experts. We are likewise grateful for our collaboration with Saferworld Myanmar, and in particular for our exchanges with Kim Tate Wistreich and John Bainbridge there.

The publication of this book would not have been possible had it not been for NIAS Press, and we particularly want to extend our gratitude to its chief editor Gerald Jackson. We are also grateful to the two anonymous reviewers, who gave us feedback that was both useful and kind and to Monica Janowski who did the copy-editing.

Finally, we would like to acknowledge the generous funding of the Everjust project from the research development fund of the Danish Ministry of Foreign Affairs and to extend our gratitude for the support we received from the Royal Danish Embassy in Myanmar, its late Ambassador Peter Lysholt Hansen and his successor Ambassador John Nielsen.

Helene Maria Kyed,
May 2020

Contributors

Mikael Gravers is Associate Professor Emeritus in Anthropology at Aarhus University, Denmark. He has undertaken fieldwork in Thailand and Burma since 1970, doing research among Buddhist and Christian Karen, in Buddhist monasteries, and in Hindu and Muslim communities. Mikael is the author of *Nationalism as Political Paranoia* (1999) and editor of *Exploring Ethnic Diversity in Burma* (2007). In 2014, he co-edited *Burma/Myanmar – Where Now* (with Flemming Ytzen). He has published on ethnicity, nationalism, Buddhism and politics, as well as on nature, culture and environmental protection. He has conducted research related to Burma in the colonial archives, in the British Library and at the Public Record Office, London. Before retirement, Mikael was involved in organising an international Masters degree in Human Security at Aarhus University and he lectured on this subject until 2019.

Annika Pohl Harrisson has a PhD from the Department of Anthropology at Aarhus University. She has conducted ethnographic research in Thailand and Myanmar. Annika is particularly interested in the localised production of legitimacy, everyday justice provision, and state-society relations. Her doctoral research investigates how different forms of state-making in southeast Myanmar affect the way in which sociality and subjectivities are constituted in everyday life. Her publications include (with Helene Maria Kyed) 'Ceasefire state-making and justice provision by ethnic armed groups in southeast Myanmar' (published in *Sojourn* 2019) and 'Fish caught in clear water: Encompassed state-making in southeast Myanmar' (published in *Territory, Politics, Governance* 2020).

Lue Htar is currently a research manager at the Enlightened Myanmar Research Foundation (EMReF), an independent research organisation in Myanmar. She has a bachelor's degree in economics from the University of East Yangon but has over the past years worked within the area of qualitative anthropological research. Lue Htar has done extensive field research across different regions of Myanmar in relation to the provision of justice, issues related to land, socio-economic issues and rural development. Since 2015, she has participated as one of the main researchers in the EverJust project. Her publications include 'Everyday justice and plural authorities: Insights from Karen State about land disputes' (in *Independent Journal of Burmese Scholarship*) and 'What Naga people should be aware about their customary practices' (in *Naga the Pang Magazine*).

Anders Baltzer Jørgensen has a degree in Anthropology from the University of Copenhagen. He conducted fieldwork among Pwo Karen in Thailand and Burma in the 1970s, and since then has visited the Karen communities in Thailand frequently. From 1980 onwards, he was senior and then chief advisor in the Ministry of Foreign Affairs, Denmark, responsible for development issues. He has formulated projects, and advised and undertaken assignments, in a wide range of Asian and African countries, resulting in a large number of internal reports (Formulations, Appraisals, Reviews, and Evaluations). He retired from the Ministry in 2014 but continues to publish papers on Pwo Karen history and natural resource management. Anders participated as an associate researcher in the EverJust project.

Helene Maria Kyed is Senior Researcher at the Danish Institute for International Studies and heads the Peace and Violence research unit there. She is trained as a social anthropologist and has a PhD in International Development Studies from Roskilde University. Helene coordinates the EverJust research project in Myanmar (2015–2021). She has done extensive research on policing, informal justice and state formation in Southern Africa and Myanmar, focusing on rural as well as urban settings. Her most recent book is *Policing and the Politics of Order-Making* (2015), and she co-edited the special issue on 'Justice in Myanmar' published by the *Independent Journal of Burmese Scholarship*.

Kirsten McConnachie is Associate Professor in Law at the University of East Anglia, UK. She is a socio-legal researcher with extensive research expertise in refugee studies, particularly on refugee-led governance systems. Her research has included extended fieldwork among Karen refugees living in camps in Thailand and among Chin urban refugees in Malaysia and India. Her books include *Governing Refugees* (2014) and the *Routledge Handbook of Socio-Legal Theory and Method* (2019), the latter co-edited with Naomi Creutzfeldt and Marc Mason. She is a member of the editorial board of the *Journal of Human Rights Practice* and the *International Journal of Refugee Law* and a series editor for Berghahn Books' series on forced migration.

Lwin Lwin Mon is Professor in the Department of Anthropology, University of Yangon. She has a PhD degree in Anthropology (2012) and MA and MRes degrees in Archeology from the University of Yangon. In 2013, she was an ALFP research fellow in Japan, and in 2015 she was a CEU research fellow in Hungary. Lwin Lwin Mon has been one of the main researchers in the EverJust research project. She has published research on socio-cultural and political anthropology in international academic journals and collected volumes. Her most recent publication is 'Legal hybridity in everyday justice provision in a Mon village' (in the *Independent Journal of Burmese Scholarship*).

Than Pale is Professor in the Department of Anthropology, University of Yangon, where she obtained her PhD degree. She has conducted ethnographic research on socio-economic aspects of different ethnic groups in Myanmar and has published various works with Yangon University Press in 1999, 2000 and 2004. In 2017, she carried out research on the healthcare practices of the Yin Baw ethnic group in Kayah State, using a medical anthropological perspective. She is currently a researcher with the Everjust project, focusing particularly on Hlaing Htayar Township in Yangon and Hpa-An district in Karen State (2015–2019). In addition, she is doing research on 'Human rights for migrant Burmese fish-workers' (2020–2021). Her most recent publication is 'Justice-seeking strategies in everyday life: Case study among urban migrants in Yangon' (in the *Independent Journal of Burmese Scholarship*).

Mi Thang Sorn Poine has a BA degree in Geography (2014) from Mawlamyine University. She worked for four years at the Mon Women's Organisation and has done research on perceptions of women's participation in politics in Mon State. She was also involved as a researcher in the Salween River Basin Network on ecological and social impacts. Since 2016 she has worked at the EMReF as senior research officer and as a member of the EverJust research group. She has published'The Gendered aspects of access to justice in Southern Mon State' (in the *Independent Journal of Burmese Scholarship*).

Elizabeth Rhoads has a PhD in Law from King's College, London. Her work focuses on the legal and social history of citizenship and property relations in urban Myanmar. She has published on nationalisation and forced evictions in Myanmar and is interested in issues of land and property, law and social marginalisation. Elizabeth is currently completing a Blakemore Fellowship in Advanced Burmese and is a Post-Doctoral Fellow at University College London, working on the British Academy-funded project 'Framing living heritage as a tool to prevent spatial violence' with The Bartlett Development Planning Unit.

Marie Knakkergaard Richthammer is an Associate Political Affairs Officer In the Southeast ASEA and the Pacific Division, department of political and peacebuilding affairs (to the Special Envoy of the Secretary-General on Myanmar) at United Nations Headquarters, New York. She has done fieldwork on repatriation in the Thailand/Myanmar borderlands and was part of the Everjust project during her masters' studies, when she did research in Karen State, on access to justice and security, particularly for women.

Myat The Thitsar is the co-founder and the Strategic Advisor of the Enlightened Myanmar Research Foundation (EMReF), a non-profit research organisation. She holds degrees from California State University and Yadanabon University, Mandalay. She is currently doing a PhD in the Global Studies Program at the University of Massachusetts Lowell. Myat The Thitsar started carrying out social research in 2008, when she returned to Myanmar, and she co-founded EMReF in 2011. Currently, she is leading the Parliamentary Research and Support Program (PRSP). She is involved as a lead researcher in various projects on governance, political economy analyses, customary justice and legal pluralism, and identity and conflict related studies. She is the lead researcher and author of the Performance Analysis on State and Region Parliaments of Myanmar.

Nan Tinilar Win is a freelance researcher and part-time Senior Researcher at EMReF. She has a BSc (Mathematics) from Hpa-An University, Karen State (2005). She began to do social research across Myanmar in 2014, including a study of 'Migration and security challenges in Yangon's informal settlements' (2017), and research as part of the EverJust project in the Pa'O Self-Administered Zone and in Karen State.

Map 1 Map of Myanmar..

Introduction: Everyday justice in a contested transition

Helene Maria Kyed

> Rebuilding and reforming the rule of law and justice sector is a top priority for Myanmar. It is also vital for our efforts towards sustaining peace and development (...) It is my observation that at the community level, the majority of people continue to use long-standing local methods for solving disputes and are reluctant to take cases to the formal or official justice system of the state (...) The public trust in people who are working in the Justice Sector has eroded. It is because of corruption, exercising the law for their own interests, [and] failing the principle of upholding justice without favour (Daw Aung San Suu Kyi, Naypyitaw, 7 March 2018).

Myanmar's *de facto* leader, Daw Aung San Suu Kyi, spoke these words at a conference on 'Justice Sector Coordination for the Rule of Law' almost two years after she and the National League for Democracy (NLD) won a landslide victory in the country's first democratic elections in six decades. The need for fundamental reforms of the ways in which justice is dispensed in Myanmar is evident. Aung San Sui Kyi's civilian government inherited a flawed justice system, which since the inception of military rule in 1962 had been more concerned with extending a centralised vision of law and order than with providing equal and impartial justice (Cheesman 2015; Crouch 2014). Widespread corruption and inefficiency, and a concern for regime preservation rather than individual rights, still haunt the official justice system, the courts and the police. Lack of state-provided justice remains a core concern. The continuing armed conflict and large-scale military campaigns against ethnic minorities, especially in Rakhine, Northern Shan, and Kachin States, are headline reminders that the transition from military junta to democracy is fragile and contested (Chambers and McCarthy 2018: 3). The serious injustices of the past are still not being dealt with, and there has been little attempt to compensate victims and acknowledge their suffering; and everyday exclusion and discrimination, often based on ethnic and religious identity, continue to be at the heart of the transition (South and Lall 2018; Chambers and McCarthy 2018: 15).

In this wider context, the ordinary people of Myanmar are trying to avoid the official state system and are seeking other avenues to obtain justice in the everyday, as Daw Aung San Suu Kyi notes in the speech quoted above. These other avenues do, as she says, include 'long-standing local methods for solving disputes' (see quote above) that are culturally and religiously informed, but they also include innovative, evolving and creative ways of dealing with matters of justice, ways that are outside the state system (Kyed 2018a).

This book tackles the vexed question of how these 'local methods' – better captured using the term 'everyday justice' – play out in the current transitional context of Myanmar. Based on ethnographies in different localities, each of the book's contributions takes the perspective of ordinary people and asks how people deal with disputes and crimes; whom they turn to for resolutions; and what the various ways are in which they perceive (in)justice. These empirical questions serve as a lens through which to analyse the dynamics of state-making, the role of identity politics and the constitution of order and authority in present day Myanmar.

The concept of the 'everyday' is not only appropriate as a way of indicating that our focus is on ordinary, typical, 'small' justice issues – as opposed to extra-ordinary, exceptional, 'big' justice issues such as mass atrocities, structural discrimination, and human rights violations. It also conveys a particular mode of thinking about social life and politics that moves beyond macro structures, elite politics and abstract processes, by acknowledging the agency of ordinary people and the interaction of a multiplicity of practices, relations, and meanings (Guillaume and Huysmans 2018). In the context of Myanmar, this means foregrounding the experiences of previously 'ignored actors' (Ibid. 688): people on the margins of the state, minorities, women and the economically deprived. It also means understanding how these people's very localised ways of dealing with disputes and crimes interact with and reflect the wider context and the 'big issues' that haunt the political environment in the country. While this book does not deal directly with the question of how to pursue transitional justice nor with how to reform national judicial institutions, its contributions serve as an avenue through which to grasp and address bigger issues relating to justice in a way that is grounded in ordinary people's experiences and everyday practices.

In line with the focus on the everyday, the book adopts a legal pluralistic approach (Merry 1988; Griffiths 1986; von Benda-Beckmann 1997) that acknowledges the possible coexistence of different forms of social ordering, meanings of justice, and interpretations of the causes of disputes, victimhood and suffering. This approach is open to various culturally specific meanings of justice that are not necessarily in accordance with state-legal norms or international human rights, but which may follow local, customary, religious and/or other perceptions of just, adequate and sufficient resolutions to disputes and crimes (Kyed 2018a: ii). It also enables the analytical inclusion of actors who are not officially part of the state legal system in the category of 'justice provider' or 'dispute resolver'. In this book we take this category to include not only judges, police and court officials but also religious leaders, customary authorities, and armed actors. Finally, an everyday and pluralistic perspective allows insights into a variety of individual and collective strategies for seeking justice, including the use of brokers or facilitators.

The contributions to this volume illustrate the existence of legal pluralism in Myanmar across both urban and rural contexts: from the cities of Yangon and Mawlamyine to the Naga hills, the Pa-O Self-Administered Zone, Thai refugee camps and villages in Karen and Mon States. In all of these sites, the official state system is only one among many avenues for seeking resolution in criminal and civil cases. More often than not, the main actors consulted in everyday justice are village elders, local administrators, religious leaders, spiritual actors and/or the justice systems or individual members of ethnic armed organisations. The contributions to this volume explore *how* these actors address disputes and crimes, and *why* people turn to them (rather than the state), based both on the *emic* opinions of people themselves and on our *etic* analysis, which draws on history, political context, and comparative theoretical literature (Morris et al. 1999).[1]

1 As discussed by Morris et al. (1999: 781–2), *emic* refers to the insider perspective, or what in anthropology has been defined as the 'native's point of view' (Malinowski 1922) in understandings of, for instance, culture and justice; whereas the *etic* is the perspective of the outsider or observer, taking into account antecedent factors such as economic, historical and political conditions that may not be salient to the cultural insider.

The volume does not pursue a systematic comparative analysis, but provides in-depth empirical insights that juxtapose differences and similarities across local field sites, based on the interrogation of a set of shared questions. This illuminates local contextual variety in the composition of justice actors, customs, identities and socio-political relations, but it has also allowed us to come up with insights into four important themes that are shared across all of the sites covered: a strong preference for *local and informal resolutions*; an omnipresence of *state evasion* in justice-seeking practices; the prevalent influence of *religious beliefs and cultural norms* in how people understand (in)justice; and the significant role played by *identity politics* both in including and excluding people from access to justice and in shaping local justice preferences.

To situate these findings in the wider literature on legal pluralism and justice reform in general, and the Myanmar transition in particular, this introductory chapter firstly outlines the main debates, concepts and methodology with which the book engages before going more into detail in relation to the four themes shared across the different field sites mentioned above. Finally, it provides an outline of the chapters and a brief discussion of the limitations of this volume and the need for further studies.

The debate and concept of legal pluralism

This book inserts itself into the debate about *legal pluralism* and the recognition of customary, informal, or non-state systems that now cuts across academia, policy circles, and development practitioners. Since the 1960s, the concept of legal pluralism has been used by anthropologists and socio-legal scholars as an analytical concept to describe situations where there is a plurality of legal orders within the same social field (Merry 1988: 870; Griffiths 1986: 2). It has been applied in a range of studies, spanning the interactions between indigenous and European law during colonialism and newer studies of the dialectic of different normative orders within industrialised societies and post-colonial settings (Merry 1988). As is evident in the work of John Griffiths (1986), the scholarly understanding of legal pluralism as an 'empirical state of affairs' implies a critique of the state as *the* singular and essentially given foundation of 'law' and unit of political organisation. Griffiths (1986: 2–4) defined this singularity of state law as 'state legal centralism', which he saw as an ideological project aimed at subordinating all other legal orders, whether defined as customary, informal or indigenous, under the sovereign command of the state (see also Merry 1988: 870). State legal centralism, Griffiths argued, inhibits us from considering alternative, non-state forms of ordering as legal phenomena and types of law equal to state law (ibid.: 3). What Griffiths called the 'strong' or 'descriptive' legal pluralistic approach, by contrast, allows for the inclusion of norms, meanings, and practices of ordering and justice that can differ from state-legal criteria; and it does not presume a predefined hierarchy of legal orders.

The contributors to the book use this strong legal pluralistic perspective as their analytical foundation. At the same time, they acknowledge the political stakes and dilemmas that are inherent in legal pluralism within transitional and conflict-affected societies like Myanmar, which, since the late 1990s have also permeated international debates among policymakers and practitioners of justice sector reform. Paralleling the United Nation's recognition of the rights of indigenous peoples (UN 2008), international agencies such as the World Bank, USAID, UNDP and DFID have increasingly adopted a more legal pluralistic perspective, seeking ways to incorporate 'non-state', 'informal' and 'customary' actors into programmes aimed at improving access to justice for poor and marginalised people, especially in so-called 'fragile states' (Andersen et al. 2007; see also DFID 2004).[2] This marks a shift from what used to be an exclusive focus on formal state institutions and on top-down state-building in donor policies, reflecting what Griffiths (1986) calls state legal centralism. The main reason for the shift has been the poor success rate in reforming official state institutions and a realisation that the 'non-state', 'customary' or 'informal' systems were often the most accessible, legitimate, and effective justice providers in the eyes of ordinary people (Kyed 2011: 5–7; Harper 2011; Isser 2011; Baker 2011). International agencies – and indeed some states in the Global South – have come a long way in accepting the reality of legal pluralism, but important political dilemmas continue to permeate the field.

One core dilemma is the often-perceived opposition between informal or customary practices and international human rights and rule of

2 For a detailed and critical discussion of the application of legal pluralism by international development agencies, see Kyed (2011) and Albrecht et al. (2011).

law principles. The former are often valued for their local accessibility, flexibility and capacity for mediation, but are criticised for failing to adhere to the principles of equality before the law (especially with regard to gender, due process, legal certainty and predictability; see Kyed 2011: 7). Another core dilemma is the tension between recognising a plurality of justice systems within the territory of the nation state and international adherence to the state as *the* superior form of political organisation. The strength of this idea of the state, as Bruce Baker (2011) has pointed out, makes it difficult for international agencies to accept a plural system where non-state systems are equal to, rather than subordinated to, state law and authority. Politics are involved here, because justice systems are not politically neutral but are embedded in particular socio-political structures (Tamanaha 2008: 400). Recognition of legal pluralism can therefore be seen by existing states as a challenge to their sovereignty, and thus to their claim to superior authority vis-à-vis non-state claimants (Kyed 2009: 115).

In state and donor policies these dilemmas have mainly been tackled by compromising existing forms of pluralism, through interventions that try to 'fix' or 'harmonise' customary/informal practices so that they fit better with state-legalistic definitions of law and justice (Isser 2011: 342–343; Harper 2011: 41–51; Albrecht et al. 2011; see also Chapter 10, this volume). The actual incorporation of non-state legal orders into justice sector reforms has frequently either been treated as a 'transitional strategy towards' pursuing conventional state-building (Isser 2011: 325; Kyed 2011: 6) or has been used by states as a means of subordinating and regulating non-state legal orders (Kyed 2009). Very few policies recognise the plethora of actual non-state practices and actors on their own terms or regard these as being on par with the state. There is also often a failure to acknowledge that local understandings of justice may not adhere to international state-legal definitions but may be multiple and diverse (ICHRP 2009: 93). As Kirsten McConnachie (Chapter 10, this volume) shows, international interventions (in the case she discusses, refugee camps) that seek to 'fix' and 'harmonise' local systems, while well-intentioned, can end up undermining what local residents view as legitimate justice provision. An alternative approach is to employ an open-ended and non-state centric perspective on legal pluralism in the 'strong' sense, as Griffiths

(1986) argues. This is exactly what this book does, in its analysis of everyday justice in Myanmar.

Moving towards legal pluralism in Myanmar

While some donor agencies and government officials acknowledge that justice provision in Myanmar is not solely a state affair, existing laws, policies and most justice sector programming do not support a recognition of legal pluralism (Kyed and Thawnghmung 2019). State-legal centralism prevails strongly, at least officially. The judicial system of the state is legally the only official court system in present-day Myanmar: it holds a monopoly on the mandate to adjudicate civil and criminal cases (Kyed 2018a; Kyed 2018b; Denney et. al. 2016; MyJustice 2018; Saferworld 2019). Even the officially recognised customary law, which applies to family law matters only – based on the four main religions (Buddhism, Islam, Hinduism and Christianity) and codified during colonial rule – can only be applied by the official courts (Crouch 2016: 62–92). The customary rules practiced within the many ethnic groups, and locally codified by some (such as the Naga), remain unrecognised by the state. Legally speaking, they are outlawed, although the application of such rules may be tolerated in practice, as they were during colonial rule. The same applies to the parallel justice systems and laws that have been developed by some of the ethnic armed organisations (EAOs), as documented by McCarthy & Joliffe (2016) (see also Kyed 2018b; Harrisson and Kyed 2019; Kyed and Thitsar 2018). In practice, these systems challenge the monopoly of the central state to define what law and justice are, and they also claim to be able to resolve disputes and crimes that are officially within the mandate of the state. It is very likely that they are not legalised for this precise reason.

State recognition of ethnic minority systems is a deeply political and contested issue in Myanmar, not least given the many years of conflict, ethnic minority struggles for self-determination, and the efforts on the part of the previous military regime to enforce superior rule and to force minorities to submit to majority (Burmese) culture. In this larger picture, what has been particularly silenced and has also remained unrecognised is the plethora of local justice actors, who may not always constitute a 'system' but who are important in everyday justice in local settings.

To analyse legal pluralism in Myanmar from the emic, insider and everyday perspective, the contributors to this book apply open-ended, rather than universalist, definitions of justice and justice provision. This approach allows us to include in the category of justice provider actors and forums other than those who hold the official title of justice provider (such as court judges). It also means that we do not take it for granted that people everywhere understand disputes and crimes in the same way or that justice conveys the same meaning to everyone. What may be regarded as a crime in one context, punishable by a given law or set of rules, may not be regarded as a crime in another context. Similarly, while a sense of justice to some may be associated with the punishment of a perpetrator of a crime, to others material compensation or reconciliation may be understood as appropriate justice. Based on this acknowledgement of pluralism, justice provision is used here as an umbrella term to describe the resolution of disputes and crimes that involves deliberate efforts to provide a remedy, a reparation, a punishment and/or an end to a conflict between two or more parties, regardless of the outcome of those efforts. Justice provision may be associated with material outcomes and based on secular mechanisms, as is, for example, a third-party decision on reconciliation, but it can also be non-material, as is spiritual, religious and social healing or repair. Across the book, we see various combinations of these forms of justice, influenced by cultural norms, religious beliefs, historical experiences and socio-political conditions.

In studying everyday justice from an emic perspective, the contributors to this volume do not, however, use a normative approach that reifies and romanticises 'the local', 'the customary', or 'the informal'. Rather, the book pays close attention to local power dynamics and to how, at various levels, politics permeates the provision of justice within local arenas and in the relationship between the state system and other legal orders. Following Tamanaha's (2008) approach to legal pluralism, we take the view that justice provision, and social ordering more broadly, are not neutral, apolitical activities. They provide a route to authority – and often an income too – as well as supporting positions of power within the social organisation of a given society (Kyed 2009: 115). Keebet von Benda-Beckmann (1981) has introduced the concept of 'shopping forums' to capture these power dynamics as forms of competition between justice providers in legally plural contexts (see

Poine and Kyed, Chapter 1, this volume and Richthammer, Chapter 4, this volume). Paying attention to power dynamics also means analysing the possible forms of inclusion and exclusion from access to justice, which may be based, for instance, on differences in gender, generation, ethnicity, religion and socio-economic status. Finally, the book pays attention to the politics of justice provision that emerges in the relationship between the state and other forums. In Myanmar, unlike some other contexts (Kyed 2009; Tamanaha 2008), this relationship seldom takes the form of open competition over the making of final decisions in settling individual disputes or crimes. Rather, it is expressed in state evasion or through different forms of identity politics.

Legal pluralism in Myanmar is characterised by deep splits between the state and local justice forums, but this does not mean that we can conceive of these as expressive of two distinct legal orders – the state and the customary. In the contemporary world, as Merry (1988: 872–873) has highlighted, it is difficult to apply the 'classic legal pluralism' perspective, which, with its focus on the effects of imposing colonial law on the colonised, tended to conceive of state and customary systems as inherently distinct and separate. The reality is much more pluralised and hybrid (Albrecht and Moe 2014). In Myanmar, as elsewhere, justice providers often draw on a body of rules and procedures that derive from a mixture of different legal orders from the past and the present. There are many mutual influences and there exist both internal and external dynamics of change and continuity. The chapters in this book try to capture this complexity, based on detailed tracing of cases and analysis of everyday dispute resolution.

The methodology: Ethnography and case studies

A legal pluralistic approach and a focus on the *everyday* calls for a research methodology that covers in-depth empirical studies of justice practices, actors, and perceptions within selected localities. Ethnography enables the kind of 'insider', emic accounts that such a research endeavour requires, but does not preclude a historical and contextual analysis (Hammersley and Atkinson 1995). With its combination of participant observation, semi-structured interviews and informal conversations through longer-term stays or several return visits to a single field site, ethnography offers insights not only into people's (stated) perceptions, as captured in structured interviews and surveys, but also into social actions and practices (Hughes 1992). The methodological focus on practices necessarily has theoretical dimensions, linked to an actor-oriented approach to social structure and social life – which holds that actions and social interactions are not simply reflections of (or deviations from) an innate or fixed social structure, but are part of producing social structure (Holy and Stuchlich 1989: 6). This also implies a view that norms (*what ought to be* or prescriptions for actions) are not necessarily always the same as practice (*what people do*). If a person is asked, for instance, how a theft case is handled in their village, the answer will typically describe a prescribed norm or rule relating to how and by whom thefts are supposed to be handled. This can provide valuable answers about people's perceptions of the ideal way for justice provision to work or what they have been told is supposed to be the norm. However, our research shows that this does not always reflect real life cases: i.e. theft cases are handled in often ambiguous and varied ways, following different routes, in practice. In addition, social actors ascribe different meanings to actions, such as why a case was reported to a certain forum. People also understand central concepts like justice in different ways. Triangulation of data on norms, perceptions and actions allows ethnographers to explore both what (different) people do and why they do it, seen from the perspective of the individual within a specific social setting.

Each of the chapters in this book draws on such ethnographic research, which, in the context of Myanmar's history of military rule and isolation from the outside world, has been very difficult, if not impossible, until very recently. The transition has implied openings for empirical research, allowing both Myanmar and foreign researchers to stay for longer periods of time in a research setting and to access areas that they were previously prohibited from entering by the government. In fact, the contributions to this volume present the very first ethnographies of everyday justice in Myanmar since the beginning of the military regime in 1962.[3] This means that the studies are very exploratory and that they could not draw upon existing post-colonial research on justice or on

3 McConnachie's chapter on justice in the refugee camps (Chapter 10, this volume) was based on ethnographic research prior to and during the very first year of the transition (2008–2012), research which was only possible because the places covered are outside the territorial governance of the Myanmar state.

the localities in which fieldwork was carried out. Thus, the researchers had to rely on the oral accounts by local informants, for instance in getting to know the history of each field site and changes in local justice provision and in social life in general.

The recent history of military government means that access is still difficult in many localities, not only in terms of official permission to conduct fieldwork but also in terms of building the kind of trust and confidence with informants that is necessary to discuss sensitive issues such as disputes, relationships with authorities and so forth in depth. Ethnography, with its focus on long-term stays in one setting and/or several return visits to one or a few selected places, is particularly well-suited to trust-building and to getting people to share their stories, views and dispute cases. Trust-building is particularly important for researchers who are foreigners (from outside of Myanmar) or outsiders (Myanmar researchers of other ethnicities) to the local setting and its inhabitants, which is the case for most of the contributors to this volume.[4] As Than Pale, a Shan Buddhist, notes in her chapter, it took her several return visits to the mixed Buddhist–Muslim village in which she carried out her fieldwork to get Muslim women to speak to her, and achieving this has been essential to her ability to analyse the relationship between Buddhists and Muslims in local dispute resolution.

However, ethnography does not remove the challenges of translation, cultural and linguistic, and of the positionality of the researchers as 'outsiders' who will always, necessarily, interpret their data in ways that can never be completely aligned with the 'insider' view (Hammersley and Atkinson 1995: 93–102). To take these challenges into consideration requires ethnographic reflexivity and attention to local language, especially in relation to the meanings of core notions like *justice*, which are culturally loaded and based on different experiences. In the chapters in this book, the authors try as much as possible to include the meanings of those local words that are most significant to their topic of analysis, in order to reduce the risk of losing their local meanings with translation into English. In the field, this has been facilitated by working with assistants and translators who are familiar with or from

4 Exceptions include Thang Sorn Poine, who is from the Mon village studied in Chapter 1; and Lue Htar, who is a Goga Naga, the group studied in Chapter 3, which she has co-written.

the local context and by actively discussing the meanings of local words with key informants.

Ethnography, being essentially qualitative, captures the complexities of social contexts with less focus on the generalizable and the comparative. The chapters in this book are built on qualitative case studies in one or two localities (for example, a village or a ward), and most of them analyse everyday justice through the presentation of one or a few selected case examples of disputes, injustices or crimes. The focus is on depth rather than breadth. This has the advantage of teasing out the ambiguities, inconsistencies and complexities that exist even within a single village and a single case, but it also means that the book cannot claim to represent and generalise in relation to everyday justice in Myanmar as a whole, or even within one ethnic group or within one state. This book is therefore not a book of systematic comparison. Instead, the authors use the case-study method to identify attitudes and patterns of behaviour relating to everyday justice seeking practices and perceptions within the case-study field sites while also maintaining a focus on inconsistencies and variation in everyday practices (Flyvbjerg 2006). In addition, the case studies answer both 'how' and 'why' questions by relating a case to its wider contextual conditions and by triangulating data sources (Baxter and Jack 2008: 544–545). Through looking at all of the individual cases in this book, we are able to identify important similarities and differences, which can serve as a basis for proposing tentative generalisations that can be tested in future research.

In most of the chapters of this book the case studies aim to cover both of 1) the 'locality' of the fieldwork within which everyday justice is explored, through interviews and observations; and 2) a selected number of real-life disputes and crime cases. Rather than beginning with how already-known justice providers or institutions, such as a village administration, resolve disputes, the primary focus of data collection and analysis is the cases themselves, which relate to disputes and to crimes. This method serves to capture actual practice, based on oral accounts, and, where possible, also the ways in which cases are handled within specific forums.[5] This was achieved, on a practical level, by speaking to as many people as possible who were involved in

5 In the EverJust project we referred to this method as 'case tracing', which means that the researchers followed different cases of disputes or crimes, where possible from beginning to end, and included the accounts of as many persons as possible.

a given case (including disputants, victims, perpetrators and dispute resolvers) or who observed it, asking them in detail about the trajectory of a case (who resolved it, what was the cause of the case, what were the outcomes, which resolution procedures were used). Interviews also served to capture the different norms and perceptions that interviewees ascribed to a case, by asking them to evaluate the process, outcomes and choices made (why was this and not that pathway to a resolution used, was the outcome seen as satisfactory/just, how was the cause of the conflict understood). The distinct advantage of this approach, over one that focuses on particular types of institutions, is that it remains open to a variety of reactions to disputes and crimes as well as to the possible use of justice providers who are not officially recognised as such (Isser et al. 2009: 14).

The case studies in the chapters are used to analyse attitudes and patterns of behaviour relating to everyday justice, through triangulation with data from other cases about which some data was gathered, as well as through triangulation via interviews with justice providers who described the norms and rules for justice provision in the field site in general. In some chapters, typical or more representative cases are used as examples, allowing an analysis of general attitudes and patterns of behaviour; in other chapters the cases selected were atypical or likely to shed light on particularly complex circumstances. Than Pale in Chapter 6, and Poine and Kyed in Chapter 1, for instance, are interested in understanding what happens when crimes cannot – against the norm – be resolved within the village, and thus they use a case that is (atypically) resolved outside of the village.

The selection of cases of crimes/disputes (and the selection of interviewees) does not follow the logic of random sampling and is therefore not statistically representative (Small 2009: 24–25). Instead, cases were selected according to information-oriented sampling (Flyvbjerg 2006), based on sequential interviewing, snowballing, observations and the identification of typical and atypical cases (Small 2009: 28). While this selection method is characteristic of qualitative case studies, it is also suitable for the fieldwork contexts we covered, where there are no available dispute/criminal case registers from which random sampling can be made. Therefore, the cases included in this book are those that the informants, in a given setting, chose to tell the researchers about. Furthermore, the selection of field sites as case-study areas was not based on sampling, but on access options, connections and security concerns. Thus, the chapters can claim neither to be representative of, for instance, (all) Karen villages or (all) urban wards in Mon State; nor can a particular field site be claimed to represent a typical or atypical field site. Instead, the case studies provide in-depth empirical insights into ongoing processes and engage in explaining those processes by analysing them in relation to their own contextual conditions.

In all of the chapters in the book, care is taken not to treat the inhabitants in the field sites as homogenous 'communities' with the same opinions and experiences. Thus, as many voices as possible are included, and it is made clear 'who is speaking when' (according to gender, generation, ethnicity, religion, socio-economic status and so forth). Due to the sensitivity of the research topic, all persons and local place names (villages, wards) are anonymised in all the chapters. Only information on the state, town and/or township is included.

The insights of the book: Shared themes across field sites

Given the ethnographic case-study approach, each of the chapters in this book provides unique insights into everyday justice in particular fieldwork sites. Each focuses on analysis of different sub-topics. These include property disputes and brokers; the role of religion; ethnic exclusion/inclusion; the influence of armed groups; customary law codification; critical affects of the state; forum shopping; and camp justice in the context of international interventions. Cutting across this variety, the book presents significant insights into four themes that are, in different ways and with different weight in different sites, shared across field sites, which come through in all of the chapters.

1. Preference for local, informal resolution

This is the first of the themes. The vast majority of dispute and crime cases never make it to court, but are, if they are ever, indeed, reported to a third party, handled by local actors within the village or neighbourhood. In the field sites covered by the chapters in the book, this applies to cases including theft, physical fights, domestic violence, public disturbances and arson; and to disputes related to marriage, land, property, and debt. Not all such cases are reported to a third-party justice provider, as some are settled within the closest structures of the family, neighbours, or the kinship-group, while others are left unaddressed. This is not simply a rural phenomenon or evident only where the state courts are geographically distant. Even in Yangon city, where the state has a strong presence and seems unavoidable, a considerable number of cases do not go to court but are handled informally by local actors or brokers (*pweza* in Burmese), as Lwin Lwin Mon and Rhoads show (Chapters 5 and 9, this volume). These empirical findings correspond well with people's justice preferences as expressed in qualitative interviews and confirmed by available surveys. A survey conducted by the EverJust research project in 2016 showed that approximately 70 per cent of both male and female respondents in selected urban and rural areas in Yangon, Karen State, and Mon State think that disputes and crimes, irrespective of type and gravity, are best resolved within their local area.[6]

Village and ward leaders are by the far the most significant local justice providers, and across all of the field sites they perform most third-party resolutions. In the Myanmar government-controlled areas covered by the chapters, this category of local leaders includes a hierarchy comprising 10-household and 100-household leaders (*sal eain mu/yar eain mu*), who are organised under a ward administrator (*yat kwet oak choke yey mu* in urban areas) or a village tract administrator (*yat*

6 A UNDP survey on Kachin, Rakhine and Shan States generated similar findings – between 71 per cent and 85 per cent of the respondents felt that it was best to resolve disputes within the community (Kachin (71.7 per cent), Rakhine (85.5 per cent), Shan (73.1 per cent) (UNDP 2017). Similarly, in a country-wide survey conducted by the MyJustice project, covering areas controlled by the Myanmar government – it was found that approximately 70 per cent of respondents felt that the ward, village tract, or household leaders were most appropriate for settling disputes between people (MyJustice 2018). Our own EverJust survey was conducted in the areas where we were also doing qualitative research. In Karen State, these included two urban wards and two villages in government-controlled areas, as well as one village in an area controlled by the Karen National Union (KNU) (an ethnic armed organisation). In Mon State it covered one village in an area controlled by the New Mon State Party (NMSP), another ethnic armed organisation, as well as three villages and one urban ward in government-controlled areas. Five urban wards were covered in Yangon Township. A final analysis of the survey is still underway. It did not cover the Pa-O and Naga Self-Administered Zones, which are covered by chapters in this book (Poine and Win, Chapter 2; Htar et al., Chapter 3), as qualitative studies there were carried out after the survey was finalised. These are therefore only estimated figures – which do, however, confirm what has emerged from the qualitative studies.

kwet oak choke yey mu in rural areas).[7] Often, these administrators are assisted in the resolution of disputes by elders (*ya mi ya pha* in Burmese) or by a committee of elders and 10-household leaders. Officially, the ward and village tract administrators constitute the lowest level of the Myanmar state administration and are elected by a member from each household (Kyed et al. 2016; Kempel and Aung Tun 2016). However, these leaders' extensive role in justice provision is, in practice, only vaguely recognised by the state. The law of 2012 that regulates the ward and village tract administrations states that these administrators must ensure 'security, prevalence of law and order, community peace and tranquillity' (The Republic of the Union of Myanmar 2012: Chapter VII, article 13a). However, it does not specify the types of cases that local administrators may deal with, hear or resolve. The only explicit reference is to thieves and gamblers, who must be reported to the police (ibid.: Chapter XV, Article 35). Ward and village tract administrators are detached from the official judiciary, with no system of appeal and referrals – which also reflects the fact that they do not have a *de jure* mandate to punish and adjudicate crimes. As such, they constitute mainly *informal* justice providers, who operate outside the law – but who are, nevertheless, widely preferred and more trusted than the official justice system.

Trust, and the fact that the village and ward leaders are embedded in the local setting, are both significant in understanding their prominent role in justice provision. The informal resolution mechanisms that they use also afford them local legitimacy. They mainly apply compensational justice and try to reach consensual agreements through negotiation and mediation, which fits well with most interviewees' stated justice preferences. The emic notion of *nalehmu* (literally, 'understanding') is often used to describe the way in which resolutions are based on mutual understanding, trust, and support from social relations (for a discussion of *nalehmu* see Rhoads, Chapter 9, this volume). There is a strong focus

7 The 10 household leaders are elected representatives for each 10 households in a village and a ward, and from among these 10-household leaders a 100-household leader is elected, who work closely with the ward (urban) and village tract (rural) administrators. In rural villages with around 100 or less households, the 100-household leader is often referred to as the village leader, which is a category of leadership that was initially removed by the 2012 ward and village tract administrator law, but reintroduced when this law was amended in 2017 to ensure village leader representation in smaller villages, below the village tract level.

on reconciliation, social harmony, and avoiding the escalation of conflict, rather than on punishing perpetrators. Warnings against repeat offences are used, but social sanctions and 'promise letters' (*kahn won*) are the main mechanisms for retaliation, rather than recourse to the punitive (official) justice system. In this regard, the dominant mechanisms are non-judicial and similar to community-based or customary dispute resolution in other contexts (Albrecht et al. 2011; Harper 2011). The prominent role of negotiation and informality is also reflected in the use of orally transmitted rules and norms.

The studies covered by the contributors to this volume found no examples of the use of written laws or village principles in the areas fully administered by the Myanmar state. Things are different in the areas under the partial or full control of ethnic organisations, where written village rules and principles were found to be used in many cases. Interestingly, the studies on the Pa-O and Naga Self-Administered Zones (SAZ) show that the degree of legal institutionalisation at the village level is higher than in Myanmar state areas (see Poine and Win, Chapter 2, this volume; Lue Htar et al., Chapter 3, this volume). The same applies to areas controlled by ethnic armed organisations such as the KNU (Karen National Union) and the NMSP (New Mon State Party), as Harrisson and Kyed (2019) show (see also Kyed and The Thitsar 2018). In these areas there is also a clear preference for local dispute resolution and village systems have fixed justice committees, use written principles, and have direct links of referral to higher-level justice forums within the ethnic organisations. Village justice committees in these areas can also issue punishments such as fines, communal labour and/or expulsion, but they do not have prisons.[8] These differences from the Myanmar government-controlled areas reflect the fact that the ethnic organisations, unlike the Myanmar state, recognise village justice systems as part of their systems of governance, even though this is not officially recognised by the Myanmar state. This point of difference becomes important when cases cannot be successfully resolved at village level.

When disputants cannot agree or when perpetrators cannot be identified, fail to respect decisions, or repeat their offences, village or ward leaders sometimes give up on resolving a case. When this hap-

8 The ethnic armed organisations, like the KNU and the NMSP only have prisons at levels above the village (Harrisson and Kyed 2019).

pens, disputants and local leaders alike try as much as possible to avoid cases ending up in the Myanmar state system. In the Pa-O and Naga areas, the typical reaction is to transfer the case to the higher-level ethnic or tribal forums, which are mostly trusted and seen to use dispute resolution mechanisms that are familiar and preferred.[9] By contrast, in Myanmar government-controlled areas it is very rare to see a case being transferred to higher levels in the official system or even leaving the village or ward. Sometimes this means that cases are left unresolved, but on many occasions the parties instead turn to a variety of alternative actors or 'informal justice facilitators' (Kyed 2018a; 2018b).

'Informal justice facilitators' are actors who have no explicitly recognised role in justice provision, but who give advice, connect people to justice providers, pressurise the opposing party to pay compensation or come to an agreement, or provide spiritual remedies and rehabilitation. They include, for instance, religious and spiritual leaders such as Buddhist monks, astrologers, and spirit mediums, as is evident in Richthammer's analysis of a theft case (Chapter 4, this volume). They can also include individual armed actors, such as the member of a KNU splinter group in Than Pale's chapter (Chapter 6, this volume) who helps to pressurise the perpetrators not to repeat an offence. In Poine and Kyed's chapter (Chapter 1, this volume), the mixture of informal actors is evident – when the village tract administrator gives up on resolving an arson case, it initially goes to the NMSP justice system, but is finally brought to a conclusion by members of the Myanmar military (the Tatmadaw) within a secret military office. Recourse to politicians, the media, demonstrations and other 'out-of-court' mechanisms are also evident in Poine and Nilar Win's chapter (Chapter 2, this volume), which shows how the Pa-O victims of land confiscation give up on help both from the state system and from their own ethnic organisation.

This recourse to informal justice facilitators reflects the complex pluralism of justice provision and also a prevalent mistrust in (most) external systems and authorities, especially those of the Myanmar state. This mistrust reinforces a preference for having one's case resolved by local forums, whenever possible.

9 A similar pattern of referral to higher-level ethnic justice committees within the ethnic organisation was seen in KNU and NMSP areas (see Harrisson and Kyed 2019; Kyed 2018b; Kyed and The Thitsar 2018).

Local forums, as McConnachie (Chapter 10, this volume) discusses with regards to local camp justice, also have limitations. This is evident when what people refer to as 'very serious cases' occur, such as murder, homicide, rape by strangers,[10] drug trafficking, and land confiscations by external actors. These cases are difficult for local justice providers to resolve, either because people expect high penalties or because, as is often the case with drug trafficking and land confiscation, they involve armed actors – military or ethnic – and/or persons with powerful political connections, whom local leaders do not dare confront (Kyed 2018b; see Htar 2018 on this point for Karen State). Again, when tackling these cases, people seldom report them to higher levels of the official Myanmar justice system, but either leave them unresolved or engage informal justice facilitators or ethnic systems where these exist – as they do in NMSP, KNU, Pa-O, and Naga areas. In Lue Htar et al.'s chapter on the Naga (Chapter 3, this volume), for instance, a homicide case is resolved through negotiation and compensation between the kinship groups (*pha thar su*) of the victim and the perpetrator. If this had not been successful, the case would very likely not have been reported to the Myanmar police but instead to the higher-level 'Naga literature and cultural committee'. There is no confidence that the Myanmar state system will provide satisfactory results, and the Naga prefer to be tried under their customary law, which focuses on compensation rather than imprisonment, and is applied by Naga people. However, recourse to ethnic organisations may not in all instances be successful, either because their authority to enforce decisions is not sufficiently well recognised, as Poine and Kyed show (Chapter 1, this volume) or because members of these organisations are sometimes themselves involved in cases, as Poine and Nilar Win (Chapter 2, this volume) illustrate. As these two chapters on a Mon and a Pa-O village demonstrate, many of those cases that are not successfully resolved locally tend to get very complicated due to power dynamics and the presence of multiple authorities and overlapping systems. This too reinforces a preference for local resolutions.

As already hinted above, there are several reasons for the preference for local and informal resolutions, related to a combination of politi-

10 Rape of women by relatives or by people whom the women and their families know is usually dealt with within the community, initially within the families. Sometimes a local dispute resolver such as a village leader is involved. However, many such cases are not heard or resolved at all (see Denney et al. 2016; Poine 2018).

cal-historical and socio-cultural factors (Denney et al. 2016: 11; Kyed 2018a). Many decades of military rule, conflict, and corruption have created a distrust in and a fear of formal Myanmar state institutions, but this is only part of the explanation. Another important part of the explanation for the preference is specific forms of belonging, often expressed in identity politics of some kind, as well as culturally and religiously informed perceptions of justice, misfortune, and dispute that exist within groups and localities. Before turning to this topic, we will look first at the tendency to evade the state.

2. State evasion

This is the second of the themes that are shared across the case studies dealt with in this book. Despite the transition, a negative narrative of the Myanmar state prevails within the localities covered in this book, and this leads to a decided and deliberate 'turning away' from the justice institutions of the state. This is not just about avoiding the state, in the sense of keeping away or not doing something, but is about explicitly evading it, with 'evasion' being understood as an act of avoiding something unpleasant or unwanted (Cambridge Dictionary, online). What are the reasons for this evasion? According to interviewees across the study areas, evasion is because of the way that the official legal system functions: it is seen as costly in time and money, and as infected by corruption and complicated legal procedures. The state system is not associated with justice but is perceived as being beneficial only to those who have sufficient powerful connections and financial means to win a case (MLAW and EMR 2014; Kyed 2018a; Denney et al. 2016).[11] Far from being associated with justice, people associate engagement with the state system and with higher-ranking authorities with psychological and emotional harm.

Many people view the official system as intimidating, because anyone who brings a case to it must face higher-level state authorities. People also view the formal court setting, displays of official documents, and the use of formalistic language and complicated procedures as intimidating. As court proceedings are held in Burmese, this feeling

11 For a description of Myanmar's legal system as it has evolved over time, including how it suffers from many challenges to providing equal justice, see Rhoads, Chapter 9, this volume (see also Cheeseman 2015; Crouch 2014).

is even stronger among those who do not speak Burmese well, such as members of the ethnic minorities. Contacting the state is seen to create problems and to worsen an already bad situation, as Harrisson (Chapter 8, this volume) notes from the point of view of the residents of a poor ward in Mawlamyine: even if you are a victim, it brings you into a web of complications, costs, shame, disruption of social relations and potentially a loss of justice or even life (as Harrisson shows in discussing a case where a man who was very likely innocent of the crime that he had been convicted for lost his life in prison). The situation is even more precarious for those people who are excluded from citizenship, and who therefore have no ID documents, as is currently the case with many Muslims and Hindus in Karen State (and elsewhere), as Gravers and Jørgensen discuss (Chapter 7, this volume).

State evasion does not reflect an aversion to formality or legal procedures as such. Rather, it highlights people's underlying distrust and oftentimes fear of the Myanmar state and its authorities. Distrust and fear are, in turn, deeply embedded in historical experiences of state oppression and abandonment. Even though most people mentioned in this book have never actually experienced a court case or reported a case to the police, the negative historical narrative related to the state (Richthammer, Chapter 4, this volume) informs their evasion of the state in the present. This is particularly, but not exclusively, evident among the ethnic and religious minorities, who have experienced particularly harsh forms of military state oppression or who are still excluded from citizenship (see Gravers and Jørgensen, Chapter 7, this volume). In many ways this book illustrates that the present-day state remains associated with the military state, and that the political transition has done little to change this. In the poor urban ward of Mawlamyine studied by Harrisson (Chapter 8, this volume), this continuity with the past is experienced as a lack of state care and an indifference towards the concerns of the poor. When people do engage the state, it is experienced as predatory. Thus it is better to evade the state whenever possible.

In practice people evade the state by carving out temporary 'non-state spaces' (Scott 2009) where disputes can be resolved and interpreted, in a different way, outside of the legal and political framework of the state. Sometimes this simply means not reporting a case to the state, even if it is a severe crime. Instead the case is concluded locally. At other times, evasion is more explicitly and deliberately articulated. In these instances, local leaders or informal brokers often play a crucial role as 'evaders of' and 'gate-keepers to' the state system. Ward and village leaders often warn people that going to the official system is time-consuming and costly, and that it may not serve their justice needs (such as their desire for compensation) but may instead escalate the problem (see Poine & Kyed, Chapter 1, this volume; Richthammer, Chapter 4, this volume). Ward and village leaders do not believe that the official system effectively supports their local-level decisions, but see it as undermining these decisions. They too mistrust the courts and the police, and state evasion is articulated as a way of protecting village residents. Rhoads (Chapter 9, this volume) shows how informal property brokers (*pweza*) in Yangon divert cases away from the state legal system, even before a dispute begins, by relying on informal transactions and paperwork. In the chapter on the Naga (Lue Htar et al., Chapter 3, this volume), tribal leaders actively divert a case involving a traffic accident (which resulted in a death) away from the official court and back to the customary system, claiming that this system serves the Naga better, as it secures compensation for the victim's family and reconciliation of the parties involved.

It is evident that state evasion reflects the preference for local resolution, but acts of evasion also serve, in many instances, to sustain 'the local', 'the tribal', or 'non-state spaces', something James Scott also suggests in *The Art of Not being Governed* (Scott 2009). This has clear political dynamics. In some situations, for instance, state evasion works to support the authority of village and ward leaders, because dispute resolution affords status and standing (Lund 2006; see also Poine & Kyed, Chapter 1, this volume; and Richthammer, Chapter 4, this volume). Thus, when local leaders advise people not to report to the state, they reinforce their own authority. However, state evasion is infused not only with individual interests but also with local collective interests focused on strengthening community cohesion and ethnic identity.

Than Pale shows, in her chapter on a mixed Muslim–Buddhist Karen village (Chapter 6, this volume), how joint resolution of disputes, without state interference, preserves internal social harmony and avoids the escalation of conflict between the two groups in the village. This is because, as Gravers and Jørgensen (Chapter 7, this volume) also show, tensions between groups and discrimination against Muslims derive mainly from the actions and attitudes of external state officials and monks. State evasion can thus be a way of preserving peace inside smaller, mixed villages. In Lwin Lwin Mon's chapter, we see how the resolution of disputes among the Karen themselves serves to strengthen a united Karen ethnic and Christian identity (Chapter 5, this volume). A similar point can be made about the Naga leaders' insistence (see Lue Htar et al., Chapter 3, this volume) on using customary law, which in this context is explicitly linked to identity politics. As Lauren Nader (1990: 291) argues, the emphasis on achieving social harmony in local dispute resolution can be interpreted as a way to resist external control by the state so as to preserve local autonomy.

State evasion does not, however, mean full state absence nor does it necessarily mean overt resistance to the state. Rather it often involves complex relationships between state presence and state absence, as well as state 'mimicry and contradiction' (Scott 2009: 182). The option to transfer cases to the state system always lurks in the background as a possibility and as a site of comparison with local resolution. It is not uncommon, for instance, for village or ward leaders to threaten to send perpetrators or disputing parties to the police, if the parties are reluctant to obey decisions or to come to an agreement (Poine and Kyed, Chapter 1, this volume; Kyed 2018b). Even if this transfer to the police seldom actually happens, the state (here the police) serves as a kind of reference point to facilitate local resolutions.

Harrisson (Chapter 8, this volume) makes the point that the state can actually be present despite its physical absence, through the ways in which it affects people in the local contexts. In the poor urban ward that she studied, the state's lack of care, its indifference and its acts of predation affects social relations, creating mistrust among neighbours and a fear of reporting crimes (for instance by victims of rape or domestic violence), even to the local administrator. Here state evasion does not lead to social cohesion, as it does in the rural villages of the Karen, Naga, and Mon, but signals a deeper disruption of sociality, following years of negative state interference. The ward Harrisson studied is, in fact, itself the result of a large-scale eviction from the city centre to the periphery of the city and this has deeply affected people's relationship to the state.

State evasion therefore takes different forms and serves different purposes, depending on the local context. Shared across the case studies in this book are, however, a historical experience of state oppression and abandonment. The state is, as a result, disassociated from access to justice, which in various ways supports the preference for local resolutions. Yet this preference is not always a matter of evading state authorities *per se* but may also be influenced by culturally and religiously informed notions of justice that differ from the kinds of justice that a state-legal system enforces. We now turn to this.

3. The centrality of cultural norms, social harmony and religious–spiritual beliefs

The third of the themes that are shared across the case studies of this book relates to the valuation of social harmony and the significant role of cultural norms and beliefs when we address questions of justice. 'Make the big cases smaller and make the small cases disappear' (*kyi te amu nge aung, nge te amu pa pyauk aung* in Burmese) is a well-known saying that is used across most ethno-religious communities in Myanmar (see Denney et al. 2016: 1; Kyed 2018a). It strongly reflects *emic* notions of justice, based on the cultural norm of social harmony, which favours reconciliation and the restoration of social relations. State-legal justice, with its focus on punishments and identification of 'winners' (victims) and 'losers' (perpetrators), is, by contrast, perceived as confrontational, is associated with conflict escalation, and is thus regarded as antithetical to social harmony. The understanding of justice as 'making cases disappear' also sometimes means that victims or disputants refrain from reporting a case at all, even to village or ward leaders.

Under-reporting is quite common in Myanmar (Denney et al. 2016; MyJustice 2018). When a case is reported to a third party, this is perceived in the first instance to amount to conflict escalation, and this is associated with feelings of shame and loss of dignity. It is particularly shameful to take a case outside one's own village or neighbourhood, as this is seen as particularly likely to escalate the conflict and undermine local social relations (see also Kyed 2018a). Such feelings of shame are stronger if parties fail to resolve a dispute within their own village or neighbourhood through reconciliation or a consensus-based agreement on compensation. It is considered most shameful to take a case to the state at higher levels.

Even when punishments (such as fines or payment of compensation) are issued by village or ward leaders, the primary focus is on restoring relations between the parties and preventing any escalation of conflict.

There is another common saying in Burmese, *kot paung ko hlan htaung* (equivalent to the English saying: 'You should not air your dirty laundry in public') that underlines the disincentive to report, pointing to the fact that this would draw a dispute into the public realm and make it visible. For example, Richthammer (Chapter 4, this volume) shows how a Karen-Buddhist woman whose gold was stolen did not want to report her case to the police because she was afraid of being seen as shameful by other village residents, because reporting the case would be regarded as 'escalating the problem'.

As Nader (1990) argues, social harmony can be understood as a kind of ideology that can work to avoid state intrusion, but it also typically supports a particular social organisation, especially in small-scale, closely-knit societies. This is very evident in Chapter 3 (this volume) on the Naga, where the primary focus of dispute resolution is to secure good relations between the patrilineal kinship groups (*pha thar su*) of the disputants (i.e. the victims and the perpetrators), as the *pha thar su* constitutes the most significant base of the social organisation. In trials it is distant *pha thar su* relatives of the disputants who negotiate the case, not the individual disputants themselves. This is to avoid actions of revenge, which would escalate the situation and potentially harm social organisation. If a case should proceed to the state court, resulting, for instance, in imprisonment, reconciliation would not be possible. A similar example is explored by Lwin Lwin Mon (Chapter 5, this volume), who shows how the village leader and the Baptist minister focus on social harmony and reconciliation in domestic violence cases, so as to preserve an image of the urban Baptist Karen community as peaceful and sustain religious norms (e.g. of not pursuing divorce).

As is evident in several of the chapters, religious and spiritual beliefs also influence how people act when they face a case and how they understand misfortune, injustices, and victimhood. Religion can also serve as a kind of private or personal retreat from seeking secular justice or from confronting the dispute in public. It can be a way to make inner peace with a dispute or crime, either after it has not been successfully resolved by a third party or as a substitute for reporting the case at all, or of negotiating directly with the other party. Often this is combined with seeking spiritual remedies to ease the suffering, such as through prayer or by going to a religious or spiritual actor (a monk, astrologer or spirit medium) to pray or to get *ye dar yar* (spiritual protection). Doing something of this kind is a private affair that does not involve direct reconciliation between the involved parties.

Theravada Buddhist beliefs, which are widespread across Myanmar, influence understandings of injustices and victimhood. Many Buddhists understand problems as being the result of misfortune, which can only be resolved within oneself by coming to peace, through detachment (Schober 2011). Accepting problems is understood to pay off deeds committed in past lives, thereby ensuring good karma (*kamma* in Pali; *kan* in Burmese) in the future.[12] If a person is robbed, for instance, this can be understood as a result of the victim having robbed someone in his/her past life. This is illustrated in Chapter 4, in which Richthammer shows how a Buddhist Karen woman who lost her gold savings accepted this explanation about deeds in a past life when she realised that she would not get her gold back. Not seeking a (secular) remedy means that a victim of theft, such as this Buddhist Karen woman, can repay such misdeeds from a past life. There is also a belief that those who cause harm in this life will be punished in their future lives, which makes a third-party resolution unnecessary. In this way, injustice can be understood as a deserved and almost inevitable consequence of fortune, which must be personally endured rather than externally resolved (Denney et. al 2016: 3). This strengthens the tendency not to report cases to a third-party justice provider and is the basis for the fact that some people seek spiritual rehabilitation by visiting monks or spirit mediums instead (see also Poine 2018; Kyed 2018b).

Among the Baptist Karen in Yangon, whom Lwin Lwin Mon (Chapter 5, this volume) discusses, there is also a prevalent understanding that problems are associated with a person's fate or with the actions of God. This is associated with a strong preference for forgiveness over seeking remedies and punishments. Prayer is often the first, and sometimes the only, action that is taken when a person faces misfortune or is a victim of crime. Here the Baptist minister and the Sunday school play a strong

12 Following Spiro (1966) karma is defined as action (deeds, words and thoughts). Karma determines one's rebirth and can be understood as the net sum of one's actions in the present life and in past lives, notably actions that have to do with one's merits and demerits. Karma is connected to a law of cause and effect. In daily lay Buddhist understandings of Karma in Myanmar, karma is also associated with good/bad luck or with fortune/misfortune, that is, it is for example understood as poor karma if a person faces bad situations.

role in nurturing religious understandings of justice and wrongdoing. In the Goga Naga tribe, discussed by Lue Htar et al. (Chapter 3, this volume), beliefs in invisible spiritual repercussions also mean that only forgiveness, rather than punishments (including compensation), can be issued if the disputants are members of the same *pha thar su* (patrilineal kinship group). If any compensation is paid, the Goga Naga believe that it will likely cause bad luck, such as illness in future generations of the *pha thar su*. Thus, punitive justice is believed to potentially cause harm even to the victim. This may also help explain why people evade state justice, which is focused precisely on punitive justice.

Religious beliefs mean that there is less of a desire for secular punishments, especially those (such as state-legal imprisonment) that do not foreground reconciliation. Buddhist, Christian, and customary beliefs in spirits all tend to support the cultural norm of social harmony. In addition, religion offers explanations for misfortunes the victims face, which gives them relief and comfort, especially in the absence of secular justice. As Nader (1990) argues, the supernatural becomes important when visible, secular or public institutions fail to resolve a case or to provide preferred justice outcomes (see also Richthammer, Chapter 4, this volume). However, this does not mean that beliefs only become relevant when state or village justice fail; they also guide interpretations of and actions in relation to disputes and crimes in the first place, as is evident in the many instances where people refrain from reporting cases at all. These beliefs also support the preference for local dispute resolution.

While local dispute resolution can be seen to protect people from the negative consequences of state-legal justice, the focus on social harmony and the role of religion can also be problematic for those people who are particularly vulnerable and less powerful in the social organisation of a given group. Lwin Lwin Mon shows (Chapter 5, this volume), for instance, how female victims of domestic violence agree to reconcile with their husbands as they do not want to appear conflictual or to contradict the advice of the (male) Baptist minister and the (male) village leader. It is therefore not coincidental, as Mi Thang Sorn Poine (2018) shows, that in a Mon village, women tend to report cases less often than men and are the ones who most frequently seek rehabilitation from spiritual or religious actors. In Naga society, customary norms also disfavour women, especially in the areas of inheritance and divorce, something which accords with a strongly patrilineal kinship organisation which is also central to local dispute resolution. As Lue Htar et al. (Chapter 3, this volume) point out, Naga tribal leaders are now beginning to gradually change the customary law articles that discriminate against women, but many challenges remain. Women are not the only vulnerable groups, as Gravers and Jørgensen (Chapter 7, this volume) show: ethnic and religious minorities within a given locality, such as Muslims and Hindus, who face discrimination from the authorities, also frequently avoid reporting cases locally, as they do not want to stir up attention or be suspected of engaging in conflict escalation (see also Harrisson 2018 on a similar point for a ward in Mawlamyine).

4. Identity politics: Exclusion and inclusion

The importance of exclusion and inclusion, frequently linked to identity politics, constitutes the fourth theme found in the case studies in this book. Identity politics has played an important role in Myanmar's history since colonial times. It has permeated the (still ongoing) armed conflicts between the military and ethnic armed organisations and has been an important theme both in the military atrocities against minorities and in claims to self-determination on the part of minorities, based on their ethnic group identity. Identity has a profound effect on everyday forms of governmental exclusion of and discrimination against certain categories of people. Identity politics in Myanmar is based on a deeply entrenched reification of ethnic, racial and religious group identities, one that dates back to the British colonial administration's divide-and-rule tactic of governance (Gravers 1999). As Gravers and Jørgensen (Chapter 7, this volume) discuss in detail, the divisive colonial categorisations of ethnicity spilled over into a pervasive Burmese nationalism during the post-colonial military regime. An ethnic hierarchy was furthermore formalised in the citizenship law (1982), one that still excludes some ethnic groups from citizenship (Muslims, Hindus and Chinese) and makes the Bamar–Buddhists the highest-ranking group within the polity (Cheesman 2017). Burmese nationalism, with its focus on national unity and integrity, has worked to justify violence and discrimination against other ethnic and religious groups, who were unwilling to 'Burmanise' and convert to Buddhism (on how this was experienced among the Christian Naga, see Lue Htar et al., Chapter 3, this volume).[13]

Despite the transition, Gravers and Jørgensen (Chapter 7, this volume) argue that nationalism and ethno–religious divisions persist today in Karen State (and elsewhere), something which is particularly evident in the denial of ID documents and provision of justice to Muslims and Hindus (see also KHRG 2017). This continuity, Gravers and Jørgensen argue, is exacerbated by the situation in Rakhine State since 2011, as well as by the strengthened role of nationalist monks, who use their spiritual power to spread anti-Muslim sentiments (often on social media), through a discourse of saving the nation and Buddhism (Wade 2017).

At the same time, ethnic identity divisions permeate not only ethnic insurgencies against the state, but also the non-violent and yet inherently political efforts by ethnic minority leaders to strengthen internal ethnic unity and recognition. This is, for instance, evident in the Naga codification of a shared Naga customary law (see Lue Htar et al., Chapter 3, this volume). Lwin Lwin Mon (Chapter 5, this volume) also provides an example of 'quieter', more subtle forms of internal strengthening of ethno-religious identity vis-à-vis the surrounding Burmese society among the urban Baptist Karen. Ethnic boundary-making penetrates deeply into society, both as a tool of governance, type of resistance and as a mode of self-identification and community-making, which involves various forms of 'othering'.

As is evident in many chapters in this book, identity politics shapes everyday justice in both inclusionary and exclusionary ways in local settings. Sharing an ethnic or religious identity with local justice providers, such as village or ward leaders, makes people feel more comfortable with reporting cases and resolving their disputes at the local level. McConnachie (Chapter 10, this volume) recounts, for example, how the Baptist Sgaw Karen refugees prefer local camp justice, both because they fear Thai state justice and because they share Karen cultural values and identity with the camp justice providers. Shared identity can work in inclusive ways, securing access to justice that may be denied or not fulfilled in a state system that is known to intimidate or discriminate against ethnic/religious minorities. Shared language, cultural norms and loyalties based on ethnic identity were also articulated as important

13 On efforts to 'Burmanise', often referred to as strategies of 'Burmanisation', see Walton (2013) and Kyed and Gravers (2018).

to the choice of non-local justice providers, as Poine and Nilar Win (Chapter 2, this volume) show, with respect to Pa-O village residents, who prefer to report cases to the Pa-O National Organisation (PNO) when disputes cannot be successfully resolved inside the village. The Naga interviewed by Lue Htar et al. (Chapter 3, this volume) made similar points. Shared identity also played a role when the victims of an arson case in a Myanmar government-controlled village in Mon State chose to turn to the Mon ethnic armed organisation, the NMSP, rather than to the state legal system, as discussed by Poine and Kyed in Chapter 1. Even though the victims in this case were well aware that the NMSP had no official jurisdiction to deal with the case, the victims believed that the NMSP would be more willing than the Myanmar state to treat them and their case well, because they are also Mon.

When access to justice follows ethnic or religious identity, it can, however, also work as exclusionary. The preference for local resolutions within one's own ethnic group frequently relies on different forms of 'othering', as Lwin Lwin Mon (Chapter 5, this volume) argues. Even though the urban Baptist Karen about whom she writes are not hostile towards their Bamar neighbours, their understanding of the need to resolve matters among themselves rests on the articulation of outsiders and non-Karen as causes of insecurity. This othering of outsiders is pitted against an image of the Baptist Karen as peaceful and united, which can only be maintained by keeping the village purely Karen. Thus, not only do they try to avoid involving external authorities in disputes; they also have an informal rule of not selling land or renting houses to non-Karen. This form of ethnic boundary-making at the grass-roots level reflects deeper divisions and forms of inclusion and exclusion in Myanmar society, even if these are not overtly hostile.

The link between access to local justice and ethnicity is particularly problematic in mixed villages or wards where geographical boundaries do not follow ethnic or religious ones. As is argued elsewhere (Harrisson and Kyed 2019; Kyed 2018b), village leaders in Karen and Mon State under the governance of the KNU and the NMSP find it hard to deal with cases that involve people belonging to other ethnicities, especially Bamar, who are now increasingly residing within their areas due to labour migration. In practice, these non-Karen or non-Mon find it hard to access local justice. Denney et al. (2016) also found that Hindus and Muslims living in villages or wards where the leaders are Mon, Karen or

Burmese prefer to resolve their cases with their own religious leaders, as they feel they are more likely to get fair treatment there. In Gravers and Jørgensen's chapter (Chapter 7, this volume), the Karen Muslims in one mixed village claimed that they always tried to avoid raising disputes, because they believed that they would lose the dispute or have to pay more in compensation than their Buddhist Karen neighbours. It is evident, however, that these local forms of exclusion are particularly likely when external forces that promote identity-based divisions are strong.

Gravers and Jørgensen (Chapter 7, this volume) demonstrate the impact of external forces on the relationship between different groups in Karen State. In some mixed Muslim–Buddhist villages, the nationalist Ma Ba Tha monks, with their strong anti-Muslim rhetoric, have created tensions between Muslim and Buddhist villagers that previously did not exist. In addition, bureaucratic-state discrimination against Muslims and Hindus – who struggle to get ID, travel freely, and get land ownership documents – is increasingly affecting some local villages and is making it difficult for Muslims and Hindus to get access to local justice and security. In another study in Karen State, Than Pale (Chapter 6, this volume) underlines the significance of the presence or absence of external influences when she demonstrates how the absence of external influences supports a peaceful relationship between Muslim and Buddhist villagers. Despite the fact that Muslims in the village studied face state-bureaucratic discrimination *outside* the village, they have managed to maintain a shared identity with their Karen Buddhist neighbours, one that is based on shared 'locality' (they have lived in the same village for 100 years). Locality, rather than religion, is here the most significant form of community identification, Than Pale argues, because the two groups resolve disputes together and are able to avoid negative external influences. It is clear that here, evading state justice is one way of keeping external influences at bay. Thus, when cases cannot be concluded in the village by Muslim and Buddhist leaders, people do not turn to the state or to their religious leaders at higher levels, but to a Karen armed actor who is originally from the village and who thus shares their identity based on locality. These localised ways of securing social harmony nonetheless co-exist with discrimination against Muslims outside the village.

Resolving disputes through one's own ethnic leaders or organisations is not, however, a guarantee of justice or effective dispute resolution, even if people may feel more comfortable with it. The capacity of local and ethnic leaders to enforce justice is often challenged by the wider political situation of overlapping authorities and unclear jurisdictions. It is also challenged by the lack of state recognition of ethnic systems of justice. As Poine and Kyed (Chapter 1, this volume) show, the NMSP's justice system lacks the enforcing authority to settle cases that involve Mon people who live in Myanmar government-controlled areas. Poine and Nilar Win (Chapter 2, this volume) show that the Pa-O National Organisation (PNO), although often trusted with cases, struggles to protect the villagers and provide justice, because it competes with state institutions and is involved in a web of different armed actors, partly connected to the PNO and partly to the military. The PNO's ability to serve the justice needs of the Pa-O villagers is particularly precarious when large business interests are at stake in a dispute. Chapters 1 and 2 provide powerful illustrations of the complex and politically charged situation of legal pluralism in the everyday lives of people in Myanmar, which is infused with identity politics, ethnic divisions and the continued role of militarised actors. The critical repercussions of this situation for access to everyday justice are particularly noticeable when cases cannot be resolved locally.

The contributions: From urban Yangon to rural Naga

After this introduction, the book opens with a chapter that takes us to a large village in southern Mon State that no longer is affected by armed conflict but which, albeit being officially governed by the Myanmar state, still has a plurality of *de facto* armed and non-armed authorities. In Chapter 1, by Mi Thang Sorn Poine and Helene Maria Kyed, the authors explore what people do when crimes cannot be resolved inside the village. They argue that 'forum shopping' outside the official state judiciary is a common strategy, but one that is fraught with high levels of uncertainty and risk. The informal alternatives, such as the NMSP and a secret military office, do not provide entirely satisfactory solutions: the NMSP because it lacks enforcing authority, and the military because it takes a high informal fee. 'Forum shopping' is not here equal to free choice but is rather a symptom of a deep and persistent instability of authority, which has roots in the long history of militarisation and conflict preceding the transition. This situation further underscores a preference for settling crimes, whenever possible, inside the village.

Chapter 2, by Mi Thang Sorn Poine and Nan Tin Nilar Win, also gives insights into the effects of plural authorities and justice systems for village residents, but in a slightly different political context: the Pa-O Self-Administered Zone (SAZ). Here, village dispute forums have to relate to a complex mixed administration of Myanmar state institutions, the Pa-O National Organisation (PNO) – now a political party, with its own informal justice system – and the Pa-O National Army (PNA) – now under the Myanmar military, but with links to the PNO. When disputes cannot be settled at village level, Pa-O village residents prefer the PNO to the Myanmar state, but the PNO's capacity to dispense justice and protect village residents is significantly compromised when perpetrators are powerful armed actors. Mi Thang Sorn Poine and Nan Tin Nilar Win argue that the continued role of armed power is a significant obstacle to justice in the Pa-O SAZ, where the population is becoming increasingly aware of their rights due to the transition. The PNO is trying to codify its customary law, in order to strengthen its system of justice, but this is challenged by lack of state recognition.

This topic of codifying customary law is also taken up in Chapter 3, but here it is not a former ethnic armed organisation who are dispensing justice, but a 'literature and cultural committee' of civilian Naga leaders – who are trying to promote a common Naga justice system as part of a Naga nation-building strategy. Lue Htar, Myat The Thitsar, and Helene Maria Kyed argue in this chapter that the political transition has created a context for these efforts, which are centred not only on creating a united Naga group identity but also on obtaining state recognition to support Naga self-determination. Drawing on the wider literature on legal pluralism, the chapter discusses the political dynamics of state recognition of customary law. In particular, the authors argue for the need to include more Naga voices in the revision of customary law and to ensure gender equality in the application of law.

Chapter 4 also explores the strong role of cultural norms in the preference for local dispute resolution, here in a small Pwo Karen village in Karen State, where spiritual beliefs – Buddhist and animist – substitute for the lack of official state justice, both as remedies and as explanations for misfortunes. Marie Knakkergaard Richthammer argues in this chapter that state evasion is not only due to negative historical experiences with the state but also to the fact that state-legal norms contradict cultural and spiritual norms. This has the effect of undermining state authority, while enhancing the legitimacy of local actors, such as the village leader and spirit mediums. She argues that the legitimacy of justice sector reform in Myanmar will depend on recognising and including ordinary villagers' culturally specific understandings of justice.

In Chapter 5, Lwin Lwin Mon explores the role of religion in local dispute resolution, in an urban Karen village where the majority are Baptists. Here religion also operates as a form of socialisation centred on strengthening a united Karen ethnic identity. By contrast with the Naga and Pa-O, this identity formation is not, however, linked to an explicit political strategy of recognition. Rather it reflects 'quiet' ways of evading the state aimed at keeping the area purely Karen, which in more subtle ways reproduce the ethnic divisions reflective of Myanmar society at large.

Than Pale in Chapter 6 explores a rather different scenario, showing how the joint resolution of disputes by Muslim and Buddhist village leaders in a mixed village in Karen State is central to maintaining a shared communal identity based on 'locality'. Joint resolutions help prevent any potential tensions caused by religious differences. Than Pale argues that the significance of shared locality rather than religious identity provides a promising paradigm for legal pluralism and community-based resolution, but to achieve this more broadly would require wider political changes in the surrounding society. Conflict avoidance between the two religious groups inside the village is dependent on evading precisely those external forces that have contributed, elsewhere, to igniting enmities against Muslims.

The fact that ethno-religious conflict and discrimination are politically constructed by external elite forces, rather than being locally driven, is particularly evident in Chapter 7, which also focuses on Karen State. In this chapter, Mikael Gravers and Anders Baltzer Jørgensen explore the growing discrimination against Hindus and Muslims on the part of state authorities, evident in lack of access to ID documents on the part of these minorities, documents that are essential to their justice and security. They detail how this discrimination is embedded in a long history of ethnic divisiveness, which has created a kind of 'bureaucratic indifference' on the part of the state towards marginalised people with no right to citizenship, and which is increasingly promulgated by nationalist monks within villages and urban wards of Karen State.

In Chapter 8, Annika Pohl Harrisson deals with the topic of how state indifference and lack of care towards marginalised people are negatively affecting access to justice, in this case within a poor urban ward of Mawlamyine. Drawing on theories of 'state affect', Harrisson argues that state evasion is never completely possible for those living in this poor urban ward, because the history of state oppression, evictions, and surveillance that they have experienced is reproduced internally in relations of mistrust and lack of care between neighbours and family members. She also shows how mistrust of the state causes people to use informal brokers (*pweza*) as a costly, but often the only, means of obtaining documents without having to directly engage the state.

In Chapter 9, Elizabeth Rhoads looks closely at the role of these urban informal brokers (*pweza*), focusing on property transactions and disputes across Yangon city. With the high level of insecurity of state justice, the low level of protection of property rights, unclear (or no official) ownership documents, and widespread informalisation of property, reliance on brokers is essential to securing and resolving disputes over property. Brokers rely on their social capital, on connections and on knowledge. The system of brokerage is based on trust (rather than on formal papers), as the brokers vouch for property transactions. In many cases, this means that brokers are the ultimate arbiters in the event of a property dispute. Rhoads argues that the role of brokers in property transactions reflects a deep-seated mistrust of the state system. The flipside is that the strong role of brokers can prevent people from resolving property disputes in the official system in the event that people should wish to do so. It also often implies very high broker fees.

Chapter 10 takes us to the mainly Karen-populated refugee camps in Thailand, where Kirsten McConnachie explores the trajectory of the international interventions that were attempting to reform existing forms of self-organised camp justice since the mid-2000s. Like other groups discussed in this book, the Karen refugees were, she found, very reluctant to engage the formal justice system – in this case the Thai system – and feared doing so. However, international agencies tried to encourage the refugees to use the Thai system, based on a state-centric approach to access to justice. In their efforts to reform camp justice, the international agencies have codified new rules and created new dispute forums, while dismissing existing camp justice as ineffective and as contradicting international human rights. This led to a clash of legal cultures and a struggle over the ownership of justice between the internationals and the refugees, ultimately undermining the willingness of local camp leaders to engage in justice provision and to bring about change in justice practices – e.g. with regards to gender-based violence. Besides focusing on everyday justice for Myanmar camp refugees, this chapter also provides an insightful discussion of the potential pitfalls of international engagement with community-based justice, which is beginning to take root inside Myanmar.

The limitations of the book and directions for future study

The chapters in this book provide profound insights into everyday justice practices and perceptions and their political and societal meanings; but one caveat is that they are limited by their narrow geographical scope. Due to the multiplicity of ethnic and religious forms of belonging and the plurality of authorities across Myanmar, more in-depth empirical case studies in other states and regions, and among other ethnic organisations that engage in justice provision – armed and non-armed – would probably reveal an even higher level of complexity in legal pluralism in the country. Another limitation of this book is that the chapters do not cover studies carried out inside the official judiciary, including the courts and the police. With the notable exception of the work of Nick Cheeseman (2015) and Melissa Crouch (2014), there is a general dearth of studies of the official system, which, as pointed out in a recent report (Justice Base 2017), may be linked to the continuing difficulties in gaining access to the courts, even though these now are officially open to the public. In addition, no ethnographic studies have so far been carried out within the police force, who are often the first line of reporting to the state and who also often engage in dispute resolution (Kyed 2018b). In-depth ethnographies of court hearings and everyday case handling by the police would add further richness to the insights on legal pluralism and would probably shed light on the challenges facing state officials as well as lawyers in Myanmar. Finally, the book does not include studies of the growing role of non-governmental (NGO) and community-based legal aid providers, which tend to focus particularly on assisting children and victims of gender-based violence to access justice, but which are also moving into the areas of land and dispute resolution by village and ward administrators. These 'new' actors add to a field that is already plural and will probably expand, as part of the growing international involvement in programs on the rule of law and human rights that are accompanying the Myanmar transition. McConnachie's chapter (Chapter 10, this volume), which focuses on this type of international intervention in refugee camps, serves as a source of inspiration for similar critical studies within Myanmar.

Despite these limitations, it is our hope that this book will become a valuable contribution to the scholarship on legal pluralism in transitional societies and that it will invigorate the debate about access to justice in Myanmar. In particular, it is hoped that the book's empirical insights may help influence policies in the justice sector, encouraging a recognition of the plurality of actors who contribute to resolving disputes and taking seriously ordinary people's preferences in relation to justice. Many of the chapters in this book conclude by reflecting on this recommendation.

References

Albrecht, P., Kyed, H.M., Isser, D. & Harper, E.

2011. *Perspectives on Involving Non-State and Customary Actors in Justice and Security Sector Reform.* Rome: IDLO; Copenhagen: DIIS.

Albrecht, P. & Moe, L.M.

2014. 'The simultaneity of authority in hybrid orders.' *Peacebuilding* 3(1): 1–16.

Andersen, L., Stepputat, F. & Møller, B.

2007. *Fragile states and Insecure People? Violence, Security, and Statehood in the Twenty-First Century.* New York: Palgrave.

Baker, B.

2011. 'Justice and security architecture in Africa.' *Journal of Legal Pluralism and Unofficial Law,* 63: 25–48.

Baxter, P. & Jack, S.

2008. 'Qualitative case study methodology: Study design and implementation for novice researchers.' *Qualitative Report* 13(4): 544–559.

Chambers, J. & McCarthy, G.

2018. 'Introduction: Myanmar transformed?.' In Justine Chambers et al. (eds), *Myanmar Transformed? People, Places and Politics,* pp. 3–20. Singapore: ISEAS – Yusof Ishak Institute.

Cheesman, N.

2015. *Opposing the Rule of Law: How Myanmar's Courts Make Law and Order.* Cambridge: Cambridge University Press.

2017. 'How in Myanmar "national races" came to surpass citizenship and exclude Rohingya.' *Journal of Contemporary Asia* 42(2): 1–23.

Crouch, M.

2014. 'The layers of legal development in Myanmar.' In Crouch, M. and T. Lindsey (eds), *Law, Society and Transition in Myanmar,* pp. 33–58. Oxford: Hart Publishing.

2016. *Islam and the State in Myanmar.* Oxford: Oxford University Press.

Denney, L., Bennett, W. & San K.T.

(2016.) *Understandings of Justice in Myanmar.* Policy Brief, November 2016., s.l.: MyJustice and Saferworld., November 2016.

DFID (Department for International Development)

2004. *Non-State Justice and Security Systems.* London: DFID.

Flyvbjerg, B.

2006. 'Five misunderstandings about case-study research.' *Qualitative Inquiry* 12(2): 219–245.

Gravers, M.

1999. *Nationalism as Political Paranoia in Burma. An Essay on the Historical Practice of Power.* London: Curzon.

Griffiths, J.

1986. 'What is legal pluralism?' *Journal of Legal Pluralism and Unofficial Law* 24: 1–50.

Guillaume, X. & Huysmans, J.

2018. 'The concept of "the everyday": Ephemeral politics and the abundance of life.' *Cooperation and Conflict* 33(4): 687–706.

Hammersley, M. & Atkinson, P.

1995. *Ethnography. Principles in Practice.* New York: Routledge.

Harper, E.

2011. *Customary Justice: From Program Design to Impact Evaluation.* Rome: International Development Law Organisation (IDLO).

Harrisson, A.P. & Kyed, H.M.

2019. 'Ceasefire state-making and justice provision in ethnic armed group areas of Southeast Myanmar.' *Journal of Social Issues in Southeast Asia* 34(2): 290–326.

Harrisson, A.P.

2018. 'Everyday justice for Muslims in Mawlamyine: Subjugation and skilful navigation.' *Independent Journal of Burmese Scholarship* 1(2): 57–85.

Holý, L., & Stuchlik, M.

1983. *Actions, Norms and Representations Foundations of Anthropological Inquiry.* London: Cambridge University Press.

Htar, L.

2018. 'Everyday justice and plural authorities: Insights from Karen State about land disputes.' *Independent Journal of Burmese Scholarship* 1(2): 162–210.

Hughes, C.C.

1992. 'Ethnography. What is in a word-process? Product? Promise?' *Qualitative Research* 2(4): 439–450.

ICHRP (International Council for Human Rights Policy)

2009. *When Legal Orders Overlap: Human Rights, State and Non-State Law.* Geneva: ICHRP.

Isser, D.

2011. *Customary Justice and the Rule of Law in War-Torn Societies.* Washington: United States Institute for Peace (USIP).

Isser, D., Lubkemann, S.C. & N'Tow, S.

2009. *Looking for Justice. Liberian Experiences with and Perceptions of Local Justice Options.* Washington DC: USIP.

Justice Base

2017. *Behind Closed Doors: Obstacles and Opportunities for Public Access to Myanmar's Courts.* London: Justice Base.

Kempel, S. & Tun, A.

2016. *Myanmar Ward and Village Tract Elections in 2016: An Overview of the Role, the Laws and the Procedures.* Myanmar: Norwegian People's Aid, 31 January 2016.

KHRG (Karen Human Rights Group)

2017. *Foundation of Fears: 25 years of Villagers' Voices from Southeast Myanmar.* Karen Human Rights Group (KHRG), October 2017. khrg.org/2017/12/foundation-fear-25-years-villagers-voices-southeast-myanmar.

Kyed, H.M.

2009. 'The politics of legal pluralism: State policies on legal pluralism and their local dynamics in Mozambique.' *Journal of Legal Pluralism and Unofficial Law* 59: 87–120.

2011. 'Introduction to the special issue. Legal pluralism and international development interventions.' *Journal of Legal Pluralism and Unofficial Law* 63: 1–23.

2018a. 'Introduction to special issue on everyday justice.' *Independent Journal of Burmese Scholarship* 1(2): i–xxii.

2018b. *Community Based Dispute Resolution. Exploring Everyday Justice in Southeast Myanmar.* Report for International Rescue Committee. reliefweb.int/report/myanmar/community-based-dispute-resolution-exploring-everyday-justice-provision-southeast.

Kyed, H.M. & Gravers, M.

2018. 'Representation and citizenship in the future integration of ethnic armed actors in Myanmar/Burma.' In Ashley South and Marie Lall (eds), *Citizenship in Myanmar. Ways of being in and from Burma*, pp. 59–86. Singapore: Chiang Mai University Press and ISEAS.

Kyed, H.M., Harrisson, A.P. & McCarthy, G.

2016. *Local Democracy in Myanmar: Reflections on the Ward and Village Tract Elections in 2016*. Copenhagen: DIIS.

Kyed, H.M. and Thawnghmung, A.

2019. 'The significance of everyday access to justice in Myanmar's transition to democracy.' *Trends in South East Asia*, 9. Singapore: ISEAS – Yusof Ishak Institute.

Kyed, H.M. and The Thitsar, M.

2018. 'State-making and dispute resolution in Karen frontier areas.' *Independent Journal of Burmese Scholarship* 1(2): 29–55.

Lund, C.

2006. 'Twilight Institutions: Public Authority and Local Politics in Africa.' *Development and Change* 37 (4): 686–705.

Malinowski, B.

1922. *Argonauts of the Western Pacific*. London: Routledge.

McCarthy, B. & Joliffe, K.

2016. *Ethnic Armed Actors and Justice Provision in Myanmar*. Report, The Asia Foundation, October 2016.

Merry, S.E.

1988. 'Legal pluralism.' *Law and Society Review* 22(5): 869–896.

MLAW (Myanmar Legal Aid Network) and EMR (Enlightened Myanmar Research)

2014. *Between Fear and Hope: Challenges and Opportunities for Strengthening Rule of Law and Access to Justice in Myanmar.* London: Pyoe Pin/DFID.

Morris, M.W., Leung, K., Ames, D. & Lickel, B.

1999. 'Views from the inside and outside: Integrating emic and etic insights about culture and justice judgement.' *Academy of Management Review* 24(4): 781–796.

MyJustice

2018. *Searching for Justice in the Law: Understanding Access to Justice in Myanmar. Findings from a Myanmar Justice Survey 2017.* Yangon: British Council.

Nader, L.

1990. *Harmony Ideology: Justice and Control in a Zapotec Mountain Village.* California: Stanford University Press.

Poine, T.S.

2018. 'Gendered aspects of access to justice in southern Mon State.' *Independent Journal of Burmese Scholarship* 1(2): 1–25.

Saferworld

2019. *Security, Justice and Governance in South East Myanmar. A Knowledge, Attitudes and Practices Survey in Karen Ceasefire Areas.* London: Saferworld. January 2019.

Schober, J.

2011. *Modern Buddhist Conjunctures in Myanmar: Cultural Narratives, Colonial Legacies, and Civil Society*. Honolulu: University of Hawaii Press.

Scott, J.C.

2009. *The Art of Not Being Governed: An Anarchist History of Upland Southeast Asia.* Newhaven, Conneticut: Yale University Press.

Small, M.L.

2009. '"How many cases do I need?" On science and the logic of case selection in field-based research.' *Ethnography* 10(1): 5–38.

South, A. and Lall, M. (eds)

2018. *Citizenship in Myanmar. Ways of Being in and from Burma.* Singapore: ISEAS and Chiang Mai University Press.

Spiro, M.E.

1966. 'Buddhism and Economic Action in Burma.' *American Anthropologist* 68 (5): 1163–73.

Tamanaha, B.

2008. 'Understanding legal pluralism. Past to present, local to global.' *Sydney Law Review* 30(3): 375–411.

The Republic of the Union of Myanmar

2012. *The Ward or Village Tract Administration Law*. Ministry of Home Affairs.

UN (United Nations)

2008. *United Nations Declaration on the Rights of Indigenous Peoples.* New York: UN. March 2008.

UNDP

2017. *Access to Justice and Informal Justice Systems in Kachin, Rakhine and Shan States.* Yangon: UNDP.

von Benda-Beckmann, K.

1981. 'Forum shopping and shopping forums: dispute processing in a Minangkabau village in west Sumatra.' *Journal of Legal Pluralism and Unofficial Law* 13(19): 117–159.

von Benda-Beckman, F.

1997. 'Citizens, strangers and indigenous peoples. Conceptual politics and legal pluralism.' *Law and Anthropology* 9: 1–42.

Wade, F.

2017. *Myanmar's Enemy Within.* London: Zed Books.

Walton, M.J.

2013. 'The "wages of Burman-ness": Ethnicity and Burman privilege in contemporary Myanmar.' *Journal of Contemporary Asia* 43(1): 1–27.

1 Forum shopping and plural authorities in southern Mon State

Mi Thang Sorn Poine and Helene Maria Kyed

Introduction

This chapter explores everyday justice in Seik Soi, a Mon village in southern Mon State, with a particular focus on what people do when disputes and crimes cannot be resolved inside the village.[1] Drawing on theories of legal pluralism, we argue that the long history of armed conflict and state suppression has led to a pluralisation of authority that makes 'forum shopping' a core justice-seeking strategy. The term 'forum shopping' refers to situations where people choose between different justice forums to try to get the best outcome relating to a dispute or crime (von Benda-Beckmann 1981: 117; Unruh 2003; Sikor and Lund 2009). In the chapter, we discuss the various consequences of forum shopping for village residents' access to justice and the role that power dynamics play in this practice. While forum shopping provides alternatives to what is experienced as an inadequate official justice system, it also reflects a high level of unpredictability and risk for litigants. Ultimately, forum shopping is caused by a high level of uncertainty about authority, as well as by the continued militarisation of power in Mon State.

For many years Seik Soi was affected by the armed conflict between the Burmese military (Tatmadaw) and the main ethnic armed organisation (EAO) of the Mon people, the New Mon State Party (NMSP). Since the ceasefire in 1995, the village has officially been a Myanmar government-controlled area, but the NMSP still constitutes a significant *de facto* authority in the minds of many Mon villagers. They sometimes take disputes and crimes to the NMSP headquarters, if village-level resolutions fail. This is despite the fact that villagers and the village leader know that the NMSP's justice system is not legally

1 All place and person names are anonymised in this chapter in order to protect our interlocutors' confidentiality.

recognised in Myanmar law, and therefore lacks the official authority to enforce resolutions for people who live in government-controlled areas. The reason is that the NMSP is generally seen as a better option than the official Myanmar system. The co-existence of official and unofficial justice systems is complicated, however, and Seik Soi villagers are not fully satisfied with any of the systems.

insterad they prefer to have cases resolved inside the village, and this is supported by the village leader, who gains authority and standing from handling disputes locally. It is only when resolutions at the village level fail that people forum shop. In doing this, they try, as much as possible, to avoid the official Myanmar system and instead try out case resolutions with various unofficial actors.

The chapter is based on empirical findings from ethnographic fieldwork in 2016–2018, which used in-depth interviews, case-tracing and participant observation.[2] We illustrate legal pluralism and forum shopping by drawing on an extended case study of the burning of a rubber plantation – i.e. an arson case – in Seik Soi. Before moving to the village, we first outline our main theoretical approach, including a discussion of the concepts of legal pluralism and forum shopping. This is followed by a brief background to the history and current situation of Seik Soi. Thirdly, we illustrate the insights of our empirical findings by drawing out the details of the arson case. We then discuss the underlying reasons for forum shopping and what repercussions it has for Mon villagers' access to justice. We conclude by reflecting on the policy implications of the study's insights.

Legal pluralism and forum shopping

Anthropological studies of micro-level dispute processes have the capacity to uncover the political dynamics and strategic manoeuvring involved in contexts where there is legal and institutional pluralism. They do this by exploring how different institutions that resolve disputes

2 A total of 54 qualitative interviews were conducted, including 36 with ordinary residents (16 with women and 20 with men); 11 with local leaders and elders; three with monks; two with spirit mediums; and one with a clerk. Twelve days of participant observation of dispute resolution were spent at the village tract administrative office. The research was conducted as part of the EverJust project, financed by the development research fund of the Danish Ministry of Foreign Affairs.

– both state/formal and non-state/informal institutions – relate to each other, as well as exploring the ways in which individuals pursue dispute resolution strategies in the context of a plurality of institutions (Merry 1988: 882). A core insight is that rather than simply co-existing, the different dispute resolution institutions influence each other through collaboration, competition, and opposition, often irrespective of their official legal status. At the same time, the preferences and strategies of people with disputes influence the actions and, ultimately, the authority of the different dispute resolution institutions (Lund 2006; S.F. Moore 1978; von Benda-Beckmann 1981; Kyed 2011). This study follows a similar inquiry. In particular, we engage with Keebet von Benda-Beckmann's use of the concepts of 'forum shopping' and 'shopping forums' to discuss the ways in which Mon villagers and village leaders navigate and influence the plural landscape of dispute resolution inside and outside the village.

Forum shopping describes a strategy where a disputing party or a victim or perpetrator of a crime switches between different dispute resolution forums. This occurs when contestants base their claims on the legal framework that suits them best among different alternatives – such as state law, customary rules and religious/spiritual norms. The choice of forum is based on what the contestant deems most likely to produce a satisfactory outcome, even though they might not always be successful (von Benda-Beckmann 1981; Lecoutere 2011). At the same time, forum shopping is a negotiation process in which power relations matter a great deal (Lecoutere 2011). To capture these power dynamics in a context of legal pluralism, von Benda-Beckmann (1981: 117) also introduces the concept of 'shopping forums'. She argues that it is not only the contestants who shop between different forums; the forums also 'shop' for clients and disputes. They do this to serve their own political ends, because resolving disputes is an important source of authority, and often of income too (Sikor and Lund 2009: 10). Put simply: when, for instance, village leaders are able to handle crimes outside of the official courts in Myanmar, this affords local authority to those village leaders, while also challenging the *de jure* authority of the courts. In von Benda-Beckmann's study in Indonesia, she shows how local authorities compete over and manipulate disputes to serve their own power agendas. In other situations, they fend off those disputes that might, they fear, threaten their position (von Benda-Beckmann 1981: 117).

On the other hand, dispute resolvers may also play a significant role in trying to prevent people from going to other forums or in guiding people's choices of alternative options, as we show in this chapter. Von Benda-Beckmann (1981: 139) argues that such strategies, which often involve what she calls 'jurisdictional disputes between institutions', can be seen as 'the legal expression of the struggle for power'. That is, shopping by forums is driven as much by a concern for consolidating positions vis-á-vis other forums as by the intention to ensure the best substantive outcome for the contestants. However, forums also need to take into account the fact that dissatisfaction with outcomes may lead contestants to shop for other forums.

As Sikor and Lund (2009) argue, the field of legal pluralism involves a dynamic relationship between institutions that resolve disputes (shopping forums) and individuals who have disputes that need to be dealt with (forum shoppers). This is because the 'claimants seek socio-political institutions to authorise their claims, and socio-political institutions look for claims to authorise' (Sikor and Lund 2009: 10). The relationship between different 'shopping forums' is also a dynamic one. Competition between forums often co-exists in the context of various forms of collaboration or cross-referencing. For instance, when village leaders cannot resolve a dispute or realise that resolving a particular dispute may harm their position, they may forward it to another institution or draw on other actors for assistance. In some situations, the mere threat of sending contestants to another institution can work as a tool to get the contestants to accept the decisions of the dispute resolver or to come to an agreement. The intention may not actually be to transfer the case to another institution, as this could undermine the authority of the dispute resolver, but rather to use the threat to leverage the contestants. As such, the different institutions may use each other strategically, while also seeing each other as competitors (Kyed 2011; Albrecht et al. 2011).

Some studies have shown how forum shopping can enhance people's access to justice, because it gives them different options in situations where, for instance, the official system is inadequate or fails to meet the justice demands of ordinary people (Unruh 2003; Meinzen-Dick and Pradhan 2002). Other studies have, by contrast, pointed to ways in which forum shopping enhances problems of insecurity and inequality (Crook 2004) or increases potential conflicts between different justice providers and authorities (von Benda-Beckmann 1981; Sikor and Lund 2009). What seems to matter is the relative power status of people involved in forum shopping (Lecoutere 2011: 262; Meinzen-Dick and Pradhan 2002). Under some conditions, forum shopping is mainly a strategy of the more powerful, who know the different options better and often tend to be less constrained by social pressure to go to particular forums (Lecoutere 2011: 263; E.P. Moore 1993; Vel and Makambombu 2010). In other contexts, forum shopping can be a tool for the marginalised to access justice. For instance, as shown by Lecoutere, women, who are treated as inferior in the Tanzanian village system, have successfully turned to state law or other institutions to get their claims met (Lecoutere 2011: 255).

It follows from this that the specific effects or outcomes of forum shopping depend on the empirical context, the people involved, and the dispute in question. In all situations, however, the concepts of forum shopping and shopping forums bring to the fore a focus on human agency that allows us to look beyond clearly defined rules within a single coherent legal system (Meinzen-Dick and Pradhan 2002: 27).

A core question is to what extent forum shopping is reflective of free choice between available alternatives, and thus what factors influence how people can shop between forums. The level of free choice depends, according to von Benda-Beckmann and von Benda-Beckmann (2006: 25), on a complex set of factors, including self-interest, commitment to or rejection of normative orders, suitability of the law to one's objectives, personal characteristics and economic factors. Social control and pressure to resolve disputes in certain forums also play a role. For instance, villagers may be reluctant to submit their cases outside the village, because they fear challenging the authority of village institutions or because they are tied to them through social relations (von Benda-Beckmann 1981: 143; see also Chapter 3, this volume). In this sense, choices are not entirely free.

Our study adds nuances to this insight by showing how state avoidance plays an important role in shaping forum shopping. While the state courts and the police are certainly options in forum shopping, both the village leader and villagers in Seik Soi try to avoid them as much as possible, because they see them as expensive, time-consuming and hazardous. Secondly, forum shopping in Seik Soi is influenced by the low enforceability of the different dispute forums. When people switch between forums it is often because the dispute forums are not able to enforce compensation or another outcome that they have decided upon. Here legality and norms become less relevant than efforts to get a verdict materialised, and thus it is the forum with the strongest enforcing power, even if this is illegal, that sometimes ensures the final outcome. Thirdly, language and identity influence the choice of forum outside the village, which is part of the reason why the NMSP, as an organisation that represents the Mon people and uses Mon language, is often the preferred option. Here, concern for legality is substituted by loyalty and identification. These different factors, along with social control and power dynamics more generally, shape and reshape the agency of, and choices available to, both forum shoppers and shopping forums, as they manoeuver and reproduce legal pluralism in Seik Soi.

The plural political and legal context in Seik Soi village

Seik Soi village is located in Ye township, which is the most southern of the ten townships in the geographical area of Mon State, as defined by the Myanmar state. It has a population of over 2,000, with a large majority of Buddhist Mon.[3] Since 1995, it has been officially governed by the Myanmar state, represented in the village by a village tract administrator (VTA), who himself is Mon. However, in the past the village was situated in a conflict area where battles occurred nearby between the Mon nationalist movement (NMSP) and the Myanmar military (the Tatmadaw). The long history of civil war has contributed to a situation of *de facto* legal and institutional pluralism in Ye township, as it has in other conflict-affected areas of southeast Myanmar (see Joliffe 2015; South 2017; Harrisson and Kyed 2019). In Ye township some villages are governed fully by the NMSP, others have mixed governance, and others are governed fully by the Myanmar state. The main highway that runs through the township divides the NMSP areas on the eastern side, where the NMSP has a township and district headquarter, from the Myanmar state areas on the western side, along the coast. Seik Soi village sits squarely on the western, and thus on the Myanmar state, side. This division has come about after many years of disputed control and armed fighting, which ended with a ceasefire in 1995.

3 Interview, village tract administrator (VTA), 28 February 2018.

Seik Soi village was already feeling the effects of the civil war in the 1950s, when the main Karen ethnic armed group, the Karen National Union (KNU), was operating in the area, mobilising support for the ethnic nationalist cause in collaboration with the Mon nationalist movements (South 2003: 109–117). The NMSP, which today continues to be the main Mon nationalist movement, was formed in 1958, after the Mon People's Front (MPF) signed a ceasefire with the government (ibid.: 118–119). Its armed wing, the MNLA (Mon National Liberation Army), was formed in 1971. After the military took power in Burma (now Myanmar) in 1962, the NMSP and the KNU made an agreement on the division of Mon and Karen territories (ibid.: 132–142). Along with fighting the Burmese military, the NMSP tried to establish control over Mon areas and in the 1970s it created 'liberated areas' where it started to develop civilian governance structures, including a tax system, an administration, schools and clinics. In was also during this time that the NMSP developed a justice system and a law book (McCartan and Jolliffe 2016). The NMSP's justice system consists of justice committees at central or Supreme Court, district, and township levels, with members from the administrative (NMSP) and armed (MNLA) wings, connected to the village level. The law covers all types of crimes and civil disputes.[4]

The NMSP tried to expand its system of civilian governance and justice to the whole area of what it regarded as the Mon Republic. However, most areas only had a meagre NMSP presence due to the ongoing fighting and the presence of the Burmese state's own structures (South 2003: 174–175). Seik Soi village exemplifies this complicated situation. Here the NMSP established a Mon school in the mid-1980s, but NMSP officials did not directly govern the village.[5] They could only move in and out of the village to collect contributions and provide MNLA patrols. Thus, except for education, the NMSP was not able to provide Seik Soi villagers with substantial services or protection inside the village. Villagers were also afraid to bring disputes and crimes to the NMSP.

Following the 1995 ceasefire, the NMSP was allowed to stabilise and consolidate its civilian governance structures, but only inside designated territories, known as 'permanent ceasefire positions' (ibid.: 225, 245). In Ye township this covered small patches in the thickly forested hills in the southeastern area just north of Ye town, where the

4 For more details on the NMSP justice system see Harrisson and Kyed (2019).

5 Interview, teacher in Mon school, 28 February 2018.

NMSP today continues to have township and district headquarters and to exert direct governance. However, the NMSP-controlled area did not include Seik Soi and other villages on the western side of the road. The ceasefire allowed the NMSP to set up Mon schools using the Mon language across Mon State. At the same time, the ceasefire enabled the military government to strengthen its control over non-NMSP areas. The government also kept the NMSP on its list of unlawful associations, which made it illegal and prosecutable for Mon people to engage with the NMSP outside the ceasefire areas (ibid.: 224).[6]

Figure 1.1 Golden sheldrake monument at the entrance to the village. The sheldrake is the symbol of the Mon National Movement, the New Mon State Party (NMSP). *Colour image p. 357.*

Between the ceasefire in 1995 and 2014, Seik Soi was regarded by the villagers as a kind of mixed-controlled area. Despite some tensions, and although the administration was under the Burmese government, the NMSP and the village administrators coexisted fairly peacefully. The NMSP could, without any major difficulties, collect household donations (a kind of tax) from villagers as well as have campaigns on social issues, such as education and the dangers of drug use. Many disputes and crimes that the village leaders could not resolve were also sent to the NMSP, rather than to the Myanmar state. The villagers we interviewed told us that at that time there was a sense of tolerance towards engaging with the NMSP, despite this being illegal according to Myanmar state law. Gradually however, the NMSP has had to operate more carefully: now, for instance, the NMSP does not collect household taxes, but only sells its own lottery

6 A bilateral ceasefire was renegotiated again in 2012 between the NMSP and the new quasi-civilian government under U Thein Sein, following a period of tension when the NMSP refused to come under the Burmese military-controlled Border Guard Force, along with other ethnic armed organisations (EAOs) (Kyed and Gravers 2015). In 2018 the NMSP signed the National Ceasefire Agreement (NCA), which took it off the list of unlawful associations. However, the fieldwork for this chapter was conducted prior to this agreement, and thus we do not include an analysis of the impact this agreement may have had on how the villagers can interact with the NMSP.

tickets and calendars in the village, to avoid problems with the Burmese government.[7] No-one could tell us exactly why this gradual withdrawal of the NMSP had occurred, but from our interviews it seems that shifting village tract administrators have become more reluctant to openly engage with the NMSP after the political transition. One member of the village development committee, however, told us that he believed that the NMSP's influence had decreased in the 2005–2010 period because the then VTA was corrupt and had an alliance with the police and township officials, with whom he shared bribes if he sent cases to the Myanmar state.[8] The VTA during our field research period had a very different reputation – he was known to be incorruptible and to be someone who tried to avoid sending cases to the Myanmar system. He was not against people going to the NMSP with cases that he could not resolve in the village, but he was careful, he told us, because he was aware that doing this was illegal. While the impact of wider national political dynamics is certainly important in influencing people's justice practices, our field work also suggests that dispute resolution both inside and outside the village remains strongly tied to the actions and positioning of the individual VTA. As we show further below, the VTA is also instrumental in balancing the relationship between actors and dispute forums outside the village, including the NMSP, the Tatmadaw and the Myanmar state's legal system.

Village dispute resolution and forum shopping

The village tract administrator (VTA) is the central person in Seik Soi when it comes to third party resolutions of crimes and social disputes. Below him are elders and 100-household leaders, who resolve smaller disputes and crimes and who may also assist in reporting cases to the VTA, if they cannot find solutions to the problems. There is also a paramilitary group in the village, which, during fieldwork, only comprised two members, who assisted the VTA in arresting suspects and in summoning parties to a dispute to come to the VTA office. They can

7 The lottery tickets that the NMSP sells are not tickets for the official government lottery, but for their own. This lottery is part of Mon National Day and Mon Revolution Day celebrations. Sometimes calendars are also sold. People buy these to show support for the NMSP.

8 Interview with a member of village development committee, June 10, 2016.

also take suspects to the Myanmar police, if the VTA judges that the case cannot be handled inside the village. Originally, the paramilitary group was formed by the Myanmar military to provide surveillance and gather information about insurgent groups; however, although they are still under the military and have guns and uniforms from the military, they are now mainly engaged in village security and they follow the orders of the VTA.

These village-level actors constitute an informal system of village dispute resolution, which uses reconciliation and mediation as its main mechanisms, combined with compensational justice and promise letters (*kahn won*) which instruct offenders not to repeat their offences. Although Myanmar law recognises these village-level actors as part of the state, they are not officially part of the judicial system. In practice, they are also relatively detached from the official justice system, not only because there are no official transfer procedures or appeal mechanisms, but also because the village actors have a very low level of trust in the official system. An extremely small number of crimes and civil disputes reach the courts and the police.

According to the VTA, who was in office until mid-2016, around 90 per cent of the cases that villagers reported during his term of office were resolved at the VTA office.[9] He told us that of the rest, 3 per cent were forwarded to the official Myanmar system and 7 per cent were dealt with by the NMSP. According to the ordinary villagers whom we interviewed, this reflects a strong preference for resolving disputes and crimes within their own village. As we have discussed elsewhere (Kyed 2018a; Poine 2018), bringing one's case to a public place is associated with shame and loss of dignity, sometimes combined with fear of authority, and these feelings are worsened if you report a case outside the village. This means that not all cases are reported to the VTA, but are resolved inside the family or among neighbours. In certain situations, people do not even try to resolve their own disputes or crimes. Women in particular – as discussed by Mi Thang Sorn Poine (2018) – are reluctant even to report cases to the household leaders, elders or the VTA. They prefer either to keep a matter to themselves, to deal with the matter within the family, or to seek advice and spiritual guidance from astrologers, spirit mediums and sometimes monks. Villagers are also reluctant to go to the official system because it is associated with high costs and very slow and difficult

9 Interview, VTA, 1 March 2018.

procedures. Language is also an issue, because many do not know Burmese well, and this is the language spoken in the official system. The VTA, on the other hand, speaks Mon, charges much lower fees, and taking cases to him leads to quicker resolutions and compensation being paid to the victims.

Figure 1.2 Village tract administrator's office where many disputes are heard and settled in the village. *Colour image p. 357.*

At the same time, our findings also suggest that the predominance of village-level resolutions is influenced by the fact that the VTA operates as a kind of gatekeeper to outside institutions. Because the VTA is the highest authority in the village, the villagers feel compelled always to first report any issue to him, even if they desire to have a case resolved outside the village. They are reluctant to ask for the VTA's advice on state justice or to get the recommendation letters from him that are needed in order to send cases to the state system unless he himself suggests that a case should be forwarded to the state. In general, we found that the VTA always seeks to resolve crimes and social disputes himself, even when such cases are beyond his official mandate (which is the case with more serious crimes and divorce). The VTA explained that it was both shameful and complicated for him to transfer cases to higher levels. He did not believe that the official system would be able to properly resolve the cases. He did not trust the system and feared that it would place high costs and burdens on the parties. Often when villagers had been to the official system they would come back and complain to him about negative experiences. In addition, the VTA felt that if cases went to the formal system the village would look bad, as a place with problems.

Several times when we were at the VTA's office we observed how the VTA would threaten or warn villagers about the problems associated with going to the official system, explaining, for example, how slow and costly it was. This made people even more reluctant to go to the official system. As we will discuss in detail below in relation to the arson case, the VTA preferred to use various informal contacts and mechanisms to resolve difficult cases, rather than sending them to the official courts. In fact, the VTA indirectly compelled people to go to the NMSP courts, even if this was presented as a free choice. We can therefore see that the VTA plays a kind of gatekeeper role to the official justice system. This means that the choice of justice provider is not entirely free, and this, we suggest, shapes the way in which forum shopping unfolds in the village.

With this in mind, it is worth noting that the VTA and the leaders and elders who work with him do have an economic and political interest in resolving disputes inside the village, as this brings them both income and authority. Each dispute resolution case carries a fee of MMK 5,000 per party (USD 3.50), which goes to the VTA; and in 2019 the fee for granting a divorce was MMK 10,000 for women and 15,000 for men (previously it had been a total of MMK 50,000). The VTA does not, in fact, have a legal mandate to handle divorce, but in practice he does do so. While these fees are substantially lower than the costs associated with the formal system (which in addition to court fees also include transportation costs to travel outside the village), they still matter to the VTA, as he can use them for village development, which augments his standing in the village. For instance, MMK 5,000 is equivalent to half a day's wage for a worker at a rubber plantation and a third of the daily wage of a construction worker, so it is a considerable amount – though not too much for an ordinary villager to afford.[10]

Thus, most cases in Seik Soi are resolved inside the village, and the VTA is central to their resolution. When difficult cases come up which need to be referred outside the village, the VTA still plays an important role, acting as the focal point and steering the process of allocating and advancing the cases. During our fieldwork, this typically involved strategies of state avoidance and finding alternatives to the formal system. The VTA would give parties the choice of either going to the official system or to the NMSP, but in his explanation of these choices we detected a certain favouring of the NMSP – or at least a more negative attitude towards the Myanmar system than towards the NMSP. This bias was

10 According to what we were told in conversations with various people in the village, a family with five or six members spends somewhere between MMK 3,000 and 8,000 a day on food and other expenses. In terms of salaries there is a bit of difference between seasonal and permanent workers – the former, who only work 6–7 months a year in the rubber plantations, typically have a yearly income of 50 lahk (USD 3,500 approximately), whereas a person with a permanent job earns 35 lahk.

shared by the villagers we interviewed, who said they preferred to go to the NMSP if the VTA could not resolve their case. Although people also hesitated to go to the NMSP, because they knew that their courts are not legal, they still preferred to do this, because the NMSP are Mon; they use the Mon language, and people often have personal connections to individuals within the NMSP. Also, the NMSP justice system is free, as there are no fees to pay. While villagers are never absolutely sure that the NMSP will provide a fair and effective resolution, they are even less confident of this in the Myanmar system. Geographical distance seems to be much less of an issue. For Seik Soi villagers it takes one hour to get to the NMSP township office and one and a half hours to get to the district office by motorbike. By comparison, it only takes 20 minutes by motorbike to reach the Myanmar police and 45 minutes to reach the Myanmar township court. Thus, while the Myanmar state is much closer, and officially governs Seik Soi, there is still an orientation towards the NMSP system.

In what follows we will look in more detail at how Seik Soi villagers face challenges to justice when village actors cannot resolve a difficult case. We will see how, in addition to seeking justice through the NMSP, there is also an informal involvement of armed actors as well as the use of spiritual advice. Here forum shopping is not based entirely on free choice, but it steered by the village authorities and shaped by the limits to justice and the plurality of authorities outside the village.

The rubber plantation arson case

On 5 April 2016, around 500 rubber trees in A's plantation were burnt and in the same fire B lost all of his garden trees.[11] This happened just outside Seik Soi village. The two victims suspected that C had caused the fire, since A had seen that the fire came from C's garden on the day of the fire.[12] A village committee member was also witness to the fire. The vic-

11 The account of the case provided here is based on interviews with members of the family of one of the victims, with the VTA, and with a few other villagers who knew about the case, as well as on participant observation of some parts of the case resolution. Unfortunately, it was not possible to interview the second victim or the accused, as they were not present in the village when we tried to interview them, and the family members of the accused did not want to speak about the case. We realise that this biases our account.

12 Participant observation, 12 July 2017, VTA office; and interview, VTA, 8 October 2016.

Figure 1.3 Spirit medium performing a ritual. Many villagers go to the spirit medium for consultation, including to hear if they will have luck in successfully resolving a crime or a dispute. *Colour image p. 358.*

tims reported the case to the VTA's office and informed the VTA of the identity of the suspected perpetrator. The VTA tried to get C to come to the office, but C did not turn up. So the VTA got help from the paramilitary leader, who warned C twice, saying that if he did not come to the office he would be arrested and sent to the police. After that, C came to the VTA's office, but he denied the accusations. The VTA and the paramilitary leader went to the field to investigate the site of the fire, and based on this and A's eyewitness account the VTA decided that C was guilty and that he should pay 30 lakh (USD 2,100) in total in compensation to the victims, an amount that is close to the minimum annual income of a village resident who works in rubber plantations (yearly incomes range from 35 to 60 lakh).[13] However, C did not agree to this.

While the process was being handled at the VTA office, A's wife went to seek spiritual advice. First she went to a fortune-teller and later to a spirit medium. Some of their neighbours and relatives believed that the fire might have been a sign that one of the victim's family members had been attacked by a bad spirit (*out-lan*). However, A and his daughter told us that A's wife did not go to the spiritual actors because she believed that there had been possession by an evil spirit but rather to hear if 2016 would be a fortunate year to win the case. The spiritual actors had said that the A family would indeed win the case. However, they also said that the perpetrator would pay less in compensation than the victims wanted. This was actually what happened in the end.

The VTA tried hard to get C to pay the victims. He threatened to send the case to the NMSP if C did not agree to pay. While this kind of threat sometimes works to get the accused party to agree on a settlement at the VTA's office, C did not comply. He simply told the VTA that he

13 At this point they did not discuss how this amount should be divided between the victims.

was not afraid of the threats, because he did not commit the crime. The VTA now told the victims that he could not negotiate anymore. The case needed to be transferred to a higher level. He explained to A and B what the two options available to them were: to proceed to the NMSP or to go to the Myanmar government at township level. In his explanation he cast a negative light on the Myanmar system, saying that the process would be lengthy and costly, and that compensation was not guaranteed and might even be lower than the fees they would have to pay to go to court. He also warned them that the officials might ask for bribes.

The victims chose to go to the NMSP, and the VTA agreed. Subsequently, the VTA told us that he was well aware that by allowing the case to be handled by the NMSP he was moving outside the legal boundaries of his position, 'because the NMSP is still considered an armed group [and] the Myanmar government has told us that we cannot send cases to the NMSP'. Therefore he could only 'secretly send litigants to the NMSP if the litigants preferred this [to the Myanmar government]'.[14] The family of A told us that they preferred the NMSP, because, as A himself said: 'We have heard that this is best, and also the perpetrator cannot speak Burmese – so we believed it was better with the NMSP'.[15]

The victims then went to the NMSP at the township headquarters with an informal, unstamped, letter from the VTA. This prompted the NMSP at the township level to call both parties for a hearing. Members of the NMSP also went to the plantation to investigate the fire and estimate the damages. Like the VTA, the NMSP also decided that C was the perpetrator. At the township headquarters, C admitted his guilt and said that he would pay if the authorities told him to do so. In doing this, he was submitting himself to the NMSP decision. The NMSP officials said that the loss of the trees totalled 84 lakh (USD 5,900) and instructed C to compensate the victims with that amount. C, however, said that he was unable to pay such a large amount. The NMSP officials then negotiated with the victims to reduce the sum to 40 lakh (USD 2,800). This was also too high for C, who only wanted to pay 20 lakh — an amount that in turn was too low for A and B. A said to us: 'The NMSP tried to convince us to accept [the 20 lakh], but we did not agree'.[16]

14 Interview, VTA, 15 December 2016.

15 Interview, Victim A, 13 December 2016.

16 Interview, Victim A, 13 December 2016.

The victims returned twice to negotiate the case at the NMSP township level, but C did not turn up, and consequently the case was transferred to the NMSP district level. C, however, never turned up for the hearings at district level and the NMSP subsequently gave up on the case. This was in the month of May.

According to A, the NMSP officials explained that they could not force the perpetrator to turn up at the district headquarters, because they had no power to arrest people from Seik Soi. A explained to us that: 'The NMSP cannot use pressure because we [victims and perpetrator] are on the other side of the road [in relation to] Burmese control. For us people on this side [under Burmese control] the NMSP can only call people and negotiate with them. They cannot arrest people on the Burmese side'.[17] This illustrates the limits of the authority of the NMSP and of their capacity to resolve cases that occur within areas officially controlled by the Myanmar government.

The case now returned to the VTA with a transfer letter from the NMSP. On July 12, we were present at the hearing of the case at the VTA's office. Three months had passed since the fire. Both A and B were at the office when we arrived and they complained to us that they were very tired of C and could not understand why he did not properly appreciate their big loss. Now, they said, they had also had to spend a lot of money on transport to go to the NMSP. Eventually C turned up with his wife. The VTA called both parties to sit in front of his desk and started the hearing. At first, the VTA listened calmly and spoke with a soft voice. However, when C said that he was not guilty, the VTA got very upset, asking C how he could refuse guilt after admitting guilt at the NMSP township level. The VTA shouted at C: 'What do you want now?' C answered in a low voice: 'I didn't burn their rubber trees, so I want to do *yorhjal*'. *Yorhjal* means to swear to say the truth and has traditionally been used among the Mon when guilt cannot be established through material evidence. If the other parties agree to *yorhjal* they must accept it as a statement of truth, which means they can no longer pressurise the accused to admit guilt and pay compensation. If what is sworn to in *yorhjal* is false, however, the person who has sworn that it is the truth will be punished through bad fortune, such as having an accident or losing property. Nonetheless, *yorhjal* always means, whether the person swearing is telling the truth or not, that the victim

17 Interview, Victim A, 13 December 2016.

gets no compensation. By asking to do *yorhjal*, the perpetrator was not only refusing guilt, but also trying to avoid paying compensation by referring to a Mon customary norm and practice. He was in a sense doing his own kind of forum shopping in terms of switching from a secular to a non-secular legal framework.

At the hearing on 12 July, the VTA did not agree to *yorhjal*. The victims were not asked if they agreed or not. Instead, the VTA got very angry with C, and said: 'I don't understand why you say that now [that C wanted to do *yorhjal*]. You have transferred the case many times and you agreed that the court could make a decision. Now the case has come back to me again, from the NMSP court, because you didn't pay the compensation. You are wasting our time and making all of us tired. Now you are saying something different again. You are making us crazy'.[18] The VTA was clearly very upset that C did not agree to the conclusions of the negotiations at his office and at the NMSP. He also felt that C had failed to show respect, stating that: 'You made people feel confused, when we were considering and understanding of your side of the case'.

The VTA told the parties that he would no longer deal with the case, but that now: 'I will let the police resolve it'. By police, he meant the Myanmar state police, at township level. Later, the VTA told us that part of the reason why he was upset was that when such a case was returned to him from a higher-level authority such as the NMSP, he lost the power to deal with the perpetrator. This is because 'it gives the perpetrator more confidence to win', the VTA explained. He further said: 'Cases are very difficult to deal with when they come back from the upper level because the perpetrator is more difficult to deal with as he has got confidence through not having had to pay [compensation] at the higher level'.[19] This whole situation forced the VTA to derive pressure from elsewhere, namely from the Myanmar state police. He explained to C that the police would not speak as nicely to him as he, the VTA, had done. C left with his wife, and before the victims left, the VTA told them to go the police the next morning together with the paramilitary leader. He advised them to treat the police to tea or breakfast. That way, the police would be friendly to them (i.e. they would treat them well and favour their case), the VTA said. The VTA was clearly not happy about sending the people to the police, but he felt he had no

18 Fieldnotes, 12 July 2016.

19 Interview, VTA, 15 December 2016.

other choice, because by continuing to try to resolve it he would lose face. But he also felt that he had no good alternative and no authority to back him up outside the village. His suggestion to flatter the police with breakfast also clearly reflects the fact that the VTA knows that the police work best with bribery.

The case, however, did not proceed to the police or the official Myanmar court. Without telling the victims, the VTA told the police to wait, as he would try to negotiate once more. The police accepted this and allowed the VTA to work further on the case. The VTA later explained to us that he never really wanted to send the case to the police, but just wanted to use this as a threat, because he hoped it would make C pay finally. On other occasions we also witnessed this kind of threat, which the VTA used to try to get the parties to agree on a resolution at his office. The villagers are very afraid of the police, the VTA told us, and this fear may help to ensure that cases are resolved inside the village.

In this case, however, the threat of sending the case to the police did not work. So the VTA had to come up with another alternative to pressurise C to compensate A and B. In early October the VTA asked the secret service (*Saya Pa Yin*) of the Tatmadaw (the Burmese military) to help in getting C to pay.[20] The Saya Pa Yin has an unofficial office just outside the ordinary Tatmadaw camp, located on the main road, some six kilometres from Seik Soi village. According to the VTA, the Saya Pa Yin is specialised in watching the armed groups in the area and is therefore not an official place for handling crimes. Nonetheless, the personnel at the office took over the arson case.

When the case reached the Saya Pa Yin office, the officers there spoke to the VTA about the case over the phone and called the victims. This was on 9 October and the case was resolved the next day. A described to us what happened: 'When we first arrived at the office there was a Bamar three-star Tatmadaw officer inside, but when he realised that we are Mon, he called a Mon guy, who was dressed in civilian clothes. The Mon person's assistant went to arrest the perpetrator. He was like a secretary of the Mon man and he was wearing a Mon *longyi*. C was kept at the office for one night.'[21] The people at the Saya Pa Yin office said that he should compensate the victims with two cows, because they had seen that the man owned two cows. But C insisted that he did not

20 Some people call the Saya Pa Yin the Thatt Yin ('Military Camp') office.

21 Interview, Victim A, 13 December 2016.

own much and that his family would not be able to survive without any cows. So the Saya Pa Yin officer called the VTA on the phone, and the VTA suggested that the compensation should be one cow. This was the final decision. The perpetrator would not give his cow up voluntarily, so the military officer from the Saya Pa Yin office went to C's field, found a cow and gave it to the victims. The victims subsequently sold the cow and split the money. A, who had lost the largest number of trees, got six lakh, and B got three lakh. They were not satisfied, because, as A said: 'We lost a lot of compensation [84 lakh, according to the NMSP valuation]. The amount was low compared to what we lost. But we had to accept or get nothing'.[22] In addition, they had to pay 10 per cent of the compensation and an additional MMK 50,000 case resolution fee to the Saya Pa Yin office. The victims felt that this was a large amount, but they acknowledged that this kind of payment was inherent in dealing with the Myanmar state. At the VTA office they would have had to each pay MMK 5,000. The NMSP system was free of charge. Having the case resolved by the military was thus the most expensive option, but the victims found that it was their only option.

The victims were not entirely sure who the people at the Saya Pa Yin office were, and neither did they know the man who arrested the perpetrator and negotiated the case. At that point, they were exhausted, after being redirected so many times, and were mainly concerned to get something out of the case. They were simply following the advice of the VTA. A said that he believed that the office was, in fact, a place where the Mon and Karen armed groups that have signed ceasefires with the government meet to work together on resolving matters, such as cases that come from the village.

The VTA, however, denied that the Saya Pa Yin office had anything to do with the ethnic armed groups. He said it was purely a Tatmadaw office and that it is located outside the military camp because it is not permitted to let civilians inside the camp to deal with civilian matters. It is a secret, unofficial place, which most villagers do not know about, he said. But he knows the people at the Saya Pa Yin office because they go to the VTA for intelligence – such as information about the movement of ethnic armed groups in and around the village. The VTA told us that: 'It is illegal for me to resolve [cases] there. It is like an informal

22 Interview, Victim A, 13 December 2016.

understanding. So I had to stay at my office'.[23] He explicitly said that the Saya Pa Yin office cannot officially get involved in village matters. He only uses it, secretly, as a last resort, when the accused party is 'very difficult' – by which he meant when the accused refuses to agree to a negotiated settlement at the VTA office. He is also reluctant to send people there, because the fees are high. The Saya Pa Yin office thus comes through as a pragmatic yet precarious last resort for avoiding the official Myanmar justice system.

Discussion: Unpredictability and unstable authority

The arson case illustrates the plethora of dispute resolution actors who may get involved in resolving a crime in Seik Soi when village level resolutions fail. It is clear, from this case, that the official state institutions, beyond the VTA, play no direct role in the provision of justice. The police and the courts are present, but only as a point of reference, in the form of a negative warning and a threat which the VTA uses to facilitate an informal resolution (for instance, when he gives litigants the choice of sending the case to the court and when he threatens to send the parties to the police). Instead, what dominates in the pursuit of a outcome (in this case, compensation for the victims) are informal and illegal forums, outside the sphere of the official juridical system: the VTA, the NMSP, members of a secret military intelligence group, and, to a lesser extent, spiritual actors.

In this section, we wish to discuss the underlying reasons for forum shopping and the wider consequences that forum shopping has for villagers' access to justice. The arson case illustrates instances of both 'forum shopping' and 'shopping forums', as described by von Benda-Beckman (1981), but we suggest that the choice of justice provider is not based entirely on free choice and strategic calculations. While effective outcomes and financial costs are important to the trajectories of forum shopping, the underlying causes of forum shopping are the deep instability of authority in the area and a widespread distrust and fear of official law and institutions. Issues like trust, familiarity, and shame are equally important, and these concerns are not only in danger of overruling legality, but also the effectiveness of resolutions.

23 Interview, VTA, 15 December 2016.

In the arson case, the immediate concern of the victims was not a desire to follow the law and official legal procedures, but how to obtain the compensation they wanted in a way that placed the minimum possible burden on them in terms of financial costs, dignity and feeling comfortable with the situation. The first choice for the victims was therefore not to go to the police with the case, but to resolve the case at the village level, which is associated with lower levels of cost, fear and shame. It was only when the village resolution proved ineffective that the victims chose an external provider. Although the NMSP is illegal, and therefore a risky choice, as well as being geographically much farther away than the Myanmar police and court, it was still the preferred choice of the victims. Guiding this choice was not only the lower costs associated with going to the NMSP, but also the higher level of trust that the victims had in the NMSP as compared with the official Myanmar system. The NMSP officials speak Mon and are perceived to be valid representatives of the interests of the Mon people. Although the NMSP does not have much ability to enforce its authority in government-controlled areas like Seik Soi village, the fact that the NMSP is a Mon organisation plays a significant role here.

This preference for the NMSP is, we suggest, heavily influenced by the long history of ethno-nationalist conflict and the military government's oppression of ethnic minorities, which has fostered a strong sense that Burmese government officials will be biased against Mon villagers. This sentiment, along with experiences with corrupt Myanmar state officials, causes many to associate state justice with high financial costs, fear and loss of dignity. These feelings are so strong that the villagers risk the long journey across government boundaries into rebel territory to have their cases heard, even though they are aware of the NMSP's lack of authority to actually enforce decisions, something that was clear in the arson case. Avoidance of the Myanmar state is therefore central to forum shopping.

Importantly, consulting the NMSP was not based only on free choice on the part of the victims. Central to the whole process of forum shopping is the gatekeeper role of the VTA. In the arson case, the VTA steered the choices of the parties quite forcefully, and directed how the case travelled between different forums and moved in and out of his own domain of dispute resolution. At first, the VTA tried as hard as he could to resolve the case at the VTA office. When this proved difficult, he used the NMSP and the official Myanmar system to threaten the accused, to make him admit guilt and pay compensation at the VTA office. On many occasions such threats are successful, and the case ends with the VTA, but in this arson case the VTA felt that he had no other option but to transfer the case outside the village. When he instructed the victims to choose between the NMSP and the Myanmar system, he clearly favoured the former. Later he was also the one who decided to send the case to the military intelligence office, instead of the police. Through these moves, the VTA office operates as a 'shopping forum' (von Benda-Beckmann 1981), because the VTA seeks to resolve and manoeuvre cases himself, even when such cases are beyond his official mandate. However, in contrast to what von Benda-Beckmann found in the study in Indonesia, shopping by forums in Seik Soi does not reflect direct competition between different dispute resolution forums and authorities *per se*. While it is evident that the VTA's redirection of cases towards the informal arena contributes to undermining the authority of the official Myanmar system, the VTA's primary concern is not to oppose the Myanmar state or compete with it. Rather, his actions reflect his own distrust of the state, of which he is, in fact, formally part. His main concern is to end the conflict and get the victims an acceptable outcome, in order not to lose face and standing in the village.

Overall, the manoeuvring by the VTA demonstrates neither strong opposition nor loyalty towards any state or authority outside the village, be it the NMSP or the Myanmar state. As a Mon, he recommended that victims go to the NMSP, but in our interviews with him he made it clear that he did not have much faith personally in the NMSP, because of its lack of effective enforcing power outside NMSP territory. In addition, by deciding to finally send the case to the 'other side' – to the Tatmadaw military intelligence office – he demonstrated that his main concern was to end the case as quickly as possible and not to demonstrate loyalty to any particular authority outside the village. This whole process of switching forums reflects the deeper instability and pluralism of authorities, among which the VTA must carefully navigate in order to safeguard his own position within the village. His standing is less dependent on support from upper level authorities, and more on acceptance by the villagers. Thus, he engages external powers only as a very last resort. This approach is broadly shared by the villagers, who prefer village level resolution by far. The insecurity associated with engaging forums outside the village is part of the explanation for this preference.

As was evident in the arson case, the whole process of forum shopping is fraught with unpredictability and chance, because you can never be sure of the outcome. Victims must be persistent in constantly trying their luck, and risk facing higher costs and burdens at every step. The accused is not sure to get a voice or a proper investigation into his culpability. The victims are not sure to get compensation. This uncertainty helps explain why the woman associated with victim A sought spiritual advice to learn whether her side would have luck with the case. In other cases that we followed, people gave up on pursuing their cases altogether or went to spiritual actors for advice on how to deal, at a personal level, with their grievances. This underlines the fact that you must be rather courageous to engage in forum shopping, as it always involves additional burdens, both financial and emotional.

Forum shopping in a context where there are plural and uncertain authorities as well as high levels of mistrust in the official system has, we suggest, both positive and negative repercussions for ordinary villagers' access to justice. On the one hand, the availability of alternatives to the official Myanmar system provides litigants (and village leaders) with less costly avenues for seeking justice outcomes. On the other hand, forum shopping reinforces the very uncertainty and unpredictability of justice outcomes and processes that are part of the reasons for forum shopping in the first place. In Seik Soi, the trajectories and results of forum shopping are also highly dependent on the attitude and capabilities of intermediary actors, here the VTA, rather than purely on free choice on the part of the disputing parties. The VTA, in the arson case, was clearly intent not only on safeguarding his own position, but also on securing a satisfactory outcome for the victims. The previous VTA was not like that, interviewees told us. He was selfish and corrupt, and sent many cases to the police, we were told, with whom he shared bribes. During his time in office, people reported fewer cases to the VTA, or tried to forum shop themselves. Thus, forum shopping does not resolve the underlying challenge of uncertain authorities and mistrust that makes access to justice so unpredictable in Seik Soi. Notably, in the arson case, this means that the last resort becomes the Tatmadaw – the very institution that is associated with the decade-long violent oppression of the Mon minority.

The arson case is atypical in the sense that few cases in Seik Soi are resolved with the direct involvement of armed men. We encountered only four that had occurred in recent years. However, the fact that such cases exist reflects the way in which the continued militarisation of power in Mon State is kept in place by a dysfunctional official justice system and a disempowered NMSP alternative. It also illuminates the reasons for villagers and village leaders alike persisting in their preference not just for resolving disputes within the village, but also for using forum shopping – primarily as a strategy for avoiding the state.

Conclusion

Drawing on the legal anthropological literature on forum shopping, we have explored the provision of everyday justice in a village in southern Mon State. For villagers, accessing justice outside the village is challenging. The socio-political context within which they navigate contains multiple competing authorities and powerholders, who either do not enjoy legitimacy – due to fear and mistrust – or do not have enough legal and institutional backing to enforce decisions. We suggest that this reflects a deeper history of conflict, militarised governance and competing state formation processes.

While informal village resolution and forum shopping constitute positive alternatives to the distrusted and costly official judicial system, forum shopping within informal arenas also perpetuates high levels of uncertainty in ordinary villagers' access to justice. Much depends on individual leaders and actors, and their capacity to manoeuvre and be courageous and persistent in obtaining justice outcomes. For this reason, less resourceful victims or parties to a dispute, such as women, often give up on seeking remedies altogether, or turn to religious and spiritual actors, as Mi Thang Sorn Poine (2018) has described in another article on Seik Soi.

To address these challenges to everyday access to justice in Myanmar, we suggest that justice sector reform should not aim at erasing legal pluralism, but should rather focus on establishing more reliable linkages between the multiple forums. This would include stronger legal backing for those justice providers who are trusted by the ordinary villagers. Supporting a more pluralised and inclusive system could also put indirect pressure on the official system to be more responsive to the justice demands of ordinary villagers. As a first step this could involve officially recognising the role in justice provision of Village Tract Administrators (VTA), who are currently disconnected from the official judiciary and have to act without official mandate and guidance when they deal with civil and criminal cases. There are no safeguards and there is no reliable outside backing for these administrators, and their ways of resolving disputes remain highly dependent on their individual attitudes and capacities. Recognition of their role in justice provision and support for their enforcement authority could reduce the insecurity felt by village leaders in carrying out their tasks. It could also lead to an improvement in dispute resolution by making procedures and mechanisms more transparent and predictable.

Secondly, the Myanmar state should consider ways to recognise the justice system of the NMSP as an alternative option for Mon villagers, one that is more familiar, less costly and more trusted. Since the initial fieldwork was done for this study, the NMSP has signed the National Ceasefire Agreement (NCA) with the Myanmar government, which could open up ways to build linkages and achieve mutual recognition between the Myanmar and NMSP systems. In fact, the NCA recognises that the ethnic armed organisations (EAOs) 'have been responsible for development and security in their respective areas' and stipulates that signatory EAOs and the Myanmar state should coordinate 'matters regarding peace and stability and the maintenance of the rule of law' (NCA, quoted in McCartan and Jolliffe 2016: 22–23). However, the NCA does not provide a plan for how such arrangements should be implemented. This needs to be decided among stakeholders in the political dialogue (Cathcart 2016). However, currently (February 2020) this dialogue seems to be stalled, because of continued fighting in other areas of Myanmar as well as persistent fear and mistrust on both sides. This shows how justice provision is often driven more by politics and power than by efforts to ensure that ordinary villagers get the kinds of justice they seek.

References

Albrecht, P., Kyed, H.M., Harper, E. and Isser, D.

2011. *Perspectives on Involving Non-State and Customary Actors in Justice and Security Reform.* Rome: IDLO.

Cathcart, G.

2016. *Myanmar's Future can be Built in the Interim.* s.l.: New Mandala. www.newmandala.org/myanmars-future-can-be-built-in-the-interim/.

Crook, R.C.

2004. 'Access to justice and land disputes in Ghana's state courts: The litigant's perspective.' *Journal of Legal Pluralism* 36(50): 1–28.

Harrisson, A. & Kyed, H.M.

2019. 'Ceasefire state-making and justice provision by ethnic armed groups in Southeast Myanmar.' *Journal of Social Issues in Southeast Asia* 34(2): 290–326.

Jolliffe, K.

2015. *Ethnic Armed Conflict and Territorial Administration in Myanmar.* Report for The Asia Foundation, July 2015.

Kyed, H.M.

2011. 'Legal pluralism and international development interventions.' *Journal of Legal Pluralism and Unofficial Law* 43(63): 1–23.

2018a. 'Introduction to the special issue on everyday justice.' *Independent Journal of Burmese Scholarship* 1(2): 1–16. 2018b. *Community-Based Dispute Resolution. Exploring Everyday Justice in Southeast Myanmar.* Report for the International Rescue Committee and Danish Institute for International Studies, July 2018.

Kyed, H.M. & Gravers, M.

2015. 'Integration and power-sharing: What are the future options for armed non-state actors in the Myanmar peace process?' *Stability* 4(1): 1–20.

Lecoutere, E.

2011. 'Institutions under construction: Resolving resource conflicts in Tanzanian irrigation systems.' *Journal of Eastern African Studies* 5(2): 252–273.

Lund, C.

2006. 'Twilight institutions: Public authority and local politics in Africa.' *Development and Change* 37(4): 686–705.

McCartan, B. & Jolliffe, K.

2016. *Ethnic Armed Actors and Justice Provision in Myanmar.* Report for the Asia Foundation, October 2016.

Meinzen-Dick, R.S. & Pradhan, R.

2002. *Legal Pluralism and the Dynamic of Property Rights.* CaPRi Working Paper 21.

Merry, S.E.

1988. 'Legal pluralism.' *Law and Society Review* 22(5): 869–896.

Moore, E.P.

1993. 'Gender, power, and legal pluralism: Rajasthan, India.' *American Ethnologist* 20(3): 522–542.

Moore, S.F.

1978. 'Individual interests and organisational structures. Dispute settlements as "events of articulation".' In I. Hamnett (ed.), *Social Anthropology and Law*. New York: Academic Press. pp. 159–188.

2000. *Law as Process. An Anthropological Approach*. Hamburg: Lit Verlag; Oxford: James Currey.

NMSP (New Mon State Party)

1998. *Law for Making Decisions in Cases*. Translation from Mon language by EverJust research. Unpublished.

Poine, T.S.

2018. 'Gendered aspects of access to justice in southern Mon State.' *Independent Journal of Burmese Scholarship* 1(2): 1–25.

Sikor, T. & Lund, C.

2009. 'Access and property: A question of power and authority.' *Development and Change* 40(1): 1–22.

South, A.

2003. *Mon Nationalism and Civil War in Burma: The Golden Sheldrake*. New York and London: RoutledgeCurzon.

2017. '"Hybrid governance" and the politics of legitimacy in the Myanmar peace process.' *Journal of Contemporary Asia* 48(1): 50–66.

Unruh, J.D.

2003. 'Land tenure and legal pluralism in the peace process.' *Peace and Change* 28(3): 352–377.

Vel, J.A.C & Makambombu, S.

2010. 'Access to agrarian justice in Sumba, Eastern Indonesia.' *Law, Social Justice and Global Development Law Journal* 1: 1–22.

von Benda-Beckmann, K.

1981. 'Forum shopping and shopping forums: dispute processing in a Minangkabau village in west Sumatra.' *Journal of Legal Pluralism and Unofficial Law* 13(19): 117–159.

von Benda-Beckmann, F. & von Benda-Beckmann, K.

2006. 'Change and continuity in plural legal orders.' *Journal of Legal Pluralism and Unofficial Law* 38(53–54): 1–44.

2 The shadow power of armed actors: Justice-seeking practices in a rural Pa-O Self-Administered Zone

Mi Thang Sorn Poine and Nan Tin Nilar Win

Introduction

This chapter explores justice-seeking and security practices in a rural Pa-O village in southern Shan State, where the majority are Pa-O Buddhist. The Pa-O have a Self-Administered Zone (SAZ), which was established in 2011 (Yue 2015; Thot 2018). The area was affected by armed conflict until 1991 when the Pa-O National Organisation (PNO) signed a ceasefire with the military government (Yue 2016). The armed wing of the PNO, the Pa-O National Army (PNA), is now officially under the Myanmar military (Tatmadaw) and is considered a people's militia (*pyithu sit*), but it also operates on its own and runs private businesses. The PNO is now a political party and governs the SAZ. It also operates its own justice system, in parallel to the official Myanmar courts. The village under study is under mixed administration and has a plurality of governing actors, including the Myanmar government administration, the civilian elected government of the SAZ and the local structures of the PNO, as well as armed members of the PNA. In addition, at village level there is an informal system for dispute resolution and security provision, which is run by headmen, village elders and youth groups, who apply their own village principles.

How are disputes and crimes resolved under these conditions of plural governance and mixed administration and how do ordinary villagers access justice? We explore this question based on ethnographic fieldwork carried out in June 2017 and March 2018.[1] Overall, our findings show that the village dispute resolution and security system is preferred by villagers. When cases cannot be resolved at the village lev-

1 We used a methodology based on qualitative interviews, case tracing, and participant observation. We interviewed 25 people, including village elders and leaders, PNO members, the Myanmar government village tract administrator, as well as ordinary villagers, including young people, women and victims in cases.

el, villagers prefer to go to the PNO rather than to the Myanmar justice system. However, while the PNO is the preferred justice option above the village level, there are individual members of the PNO and PNA who, along with other military actors, cause villagers to have a sense of fear and insecurity. This is most evident when claims by villagers go against the business interests of the armed actors.

Overall, we argue that armed actors continue to play a role as shadow power holders in the Pa-O SAZ, which has an important influence on the situation in terms of security and justice for ordinary villagers in our field site. In this situation, the PNO and the PNA play a dual and ambiguous role: while the PNO, often in alignment with the PNA, acts to protect and represent the interests of the Pa-O villagers, there are also instances where the villagers find that members of the PNO and PNA act against villagers' interests and do not support their rights. The villagers we interviewed did not distinguish between the PNO and the PNA but saw them as part of the same organisation. In fact, when they spoke in the Pa-O language our interviewees used the English words PNO and PNA, and mentioned them together, saying, for example, that 'the PNO–PNA said or did this and that'.[2] This, as we will address, reflects the fact that the two organisations still very much overlap, in practice, seen from the perspective of the villagers. At the same time, we found that it was important, for our analysis, to distinguish between the PNO as an organisation and a political party that represents the Pa-O people, on the one hand; and the individual members of the PNO and the PNA, who have varied individual interests, on the other hand. We illustrate these insights by drawing on two in-depth case studies where the PNO and different armed actors are involved, although not openly: one that concerns drug trafficking and one that concerns land confiscation. These cases show that when perpetrators and adversaries are linked to powerful armed actors it is very difficult for the villagers to get justice in any of the existing systems. However, we also show that the political transition is opening up ways in which villagers can demand justice, including through their use of the media, and that they have an increased awareness of their rights.

2 According to our local research assistant, there are Pa-O names for the PNA and the PNO respectively – the PNO is Pa-O Joe Khoe Ajoe and the PNA is Pa-O Joe Kboe Tatmadaw. However, the villagers we spoke to did not use these names, but the English abbreviations PNO and PNA, usually bracketed together.

In the chapter we combine theories of legal pluralism with recent debates about rebel governance to discuss how dispute resolution occurs in ceasefire areas. After a short introduction to these theories, we provide a brief historical background to the Pa-O area, followed by a general overview of the significant actors in the area, of justice-seeking strategies, and of the security practices that local villagers use. We then move on to the two case studies in order to provide a more in-depth understanding of how armed actors influence dispute resolution. In the discussion and conclusion, we discuss how challenges to access to justice may affect the legitimacy and governance of the PNO, and what is needed to improve access to justice for the Pa-O ethnic group in the SAZ area.

Legal pluralism and rebel governance

The definition of legal pluralism as 'the existence of multiple normative and judicial orders that coexist within one social-political space' (von Benda-Beckmann 1997) fits well with the Pa-O SAZ context. Here there is more than one legal order in the same social field – that is, different rules and institutions that can adjudicate the same types of cases co-exist (Griffiths 1986). The reality is complex, because law and legal institutions are not within one system. The different systems sometimes cooperate and sometimes separate or compete for the same disputes. While some scholars have studied legal pluralism in contexts where there has been armed conflict (Isser 2011), there is hardly any literature that discusses the role of armed actors in dispute resolution (exceptions on Myanmar are: Harrisson and Kyed 2019; Kyed and Thitsar 2018). In order to understand the position and role of the PNO–PNA in dispute resolution, we draw on the rebel governance literature that deals with non-state armed organisations like the PNO–PNA (Forster 2015; Mampilly 2011, 2011; Sivakumaran 2009).

Following Mampilly (2011), rebel governance is here understood as civilian control and administration of territories and populations by non-state armed or rebel groups that have been formed in opposition to the central state. Rebel governance takes place predominantly in areas where the official state has limited or no control, which usually means conflict-affected areas or areas where armed rebellion has taken place. Rebel governance covers the provision of services and goods to the local populations that the rebel groups claim to represent, and such provisions are part of the rebel groups' efforts to become political movements (Mampilly 2007). This illustrates the fact that rebel groups frequently rely on civilian support and try to establish themselves as locally legitimate authorities, rather than focusing only on control, violent combat, and recruitment (Mampilly 2011). However, rebel groups enjoy different degrees of legitimacy. Mampilly (2007) also stresses that rebel groups often play a dual and ambiguous role. He uses the term 'stationary bandit' to describe this dual role. On the one hand, a rebel group supports the civilian population by providing education, development, security, justice and health services, for which it gains support from the population. On the other hand, it will frequently exploit or take advantage of the population, such as through recruitment of soldiers and extraction of food and labour. Forster (2015) notes that while the political apparatus of rebel groups provides security and protects populations against violence, they also, at the same time, use threats of violence against the people to control the territory and safeguard their own interests. We see this dual role with the PNO and the PNA, but here the situation is even more complicated. While the PNO supports the village security groups (*ywar sout*), engages in justice provision and tries to support the Pa-O people with development projects or businesses, some members of the PNO and its former armed wing, the PNA, also focus on serving their own interests, which are sometimes at the expense of local villagers' interests (see also South and Joll 2016 on this point for Myanmar as a whole). Overall, the PNO enjoys popular support both because of service provision and because of its history of struggle for the Pa-O people, but the villagers we interviewed also expressed discontent with some of the individual members of the PNO and the PNA. It is also difficult to distinguish between the PNO and the PNA. Although officially the PNO is now a political party and the PNA is a military body under the Tatmadaw, there are many overlaps in membership. Furthermore, the PNO, in addition to being a political party, also still operates an informal governance system with administrations and dispute resolution functions.

Mampilly (2011) notes that one of the key foundations of rebel governance is the development of justice systems. Building such systems demonstrates that the rebel groups are able to maintain order, which bolsters their local legitimacy. Thus, the PNO has supported village level dispute resolution, using oral customary law. While the justice system of the PNO is much less extensive than the systems developed by the larger ethnic armed organisations (EAOs) in Myanmar, such as the Karen National Union (KNU) and the New Mon State Party (NMSP) (see McCartan and Jolliffe 2016; Harrison and Kyed 2019; on the NMSP see also Poine and Kyed this volume), it is still preferred by many villagers to the Myanmar state system. It should be noted that the PNO is now working on a written form of customary law, which shows that its leaders are interested in strengthening their justice system.

Brief introduction to the Pa-O area

The Pa-O (originally called Taungthu) are and have been for many decades spread across different areas of Myanmar, particularly along the banks of the Salween River (across Mon, Karen, Karenni and Shan States). In the period around 1900 a large group of Pa-O settled in Southern Shan State (Cho 2014) and today they are the second largest group in Shan State (Thawnghmung 2018). During colonial times, the Pa-O people moved from place to place in order to avoid both the exploitative feudal system of the majority Shan group and the effects of ongoing wars, such as the Japanese occupation during the Second World War. There was discrimination against them on the part of the Shan royal leaders (*sawbwas*), who were responsible for administration, law enforcement, and services in Shan State during the colonial era (Stankus 2016). After independence from the British, the Pa-O, like many other ethnic groups, also became involved in fighting against the Burmese regime.[3]

The PNO was formed in 1946 as a political organisation and mainly operated in Shan State. It was only legally recognised by the Myanmar government when it signed a ceasefire agreement in 1991 (Yue 2015: 2–3). However, according to the chairperson of the Pa-O SAZ's leading body, this agreement was verbal only and was based on trust.[4] After this period the village tract level came under the mixed government of the PNO and the Myanmar state.

3 According to a village tract administrator from the PNO side whom we interviewed, the Pa-O revolutionary leaders had first fought the Shan Sawbwas, and soon after they formed movements to fight the Burmese military. Sawbwas can be defined as princely rulers, who were responsible for administration, law enforcement and other governance matters, also during British colonial rule (Christensen and Kyaw 2006).

4 Interview with the SAZ leading body chairperson and PNO leader, 12 June 2017.

In 2009, the PNO separated from its armed wing, the PNA, and was registered as a political party. It won three seats in the 2010 national elections. In 2011, the Pa-O were granted a Self-Administered Zone (SAZ), something granted to only six of the total of 135 officially recognised ethnic groups in Myanmar (Yue 2015; Jolliffe 2015; Thawnghmung 2018). In 2009, the PNA became a People's Militia Force (PMF) (*pyithusit* in Burmese) under the command of the Tatmadaw (the Burmese military). The policies on people's militias and on Self-Administered Zones (SAZ) are based on the 2008 constitution.[5] It is not entirely clear why the Pa-O, out of many other groups, gained a SAZ. One reason might be that the Pa-O leader, U Aung Kham Hti, attended the national congress in 1995 that discussed the drafting of the 2008 constitution. Here U Aung Kham Hti put forward the suggestion that those ethnic groups that did not have their own state (like the Karen, Kachin, Chin and Mon) should be given a self-administered state or region (Thot 2018). However, a current member of the PNO's Law Department claimed that it was because the wife of the head of the military government, General Than Shwe, is Pa-O (see also Thot 2018).[6] It should also be noted that the granting of a SAZ to the Pa-O might also have been a way for the Myanmar military government to be able to better control and administer the Pa-O ethnic group and the armed groups associated with it. As Yue (2016) notes, the granting of the SAZ meant that the PNA's generals were transformed from 'the state enemy into a successful entrepreneur' (Yue 2016: 103). One of the PNO's law department members told us that the PNO actually expected to be granted their own region or state, rather than a SAZ. He also believed that the reason why the Pa-O got a SAZ was because the PNO, after the verbal ceasefire agreement, was able to show the Myanmar government that they could improve and develop the area in terms of education, health, transportation, and economy.[7]

During our fieldwork (2017–2018), the SAZ was chaired by the PNO leader, U Khun San Lwin, and all its other six members were from the PNO party, which won all the elected seats in the 2015 elections. They represented three townships (Hopong, Hsi Hseng and Pinlaung). In fact,

5 See the 2008 Constitution's Chapter II on State Structure and Article 56 for more details about the Self-Administered Zones (SAZs) and Self-Administered Divisions (SADs).

6 Interview, member of the Law department of the PNO, 13 June 2017.

7 Interview, member of the legal department of the PNO, 13 June 2017.

the PNO was the first ethnic political party to win all the seats within its constituencies in Myanmar history. This points to the strong popular legitimacy of the PNO and its Pa-O leaders. However, the PNO is not alone in governing the SAZ, as the Tatmadaw retains a quarter of the seats in the SAZ, which are secured by the 2008 constitution. Someone from the General Administration Department (GAD) also serves as secretary in the SAZ (Jolliffe 2015: 34–40). The chairperson, U Khun San Lwin, was outspoken about the actual limitations of SAZ's subnational governance. Although the government allows the SAZ to govern and pass legislation, it has very limited jurisdiction and little independent decision-making power. The townships headed by the Pa-O in reality have to follow the directives of the Myanmar government at district level.[8] For instance, when there are crimes that require sentences of above seven years, the township courts must hand them over to the district (Stankus 2016: 12; see also Lue Htar et. al. on the Naga SAZ, this volume). Development projects also need to be approved by the central Myanmar government, and the SAZ has very limited authority in terms of legislation. In addition, the Pa-O is not legally allowed to operate on the basis of customary rules.[9]

Although the PNA has now come under the Tatmadaw as a militia, it still acts as an armed wing that supports the PNO's administrative system. In principle the PNO and the PNA are now separate entities, but, as noted earlier, many villagers we spoke to did not make any distinction between the two. There are many overlaps in practice. For instance, the leader of PNA battalion number four is also the head of the PNO's economic department. In addition, the PNA exercises power not only within the three SAZ townships but also in surrounding townships such as Taunggyi, Loilin and Kalaw, where Pa-O people live. The role of the PNA militia is here informal but vital, according to Jolliffe (2015). The PNO has its own administrative structures within the area, which overlap with the official government structures.[10] This is also the case in the village of our study. In Southern Shan State there are also

8 Interview, 12 June 2017

9 Interview with the PNO leader, who is also a chairperson of the Pa-O SAZ leading body, 12 June 2017.

10 Even though these administrative structures are under the PNO, village residents and leaders do not make a distinction between the PNO and PNA, and there are even signboards that mention the PNO/PNA as if they were one organisation. Interview, village leader, 25 March 2018.

other armed groups that represent the Pa-O, including the Union Pa-O National Organisation (UPNO), which signed a ceasefire agreement in 2013. However, when compared with the PNO, the UPNO has little authority in our study area. Although the UPNO is registered as a political party, it did not win the people's vote, because, we were told, the PNO has powerful strategies to get support from the communities, and they also own a lot of businesses.

The village context: Mixed government and leadership

Aye Thar Yar village is part of Hsi Hseng Township, in the Pa-O Saz area. It is financially supported by the Myanmar governemt. The administration and leadership of the village is complex, because it falls under both the PNO and the government of Myanmar (GoM).

The village is part of the Myanmar government's Dhone Tan village tract, but is also part of the PNO administration's Dhone Tha Htar village tract. These two village tracts are different from each other and they have different village tract administrators: one for the Myanmar government side, who resides in a village about 20 km away from Aye Thar Yar village, and one from the PNO side, who is native to, and lives in, Aye Thar Yar village. The Myanmar government village tract covers a total of 50 villages, while the PNO village tract only covers 21 villages. Some of these villages are the same but others are not. There are both differences and overlaps in terms of the administration of the two systems. With respect to Aye Thar Yar village, the PNO regards it as one village, whereas the Myanmar government's administration regards it as three different villages, even though they are physically connected: East Aye Thar Yar (the eastern part of the village, which we shall call the East Village), West Aye Thar Yar (the western part, which we shall call the West Village), and North Aye Thar Yar (the northern part, which we shall call the North Village). In practice, however, the village leadership structure follows the division of the Myanmar government, as each of the three parts of the village has its own village headman (*ywarthagyi*). These village headmen are at the same level of leadership, and thus there is no overall headman for the whole village. The village tract administrators (VTAs) on both sides – the PNO and the Myanmar government – are regarded as superior to the headmen, who in practice answer to both VTAs. There was a general perception in the village that the village headmen belonged neither to the PNO nor to the Myanmar government, as they are chosen by the villagers using local principles of selection and they also apply their own principles for dispute resolution. One youth leader explained to us that when they selected the village headmen, the village elder group shouted out the name of the person whom they had selected and asked the villagers to either agree or come up with reasons why the candidate should not be selected.

We found out that the PNO had been attempting to identify one person to be headman for the whole village, because the PNO regards the village as one. According to a high-ranking member of the PNO, they used to have one overall headman in the past. The candidate favoured by the PNO as future headman for the whole village is a middle-aged educated man whom the PNO VTA has been informally training in administrative matters and who is now engaged in the water and school committees as well as in dispute resolution. He is from the North Village, but he has not yet been appointed headman either for the North Village or for the whole village. The current headman of the North Village is, instead, U Khun Aung Tit, who is a former PNA soldier. U Khun Aung Tit told us that he was appointed by the PNO's administration and had received special administrative training from the PNO. He is at the same leadership level as the headmen from the East Village and the West Village and is therefore not regarded as above them or as being headman for the whole village. There seemed to be a certain confusion due to the dual system. The Myanmar government regarded the village as a three-part village, and while the three headmen were accepted by the PNO, the PNO wanted there to be one overall village headman, because the PNO regards the village as one. It took us a long time to figure this out, because it appeared to us that the village was one village.

Another complication arises with respect to the village tract level, because there are two village tract administrators (VTAs). The Myanmar government's VTA lives in another village, while the PNO VTA also happens to live in the North Village. This position could shift between the 21 villages after the next PNO VTA elections, which occur every two years. VTA elections on the side of the Myanmar government only take place every five years.[11] The PNO's VTA is elected by the monastery

11 2018 was an exception to this rule of elections every 5 years: elections were held both in 2016 and in 2018, because of the amendment to the Ward Administrator and Village Tract Administrator law.

donors from the 21 villages in the tract. Such donors are those who donate most to the monastery, and who are seen to have integrity, probity, and righteousness. A village tract committee decides which donors live up to these criteria. In the Myanmar government's system the VTAs are elected through a different system: according to the law one member from each household votes for 10 household leaders who then vote for 100 household leaders, who then elect a VTA among them.

Another difference between the two systems is that the PNO officially regards the village headmen as part of its administrative system, which includes village headmen, VTA, township and district, whereas the Myanmar government system only officially begins at the VTA level. In practice, however, it appeared to us that the Myanmar government's VTA also relies on the headmen. For instance, the VTA from the Myanmar government's side told us that all three village headmen are invited to participate in the monthly VTA meetings.[12] The biggest difference between the two systems, therefore, seems to be that the headmen communicate with two different VTAs.

Inside the village the headmen work in similar ways and often work together on matters such as education and water supply maintenance. Each part of the village (North, West and East) has a village committee, which includes the headman, 10 household leaders, a secretary, a treasurer, village elders and respected persons (VER) (*Change to: ya mi ya pha*), and a *thamadi ahpwe* (directly translated, a 'group with integrity', consisting of the most respected elders in the village).[13] The village headmen also have sub-committees for development, water, education, guarding the village and the local fire brigade. They also have a youth group, called *ka la tha kaung saung* (in Burmese) (see more in Stankus 2016). These committees, including the youth group, are often involved in dispute resolution, as we discuss below. In the East Village, there is also the *na ya ka* (a group of village advisers), which deals with complaints about the village leader and which is actively involved in resolving land

12 Interview, village tract administrator on the Myanmar government side, 14 June 2017.

13 According to our Pa-O assistant, *thamadi ahpwe* are found in most Pa-O villages. *Ahpwe* means a group in Burmese, but *thamadi* is Pali and does not translate easily into English. It refers to something like concentration of the mind, probity, integrity, and fairness of mind or attitude. In our village of study, this is the most important group in the village, and it is above and has more influence than the village elders. Some of its members are also village elders. The group plays a key role in village events and festivals and is involved in dispute resolution in an advisory capacity.

disputes. In certain matters the village headmen and their committees work as one group, because the village only has one school, one health care centre and one monastery. These are located in the East Village.

The village headmen operate following their own village rules, rather than the rules of the PNO and the Myanmar government, and they took pride in telling us this, because it illustrates that they also have a degree of autonomy from the two parallel governance systems. We return to these rules in more detail below and look at how they apply to dispute resolution.

Apart from the headmen and their committees, Buddhist monks are also important in the regulation of village life. It was clear to us that religion is central to the daily life of villagers. Every house has an altar with an image of Buddha, at which food and flowers are regularly offered (see also Stankus 2016). The central importance of the Buddhist religion is also expressed in the fact that it is those villagers who donate a lot to the monasteries who become part of the local village leadership system. These persons are key in the PNO's system of selecting village tract administrators (VTAs). The monks support the enforcement of village rules, such as the prohibition against drinking and selling alcohol. At one point the main monk even threatened to leave the village when people were not respecting the alcohol prohibition. This shamed the villagers.

Let us now turn to the main actors who are engaged in dispute resolution at village level and within the PNO system. As we will show, the PNO has a more significant influence at village level than does the Myanmar government.

Local justice and security arrangements

In Aye Thar Yar village there is a well-established dispute resolution system, which applies local village rules or principles. Each of the three parts of the village has a kind of judiciary group (in Burmese *khone tamati apwe* and in Pa-O *ah-kjel*), which has at least eight members. In Burmese these village committees are called *yat ywar* committees and in Pa-O they are called *hrapra dounchew*. The members of the village committees in each part of the village include the village headman, village elders and respected persons (VER), a secretary, a treasurer, one or two 10-household leaders, a member from the youth group and two members from other committees, such as those dealing with development and water. These judiciary groups are temporary in the sense that they are only formed if there is a case to be dealt with. A judiciary group can issue punishments. When decisions are made there must be seven committee members present, including 10-household leaders and members from the youth group. If a case occurs between villagers from different parts of the village, the judiciary group that is set up will include the headmen and other committee members from each of the parts: if, for instance, the perpetrator is from the North Village and the victim is from the East Village, the headmen and committee members from the North and the East Villages come together in one judiciary group.

Each part of the village also has a village security group (*ywar sout* in Burmese and *doun pawl* in Pa-O), which includes people of both genders and different ages. The purpose of this group is to collaborate with the village headmen and other committees in dealing with situations that may be harmful to the village, such as fires or strangers who are suspected of committing crimes or of being involved in the sale or use of drugs. It is intended both to provide protection and to support the judiciary group. The security group gets together when this is required, depending on need and on the situation, just as the judiciary group does. There are no permanent members and the task is voluntary.

It is unclear when exactly the village justice system was established, as there is no recorded history for the village, but our interviewees guessed that it was probably sometime after 1961, when three small villages were merged.[14] The justice system is not recognised officially by the Myanmar government, but the PNO recognises it, as cases are forwarded to the PNO system when the judiciary group fails to resolve a case.

The judiciary groups apply a set of written village principles that were developed by the village headmen and elders some fifty years ago, according to our interviewees. These principles can be changed every time the village headman changes; any changes are subject to approval by the villagers at public meetings. However, according to the village headman of the North part of the village, the only changes to have been made so far are the monetary value of fines and compensation.[15] The principles do not need approval from the PNO or from the Myanmar government, and they are therefore only locally recognised.

14 According to our informants, these three original villages correspond to the East, North and West Villages today.

15 Interview, North Village headman, 11 June 2017.

The village principles used in the three parts of the village are very similar. They are written in the Pa-O language and there are 20 of them. They include procedural principles, including who should resolve cases and to whom people should report cases – this is the village headman. They also include prohibitions and punishments for the following types of cases: drugs (sale and use); theft; trading of alcohol; crime while under the influence of alcohol; quarrels and harassment; verbal assaults on village leaders; rape; and destroying another person's property. Punishments can be fines (between MMK 20,000 [USD 14] and 500,000 [USD 355]), compensation for victims, and expulsion from the village, which must be decided by the village committee based on a recommendation from the judiciary group that is set up. A fine can be substituted by a labour sentence, such as road repair, for those who cannot afford to pay fines. However, except for rape cases, punishments, including compensation, are seldom issued straight away, because the judiciary group applies a three-step warning system, which gives the perpetrators an extra chance to demonstrate improved behaviour. First the judiciary group warns the perpetrator verbally, telling him/her not to repeat the offence again. Then, if the person repeats the offence, the warning process will include more people from the village committee and the perpetrator must sign a *kahn won* or 'promise letter' (*lake one cann* in Pa-O) in which she/he promises not to commit the offence again. Finally, if the person breaks the *kahn won*, the village committee, based on a recommendation from the judiciary group, can decide to expel the person from the village. Drug and murder cases will always lead to expulsion and cannot, as with other cases, be concluded with fines and compensation. In drug cases, the judiciary group can also decide to have the youth group destroy the house of the perpetrator. All types of cases (except rape) follow this warning system but the punishment varies. For example, whereas the sale of drugs will lead to the person being expelled, domestic violence while under the influence of alcohol will lead to a man either being separated or divorced from his wife.

According to villagers whom we interviewed, expulsion as punishment in drug cases is seen as an appropriate way to 'keep society clean' from bad influences and actions. They used the Burmese term *ywar say* to describe this, which means 'cleaning' or 'clearance' in English. This does not always imply expelling people from the village but can mean that villagers are 'cleansed' of their bad behaviour. One couple told us of a case where a man was fined because he was drunk and disturbed the village. He paid MMK 1,000 (USD 0.71) to the 'four corners of the village'. After that, he 'became a good man' and never committed an offence again.[16]

Our findings show that in practice Aye Thar Yar villagers prefer to resolve disputes and crimes inside their village. There are more challenges and risks for both parties if the case goes to higher levels, especially if they go to a court within the Myanmar state system. Even in more significant disputes, such as those over land, the villagers prefer to resolve cases through the village headmen and the judiciary group, because this means quicker resolutions and ensures compensation will be paid. Local resolutions are easiest when a dispute involves people from the same village; when a dispute involves people from different villages, it takes more time, and sometimes they end up having to go to the Myanmar court. Villagers have found that this can take a whole year, sometimes without obtaining any final resolution.[17] A former female youth leader told us about a motorbike accident case that went to the Myanmar court; it ended tragically for the victim's parents, who 'got no compensation for their child who died during the accident'. In addition, the woman told us, 'other friends who got hurt were also not compensated, because the perpetrator agreed to go to prison. The perpetrator was given the option to either compensate the victim or go to prison, according to state law. He chose prison. If the parties had been compensated according to the custom of the PNO, they would at least have had enough money for the funeral and for medicine'.[18]

This quote also reflects the fact that villagers tend to prefer the PNO when cases cannot be settled inside the village. They fear the Myanmar system, including the police, more than the PNO. They also prefer the PNO because they share the same language with PNO members (i.e. Pa-O). Finally, the PNO system is less costly than the Myanmar system. Above the level of the village there are, in practice, two co-existing justice options: the official Myanmar judiciary and the justice or dispute resolution services of the PNO. In this context, the PNO and the PNA

16 Interview, male village resident, 25 March 2018.

17 Interview, treasurer of village administrative group, 11 June 2017.

18 Interview, female former youth leader, 12 June 2017.

act together. They are, at the same time, a rebel group, an administrative system, and part of the SAZ.

As noted earlier, the village residents do not draw a strict distinction between the PNO and the PNA, although they are officially separate entities. While the PNA is a military unit, the PNO is an administrative–political unit that is organised at different levels. However, the distinction between the two groups is blurred in practice, because some PNA members are at times also involved in the PNO's administrative system. The PNO has a central office in Taunggyi, the capital city of Shan State, which is the highest level of PNO administration and is also the highest level for resolution of disputes and crimes. However, it is very rare that cases are resolved at this level. Most cases are resolved at the lower levels of district, township, village tract, and village. Sometimes the higher levels will advise resolution at lower levels. The PNO does not have specific courts or justice committees, but matters are dealt with as part of their administration. The PNO also has a law department inside its administration. The PNO's justice provision functions are closely linked to the village level, where case resolutions always begin. The PNO mostly resolves disputes and crimes informally, based predominantly on orally transmitted Pa-O customary practices, rather than on a codified law book (see McCartan and Jolliffe 2016: 6). However, during our fieldwork we noticed that the PNO had begun to prepare for the codification of a Pa-O customary law, based on data collection about existing village principles.

The village headmen can decide if a case should be forwarded to the PNO or to the Myanmar system and can prepare transfer letters for either or both. If the parties go to the PNO, but are not satisfied with the resolution, they can ask the village headman that the case be transferred to the Myanmar system. We also found that the PNO's law department can assist Pa-O people who go to the Myanmar court. One of the members of the PNO is a retired government lawyer who can give people advice and assist them during court hearings. This has, for example, happened in rape cases, which the village headmen tend to report directly to the police and thus to the Myanmar government system.[19]

Overall, we found that the village justice system can handle most cases and that the PNO is seen as a viable support when cases cannot be handled at village level. However, we also observed that both challenges

19 Interview, member of PNO legal department, 14 June 2017.

and changes to access to justice have been emerging during the gradual transition to democracy which began in 2010. On the one hand, people are becoming more aware of their rights and are much less afraid to speak up about injustices than in the past. This is true, for instance, regarding complaints about land confiscations and drugs. Some villagers have received training in human rights from a Myanmar NGO, the Metta organisation, according to a representative of the PNO legal department to whom we spoke. There is also a tendency for people to be less afraid to submit cases to the Myanmar police. On the other hand, there is also resistance to these changes, and there are many barriers when villagers raise cases that involve outsiders and affect the business interests of local armed actors or other powerful persons. The PNO VTA told us that the rights awareness training has made it more difficult for the VTA and the village headmen to govern the village according to their own principles, because people sometimes now make complaints about violations of their rights. However, as we shall see in the cases below, we also found that at least one headman, the headman of the East Village, is now taking part in taking rights claims to the higher authorities.

In what follows we will focus on two cases, to allow us to zoom in on the challenges to seeking justice faced by villagers when the village headmen cannot resolve the cases, especially when villagers make claims against powerful actors. First, we will look at a drug case, which highlights the limitations of the village system when the perpetrators are non-Pa-O and not from the village. It also points to the insecurities of involving the formal Myanmar system. Secondly, we discuss a big land confiscation case, which demonstrates that when the business interests of powerful actors are involved, the villagers struggle to get justice in the PNO as well as the Myanmar government systems.

Case 1: Drug trading and insecurity in the face of powerful outsiders

In 2016, the members of the East Village within Aye Thar Yar village committee caught a drug seller who was a local villager but who was connected to a large drug trafficker, known as Min Oo.[20] Two other villagers were also involved in the sale of drugs. The village committee at first gave verbal warnings to the dealers, according to village principles,

20 We have changed the original name to ensure anonymity.

and the committee members explained to them what the disadvantages are of selling drugs to the villagers. While two of the sellers agreed to sign a *kahn won* (a 'promise letter', stating that they would not repeat the offence), the third man refused to do this. After three warnings, the third man ran away. Then Min Oo also came to the village, but because he is not a resident of the village and is not Pa-O, he could not be punished inside the village. Instead, the villagers simply told Min Oo to leave the village. U Khun Myint, the headman of the East Village, said: 'We told him not to come and sell drugs, but he didn't listen to us. Instead, he threatened us, saying he had a gun and he did not care about us. He used to serve in the Myanmar army, and he killed a man from Htee Tain village'.[21] A group of villagers, including the headman of the East Village, then decided to inform the Myanmar Police Force (MPF) of the case. At first, U Khun Myint, told us, the villagers had had no plans to have Min Oo arrested by the police, but when he had told them that he did not care about them and that he was not afraid of them, they decided to phone the police. When the police came to the village, the headman and some of the villagers had a clever plan to get Min Oo arrested. U Khun Myint explained: 'The police and I were watching from the monastery and the 10-household leaders and other villagers were waiting near the car. When he [Min Oo] arrived, the villagers near the car told him to wait for a moment, saying that they were going to fetch the village head. The headman and the police came with a car. Min Oo did not see the police at first. When he saw the police, he attempted to flee, but then he was arrested'.[22] After that, a case was opened at the police station and it was forwarded to the Myanmar court. Min Oo was charged with having carried 26,800 tablets of drugs (WY pills) and with not having a car licence. Thus, he was accused of two crimes. The village youth group, in addition to this, enforced the village principles by destroying the houses of the local drug dealers.

The headman and the members of his village committee were asked to act as witnesses in court, but they feared to do this, because they believed that Min Oo would hire a good lawyer and that he had enough money to win the case. If he won, they feared that he would come back to the village and perhaps threaten them. He had guns so the village headmen were afraid. They worried especially for their families. No one

21 Interview, East Village headman, 15 June 2017.

22 Interview, East Village headman, 15 June 2017.

was sure with whom Min Oo had connections – whether he might have connections with the PNA or with the Tatmadaw. Later we were told by an elder that he used to be a Tatmadaw soldier until he was caught selling drugs. The police told the village headmen that it would be risky for them if they were not tactful in how they spoke and what they said about what they had witnessed.

In the court, the case was resolved within a month, and Min Oo got a prison sentence. The headman of the East Village did not know how long his sentence was, and in which prison he was being imprisoned. The headman was not interested in asking for more information, because, he said, even if the villagers wanted Min Oo to get at least 15 years in prison for his crime, they had no influence over the court's decision.[23] In short, once the case is in the formal system, the villagers have no influence over the outcome. Participation in the court hearings had cost a lot in transportation for the village headman, and they had had to use the community fund to cover this. Despite the prison sentence, the villagers feared that the perpetrator would go free, because he had money and connections. This fear illustrates a deep distrust in the formal system and the general view that people with financial means can negotiate better outcomes in the formal system (Kyed 2018; Cheesman 2015).

However, the village headman, in this case, felt compelled to ask the police for help and to turn to the formal system. This was because the perpetrator, as an outsider, could not be charged using village principles. It is clear that in this case the perpetrator did not respect the authority of the village headman: he was situated above village ties and obligations, and his power lay in the fact that he had a gun and was believed to have money and strong connections to powerful outsiders.

This drug case illustrates the fact that the village system works most effectively when the perpetrators are local villagers. It struggles to secure justice when powerful and resourceful outsiders are involved as perpetrators or linked to perpetrators. The drug case also points to the distrust in and insecurity associated with the use of systems above the village level. This not only relates to the Myanmar government system but also to that of the PNO. We were curious to know why the village committee did not transfer this case to the PNO, especially given that the villagers had told us that they prefer the PNO to the Myanmar government. A group of elders and the headman of the East Village and his

23 Interview, East Village headman, 24 March 2018.

wife gave us three reasons. Firstly, the perpetrator was not Pa-O; and he used to be in the Tatmadaw in the past, before he was thrown out due to a drug case. Thus they felt that he should be sent to the Myanmar government system.[24] Ethnicity and the military background of the perpetrator therefore seemed to play a role. Secondly, the wife of the headman said that the case had to be sent to the Myanmar government system because the PNO does not have a proper prison system, but only prisons for use for short-term punishment, and the villagers wanted to see the perpetrator go to prison for a long time.[25] This view reflects the limitations of the PNO's capacity to enforce punishments in bigger cases, given that it does not have a formal justice system. Finally, the headman of the East Village said that he no longer trusted the PNO and the PNA when it came to drug cases. He said that recently a PNA soldier had arrested a drug seller inside the East Village without even telling the headman – who had, in fact, given warnings to the seller before that. The PNA soldier took the drugs and sold them in another village. He also believed that the PNA soldier sometimes gave drugs to the villagers to sell.[26] It was clear that this headman was being critical of a particular individual soldier, but this also affected his wider trust in the PNO and the PNA as organisations. He, like other villagers, did not draw a clear distinction between the PNO as an organisation and individual PNA soldiers. Therefore, trust in the PNO as a justice provider is harmed by the actions of individual armed actors and their personal interests. Similar dynamics are evident in the following case.

Case 2: Land confiscation and contested access to rights

In 2000, Company X, owned by a high-ranking member of the PNO, seized 5,000 acres of land which had previously been used for shifting cultivation by Pa-O people from seven different villages for several generations – at least 100 years – according to a village elder from the East Village. It is also considered Pa-O ancestral land, as a Pa-O king and two Pa-O princesses are believed to be buried there. Some 50 years ago villagers had also mined for diamonds on the land, under the instructions of the highest leader of the PNO (in post since 1973),

24 Interview, elderly man, 25 March 2018.

25 Interview, wife of the headman of East Village, 15 March 2018.

26 Interview, headman of East Village, 24 March 2018.

a man whom some villagers today consider the founding father of the Pa-O nation. He is a very well-respected leader and former monk who worked for the Pa-O national cause but who later also had strong connections to the highest leadership of the Myanmar military government (Thot 2018). Some villagers believed that it was this PNO leader who assigned the land to Company X, when no diamonds were found. The idea was that the head of Company X was going to keep the land safe and in the hands of the Pa-O, as many villagers and PNO members feared that the land would be taken over by non-Pa-O, particularly by Shan- and Burmese-owned companies. Other villagers from the East Village had heard that a captain in a PNA battalion from Aye Thar Yar village had sold the 5,000 acres of land for about MMK thirty-seven million (USD 25,000) to the owner of Company X without discussing it with the villagers. When the land was confiscated in 2000 none of the villagers dared to complain about the confiscation, because it was during the time of military rule. They feared that they might go to prison if they complained. Even though they had cultivated the land for many years, they did not have any official papers relating to it, not even indigenous land records. PNA soldiers surrounded and guarded the land, something they were still doing during our fieldwork. Some villagers accepted this, because Company X is owned by people who are Pa-O, and thus ownership on the part of this company can be seen as a way to conserve the land for the Pa-O. However, occupation of the land by Company X has led to the Pa-O villagers being no longer able to use it. Several villagers told us that after the confiscation in 2000, Company X took various actions to prevent the villagers from continuing to use the land, including destroying crops and prohibiting cows from entering on the land. The soldiers used gun threats and vehicles to chase away the cows. The villagers were denied ownership.

Dissatisfied with the situation, the villagers began to negotiate with the PNA and Company X in 2004. In that year, the headman of the North Village appealed to the *lu gyi* (big people) of the PNA to give back some of the land in order to secure the villagers' livelihood. After this, 900 acres were given back in total to the three parts of Aye Thar Yar village. The villagers from the North Village and the West Village accepted the offer, but those from the East Village did not want to use the land they were offered, because it had poor soil. However, when the PNA soldiers left the area to help fight a Shan armed group, villagers from the East

Village did begin to cultivate the land they had been allocated. In 2006 and 2007, villagers from all three parts of Aye Thar Yar village requested permission from Company X to be allowed to grow crops in areas where the Company was not cultivating the fields. The Company agreed to release more land, because it was not profiting from the agricultural business that it had set up to use the land. To gain access to the land, the villagers had to apply to the PNA battalion. They had to register their names and National Registration Card numbers, and sign on paper how many acres they would cultivate of the land belonging to Company X. Around 100 households got permission to use land, but they were not allowed to grow for commercial purposes, and they were not granted ownership. According to the headman of East Village, a PNA Lieutenant also told the villagers that they would have to move off the land when the Company started its agricultural business there again.

In 2016, Company X decreased the amount of land that the villagers could use. To begin with, it announced that the villagers could only use two acres of land each. The villagers were dissatisfied and appealed to the Company, which agreed to allow them to use three acres each. Again the people of the North Village and the West Village accepted the offer, but those of the East Village turned it down, because the deal would have meant that the North Village and the West Village would be moved to the land that was claimed by the East Village. At this time, Company X had a plan to cooperate with a foreign company to grow cassava on the land being used by the West Village and the North Village. This was why they wanted to move the villagers of the North Village and the West Village to the land being cultivated by the East Village. In 2017, tensions escalated between the Company and the villagers, especially those of the East Village. In early May, the Company set up a signboard next to the land being used by the East Village that read: 'No trespassing on Company land'. The villagers from the East Village removed the Company's signboard and set up another signboard, which read: 'No trespassing on village land'. A protest action against the Company was organised in which someone from almost every household from the East Village participated. The crowd surrounded the place where the Company had set up the signboard. Even though this was very close to the PNA battalion camp, the soldiers did not attack the crowd. However, the PNA soldiers, on the third day of the protest, attacked two men from the East Village when they went to buy betel nut at a shop. We spoke to the two men, and they told us that the soldiers had questioned them about the protest and had attacked one of them by squeezing his neck and grabbing his T-shirt. The lieutenant in charge of the group was, the two men said, drinking beer inside the shop at the time, and he must have known what was happening, but he did not take any action to stop the violence. One of the soldiers had said to the two men: 'Are you trying to get the land back so that it is yours again? All you'll get is six feet by two [in other words, sufficient land to bury a person]! We will definitely shoot if the villagers set up the signboard again. We know nothing about democracy. Democracy is in the muzzles of our guns!' [in other words, if the people threatened them with democracy then the soldiers would point their guns at them].

After the villagers' protest had ended, the village headman and the elders from the East Village sent letters of complaint to the various authorities, on both the Myanmar and the PNO side: the village tract office, the township-level GAD, the SAZ office and the headquarters of the PNO. They also published their complaint in the newspaper Public Voice (*Khung San Ngaun*), which is well known among the Pa-O. The villagers from the East Village were the most active in making these complaints, both because they were the ones most affected by the situation and also because their headman was most active in raising complaints. Our impression was that the headmen of the North Village and the West Village were reluctant to complain because they have stronger connections and loyalties to the PNO than does the headman of the East Village, and so they were reluctant to be critical of the PNO.

On 4 July 2017, a meeting was held at the village monastery hall. Representatives from all three parts of Aye Thar Yar village were present. Over two hundred villagers (eighty of whom were from the East Village) and representatives from a number of authorities attended the meeting: the chief of the leading body of the SAZ, who is a PNO member; the owner of Company X; a GAD official; a Land Record Department official; a Forestry Department official; a Pa-O parliamentarian; and a former captain of a PNA battalion. However, a resolution was not reached, and the villagers were not given a chance to express their grievances. For instance, when a villager got up and said: 'We villagers should own the land because we are now cultivating it', the chief of the leading body of the SAZ interrupted him, and the request was ignored. Company X was still only willing to agree that the villagers could cultivate three acres each, which the villagers claimed was not enough to allow them to have a decent livelihood.

When we spoke to villagers who had participated in the meeting, they said that they felt that the way they had been treated reminded them of the military era. They did not notice any real difference between the Burmese military era and the current democratic era, because the authorities at the meeting still did not listen to what the villagers said. The headman of the East Village told us that the authorities did not seem willing to negotiate but simply told the villagers what to do. The villagers also worried about what would happen if Company X sold the land to other companies, because at least Company X allows them to cultivate some land. It is therefore very important, from the villagers' perspective, that they should get their land back legally, with documentation to prove that this is so.[27] A 63-year-old villager who had tried to claim his land back complained to us that Company X has never informed the Pa-O people what its profits are from any of the other businesses it has or shared any of its profits with them. The Company just oppresses the villagers, he said, and the villagers are afraid of it because it is protected by PNA soldiers, who have guns.[28] After the May meeting, the headman and the household leaders from the East Village went to the PNO member of parliament (MP) for help. They also wrote an article about the case, which was published in the Pa-O Newspaper. The MP promised the villagers that the case would be presented to the Shan State parliament, but the villages were still waiting for a solution during our visit in March 2018. They had also sent a letter to the Nay Pyi Taw Union parliament. Thus the representatives of the East Village were now trying to go outside the Pa-O SAZ to get their land confiscation case resolved.

This case illustrates the ambiguous role that the PNO and the PNA play in the justice and security field, and the challenges that villagers face in preserving their rights to land and their ownership of it. Company X represents the dual face of the PNO and the PNA: as organisations that try to preserve and protect the Pa-O area for the Pa-O people, and as a set of individuals who also have business interests that may challenge the livelihoods of the Pa-O people. For the villagers it is difficult to separate the PNO as an organisation and the individual members of the PNO – for example, Company X is owned by someone with a position

27 Interview, headman of East Village, 15 June 2018.

28 Interview, 63-year-old village elder, 25 March 2018.

in the PNA, is connected to the PNO, and uses PNA soldiers to guard the land. While Company X was given the land to prevent non-Pa-O companies from exploiting land belonging to the Pa-O people, paradoxically it also prevents Pa-O villagers from owning and cultivating the land as they like.

The case demonstrates the continuing role, at the same time both direct and shadowy, of armed men, when it comes to bigger cases such as land disputes. This role co-exists with the civil role of the PNO, including provision of justice, in which role it tries to assist and protect the Pa-O people. The villagers are positioned in an ambiguous and difficult position, because they see the PNO as their protector but are up against armed PNA actors. This is in a context where the PNO and PNA do not constitute a homogenous actor or organisation, even if they are often perceived as such by villagers: the two bodies have officially been separated since the PNO became a political party, and the PNA came under military command (Thawnghmung 2018). However, this boundary is often blurred. This ambiguity occurs in a context where there are plural authorities, as the PNO and the PNA co-exist with Myanmar government institutions. People are of course aware of this plurality of governance, and try to involve all of the various authorities and actors in resolving their grievances over land. As Lue Htar (2018) shows is also the case in Karen State, the Pa-O villagers did not use Myanmar government land law to get their land back and they did not go through formal procedures (either in the Myanmar or the PNO system). One reason for this is likely to have been that they have no official papers relating to the land, only historical claims to Pa-O ownership. Another reason is likely a lack of trust in the formal justice system. A third reason is the fact that the land confiscation case involved armed actors. Instead, then, of turning to the formal system and procedures, they tried first to negotiate directly with Company X. When this did not work, they tried to mobilise a range of actors to help them to make their claim to the land, including the Myanmar state, the SAZ, the state parliament, the PNA and the PNO leaders. It was the villagers from the East Village and their headman who were most active in raising the complaints – which was, we suggest, both due to the fact that they were more affected by the land case and because the headmen of the North Village and the West Village were more reluctant to go against the PNO and the PNA.

Conclusion

This chapter has shown that access to justice and dispute resolution in a village in the Pa-O Self-Administered Zone (SAZ) works well as long as cases can be resolved by the village dispute resolution system, which has its own set of written principles and punishments. Within the village, the village system is strong, as it is informally supported by the PNO even though it is not officially recognised by the Myanmar government. The village system is by far the preferred justice option for the villagers. However, it only works effectively when the cases involve local villagers and not external actors and interests. When the opposing party or perpetrator is non-Pa-O or is linked to powerful external actors with guns and/or money, the village system does not have sufficient authority to resolve cases and protect the villagers. We noted that in such cases, villagers do not feel that the external justice systems of the PNO and of the Myanmar government are able to secure justice for them. This leaves the villagers in an insecure position when it comes to bigger, more complex justice and security issues.

We suggest that there are two core underlying factors which can help explain this insecure situation. Firstly, challenges to accessing justice outside the village system arise because of a complex plurality of authorities, institutions and actors, with which the village headmen and their committees are interconnected in various ways. The official Myanmar system of police, courts and administration co-exists with the PNO party and its civilian structures. These are partly integrated into the SAZ structure but to some extent operate separately from this structure. In addition, the PNO has its own mechanisms for resolving disputes, which are connected to the village level headmen and committees – but these are not officially recognised as a justice system by the Myanmar state. In parallel to the PNO and the government of Myanmar is the PNA, which is now a militia connected to the Tatmadaw but whose soldiers also operate according to their own agendas, and which is still connected to the PNO and conflated with the PNO by ordinary villagers. This plurality of actors with influence and power opens a space for villagers to negotiate claims with different actors, which should ideally help them to get better outcomes. However, judging from what we observed, it seems that this plurality of actors can create challenges in accessing justice: it can mean that the external authorities are able to ignore or undermine the claims and voices of the villagers. This is especially the case when there are economic interests at play, such as businesses linked to drug trafficking and natural resources. Such a situation may also help explain why people prefer, when they can, to resolve cases inside their village. They feel they can never really trust the external authorities.

Secondly, our empirical findings demonstrate that behind the plurality of authorities there continue to be men with guns. This is not very open, because armed combat has ended, but when ordinary villagers start to complain about land confiscations and target drug dealers, armed threats re-appear and are pervasive in influencing how crimes and claims to rights are dealt with. For instance, in the land confiscation case we saw how the PNA soldiers attacked and threatened two innocent village men to stop the villagers from claiming back their land. We also saw how the drug dealer in the first case was able to avert a village resolution partly because he was armed. Thus we can see that the history of armed conflict and the continuing presence of armed actors in the Pa-O SAZ influence the justice-seeking practices of the people of villages such as Aye Thar Yar. Where does this situation leave the PNO and its legitimacy as an ethnic organisation and political party representing the Pa-O people? And what do our findings tell us, more broadly, about the democratic transition and how it is affecting the villagers?

We found that the PNO is clearly the preferred option for dispute resolution when cases cannot be resolved at the village level, although the drug case also shows that in some instances, when the perpetrator is non-Pa-O, the villagers may turn to the Myanmar police. Judging from our interviews and from the electoral victory of the PNO in 2015, ordinary Pa-O villagers consider the PNO to be their 'parent'. The PNO has gained further legitimacy because it has secured significant development since the ceasefire. The PNO has also gained local legitimacy due to its leading role, over many years, in opposing the military state and the dominance of Shan armed groups over the Pa-O people. Overall, Pa-O villagers are loyal to the PNO as their ethnic leaders. However, this legitimacy and the preference for the PNO as a justice-seeking option is challenged, at times, due to the actions of PNA soldiers, and because the PNO struggles to protect the villagers in bigger justice and security matters, such as drug and land confiscation cases. In this regard, it is important to emphasise the fact that the villagers whom we interviewed did not distinguish between the PNA and the PNO, or between individual members and the organisation. The situation is complicated, because some of the members have overlapping positions in the PNO and the PNA, and some PNO businesses are guarded by PNA soldiers. The villagers always mentioned the PNO and the PNA together in our conversations with them. Therefore, we suggest that when individual PNA members act against the rights and wishes of the villagers this may be having a negative effect on the reputation and legitimacy of the PNO. From the perspective of the villagers in our research area, the PNO/PNA has a dual face: it is regarded as being protective of and representative of the Pa-O people but is also regarded as exploitative when its members take land or are connected to the selling of drugs. This reflects the way in which economic, political, and military powers continue to overlap in the Pa-O SAZ region, despite the ceasefire, the conversion of the PNO to a political party and the Myanmar political transition more broadly.

As noted in this chapter, Pa-O villagers and village headmen whom we interviewed were quite clearly becoming more aware of democracy, and they are now more courageous about expressing and claiming their rights. The land confiscation case is a good example: after the transition, the villagers summoned up the courage to negotiate with Company X to get back their land, and they later called on different authorities to claim their land rights. However, the outcome of the case – which left villagers without ownership of the land – reflects the fact that the democratic transition is partial and is challenged by a continuing culture of militarised and top-down governance in which the interests of powerful business and armed actors may trump village claims. Among the villagers we found that there is a sense that the external authorities have been resistant to democratic changes when it comes to safeguarding their rights. Overall, this situation seems to be reducing trust in the political system as a whole. Villagers told us that they are unhappy with the situation, and said that they would find it difficult to decide for whom to vote in the 2020 election. One village elder, for instance, told us that he would not vote for any political party, not even the PNO.

It is our view that the legitimacy of the PNO will probably depend on its ability to improve its system in terms of securing access to justice for Pa-O villagers. It is especially important that the PNO be able to defend the villagers against the self-interest of armed actors. At the same time, we realise that this is a difficult challenge for the PNO in the current political situation, where there are still many armed actors on the ground. The PNA is not actually the armed wing of the PNO any longer, but is within the Myanmar military system, which means that the PNO does not hold the official authority to control the actions of soldiers on the ground. Also, the 2008 constitution limits the authority of the SAZ and of the PNO to apply their own justice system. The system therefore sets limits to the protection that the PNO can provide for Pa-O villagers, even though the PNO is the major political party in the SAZ.

Other scholars have argued for the need to formally recognise the justice systems of ethnic armed organisations (South and Joll 2016; Poine 2018). In the context of the PNO, this is complicated, because of the overlapping authorities and interests at play. Based on our findings, we recommend the development of an independent system to monitor the SAZ administration, not through centralised methods, but through locally accountable bodies that can safeguard against collaboration between powerful groups that do not serve the rights and interests of ordinary Pa-O people, such as their rights to land ownership and to a livelihood. International support for local civil society organisations can help to monitor this, so that the voices of the people are heard in public and the misuse of power by armed actors is avoided.

References

Cheesman, N.

2015. *Opposing the Rule of Law: How Myanmar's Courts Make Law and Order.* Cambridge: Cambridge University Press.

Cheesman, N. & Farrelly, N. (eds)

2016. *Conflict in Myanmar: War, Politics, Religion.* Singapore: ISEAS, Yusof Ishak Institute.

Cho, N.A.

2014. 'Pa-O community in the southern Shan State (1886–1962).' PhD dissertation, Department of History, University of Mandalay, Myanmar.

Christensen, R. and S. Kyaw

2006. *The Pa-O: rebels and refugees.* Chiang Mai: Silkworm Books.

Forster, T.

2015. *Dialogue Direct: Rebel Governance and Civil Order in Northern Cote d'lvoire.* Cambridge: Cambridge University Press.

Griffiths, J.

1986. 'What is legal pluralism?' *Journal of Legal Pluralism and Unofficial Law,* 18(24): 1–55.

Harrisson, A. & Kyed, H.M.

2019. Ceasefire state-making and justice provision in ethnic armed group areas of southeast Myanmar' *Journal of Social Issues in Southeast Asia* 34(2): 290–326

Htar, L.

2018. 'Everyday justice and plural authorities: Insights from Karen State about land disputes.' *Independent Journal of Burmese Scholarship* 1(2): 162–210.

Isser, D.

2011. *Customary Justice and the Rule of Law in War-Torn Societies.* Washington DC: USIP.

Jolliffe, K.

2015. *Ethnic Armed Conflict and Territorial Administration in Myanmar.* San Francisco: The Asia Foundation.

Kyed, H.M.

2018. 'Introduction to the special issue on everyday justice.' *International Journal of Burmese Scholarship* 1(2): i–xxii.

Kyed, H.M and Myat The Thitsar.

2018. "State-Making and Dispute Resolution in Karen 'Frontier' areas", *Independent Journal of Burmese Scholarship,* 1 (2): 29–55.

Mampilly, Z.C.

2007. 'Stationary bandits: Understanding rebel governance.' Ph.D thesis, University of California, Los Angeles.

2011. *Rebel Rulers, Insurgent Governance and Civilian Life during War.* Ithaca and London: Cornell University Press.

McCartan, B. & Jolliffe, K.

2016. *Ethnic Armed Actors and Justice Provision in Myanmar.* San Francisco: The Asia Foundation.

Poine, T.S.

2018. 'Gendered aspects of access justice in Southern Mon State.' *Independent Journal of Burmese Scholarship* 1(2): 1–25.

Sivakumaran, S.

2009. 'Courts of armed opposition groups.' *Journal of International Criminal Justice* 7(3): 489–513.

South, A. and Christopher, J.M.

2016. 'From rebels to rulers: The challenges of transition for non-state armed groups in Mindanao and Myanmar.' *Critical Asian Studies* 48(2): 168–192.

Stankus, J.

2016. 'The making and remaking of a state in Myanmar: Traditional leadership structures in Pa-O ethnic group.' MSc. thesis, Katholieke Universiteit Leuven, Flanders, Belgium.

Thawnghmung, A.

2018. *Opportunity and Challenges for Sustainable Peace, Security, and Development in the Pa-O areas: Southern Shan State, Myanmar*. Stockholm, Sweden: Institute for Security and Development Policy.

Thot, K.M.

2018. 'Pa-O National Leader: U Aung Kham Hte's Road to Politics.' (published in Burmese). Yangon: Mizzama Patibada publishers.

von Benda-Beckmann, F.

1997. 'Citizens, strangers and indigenous peoples: Conceptual politics and legal pluralism.' In F. von Benda-Beckmann et al. (eds), *Natural Resources, Environment and Legal Pluralism. Yearbook Law & Anthropology 9*, pp. 1–42. The Hague, Boston, London: Martinus Nijhoff Publishers.

Yue, R.

2015. *Warlord's Learning Curve: A Case Study of the Pa-O Self-Administered Zone*. Research Paper, City University of Hong Kong. www.burmalibrary.org/docs21/Yue-Ricky-2015-Warlord's_Learning_Curve_A_Case_Study_of_the_Pa-O_Self_Administrated_Zone-en.pdf.

2016. 'Pacifying the margins: The Pa-O self-administered zone and the political order in Southern Shan State.' In N. Cheesman and N. Farrelly (eds), *Conflict in Myanmar. War, Politics, Religion*, pp. 91–120. Singapore: ISEAS Yusof Ishak Institute.

3 Why is customary law so strong? Political recognition and justice practices in the Naga Self-Administered Zone

Lue Htar, Myat The Thitsar and Helene Maria Kyed

Introduction

The Naga Self-Administered Zone (SAZ) is located in the north-western corner of Myanmar on the border with India. Since 2003, Naga leaders from the different sub-tribes have worked together to codify a common customary law for all the linguistically different Naga sub-groups. A core aim is to unite the various Naga groups around a common identity and to obtain Myanmar state recognition of Naga customary law. Engaging the debate on legal pluralism, this chapter provides nuanced and ethnographically-based reflections on the pros and cons of state recognition of customary law. It does this by exploring the strengths of the Naga customary justice system in one rural and one urban context within Layshi Township in the Naga Self-Administered Zone (SAZ). The fieldwork underpinning the findings and analysis presented in the chapter was conducted from mid-2017 to early 2019.[1]

The current political transition in Myanmar has allowed for bigger efforts to institutionalise Naga customary law and legal practices, but the process had already begun in the 1990s, when the Naga leaders organised the Naga Literature and Culture Committee Central (NLCC-C) to improve access to justice for all the different Naga tribes and to create a shared Naga spoken and written language. The NLCC-C is now working to achieve Myanmar state recognition of a codified version of Naga customary law (NLCC-C 2003). We argue that the strengthening of customary law is part of a Naga nation-building effort that seeks to unite the Naga sub-groups around a shared group identity and to protect this identity against erosion by the majority Bamar culture and by the political influence of state-led nation building.

1 The research was conducted as part of the EverJust project, financed by the development research fund of the Danish Ministry of Foreign Affairs. The first author to this chapter is herself from the Naga Goga tribe and therefore speaks the relevant local dialect.

While key aspects of the history of the Naga, including in particular questions related to political and cultural identity, are dealt with in existing literature (Hutton, 1965 and 1969 [1922]; Kotwal 2000; Stirn and van Ham 2003; Tohring 2010; Thomas 2016), not much has been written on justice and the ways in which it is dispensed within Naga society. Based on data from in-depth interviews with rural and urban residents and leaders, women as well as men, in the Naga SAZ, this chapter provides novel insights into an area that has so far been overlooked in the scholarship on Myanmar and legal pluralism.[2] The fieldwork underpinning our analysis was conducted in Layshi Township, focusing on two sites: the main rural village of the Naga Goga tribe, which we here call Dah Tri Gyu village, and a ward in Layshi town.[3] Focusing on these two sites allowed us to explore possible differences in dispute resolution across the rural–urban divide. We do, however, remain aware that our analysis is limited in both time and space and does not enable us to generalise across all Naga sub-groups.

To situate our findings within the wider literature, the chapter begins with a brief discussion of legal pluralism, followed by a shorter overview of the Naga and the main characteristics of their social organisation. Following that, we describe the Naga justice system, including Naga principles of justice and procedures and the Naga Book of Customary Law (NLCC-C 2003), and we discuss the ways in which these have been applied in practice in three specific cases of dispute resolution. In the conclusion we return to the overall question of state recognition of customary law within the current Myanmar transition, in order to discuss the various dilemmas it presents both for the Naga and for the Myanmar state and international donors.

Legal pluralism and recognition of customary law

In scholarly and policy circles, questions concerning access to justice and the right to self-determination are often framed within the notion

2 Semi-structured interviews were conducted with 78 residents, 13 tribal and religious leaders, five administrative leaders at different levels, two members of the executive body of the Naga SAZ, as well as with elected members of parliament, government officials, police and justice department officials.

3 We have changed the village name to ensure anonymisation but kept the township name to make clear in which area of the Naga self-administered zone the research took place.

of legal pluralism. According to Merry, legal pluralism can be defined as 'a situation in which two or more legal systems coexist in the same social field' (1988: 870). While this may sound simple, it is not. Legal pluralism implies that 'every functioning sub-group in a society has its own legal system which is necessarily different in some respects from those of the other subgroups' (ibid.). For this reason, legal pluralism is often highly complex and difficult to capture in practice (Merry, 1988: 871). Identifying the relevant subgroups and determining their particular rules is complicated and calls for extensive fieldwork, especially when the rules are not codified. Importantly, however, it also calls for analysis of both the interaction and the dialectic between different normative orders, taking into account the ways in which these have evolved historically. These theoretical insights are important in our analysis of Naga customary law and practices. They highlight the difficulties of clearly outlining a specific homogenous Naga legal culture, and they also draw attention to the need to understand how customary law evolves and varies between different groups as well as through interaction with official state law. This matters hugely to discussion of the codification and recognition of a common customary law for the Naga sub-groups.

The United Nations Declaration on the Rights of Indigenous Peoples in 2007 provided an international basis for recognising the juridical systems and customs of indigenous people within a majority society or nation-state. Article 34 of the declaration states that: 'Indigenous peoples have the right to promote, develop and maintain their institutional structures and their distinctive customs, spirituality, traditions, procedures, practices and, in the cases where they exist, juridical systems or customs, in accordance with international human rights standards' (UN 2008: 24). Thus we see that recognition of indigenous judicial systems is considered a human right for the protection of indigenous people. However, such systems must not contradict international human rights standards, such as non-discrimination, fair trial and individual rights. This emphasis on international standards has the potential to raise dilemmas in recognising the customary law of a particular group (Muriaas 2003).

Customary justice systems tend to be overwhelmingly focused on the group, rather than the individual. Accordingly, they are often criticised for undermining individual rights, for being exclusionary, and for being vulnerable to local power dynamics (Muriaas 2003). They often rely on an identity-based perception of jurisdiction, whereby it is only the members of a certain group that can use it and are protected by it. This can lead to the exclusion of people who are not accepted as members of the group. Customary laws also tend to reinforce and build upon local social hierarchies that support the power of local elites. In some contexts, this sustains gender imbalances, which means that women are not treated equally with men before the law. At the same time, part of the reason why customary legal forums are often regarded as more effective than official state courts in restoring social relations is precisely the fact that they promote reconciliation and are focused on group harmony rather than on the rights of the individual (Muriaas 2003: 217–218).

Another dilemma is between state recognition on the one hand and local legitimacy and the independence of customary law on the other. In the socio-legal literature scholars have used the concept of 'weak legal pluralism' (J. Griffiths 1986; Merry 1988; F. von Benda-Beckmann 1997; Kyed et al. 2012) to describe situations where state recognition of customary law establishes a hierarchy where state law and institutions are seen (and defined in national constitutions) as superior to other legal orders. In practice, this can imply that states use the recognition of legal pluralism or customary law as a means to increase central state control over non-state or customary legal orders, and by extension of those groups of people who apply these orders (Kyed et. al. 2012: 22; A. Griffiths 2012).

The most prominent example of weak legal pluralism is the forms of indirect rule that were applied in Africa and Asia under British colonial rule. Here the recognition of customary laws served as a means for the colonial rulers to control and transform indigenous groups. A repugnancy clause was used widely in these systems, which meant that customary law was only recognised if it did not contradict colonial state law (A. Griffiths 2012: 35). Sheleff (1999: 122) contends that such repugnancy clauses undermined indigenous law, as they used the values of western culture as the yardstick for determining the legitimacy of customary norms and practices. In this way, the recognition of customary law can be political and undermine the ability of indigenous people or ethnic minority groups to themselves define their customary law independently.

'Strong legal pluralism', by contrast, describes the diversity of already existing norms and practices that are not part of the state system, but which are seen as locally legitimate and which evolve according to their own internal dynamics (A. Griffiths 2012). State policies that recognise strong legal pluralism are based on principles of equality rather than on a hierarchy of laws, and on the right of particular groups to define and live according to their customs and norms as they themselves define them (J. Griffiths 1986; Woodman 1999; Kyed et al. 2012: 23; A. Griffiths 2012). Current examples of states that recognise legal pluralism in the 'strong' sense are, however, rare. Bolivia is one example. Here indigenous legal orders are granted the same status as state law, and a high degree of independence. This applies to all of Bolivia's ethnic groups and their particular legal frameworks. This is reflected at the national level, where different ethnic groups are represented in the Constitutional Court (Albrecht and Kyed 2010). Strong legal pluralism requires that customary law be defined through participatory and inclusive processes whereby it is the indigenous people themselves who set the agenda – and not the state.

Strong legal pluralism is not uncontroversial, however, because it has political implications. Effectively it means 'that the state will no longer maintain a monopoly on the production and application of law' (Sieder 2002: 185), and therefore the state may perceive legal pluralism to be a threat to its sovereignty. For this reason, it is vital to take into account and to understand the incentives of the state when discussing state recognition of customary justice. What can the state gain by recognising it? As noted by Muriaas, one positive incentive for states is related to the capacity problem of official state courts (2003: 214). In many countries in the Global South, customary courts are seen to ease the case-load of the state courts. Another incentive could be to heighten state legitimacy in contexts where the state has low legitimacy – recognising customary justice systems demonstrates to indigenous people that the state is inclusive and supportive of them. This is particularly important in contexts like Myanmar, where state oppression and attempts to extend state law to indigenous communities during periods of conflict and authoritarian rule have ignited resistance and largely failed to embed the state in society.

When considering state recognition of customary law it is also important to be cognisant of local elite dynamics. The push for recognition of customary law most often comes from the leaders or organisations of indigenous people themselves, for instance during democratic and post-conflict transitions (Sieder 2002). These leaders have their own political agendas, which may be related to self-determination as well as to upholding the rights of indigenous people and their access to justice. The aim of these leaders is rarely, if ever, simply a return to or a continuation of traditional or customary law, as Sieder (2002: 199) notes for Latin America – it is, rather, the much broader desire of indigenous groups to gain the legitimate power to regulate their own affairs. We would suggest that this applies to the current situation of the Naga and their efforts to consolidate a common customary law during the time of the Myanmar transition. To understand the current situation, we begin with some brief background on the Naga and their social organisation.

Brief background on the Naga

The ethnic group referred to as Naga includes over 40 tribes who inhabit an area divided between northwest Myanmar and northeast India, a mountainous region known as the Naga Hills (RRtIP 2018: 11).[4] As census data is unclear, it is not known how many Naga live in Myanmar and inside what today is the Naga Self-Administered Zone (SAZ). However, according to the Naga Literature and Culture Committee (NLCC), Myanmar is home to nine Naga tribes and a population of 400,000 people identifying as Naga.[5]

The Naga people have always been a very heterogeneous group, divided into various tribes, sub-tribes and clans with varying customs, traditions, dress and languages, and divided into different polities (Kotwal 2000: 753). In fact, the term 'Naga' is of foreign origin – it was invented by the British. The different tribal languages are very distinct

4 While the 1991 Indian Census of India records 35 Naga tribes (Shimray 2007), some independent studies listed 66 Naga tribes in total (Tohring 2010).

5 The nine Naga tribes listed by NLCC-Central are Tangshang, Lainong, Konyak, Khiamniung, Para, Makury, Tangon, Gonwonnbonyo and Paungnyonmachan tribes. The Goga tribe discussed in this chapter is not mentioned here because the Goga tribe is not yet recognised as a main tribe by the Central level NLCC. By this level, the Goga are considered part of the Tangon Naga tribe. For almost two decades the Goga people have been demanding to be separated from the Tangon Naga and to have their own tribe recognised. The religious leaders and the NLCC in Layshi township are already recognising the Goga as a main tribe.

and even today Naga on the Burmese side belonging to different tribes usually communicate in Burmese.[6] The Naga tribes do not have their own script (Longvah 2017: 125), and only a few tribes, such as the Tangon Naga, have codified their language, using the English alphabet.[7] Today a large majority of the Naga are Christians. While the earliest conversions to Christianity took place in the late 1800s, with the advent of American Baptist missionaries, a number of the tribes on the Myanmar side, including the Goga tribe with which this chapter concerns itself, only converted from the late 1960s.[8] A much smaller number of Naga became Buddhists after independence from the British. Before this time, the majority adhered to beliefs in spirits, beliefs that were categorised by the British as 'animist' (see Longvah 2017: 126).[9] While very few today self-identify as animist, we found that these beliefs are still evident in dispute resolution. Christianity has been used to explain why certain customary practices have been disappearing, but we did not detect any significant influence of Christianity on the norms that govern dispute resolution, perceptions of justice and customary laws. Instead, our impression was that Christianity played a role in nurturing a shared Naga identity during late colonial rule. Later it also informed shared experiences of oppression by the Burmese military regime, which particularly targeted ethno-religious minorities.

Efforts to unite the different tribes under a 'Naga' ethnic identity, using the term that the British had introduced, were initiated by the leaders of the disparate Naga tribes in order to defend their land and culture from foreign occupation during colonialism (Longvah 2017:

6 A common Naga language, known as Nagamese, has, by contrast, been developed on the Indian side.

7 As Hutton (1969 [1922]: 19) noted long ago in relation to languages among the Naga: 'I suppose there is no part of the world with so much linguistic variation in so small a population or in so small an area. The result of the isolation of village communities, living entirely independently and often with almost entirely self-contained economies, cut off from their neighbours by forest, mountain, and river'. Furthermore, the lack of a Naga script reflects the dominance of an oral tradition, which also means that there are no written records from pre-colonial times (Longvah 2017: 125).

8 The first missionaries who came to the Goga tribe were Karen from southeastern Myanmar who had converted to Christianity much earlier.

9 For a critique of the use of the term animist to describe the Naga, see Longvah (2017: 127), who argues that the Naga also believed in a superior creator and in an afterlife, beliefs that do not, he argues, fit in with the definition of animism.

122–124; Thomas 2016: 2).[10] Around the time of independence from the British, this unification effort developed into nationalist movements with aspirations for self-determination and an independent Nagaland. The day before India gained independence from the British, the Naga nationalist movements on both the Indian and Burmese (now Myanmar) sides unilaterally declared Naga independence, but this was unsuccessful (Shapwon 2016). After a period of armed conflict, the Indian government in December 1963 officially recognised Nagaland as the sixteenth state of India and subsequently delegated extraordinary executive and judicial powers to village levels, including recognition of customary courts. Parallel political developments did not, however, occur in Myanmar (then Burma), which left Nagaland on the Myanmar side as a 'forgotten land', with very little development and no recognition of Naga customary systems (Zarleen 2010).

During Burmese military socialist rule (1962–1988) the Naga Hills were put under full Burmese administration, but the Naga had very little access to citizenship rights such as education, health, and infrastructure. During this period, armed struggle for a united, independent Nagaland continued on both the Indian and the Myanmar sides, and an armed resistance group, the National Socialist Council of Nagas (NSCN), was established in 1980. In the next period of military rule (1988–1997) – under the State Law and Order Restoration Council (SLORC) – the Naga were subjected to extensive human rights violations and were forced, sometimes by force of arms, to convert to Buddhism. The military government built many pagodas in Christian Naga villages, as part of an effort to crush Christianity and Burmanise the Naga. If the Naga refused to convert, they risked being used as military porters and they (and their children) could not apply for government jobs (Stirn and van Ham 2003).[11] Torture for disobedience was applied. A number of Naga

10 During British colonial rule, the colonial government used a policy of non-intervention in much of the Naga Hills on the Burmese side, especially in the north. In the southern part of the hills the British established indirect rule, whereby the tribes and villages were permitted to govern according to their own customary systems, but with some colonial regulation (RRtIP 2018: 13). However, at that time they did not have a common Naga customary law, but separate systems.

11 According to those we interviewed, many Naga wanted their children to obtain government employment, as this was often the only route to income and security, given that there were few business opportunities at the time. Therefore some people converted to Buddhism, even though they did not know how to worship the Buddha.

families converted nominally to Buddhism and kept their Christian faith hidden. Even today, some Naga have 'Buddhist' on their national ID cards even though they practise Christianity.[12]

In 1988, the armed rebellion was weakened as the NSCN split into the NSCN-IM and the NSCN-K (Wouters 2017). The NSCN-K, which only signed a ceasefire with the Myanmar government in 2012, was the most active in Burma but it did not have widespread support among the various Naga tribes.[13] Instead, what dominated in this period were civilian and non-violent efforts to strengthen the Naga group. As early as 1993, influential Naga tribal leaders from the different tribes inside Myanmar formed the Naga Literature and Culture Committee (NLCC), an unarmed, civilian organisation that aimed to unite the Naga across the different Myanmar-based tribes. The NLCC aimed to develop a common language, consolidate common customs, and organise the Naga New Year Festival, where Naga people can meet and gather consensus about developments for the Naga people. The vision of the NLCC was that it should become a Naga national institution that would help organise the Naga tribes into one national identity.[14] It was also the NLCC that consolidated a common Naga customary justice system, which we will discuss further below.

During the last period of Burmese military rule (1997–2011), under the State Peace and Development Council (SPDC), which led to the 2008 Myanmar Constitution, the Naga Hills were established as a Self-Administered Zone (SAZ). The existence of the SAZ does not, however, imply self-determination for the Naga, as it only provides for very limited administrative and legislative rights on the part of the SAZ Local Leading Body (Dae-tha Oo-se Ah Phwe). It should also be noted that this body does not only include Naga, but also elected members of State/Region Parliaments, the military officer in charge of Border Affairs and Security, who is appointed by the Commander in Chief of the Myanmar Army, and the District Head of Administration. According to Schedule 3 of the Myanmar Constitution, only ten legislative rights are

12 Interview with community members, Goga village.

13 In late January 2019, the ceasefire apparently broke down, as the Tatmadaw overthrew the headquarters of NSCN-K, alleging that it was connecting with rebel groups in India and providing them with shelter and military training.

14 This information is based on our interviews with members of the NLCC at central level.

granted to the SAZ Local Leading Body. These are vaguely defined and limited by a clause that holds that their application cannot override the legislative powers of the central government. Judiciary power is exclusively held by the Myanmar state's townships and district courts. This leaves Naga customary law and justice systems without official state recognition.

Figure 3.1 Naga New Year celebration in 2018 showing the traditional garments of Naga men. The celebrations bring together the Naga from the different tribes every year and can be seen as part of Naga nation-building. *Colour image, p. 359.*

Since the establishment of the SAZ and the end of military rule in 2011, the Naga have seen a number of new developments, including the improvement of infrastructure, transportation, education and trade. The different villages and townships are now better connected, which facilitates improved collaboration between the Naga. At the same time, the SAZ has meant a greater encroachment of the Myanmar state in the Naga Hills. The government has built many government buildings and put up official signposts with its logo in the region, marking the physical presence of the government. The government does not recognise the voice of local Naga sufficiently and it is trying to place all administrative matters under its supervision.

Figure 3.2 Naga New Year celebration in 2018 showing the traditional garments of Naga women. *Colour image, p. 360.*

The Bamar-dominated Union Solidarity and Development Party (USDP) and the National League for Democracy (NLD) are the dominant political parties. Nevertheless, the transition has left a space for Naga political and judicial consolidation. In 2018, a number of Naga politicians organised the Naga National Party (NNP), which is now registered to participate in the 2020 elections. The NLCC also continues to work to promote shared Naga institutions and to unite customary laws across the Myanmar-based Naga tribes. There is a growing number of different CSOs that work across the Naga tribes on ethnic issues, on peace, on issues related to the young, with students, and on political and religious topics. The social organisation and justice system of the Naga also continues to be significant in regulating everyday life, as we address next.

Local social organisations of the Naga

In our research among the Naga Goga tribe in Layshi township we found that the most significant units in Naga social organisation are the village, the patrilineal kinship group (*pha thar su*), the clan and the tribe. Of these, we found that the *pha thar su* plays a particularly pivotal role in resolving disputes. The *pha thar su* bonds all males and females together on the patrilineal side within the same tribe. They protect each other, help each other in dispute resolution, secure social harmony with other people, and support each other with food and other key items related to survival. Male members of the *pha thar su* also protect female members if, for instance, their husbands do not treat them well. Whereas the *pha thar su* is within the same tribe, the clans cut across tribes and serve to facilitate cross-tribe communication (see Hutton 1969 [1922]: 20–21).

In terms of leadership, each of the larger villages still has a traditional headman, whose position is based on hereditary status within the patrilineal kinship line. He traditionally worked together with elders or *pha thar su* leaders (the eldest man in a *pha thar su* is its leader), but since the SAZ was introduced, he also works with the village NLCC and the government-appointed village or village tract administrators. Thus, village leadership has changed somewhat and has become a dual system that incorporates Myanmar village administration structures. Dah Tri Gyu village is categorised as a 'village tract' and therefore has a village tract administrator (VTA), who is appointed by the Myanmar government.[15] Until recently, the VTA and the headman (*ah ma aé* in the Goga Naga language) was the same person, but because the headman of Dah

15 According to the 2012 Ward Administrator and Village Tract Administrator law of Myanmar (see Kyed et. al. 2016), the VTA is now supposed to be elected, but this is not the case as yet in Dah Tri Guy village.

Tri Gyu village was getting old, his son had become the VTA. This shows that hereditary traditional leadership continues despite government intervention. Officially, the VTA deals with issues related to orders from the government, including matters relating to education, ID, health and infrastructure. The headman is involved in internal village matters, including dispute resolution. Since the formation of the NLCC at village level, the headman works with and is himself a member of the NLCC.

Figure 3.3 View of the rice storage houses in Dah Try Gyu village. *Colour image, p. 360.*

In Dah Tri Gyu village, which is the main village of the Goga tribe, the majority are Christian, with only six households being Buddhist, among them the headman and his family, whose son is also the government village leader. They probably converted because being a Buddhist is an advantage if you want a position with the government. According to our interviewees, no one identified as 'animist' any longer, but the elders had a good knowledge of spirit beliefs. Some traditional dispute resolution practices also relate to spirit beliefs.[16]

The Goga tribe write in Burmese (or, less frequently, in English). Only in 2017 did the Goga tribe begin to create their own written language, with help from a foreign linguist. They now have a Goga primary school textbook and a small number of Goga were trained to teach using it in February 2019. They use the English alphabet.

As the Naga have a patriarchal system, Naga women are subordinated to their parents and brothers, and, when they marry, to their husbands. Women have no right to assume leadership positions, neither religious nor administrative. They also lack rights with respect to inheritance and divorce.

16 Naga were famous for being a headhunting tribe in the past, but according to the elders of Dah Tri Gyu village, headhunting disappeared about 100 years ago. They still, however, keep the headhouse and the stone block where heads used to be displayed.

The Naga justice system and dispute resolution procedures

Traditional dispute resolution is still very much intact in the Naga villages like Dah Tri Gyu, and even in towns like Layshi. Before the NLCCs were formed at tribal village, township and central level, the Naga applied only orally transmitted rules and norms, and there was no clearly institutionalised hierarchy of 'justice committees' for the Naga as a whole. As a result, customary laws, transmitted orally, varied from village to village. From what informants told us, however, it is clear that the central principles of justice were similar across the diverse tribes These principles include a focus on compensation, reconciliation and shaming as remedies, and a concern with truth-seeking, using witnesses, trial by ordeal and oaths as the main dispute resolution mechanisms. Naga principles of customary law do not include the use of prisons or physical punishment.

According to the village elders and leaders whom we interviewed, the purpose of compensation is not only to punish the perpetrator and reconcile the parties, but also to prevent new offences, which is achieved by setting the level of compensation high. Shaming measures are additional penalties (to compensation) and are also seen as preventive. They include *ywar say* ('cleaning the village') and *mee sar yay sar* ('eating fire and water').[17] Naga tribal leaders explained that they used village cleansing rituals to make the offender or his/her family feel shame for an offence. If a perpetrator repeats an offence several times, his/her own *pha thar su* can expel him or her from the *pha thar su*, from the whole village and/or from the tribal community. Another option is to send repeat offenders to the state legal system, but this, like expulsion, is a last resort. Forgiveness without compensation is only possible if the disputants are members of the same *pha thar su*. In such cases, the victim's family will refuse to take any compensation even if the perpetrator and his/her family offer to pay it. In fact, according to the Dah Tri Gyu village headman, it is bad luck for the family to take compensation from within the same family: doing so could, he said, cause misfortune for the next generation. This is connected to tradi-

17 *Mee sar yay sar* must take place within 15 days of a settlement being decided upon. Each of the two sides must pay for a pig at least four years old. These animals are slaughtered and the meat is served to leaders and to the *pha thar su*; and both sides must agree the case is over and that there is no longer any animosity between them. The offender must, in addition, pay a knife to the victim's family. *Mee sar yay sar* is commonly used for very serious cases involving such crimes as rape and murder.

tional spirit beliefs. In the same way, if a crime takes place within the same *pha thar su* it is bad luck to forward the case to higher levels such as the NLCC or the state courts.[18]

During the dispute resolution process, truth-seeking is a core moral value and is the obligation of the individual and the community as a whole. However, material evidence of a crime or of what really happened in a dispute is often lacking. For instance, in the land dispute cases we encountered in Dah Tri Gyu village, the disputants found it difficult to prove land ownership, as they have no official documents relating to ownership and traditional markings showing land boundaries are often unclear. Therefore, in settling disputes, the system relies heavily on witnesses. If witnessing does not work satisfactorily, trial by ordeal may be used, together with oaths. These are practices that predate conversion to Christianity. Traditionally, they included 'diving into the water by disputants' (*sulidah* in Goga),[19] 'daring to eat soil' (*lahlaw dze* in Goga),[20] 'biting a tiger-tooth' (*rhuke mahgaw* in Goga)[21] or offering a domestic animal to the spirits. Naga believed, traditionally, that an oath taken to the spirits of the forest, to the earth, or to the ancestors would have serious consequences for their lives and well-being. While these traditional practices are now used less frequently in dispute resolution, Naga leaders still draw on them to explain how the Naga have traditionally taken pride in revealing the truth. According to interviewees in Dah Tri Gyu village, trial by ordeal is now disappearing, due to Christianity. They said that they never use the tiger tooth any more, but 'diving into water' is still used, although as a very last resort when other attempts at resolution fail.[22] The reason that it is considered a last resort is that many Naga still believe that using this method leads to bad luck for the disputants or their family members in the future.

18 Interview, headman, Dah Tri Gyu village, 24 February 2019.

19 The two disputants have to dive into a pool of water and the one who stays longest under water is telling the truth – for instance, in land disputes, the one who stays longest in water is said to have made the true claim to the land ownership.

20 You eat soil and take an oath, and if you are not telling the truth you will vomit, get sick and your great grandson will have bad luck (interview, Dah Tri Gyu village elders, 24 February 2019).

21 If you bite the tiger tooth, and you are not telling the truth, you will get a very dry mouth (interview, Dah Tri Gyu village elders, 24 February 2019).

22 The most recent example at the time of writing was in April 2019 in Layshi township, when two land disputants dived into water. The event was filmed and posted on Facebook.

This notion of bad luck is informed by traditional spirit beliefs, despite the fact that the majority now self-identify as Christians and no longer practice animism, no longer worshipping or making offerings to the spirits. Christian churches have also encouraged people to move away from traditional practices such as 'diving in water'.

Regardless of whether the emphasis is on remedies or on truth-seeking, we learnt that the *pha thar su* plays an important role in dispute resolution, as it is the first port of call. It seems to be a shared principle across tribes that a case must be dealt with at the *pha thar su*-level before it is moved to the village level for resolution. Only if a case involves different tribes is it common to go directly to the township level NLCC, as all tribes are represented at this level.

We found that it was considered shameful not to go first to the *pha thar su* when dealing with a crime or dispute. If a case is between members of two *pha thar su*, the two *pha thar su* come together first to try to settle the case. Only if they fail to find a settlement is the case forwarded to the village level headman; and only if that fails is the case forwarded to the NLCCs at higher levels (first the tribe, then the township, and then the central level), following a step-by-step procedure. The involvement of the *pha thar su* remains important at every step. The NLCC committee negotiates with the two *pha thar su*, and unless they are both satisfied the committee cannot make a decision. It is not enough that the victim is satisfied. If a perpetrator runs away from a court case, the closest members of his/her *pha thar su* take responsibility in the case and must also pay the compensation that has been determined. Irrespective of tribe, the Naga traditionally regard the *pha thar su* as 'second parents'. According to the village headman in Dah Tri Gyu, an important responsibility of the *pha thar su* is to make sure that the cases do not become 'big', by which he meant that they should be resolved peacefully at the *pha thar su* level and should not escalate to higher levels.

When a case reaches the NLCC system, a jury committee is formed, which analyses the case based on testimonies from the plaintiff and the accused.[23] The jury members report their findings to the executive com-

23 The jury committee consists of people who are part of the NLCC committees, which are elected by the tribal leaders from each tribe. Which NLCC members are part of the jury varies from tribe to tribe, but the jury must include, as a minimum, the chairman and the secretary of the NLCC committee at the relevant level (township,

mittee, which in turn makes recommendations to the jury members, who then make the final judgement. Both sides in the case must pay *khone kha* ('charges for jury members') to the jury committee. The amount depends on the type of case. NLCC houses, known as 'Naga traditional museums', are situated in some larger villages and township towns, and are not only used as courts, but also for keeping Naga costumes and traditional instruments.[24] They are also used for the Naga New Year opening ceremony, during which traditional totem poles are beaten.

Figure 3.4 Naga Traditional Museum at Township level. Here disputes are resolved by the Naga Literature and Culture Committee and the houses are also used for other traditional activities as well as serving as museums. *Colour image, p. 361.*

The Naga Book of Customary Law

In their everyday work, the various committees and juries of the NLCC system apply the Naga Book of Customary Law. This was produced in 2003 by the different tribal leaders of the NLCC, who collected the oral customs and practices from each of the tribes to provide a codified version of Naga customary law.[25] The NLCC leaders see the Book of Customary Law as one of their major achievements. The current version lists 95 offences and details the punishments for each of these. In

district, central). They will also consider which tribes the disputing parties are from, and will then try to ensure that there is a jury committee member from each of those tribes.

24 As there are many different Naga tribes, they use the following name in Burmese *Naga yoe yar yin kyay hmu pyaut tike* to describe the Naga Traditional Museums.

25 There was no evidence to suggest that this Book of Customary Law was a copy of the Naga book of customary law which exists on the Indian side, although the leaders may have been inspired by the fact that the Indian Naga have had a codification of their customary law for a much longer time.

doing this, it adheres to the traditional Naga principle of compensation. For instance, for murder and rape it states:[26]

> Article 1. Murder: Whoever intentionally causes another person to die yet makes the evidence disappear; is culpable of homicide not amounting to murder; or causes death by performing an act with the intention of causing death or with the intention of causing bodily injury as would be sufficient in the ordinary course of nature to cause death, commits the offence of murder.
>
> Punishment: Whoever commits murder shall be liable to pay (a) five buffaloes over four years old (or) the equivalent in cash to this, as a fine; and (b) one 90-inch gong, one 140-bead coral necklace, one loincloth decorated with beads and one blanket decorated with beads (or) the equivalent in cash, to the victim's wife, son, daughter or closest heir.
>
> Article 17. Rape: Whoever has sexual intercourse with a woman without the consent of that woman is guilty of the offence of rape.
>
> Punishment: Whoever commits such an offence shall be liable to pay three buffaloes over five years old and one pig of a girth exceeding five-fists, (or) the equivalent in cash, as a fine.

Today the Book of Customary Law is widely used across the Naga region. The purpose, as is stated in the Book, was to bring the different tribes together under one law, based on an understanding that the Naga prefer to follow their tradition and culture in juridical matters:

> Different Naga ethnic groups have similar traditions and cultures, and they all accept, to this day, that a case is only finalised when the offender is punished according to their traditions, which they acknowledge even if the offender is punished by existing [State] law. The traditions and culture of different Naga ethnic groups differ according to the different places of residence. Therefore, this law is being established in order to ensure consensus about judicial punishment. In proceeding with established judicial punishment, the court uses this judicial [Naga] law in cases between Naga individuals and between Naga and individuals belonging to other ethnic groups only if the plaintiff states his desire to use this law (see NLCC-C 2003: Preface).

26 These extracts from the Book of Customary Law were translated from Burmese to English in July 2017 by Waili Soe Win.

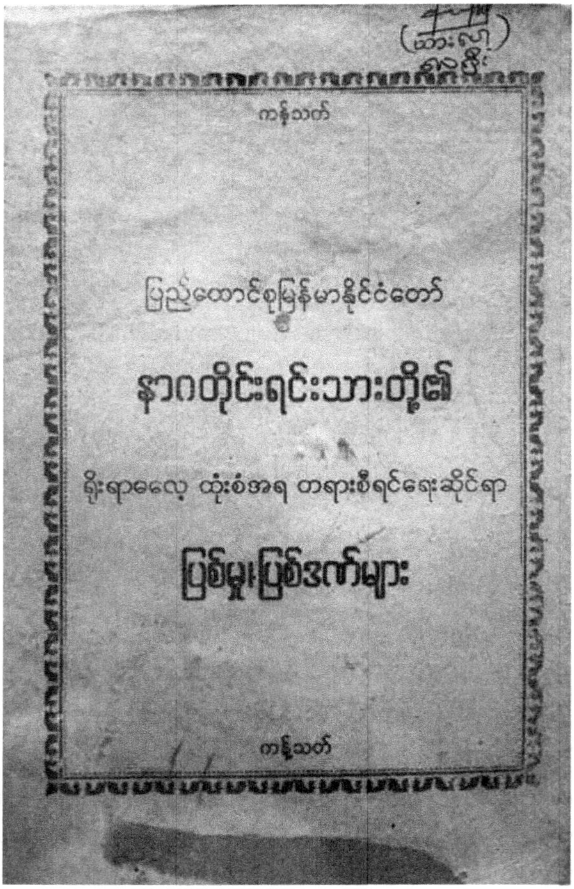

Figure 3.5 Cover page of the Naga Book of Customary Law. Photo by Lue Htar.

It can be seen from this statement that the Book of Customary Law acknowledges differences between Naga tribes; and that adjudication according to the Book of Customary Law should always be consent-based: both the plaintiff and the accused should be free to choose to seek justice under other systems of law (such as Myanmar state law).

Currently, according to the NLCC at central level, the Book of Customary Law is in the process of being amended, because at the time of the codification the NLCC did not adequately consult with all the village and tribal leaders or with certain other relevant stakeholders. There is also a desire to invite legal experts to amend the law. The Dah Tri Gyu headman complained to us that some of the compensations mentioned in the Book of Customary Law are not appropriate to the Goga tribe but draw on the practices of other tribes. Gender inequalities also persist in Naga customary law, such as unequal inheritance and lack of female representation. Finally, the law lacks a procedural code stating how cases should be resolved and how the NLCC committees should refer cases to each other. Nevertheless, our findings show that the Book of Customary Law is widely used, especially in guiding the setting of compensation.

Examples of dispute resolution from Layshi township

In what follows we provide examples of dispute resolution, pointing to the importance of the *pha thar su*, of the NLCC and of Naga customary law. The first case, from Dah Tri Gyu village, serves primarily to illustrate the role of the *pha thar su*, while the second case, from Layshi town, illustrates in addition how Naga leaders try to circumvent the state judicial system and to revert to Naga customary law. Finally, the third case shows that customary law is not static, but gradually changes in accordance with changes in wider society, here with respect to gender equality. This adaptability is, we suggest, one of the factors that contributes to the prevalence of customary law. In addition, the strength of customary law is in the role it plays in nurturing a shared Naga identity and in providing an alternative to state justice.

Case 1 – A case of accidental death and the role of the pha thar su

In 2014, U Law Ri went on a two-day hunt with five people, including U See Kyu, who had recently moved to Dah Htay village to serve as village pastor.[27] On the second day, they followed a group of monkeys. U Law Yi aimed at a monkey, but he decided that it was too small and dropped his gun. Suddenly, he saw a monkey that seemed to be mocking him, and he shot at it. When he got closer to the target, he found that he had shot U See Kyu, who died on the spot. When they got back to Dah Htay village, the hunting group informed the village leaders of the death. The perpetrator's *pha thar su* informed U See Kyu's family of the incident.

27 This case was narrated to us on 20 May 2017 by an NLCC member in Layshi who is in the same *pha thar su* as the deceased and who was also involved in the resolution. We also interviewed the victim's first cousin's brother about this case on 8 January 2018.

They live in another village, but are also from the Goga tribe. The close relatives of the perpetrator stayed away. U Law Ri's *pha thar su* went to meet U See Kyu's family and *pha thar su*, to settle the case. U See Kyu's close family members wanted revenge and demanded that U Law Ri be put to death for having killed U See Kyu.

Both U Law Yi's and U See Kyu's *pha thar su* quickly realised the tension and the emotional reaction of U See Kyu's close family members. Therefore they negotiated the case on behalf of (and in the absence of) the victim's closest family and the perpetrator. Within three days, they had agreed to settle the case, with compensation of MMK 3,000,000 (USD 1,950) in cash, a Naga traditional man's blanket, and one buffalo, to be killed for the funeral. The amount of money followed the Naga Book of Customary Law, whereas the blanket and the buffalo for the funeral were extra, to please the victim's family. When they had reached agreement, both *pha thar su* sides promised not to have any animosity or hatred over the case.

U See Kyu could not, however, afford to pay the compensation, as he is quite poor. Therefore other members of his *pha thar su* paid it. The other members of the hunting group also contributed to the compensation, paying one third of this. This was based on the fact that the Goga tribe has a hunting rule that holds that hunting group members share whatever they get in terms of prey. When the money had been paid, a *mee sar yay sar* ('reconciliation ritual') was performed. As is usual, a large meal was served, and the two most responsible persons from each family in the case exchanged plates and ate each other's food on the plates. The purpose of this ritual is to ensure that these people and their descendants will not mistrust each other. Both sides accepted the decision, without any threats, and this reduced the likelihood of social tension between the two *pha thar su*.

This case emphasises the significant role of the *pha thar su* in settling what in legal language would be called involuntary manslaughter. In Naga terms, however, the case fell under the category of *taw mout tel* ('bewitching by forest ghosts or spirits', causing loss of sight), which is a concept that is used specifically to explain accidents that take place during hunting expeditions. Traditionally, when such accidents occur, the person who has killed someone is hidden while the relatives from the two sides discuss and negotiate. However, if the victim's side wants revenge (a man for a man), the *pha thar su* leaders step in to mediate and persuade the victim's side to find a peaceful settlement that restores the relationship between the two *pha thar su*. The satisfaction of the victim is less important than social harmony. We saw in this case that the *pha thar su* used the compensation laid out in the Naga Book of Customary Law, together with traditional reconciliation rituals and hunting rules. According to the Dah Tri Gyu village administrator and one of the NLCC township members, the NLCC prefers that the *pha thar su* resolves important cases like these, with a focus on peacefully reconciling the two sides.[28] They fear that if the NLCC were to resolve it, one of the parties might be dissatisfied and seek revenge. It is only if the *pha thar su* is unable to resolve the case that the NLCC must step in.

According to Myanmar state law, this type of case – the taking of life – should have been adjudicated in the courts. However, this option was seen as too risky, according to the NLCC member with whom we spoke: if the perpetrator were to go to prison, he could die, and this would create tension between the two *pha thar su*. Also, the victim's family might be dissatisfied with the lack of compensation if the perpetrator were to go to prison, and this could lead the victim's side to seek revenge and maybe even kill the perpetrator. This might mean, the NLCC member said, that there could be another murder case, if the case went to the state system. When we spoke to the police about such cases, we found that there were different opinions. One officer in Layshi said that sometimes the police officers avert their eyes to the handling of cases by the Naga themselves, because they know that the Naga prefer to resolve their cases in the customary way. He agreed that the Naga's own customary resolution system is the most suitable for local people. However, some judges and policemen were not happy about village leaders dealing with such a case. They insisted that there is only one law: the Myanmar state law. The next case discussed below will reveal some of the tensions between state and customary adjudication. This case was resolved by the NLCC, probably because it had already ended up in the hands of the state police and because the parties were from different Naga tribes. The case also illustrates how Naga leaders have an interest in diverting cases away from the state system, so as to strengthen the Naga institutions, and thus also their own authority.

28 Interview with NLCC member on 7 January 2018.

Case 2 – A traffic accident and avoidance of state justice

Mg Yi Pae, a 23-year-old man from the Goga tribe who ran a transportation service, had a collision with a motorbike carrying a husband and a wife who were from the Tangon-Naga tribe.[29] The man died on the spot, and the woman was seriously injured. Once Mg Yi Pae's *pha thar su* heard about the case, leading members of it went straight to the Layshi township NLCC and requested its support in resolving the case following Naga customary law. However, when they arrived at the site of the accident two hours later, Mg Yi Pae had already been arrested by the township police. According to an NLCC member, a witness on the road had informed the police of what had happened. The police refused to allow the case to be negotiated by the NLCC, saying that the case had already been submitted to the district level in Sagaing region, which is located outside the Naga SAZ. Over the next two days, the township NLCC (*yin kyay mhu*) met with representatives of the *pha thar su* of the victim (the husband) and of the perpetrator, and both sides accepted that the case should be settled following Naga customary law. Then the NLCC went to negotiate with the township police, asking the police to transfer the case from the state's jurisdiction to the NLCC. The police officer on duty refused to do this, saying, according to an NLCC member: 'The case cannot be resolved with Naga customary law. Who recognises your law?' One member of Mg Yi Pae's *pha thar su* also told us, during an interview: 'When we talked with the township police, the station officer replied very roughly, shouting back at us, saying: "We have one law for the whole country, no separate law for Naga. You Naga leaders have to obey that law too". Then the Naga leaders just said straight back: "The Naga have Naga Law, and Naga law should be respected. Will you take responsibility for what will happen in the future? We speak for them [the Naga people]"'.[30]

By that time, the case was already being handled by the state township court. However, the NLCC did not give up easily, and they kept negotiating. After one month, the police agreed to the NLCC's request. The township police went to the district hospital where the injured woman was hospitalised and brought her back to Layshi, so that she could help

29 This case was narrated to us by the perpetrator's uncle, a member of the township NLCC and a local resident.

30 Interview, 21 March 2018.

to remove the case from the state court. The woman followed state court procedures, by reading aloud that she did not wish to take forward any grievance related to the case (either on her own behalf or on her husband's behalf), and therefore did not want to pursue a court case. After that, Mg Yi Pae was released from police custody. For the process of moving the case from the state system to the NLCC, the perpetrator's family had to pay several informal fees – what we might consider bribes: MMK 4,000,000 (USD 2,600) to the township law office, MMK 500,000 (USD 333) to the township police chief, MMK 350,000 (USD 233) to the second police chief, and around MMK 50,000 (USD 33) to other police personnel.

The day after the case was revoked at the court, the hearing at the township NLCC office began. Within one day both sides' families and *pha thar su* had been heard, separately, and compensation for the victim's side had been decided. This case, like the previous one discussed, was regarded as involuntary manslaughter, meaning that compensation of four buffaloes was due, equivalent to MMK 800,000 (USD 533) at the time, as well as MMK 3,500,000 (USD 2,330) in cash. For the serious injury to the woman and compensation for her medical treatment, the perpetrator had to pay another MMK 3,500,000 (USD 2,330). Each side had to pay MMK 25,000 (USD 17) for the *mee sar yay sar* (reconciliation ritual), as they had to buy a four-year-old pig each. The perpetrator's family also paid a smaller amount (*khone kha* – 'charges for jury members') to the NLCC as a kind of court fee. After the decision had been made, both sides agreed to settle the case: they promised not to pursue any revenge against each other in the future. Then the victim's side paid 10 per cent of the compensation to the NLCC's association fund.[31]

In total, the case cost Mg Yi Pae's side MMK 20,000,000 (USD 13,315). The vehicle he had been driving had been seized by the state and it was never returned, because it did not have registered Myanmar licence plates (and was therefore regarded as illegal by the state). However, Mg Yi Pae's *pha thar su* was satisfied that the case had been settled so quickly, and that Mg Yi Pae did not end up in prison, due to the help of the NLCC. Despite the costs incurred by Mg Yi Pae's family, the family members preferred customary justice to state justice, which

31 NLCCs at every level have their own funds. These are used for the renovation of office buildings and for buying other things, as well as for the New Year ceremony and for developing Naga literature.

meant both avoiding imprisonment and ensuring reconciliation with the victim's side. Customary justice was also preferred by the victim's side: the injured woman, who had lost her husband, was satisfied that she did not have to travel again and again to the district court, which is located far from her home. This would have been costly for her. Also, she knew that, had the case been adjudicated in court, she would have been unlikely to have received any compensation. Her *pha thar su* and the members of the NLCC were instrumental in convincing her of these potentially negative aspects of going to court. They convinced her that the court was not the best option for her.

This case helps to shed light on the different reasons why the Naga and their tribal leaders prefer the customary system to the state system, even when a case has in fact initially gone to the state police and courts. We suggest that both endogenous and exogenous factors are at play. There are two endogenous factors. The first is that the preference for customary justice in the above case was linked to the type of remedies that are applied through customary law: compensation for the victims, and reconciliation aimed at restoring social harmony and peace between the parties involved in the case and their *pha thar su*. These remedies were regarded as comparing favourably with imprisonment, which could, it was feared, have led both to the death of the perpetrator and an absence of compensation for the victim.

The second endogenous factor is that it is evident that in a case like the above reverting to the Naga customary system contributes more generally to efforts on the part of Naga leaders to strengthen that system and by extension to support Naga social organisation and cultural identity. Had it not been for the insistence and the negotiation skills of the members of the NLCC, the case would probably have been adjudicated in the state court. The members of the NLCC are the most important Naga tribal leaders, and they had an interest in making sure that the case was handled within the system that they represent and from which they gain their authority. Apart from a concern for the parties' access to justice, these leaders were also concerned with preserving Naga organisation, ethnic identity and leadership, when they insisted on handling the case within the NLCC. The leaders worry that their traditions, and the forms of organisation they sustain, will disappear if cases are resolved by the state. We would suggest that keeping cases within customary jurisdiction is part of building ethnic identity – an identity that also sustains the authority of the Naga leaders. Achieving this, as we have seen in the above case, requires very good negotiation skills on the part of the Naga leaders, who had to convince both the victim and the state officials to allow the case to be handled in the customary system. The process of reverting cases to the customary system can also be rather costly, once the case has gone to the state institutions, as it involves, as we have seen, the payment of a number of informal fees.

There are also exogenous factors involved here. The preference for resolving cases in the customary system cannot be divorced from the historically embedded understandings of the state system on the part of the Naga. The bitter experience of suppression that they suffered under six decades of military rule have alienated the Naga from official state institutions, including the state courts and the police. This alienation is today reinforced by the high costs associated with involving the state system in dispute resolution and by the use of formalistic Burmese language in the courts – which most Naga, who lack higher education, do not understand. As a Naga senior clerk at the township court in Layshi explained to us, most Naga face difficulties in understanding and trusting state court procedures. However, as is evident in the above case, transfer of a case to the customary system is dependent on the willingness of state officials to negotiate with the Naga leaders. We were told by one of the NLCC members involved in the case that it was fortunate that the main officer at the district court was sufficiently sympathetic to the Naga to allow the case to be handled by the Naga themselves. This contrasts with the attitude of the police officers, who were initially against the transfer and only allowed it after the payment of informal fees. The contrasting views of different state officials, and the need for informal payments to ensure that cases are settled in the customary system, reflects the insecurity facing the customary system, as a system that remains unrecognised by the state.

We would suggest that this lack of official recognition informs ongoing efforts on the part of the Naga leaders to strengthen Naga traditions and their customary system in everyday dispute resolution. In discussing the next case we intend to show that these traditions are also being internally negotiated and challenged in order to keep up with changes in society. Gender is one such area of change.

Case 3 – A case of domestic violence – adapting to the rights of women

In 2008 a 20-year-old girl named Ma Lo Se and her husband, U Kha Thee, aged about 60, both from the Goga tribe, moved into a house near Daw Khaw Htar's home in Layshi town.[32] Ma Lo Se was U Kha Thee's fourth wife, and she was the niece of his second wife (who is still married to U Kha Thee, though not in contact anymore). Ma Lo Se gave birth to a boy a year later.

When the boy was six months old, Daw Khaw Htar noticed that Ma Lo Se was very often being beaten by U Kha Thee. She could see this with her own eyes, and she also saw that U Kha Thee was behaving in a sexually improper manner. Once she went to try and stop U Kah Thee from beating his wife. Then one day, in the middle of the night, Ma Lo Se fled to Daw Khaw Htar's home with her child. However, U Kha Thee followed her; and when Ma Lo Se refused to go back with him, U Kha Thee pushed her down, grabbed the child and left. Ma Lo Se stayed with Daw Khaw Htar. However, she worried a great deal about her child. Sometime later, U Kha Thee threatened her, saying that he would send the child away if she did not come back home. Ma Lo Se went home. The next day, Ma Lo Se's *pha thar su* heard about the situation, met with U Kha Thee and asked on behalf of Ma Lo Se for a divorce. While they were talking to U Kha Thee, Ma Lo Se fled out the back door with her child. The next day, Ma Lo Se's *pha thar su* brought the case to the township NLCC. Within a few days, the NLCC heard the case. Daw Khaw Htar was the key witness, and a few days later the NLCC granted the divorce, deciding that U Kha Thee should compensate his wife with four buffaloes. Ma Lo Se was allowed to keep the child until he was three years old, and after that the child would have to live with the father's family. She was also given MMK 600,000 (USD 400) to cover the costs of caring for the child. U Kha Thee's *pha thar su* was not present, apparently because they disliked him. One of the NLCC judges in this case, shared his view about the decision with us, and explained that it had involved some changes in the customary law:

> Normally, compensation has to be paid by the person who seeks divorce [the wife, in this case]. In a case of divorce where there is mutual agreement, the husband and wife have to divide the

32 This case was narrated to us by the perpetrator's sister in law, but we were first made aware of the case by a Naga MP, when we were discussing changes in society.

> property in half. In this case the NLCC agreed to the divorce and also decided to penalise U Kha Thee for torturing his wife. But we still need to change more [of our customary law], and we need to improve the law to adhere to international conducts and standards, even though now we think more about the [rights of] women.[33]

The justice practitioners we spoke to, both old and young, appreciated the need for such changes in order to protect the rights of women more effectively. Traditionally, women had no right to divorce their husband, and if they wanted to divorce, they would not get any property; and ultimately, all the children would stay with the husband – because when a woman marries, she automatically becomes (as do her children) part of the husband's lineage. Traditionally, only sons, not daughters, have the right to inherit from their parents. Previously, even if the parents wanted to give a share to their daughters, the *pha thar su* would not accept this, seeing it as a violation of group principles. Some changes are now taking place, which are reflected in Naga customary law. Now parents can give property they accumulate during their lifetime to their daughters, although they still cannot pass on ancestral property (land and houses) to them. Naga customary law also now allows for both husbands and wives to petition for divorce (if they do not live up to their duties and responsibilities), and both sides can seek compensation from each other and share the property.

However, these changes have not done away with gender inequality in the Naga justice system. As we have seen, in the above case the woman was only allowed to keep her child until he was three years, rather than getting full custody. There continue to be no female members of the Naga NLCC or any female village headmen. There are no changes to the rights of women in many families, especially not in rural areas, where women are still marginalised. For instance, if a couple does not have a son, their property is automatically taken by the husband's brother's family, even if they have many daughters. The following story by a young Naga woman illustrates the hardships many Naga women endure:

> Sometimes, I pray that my mum will not have a long life, because my dad's cousins are not good to our family. My mum and dad had seven children, but only one was a son and he passed away. My dad is the eldest son, so when he married he got the family inheritance.

33 Interview with MP and former NLCC chairman, 13 May 2017.

> My parents bought new land after they married. When they wanted to send us to school, they wanted to sell some of that land to pay for our schooling, but my dad's cousins did not agree. They said that the women will be taken care of by the families that they marry into. My dad did not want to have a conflict with his cousins, so now we cannot finish our education ... My mum is very sad all the time. So what I feel is that we women are not born as human beings.[34]

Adjusting to changes in wider society is important for the continued strength of Naga customary law and practices, and with more and more women getting education this will be especially important. Such endogenous developments of customary law are therefore also important to the relevance of the Naga customary system, in addition to the potential for state recognition.

Concluding discussion

The key finding of this chapter is that the customary justice system of Naga plays a key role in regulating social life among Naga in the Naga Self-Administered Zone (SAZ), at all levels of society, from the patrilineal kinship group (*pha thar su*) to the district level. To explain this key role, we have pointed to the interrelationship of endogenous and exogenous factors. Together, these factors show that, despite continuities with the past, customary justice is a dynamic and evolving field that is linked to political developments. Our analysis has shown in particular that efforts to further strengthen customary justice are part of ethnic identity formation and of the consolidation of a Naga political position in the current Myanmar transition.

The first important endogenous factor explaining the strength of Naga customary law is Naga social organisation, which knits people together through the *pha thar su*, based on patrilineal descent. The role of the *pha thar su* demonstrates a social obligation to seek customary justice that is focused on reconciliation and the restoration of relationships through compensation and rituals. This can be contrasted to seeking official state justice, which is focused on punishing individuals. The *pha thar su* protects its members, but the main purpose of justice is social harmony, and this makes it difficult for the individual to pursue other forms of justice than customary justice. Customary procedures

34 Interview, 14 December 2017.

support the continued relevance of the *pha thar su* and secures peaceful relationships between the different *pha thar su*. In addition, many Naga still adhere to the traditional spiritual belief that it can be dangerous to by-pass one's *pha thar su* in dispute resolution, as this may result in misfortune for future generations. The role of the *pha thar su* is, in turn, supported by the headmen and other tribal leaders, and is therefore closely linked to local positions of power.

This relates to the second important endogenous factor underlying the strength of Naga customary law, which is the desire of Naga tribal leaders to promote Naga ethnic identity and Naga nation-building. This is the basis of recent efforts by Naga tribal leaders to consolidate the Naga customary system by codifying it in the Naga Book of Customary Law and by holding NLCC trials at different levels. It is clear from our analysis that these institutionalising efforts help to strengthen Naga access to justice when cases cannot be handled within the *pha thar su* or the village. However, the institutionalisation of the customary system across tribes is also part of promoting a common Naga ethnic identity, and therefore has a political goal that is focused on Naga nation-building. In everyday justice, this is evident in the way in which the tribal Naga leaders try as much as possible to draw disputants towards the customary system and to push them away from the state system. When disputants use the customary system, they are simultaneously increasing the strength of the Naga organisation and of the tribal leaders who represent this.

There is also an exogenous factor at play here in strengthening Naga customary law. The strength of the customary system cannot be understood independently of the views and experiences that most Naga have of the official state justice system. This system is not seen as a provider of justice, but as an uncertain and mistrusted alternative to customary justice. Even though few Naga are involved in armed rebellion against the Myanmar state, the history of the military oppression of the Naga continues to inform negative views of the state justice system. State avoidance is therefore not equal to state opposition, but it does help to support the preference among the Naga for the customary system, as opposed to the state system. In this sense, state avoidance can be seen as a factor strengthening the political position of the Naga within Myanmar.

There is a fourth factor strengthening Naga customary law. This is the willingness of Naga tribal leaders to try to adjust customary law to wider changes in society. This is, and will probably continue to be in the future, an important part of strengthening customary justice among the Naga. We have in this chapter focused on gender as an area that is being gradually changed, but other areas, such as increased inclusion and a wider representation of Naga people in defining and implementing Naga customary law, could be another important area of change.

We would like to conclude by returning to some reflections on the possible state recognition of the Naga customary system within the current transitional context of Myanmar. It is evident that the political transition has opened up a space for ethnic minority leaders and organisations to raise claims from below. In this process, minorities like the Naga are using familiar strategies of nation-building, such as promoting a common language, common cultural practices and a common law. In the context of Myanmar, these forms of minority nation-building are also a strategy for the survival and protection of minority rights in the context of a long history of centralised Myanmar state-led nation building, which sought to suppress and assimilate minorities into the majority Bamar culture.

Against this background, state recognition of Naga customary law can be seen as one factor protecting and supporting minority rights. However, it is also important to be aware of the political challenges of such state recognition, as is reflected in the wider literature on the topic (Sieder 2002; Kyed et al. 2012; Muriaas 2003; Sheleff 1999; Leonardi et al. 2011). Three important sets of questions must be addressed. Firstly, what is the goal behind the recognition of customary law and whom does it intend to serve? Is the aim to improve and enhance ordinary people's access to justice and rights, according to what they find legitimate, or are the political goals of elites dominant? And, related to this, do the political goals of the elite support the interests of ordinary people and their rights? Secondly, how and by whom is customary law defined, and thus where does the power of definition lie? Are ordinary people participating in defining customary law, including women and vulnerable groups, or is it mainly a local elite exercise? Thirdly, it is important to ask how the recognition of Naga customary law may contribute to sustainable peace and development in the Naga area, and consequently how it plays into wider negotiations for federalism and ethnic minority rights within the wider political context of Myanmar.

As Sieder (2002) notes, historical experiences from elsewhere show that the extent to which political autonomy granted to minorities results from state recognition of customary law depends on how and by whom 'customary' or 'tradition' is defined and applied. In some contexts, and certainly during colonial rule, recognition of customary law has mainly been used as a tool of the elite and of the central state to control indigenous people. It has not been used as a tool to enhance ordinary people's access to justice. This is what has been referred to as 'weak legal pluralism' (Merry 1988; J. Griffiths 1986). Sieder (2002: 200) writes that: 'Legal recognition of indigenous norms and practices – subject to national and international human rights norms – [sometimes] represents a way in which ruling elites map out new territories and communities, extending their control to areas formerly beyond their reach or currently beyond their control' (Sieder 2002: 200). However, this political instrumentalisation of customary law should not only be understood as an extension of power from the top down, or from the centre outwards. It is also important to be aware of local power dynamics. In some contexts, local leaders and elites assume the power to define customary law, without adequate inclusion of ordinary people, and sometimes they use this position to consolidate their own position of power. This may result in the exclusion of some members of the minority groups (for instance along the lines of gender, generation or sub-tribe) not only from defining customary law, but also from equal access to justice, property and resources (Kyed et. al. 2012: 24). With these risks in mind, it is very important that the process of recognition among the Naga be carried through in such a way that it benefits and includes the whole population. It must be an inclusionary and participatory exercise. Otherwise, the recognition of customary law, which is based on group rights, may undermine some individuals' or sub-groups' right to equal justice.

Currently, the codification of customary law in the Naga Book of Customary Law has not been based on wide participation, but there is a willingness among tribal leaders to take into account a greater respect for human rights, as we have seen in relation to gender. These leaders will need to collaborate to achieve wider inclusion of Naga voices, such as those of women. This could be supported by international organisations and by the growing number of educated young Naga (see also Tobin 2014: 76). These internal processes of inclusion are important. However, it is also important to look at the external challenges.

The most pressing challenge to access to justice and customary law nowadays does not come from within Naga society, but from the Myanmar state and its (un)willingness to recognise the customary law of ethnic minority groups. Apart from the risks associated with weak legal pluralism, the challenge is to create incentives for the Myanmar state to recognise legal pluralism in the strong sense, that is, to genuinely recognise locally-defined customary laws and institutions. This is necessarily a political choice and involves a change in perspective and political culture to include more recognition of the rights of minorities. As we discussed in the theoretical part of this chapter, a classic dilemma for states (anywhere) is that recognition of customary law in the strong sense will imply the need to devolve judicial power from the centre to the peripheries. For the state to do this in Myanmar would require a fundamental shift in how power has been organised and nation building has been pursued, namely through centralisation and assimilation into the majority Bamar culture. It would also require a change of perspective. Rather than seeing customary law as undermining state unity, the central government would need to be convinced that the recognition of the customary law of minority ethnic groups would create more trust in the state and the peace process. Recognition of minorities could, in fact, afford legitimacy to the central state. At a more practical level, the recognition of customary law and institutions could also ease the burden of the state justice system. The transition may provide the momentum for such shifts and incentives to be articulated. Sieder (2002: 201) notes for Latin America that during times of democratic transition there, the weaknesses of state judicial systems and (at least some) international donor preferences for strengthening informal justice can constitute a means by which spaces for customary law can be strengthened, even when the government seems to continue to block recognition of ethnic minorities' right to exercise it. This statement applies equally to Naga and other ethnic minority groups' customary law in Myanmar.

References

Albrecht, P. & Kyed, H.M.

2010. *Justice and Security. When the State isn't the Main Provider*. DIIS Policy Brief, Copenhagen: Danish Institute for International Studies (DIIS). December 2010.

Griffiths, A.

2012. 'Legal pluralism, justice and human rights: Reappraising law in a transnational age.' In H. Kyed et al. (eds), *The Dynamics of Legal Pluralism in Mozambique*, pp. 34–49. Maputo: Kapicua.

Griffiths, J.

1986. 'What is legal pluralism?' *Journal of Legal Pluralism and Unofficial Law* 24: 1–50.

Hutton, J.H.

1965. 'The mixed culture of the Naga tribes.' *Journal of the Royal Anthropological Institute of Great Britain and Ireland* 95(1): 16–43.

1969 [1922]. *The Angami Nagas, with some Notes on Neighbouring Tribes* (2nd ed.). Oxford: Oxford University Press.

Kotwal, D.

2000. 'The Naga insurgency: The past and the future.' *Strategic Analysis* 24(4): 751–772.

Kyed, H.M., Coelho, J.P.B., Neves de Souto, A. & Araújo, S.

2012. 'The dynamics of legal pluralism in Mozambique.' In H.M. Kyed et al. (eds), *The Dynamics of Legal Pluralism in Mozambique*, pp. 1–32. Maputo: Kapicua.

Kyed, H.M., Harrisson, A.P. & McCarthy, G.

2016. *Local Democracy in Myanmar: Reflections on the Ward and Village Tract Elections in 2016*. Copenhagen: DIIS.

Leonardi, C., Isser, D., Moro, L. and Santschi, M.

2011. 'The politics of customary law ascertainment in South Sudan.' *Journal of Legal Pluralism and Unofficial Law* 43(63): 111–142.

Longvah, S.

2017. 'Christian conversions, the rise of Naga national consciousness, and Naga nationalist politics.' *The Southasianist* 5(1): 121–139.

Merry, S.E.

1988. 'Legal pluralism.' *Law & Society Review* 22(5): 869–896.

Muriaas, R.L.

2003. 'Dilemmas connected to recognising customary law and courts in South Africa.' *Human Rights in Development Online* 9(1): 205–233.

NLCC-C (Naga Literature and Culture Committee - Central)

2013. *Naga Book of Customary Law*. Khamti: Naga Literature and Central Culture Committee.

RRtIP (Resource Rights for the Indigenous People)
2018. *Land and Forest Governance in the Naga village republic*. Yangon: RRtIP.

Shapwon, W.
2016. *The Illegal Formation of the NSCN*. Kohima: Vision Press.

Sheleff, L.
1999. 'The future of tradition: Customary law, common law and legal pluralism. Between recognition and repugnancy, the right to group right.' *Reference and Research Book News* 15(2): 121–152.

Shimray, U.A.
2007. *Naga Population and Integration Movement.* Mittal Publications.

Sieder, R.
2002. 'Recognising indigenous law and the politics of state formation in Mesoamerica.' In R. Sieder (ed.), *Multiculturalism in Latin America,* pp. 184–207. Institute of Latin American Studies Series. London: Palgrave Macmillan.

Stirn, A. & van Ham, P.
2003. *The Hidden World of the Naga: Living Traditions in Northeast India and Burma*. Munich: Prestel.

Tobin, B.
2011. 'Why customary law matters: The role of customary law in the protection of indigenous peoples' human rights.' PhD thesis, Irish Centre for Human Rights and National University of Ireland, Galway.
2014. *Indigenous Peoples, Customary Law and Human Rights – Why Living Law Matters.* New York and London: Routledge.

Tohring, S.R.
2010. *Violence and Identity in Northeast India: Naga-Kuki Conflict*. India, New Delhi: Mittal Publications.

Thomas, J.
2016. *Evangelising the Nation: Religion and the Formation of Naga Political Identity.* New Delhi: Routledge.

UN (United Nations)
2008. *United Nations Declaration on the Rights of Indigenous Peoples.* New York: UN.

von Benda-Beckman, F.
1997. 'Citizens, strangers and indigenous peoples: Conceptual politics and legal pluralism.' *Law and Anthropology* 9: 1–42.

Woodman, G.R.

1999. 'Ideological combat and social observation: Recent debate about legal pluralism.' *Journal of Legal Pluralism and Unofficial Law* 42: 21–59.

Wouters, Jelle J.P.

2017. 'Who is a Naga village? The Naga "village republic" through the ages.' *The South Asianist* 5(1): 99–120.

Zarleen, A.

2010. *Developing the Forgotten Land – Eastern Nagaland in Northwest Burma.* www.burmalink.org/developing-forgotten-land-eastern-nagaland-northwest-burma/.

4 Buddhist and animist non-state authority in a legal plural setting in Karen State

Marie Knakkergaard Richthammer

Introduction

Due to the many years of armed conflict and legal pluralism, several ethnic states in Myanmar have parallel governing systems outside that of the formal state, which are either controlled by Ethnic Armed Organisations (EAOs) or by local informal institutions. Some of the EAO-controlled areas, such as parts of Karen State that are controlled by the Karen National Union (KNU), have their own administrative systems, police forces, judicial systems, schools, healthcare and so forth (McCartan and Jolliffe 2016; Saferworld 2018; South et al. 2018). Recent research has shown that the KNU's judicial institutions enjoy authority and legitimacy in many parts of Karen State, where civilians perceive the KNU to be the main governing actor (Saferworld 2019; Kyed and The Thitsar 2018). This situation creates a complicated plural institutional landscape, where the legal and administrative institutions of the central Myanmar state (*Myanmar asoe ya* in Burmese) do not penetrate all areas and where local citizens do not engage with Myanmar state institutions for dispute resolution and access to justice.[1] In general, there are high levels of scepticism of the central state. Importantly, this scepticism is also present in the Karen village that I discuss in this chap-

1 I use 'state' rather than government to designate the central state administration and system, including the justice sector. The concept of government carries many connotations in Myanmar as there are many *de facto* governing powers, including some of the Ethnic Armed Organisations, the Tatmadaw (Myanmar military) and the government elected under the National League for Democracy (NLD). *Myanmar asoe ya* translates as 'Myanmar government'. In Burmese, 'state' (*pyinaal*) refers to a governed area within the country and does not refer to the central state. 'State' in English can refer to a country and has a permanent connotation whereas 'government' in English is usually understood as referring to something temporary or replaceable. Although my informants used *Myanmar asoe ya*, they were not referring to the current government *per se* but to the state as a concept.

ter, even though it is not controlled by the KNU but officially under Myanmar state control.

This chapter explores access to justice and dispute resolution in a Myanmar state-controlled village in the south-eastern part of Karen State. I call the village Hlaing Kone.[2] It is predominantly inhabited by Buddhist Pwo Karen. The residents of Hlaing Kone say that they prefer to have their disputes and crimes resolved by local informal institutions which are neither linked to the KNU nor to the Myanmar state. While village leaders do provide secular third-party resolutions for disputes and crimes, I also found that Buddhist and animist beliefs play a significant role in regulating social behaviour and in dealing with and understanding misfortunes.

Drawing on theories of legal pluralism, this chapter examines how legitimate authority is constituted through dispute resolution and access to justice, something which also sheds light on the relative authority of the Myanmar state seen from the perspective of the Karen village. As Christian Lund (2016) argues, the provision and protection of rights are fundamental to the constitution and maintenance of authority, and this makes a functioning judicial system an important institution in the pursuit of state authority. A survey of people's perceptions and use (or lack of use) of the state's judicial institutions can therefore serve as a proxy for understanding the authority of the central state. I pursue this endeavour through a locally-grounded study into the way in which disputes and crimes are resolved locally and how village residents perceive the judicial system of the state vis-á-vis alternative local options. A core insight of my empirical findings is that the informal institutions in Hlaing Kone village enjoy authority, as they manage to provide the village residents with explanations for misfortune based on religious beliefs and beliefs in spirits. Conversely, village residents try as much as they can to avoid seeking justice within the state's juridical systems. There are several reasons for this, which I discuss in the chapter. Not only do village residents perceive state institutions to be confusing, costly, and distant; they also feel that it is somewhat shameful to engage with them. Informal institutions are also preferred because they support locally legitimate norms that are different from those which are the basis of the legal system of the state. Negative perceptions of the

2 The original name of the village is changed here for the purpose of anonymising my informants.

judicial system of the state are also rooted in the fact that the central state has never provided equitable access to justice nor managed to build an institutionalised connection with the village residents, due to many years of armed conflict and state repression. This situation in turn undermines the current state-building process, which, in part, depends on nurturing authority through provision of rights and access to justice through the state. These do not, in fact, necessarily have to come directly from the central state; they could be provided by recognising the ethnically and legally plural landscape. I suggest that the state-building process will probably not succeed in achieving legitimate authority if the state does not engage with those local non-state actors that enjoy authority (see also Podder 2014).

The findings presented in this chapter are based on a combination of qualitative and quantitative research carried out during fieldwork in 2016 as part of the EverJust project (see Introduction to this volume). I have triangulated data emerging from a combination of semi-structured interviews, stakeholder mapping, case-tracing, a quantitative survey and participant observation.[3]

Theoretical framework: Legal pluralism and authority

The chapter adapts a non-state-centric Weberian-inspired understanding of legitimate authority that sees this as based on recognition of that authority by both the ruler and the ruled. This means that both state and non-state actors can claim authority, and it is not only state institutions that are attributed legal authority. This understanding of legitimacy is constituted by members of the society in which the relevant (state or non-state) institutions make their claim. Theoretically, the chapter draws on empirically-grounded theories of legal pluralism (Merry 1988; Tamanaha 2008; Helmke and Levitsky 2004), and builds on Lund's (2001, 2016) conceptualisations of authority and legitimacy.

Brian Tamanaha (2008) argues that the various normative systems within a legally plural setting compete for authority. The judicial sys-

3 The fieldwork took place between September and October 2016 and included both a quantitative survey of 40 participants and 27 interviews conducted by the author and Lue Htar, who are both members of the EverJust research team. The interviews were conducted with the village leader, previous village leader, village elders, the headmaster of a local school and ordinary villagers.

tem of the state claims and strives to hold the monopoly of authority, but this is often not realised in practice. Tamanaha also argues that informal or parallel institutions would not exist if they did not possess authority. Lund argues (2001, 2016) that the *de facto* legitimate authority of institutions is never a constant but is continuously changing and renegotiated over time, and it is built within the public imagination and through interaction and investment in this.[4] Legitimacy is by extension closely connected to an institution's ability to provide citizens with certain rights, as it is through the provision of these that people come to invest in it, through interaction with it. This makes everyday conflict resolution an important arena for the constitution of authority: when people bring their cases to specific forums, this impacts the legitimacy and thus the authority of those forums (ibid.).

Legitimate authority is frequently built by non-state actors through articulations of being opposed to the state (Lund 2001). This has methodological implications for studying the authority of institutions, as it becomes necessary to look at people's perception of and interaction with the state and other actors or institutions who/that claim authority (Lund 2016). Building on the work of Sally E. Merry (1988), Tamanaha (2008) and Lund (2016), it is clearly important to take into account the historical and cultural context in analysing the legally plural setting in Hlaing Kone. To achieve a proper understanding of the presence of multiple authorities and institutions, Tamanaha (2008), Gretchen Helmke and Steven Levitsky (2004), and Lund (2016) all highlight the importance of observing everyday interactions among the people in a village, including any interaction between competing institutions and the narratives that they have about each other. In this chapter, I investigate how a historically embedded narrative about the state has led to a deficit of trust in the villagers' attitude towards the state and to an avoidance of the state on their part.

This chapter draws on the differentiation between formal and informal institutions, building upon Helmke and Levitsky (2004). Formal institutions are, in this case, state judicial institutions, while informal institutions include customary institutions and those related to belief, both that associated with formal religion and that associated with traditional animism. I am aware that these conceptualisations have lim-

4 For the purposes of this chapter I simply use 'authority' as the term for legitimate authority.

itations, as the institutions within the case area may be informal or non-state seen from a state-centred vantage point but regarded as involving more formal mechanisms seen from a local perspective. It should also be noted that formal institutions, here meaning state institutions, sometimes act rather informally, blurring the distinction between what is formal and what is informal. However, for the purposes of this study, the chapter adopts a simple distinction between formal and informal and between state and non-state institutions.

Hlaing Kone village

Hlaing Kone is situated at the foot of the hills, around an hour's drive from Hpa-An, the capital city of Karen State. The village is small, only consisting of around 40 households. In the rainy season it is difficult to reach the village as the rivers overflow, turning the low-lying rice fields in the area into large lakes, and the roads are flooded or are muddy.

The village was previously a 'brown area', a category used by the Myanmar military state to describe a contested area where multiple EAOs were operational, as well as the Tatmadaw (Saferworld 2018).[5] Back then, the KNU had contact with the village and collected taxes. After the 2012 ceasefire agreement between the KNU and the government, the status of the area changed and it became a 'white area', as it was no longer contested and was officially controlled by the Myanmar State. However, according to the village residents there are still armed actors in the area, including Tatmadaw soldiers and members of the KNU and KNU splinter groups, the Democratic Karen Benevolent Army (DKBA), and the Border Guard Force (BGF) (Human Rights Watch 2016).[6] Today, the village residents no longer pay taxes to the KNU, but the village leader always attends the annual meetings of the KNU, and the village has a stronger affiliation with the KNU than to the central Myanmar State, according to the village leader.[7] In general, connections to the state are weak.

After the 2012 ceasefire, economic conditions improved but this was not due to assistance from or opportunities provided by the Myanmar

5 Interview, village leader, 12 September 2016.

6 Interview, Aung Min, 15 September 2016. The DKBA later changed name to Democratic Karen Buddhist Army.

7 Interview, village leader, 12 September 2016.

State. The main source of income has instead been remittances from village residents who are migrant labourers in Thailand. In fact, during fieldwork in 2016 there were mainly older people and children in the village because most young and middle-aged people were working in Thailand. Due to the improved economic situation, the village has managed to build a primary school, whose construction was fully funded through collections by the village leader from village residents. During our stay in 2016 the village leader found it important to emphasise to us that the building of the school and the maintenance of roads were not funded to any degree by the Myanmar state. Only the salary of the Bamar headmaster of the school was being paid by the Myanmar state, he said. In addition, village residents told us that there is a strong sense of kinship within the village. They feel like 'brothers and sisters' and depend on each other, rather than on the state, for local development. The same applies to dispute resolution.

Local dispute resolution institutions, practices and beliefs

From our interviews in Hlaing Kone it became apparent that the main institutions to which people turn when they face disputes and crimes are customary and are rooted in Buddhist and animist beliefs. In principle, the village leader is the main person to whom village residents will report cases when they decide to seek a third-party resolution. The village leader is formally elected by the village residents and is registered by the Myanmar state as part of the state administrative system (Kyed et al. 2016). However, in reality the position is more customary than related to the state, as it has been inherited within the same family for at least 40 years.[8] This family enjoys a high level of respect in the village. The village leader is also a respected spirit medium, who is regularly consulted when it is believed necessary to expel bad spirits. Although in principle it is possible to refer cases to higher-level institutions within the Myanmar state administrative system, this is not done, in practice. Instead, if the village leader fails to find a satisfactory solution to a case, he will encourage the disputants or the victims to seek help from

8 The village leader later resigned the position, something which we discovered during follow-up field work in April 2018. The village leader explained that he had resigned because the position interfered with his work as a spirit medium, as being village leader meant that he had to do administrative tasks that he found frustrating.

other local institutions, including the local Buddhist monk, astrologers, and spirit mediums. While these actors do not provide secular justice, such as enforcing compensation or seeking to negotiate a settlement between the two parties, they help disputants to find relief, make sense of the misfortune they are facing, and advise on whether they will find a resolution (such as whether stolen goods will return). Village residents typically provide offerings and donations to monks to minimise future suffering. Astrologers read palms in order to assess the past and future trajectory of a case, and spirit mediums try to help disputants deal with a case through protection rituals, exorcism of spirits and ceremonies.

In Hlaing Kone, people make a distinction between astrologers and spirit mediums (or healers), and between 'lower' and 'upper' level spirit mediums. The term for astrologers and spirit medium is the same in Pwo Karen (*oung khar doth char*), but in Burmese an astrologer is *pay din sayar* and a spirit medium is *a kyar a myin*. Although there is only one term for the two in Pwo Karen, there is a difference: an astrologer assesses people's future or past through palm reading, whereas spirit mediums ask their spirits to assist with telling the future or the past or to heal people, either from disease or from being possessed by evil spirits. An important distinction is made between upper-level (*a htet lan* in Burmese) and lower level spirit mediums (*auk lan* in Burmese). The former protect people from bad spirits through protective objects or spells (*ye dar yar* in Burmese) and cure illnesses or misfortune caused by spirits or witchcraft through exorcism. By contrast, a lower level spirit medium – an *auk lan* – uses black magic, for example to kill people or make them fall ill. Simply talking about these lower level spirit healers induces fear, and it is not considered normal practice to engage with them or to admit engaging with them (see also Spiro 1996: 21–24).

The use of monks, astrologers, and spirit mediums reflects the fact that the village residents in reality mix Buddhist norms or moral codes with animist traditions and beliefs in spirits, even though they identify themselves publicly as being Buddhist Pwo Karen.[9] This mix is evident in everyday practice as well as in dispute resolution. The villagers engage in daily Buddhist rituals of donations to their house shrine and to the local monastery, which has an important role as it also provides elec-

9 Although Buddhist and animist practices are separate belief systems it is common to find in Myanmar that Buddhists engage in a range of practices, from both systems, but identify their religion as Buddhism (see Spiro 1996: 3).

tricity to half of the village. However, the worship of spirits is also an important part of villagers' lives. They have 'spirit houses' where their deceased relatives live, who protect the family from bad spirits, and they wear protective necklaces and bracelets that are blessed by upper level spirit mediums, to help protect themselves from malevolent spirits and to strengthen good spirits. They also attend seasonal ceremonies, especially in the rainy season, to make their spirits stronger, in order to withstand the influence of malevolent forces. In the rainy season, it is believed that the spirits get weaker and that therefore people can more easily be possessed by malevolent spirits, which force them to do or say evil things. There is also a strong belief in witches. There is a local folk tale relating how a village can only be established if there are seven witches living there.[10] Village residents believe that not all witches are dangerous or inflict harm on others, and they also believe that most witches do not realise that they are witches. According to many interviewees, there is at the present time a dangerous female witch in Hlaing Kone who bewitches people if she becomes jealous of them. This witch was in the past expelled from the village by the former village leader, but she is now old and has moved back to the village to live near her children. However, people still fear her. When we were visiting the village, some villagers specifically told us not to ask them about the witch, especially not at night. They believe that the witch's hearing is enhanced in the dark, and thus they feared that she would hear that they were giving us information about her. This might lead her to bewitch them. Several villagers told us about instances where the witch had either possessed or killed people, or had made people sick with her black magic.

When asked directly what law applied to the village, the village leader said that it was Myanmar state law, but in reality we found that it was a mixture of Buddhist and animist spirit beliefs that were most significant in regulating social behaviour and in dealing with misfortunes, crimes, and disputes.[11] As will be evident in the gold theft case I will discuss below, a mixture of Buddhism and animism provides different alternative approaches to deal with and comprehend a misfortune or suffering.

As Melford Spiro's (1996) study of Buddhism in Myanmar suggests, Burmese Buddhists believe that suffering originates through *karma*, as a consequence of bad deeds in a past life. This means that Buddhism

10 Interview, Nan Mu Kho Sae, 13 September 2016.

11 Interview, village leader, 12 September 2016.

does not offer any immediate solution to suffering, as it is not possible to escape one's current *karma*. However, one can hope to minimise future suffering through good deeds. A person's current situation with regard to health, wealth, social status, etc. is, within Buddhism, believed to be dependent upon past actions. Actions, and even thoughts and desires, are categorised as either beneficial for future *karma*, in this life or in the next, or as harmful for future *karma*, as Spiro explains (1996: 3–6). This belief internalises responsibility for one's fortune or misfortune and discourages engagement in secular judicial systems, as accumulating good *karma* is essential within Buddhism if one wishes to improve one's conditions in a future life (Walton 2016).

If one follows this line of thinking, seeking justice through secular revenge, retribution, or similar remedies does not make sense. By contrast, animist beliefs offer immediate alternative explanations and solutions, because suffering, illness, loss of goods, etc. are believed to be caused by evil spirits or witches. Blame is not laid solely on the victim's shoulders, because suffering is believed to be caused either through the malevolence of an evil witch or through failing to propitiate certain spirits or *nat*.[12] This means that it is possible to seek resolution to suffering outside of the individual self, through performing various rituals, either to combat evil forces, such as a witch, or to satisfy the spirits (Spiro 1996: 24–32).

The mixture of these beliefs on the part of the various actors involved in a case, and the way in which they feed into secular dispute resolution and avoidance of the state, is evident in the following case concerning the theft of gold. Here we will also see that not only the victim but also astrologers and spirit mediums mix Buddhism with spirit beliefs and share a tendency to divert cases away from secular justice.

The gold theft case

Daw Lai Kyi is a 59-year-old Pwo Karen woman who believes in both Buddhism and animism. She and her husband were born and raised in Hlaing Kone, where they work as farmers. They have five children. Three of them work in Thailand and send back remittances.

12 *Nat* are a Burmese category of powerful spirits that can cause pain and suffering but also good (Spiro 1996: 40–45). For the purposes of this chapter, I will refer to them as 'spirits'.

In May 2016, Lay Kyi had a large amount of gold stolen, which had severe consequences for her and her husband. Putting one's savings in banks is not common practice in Myanmar and because of the theft, the family was not able to finish building a house for their daughter, who was working in Thailand. Lai Kyi had kept her gold hidden in the house, and one day when she wanted to wear the gold for a ceremony, she realised that it was missing. She immediately informed her neighbours and the village leader, but no one had seen or heard anything unusual. The village leader said that he could not resolve the case of the theft, although we were later told that he did try to investigate it by asking other village residents about it. Lay Kyi explained that she was not interested in punishing the thief, but simply wished to get back her gold. When she realised that the village leader could not help her, she went to consult an astrologer. Drawing on Buddhist beliefs in *karma*, the astrologer told her that she should appreciate the theft, because it meant that the thief had removed Lai Kyi's bad *karma* and in doing this, had saved her life and that of her husband. The astrologer explained that the theft had happened because of Lai Kyi's deeds in a past life: she had herself stolen gold in a past life. If the gold had not been stolen now the bad *karma* could have killed her or her husband. The astrologer also said that the gold would eventually come back to Lai Kyi in some way. After a few days, the gold had still not returned, and Lai Kyi then went to five other astrologers in places close to the village. She hoped that they would be able to help find the thief, but they told her the same thing as the first astrologer: the theft had occurred because of Lai Kyi's deeds in a past life.

Lai Kyi accepted the Buddhist explanation for the theft, saying to us that she believed that a person's living conditions depend on *karma*. 'Lucky people have good businesses and unlucky people don't have success with their businesses. And the luck[13] you have in this life depends on your actions in your past life', she said.[14] Nevertheless, she was still determined to try to get her gold back. She went to both an upper-level

---

13 *Karma* should not be mistaken for 'good/bad luck' following Spiro (1996), but rather as a sum of actions, thoughts and desires, either beneficial or harmful for future *karma*, in this life or in the next. However, a person's current situation is believed to be dependent upon past actions or of bad deeds in a past life and it is commonly understood in lay Buddhist belief that one's good/bad luck is associated with *karma*.

14 Interview, Lai Kyi, 15 September 2018.

spirit medium and a lower-level spirit medium, both of whom operate in the domain of animist beliefs and practices in addition to Buddhist customs. Like the astrologers, both spirit mediums confirmed that her husband or herself could have died if the gold had not been stolen, due to their bad *karma*. While Lai Kyi accepted this explanation, she was so determined to get her gold back that she asked the lower-level spirit medium to perform black magic, which, according to animist beliefs, would make the thief so dangerously sick that he or she would die if the gold was not returned. However, after waiting for a while, Lai Kyi realised that no one had got sick or died, and no one had returned the gold. As the upper-level spirit medium agreed that bad *karma* was the cause of the theft, he did not engage in any rituals to help Lai Kyi. Lai Kyi instead decided to make a donation to the village monastery, hoping that this would improve her *karma* and help her get the gold back. However, in 2018 her gold had still not returned.[15]

It is clear from this case that Lai Kyi sought a resolution for the presumed theft within the informal and spiritual forums that are locally accessible to her, and that these forums are not guided by state legal norms, but by a mixture of Buddhist and animist beliefs and practices. Lai Kyi said that she believed the explanation given to her about her past life deeds and her family's bad *karma*, but she was still dreaming of getting her gold back so that they could finish their daughter's house. This was probably why she pursued so many astrologers and spirit mediums, and why she also asked the lower-level spirit medium to perform black magic. When we discussed the case with her, she made it clear that she had no desire to see the thief punished within the state legal system, with something like imprisonment or a fine. In fact, she did not even consider this as an option.

I was particularly interested to know why she had not reported the case to the police, not even when the local informal forums had failed to bring back her gold. I kept asking her to consider answering this question. She initially said that she felt that she had done everything she could in relation to the case. It was as if it were unthinkable to her that the police should be involved in anything except a murder case. Lai Kyi explained:

15 In April 2018, in a follow-up interview with Lai Kyi, she reported that the gold had still not been returned to them.

> The police should never get involved in any case unless it is murder. Everything else should be solved within the family or at village level. If a man beats his wife, it is her own fault because of her own bad *karma* due to deeds in a past life. Such cases should not involve anyone else.[16]

She told me that she had no desire for the police to initiate a process that would punish the thief. In fact, this could be harmful, she said, because if the thief were punished in a secular fashion it would annul the benefit to her of the fact that the theft had allowed her to pay for her deeds in a past life, which would improve her *karma*. Had the thief been punished within the judicial system, her bad *karma* would have persisted. Secular punishment of the thief would have meant that she had not accepted the bad *karma* that she faced in this life. Another reason that she gave for not reporting to the police was that it would have been shameful to do so. She worried that other village residents would think that she was making too big a case out of the gold theft by going to the police. Things should be kept in the village or it would cast shame on her.

While the wife of the village leader believed that Lai Kyi's reluctance to report the case to the police was also associated with costs, as the police are believed to charge money for opening cases, Lai Kyi did not give this explanation. In fact, turning to all the different spiritual actors had been quite costly for Lai Kyi, amounting to MMK 300,000 (USD 210) in fees and donations. This shows that it was belief that was the strongest element in determining her actions in the case, along with the shame that comes with engaging institutions outside the village.

It is also noticeable in this case that Buddhist beliefs in *karma* co-exist with a desire for compensation – i.e. for retrieving the gold – in this life, but that this does not translate into a desire for secular punishment of the thief, but rather into a desire that the thief be harmed through magical means if he/she does not return what was stolen. I would suggest that this also points to the prevalence of animist beliefs mixed in with Buddhist ones. That Lai Kyi was not only a strong Buddhist but also believed in malevolent spirits and beings was evident in her understanding of witchcraft. This came up when we asked her if she had ever experienced domestic violence. She told us that her husband had sometimes abused her, physically and verbally, when he had been drinking at night. She had never reported this to anyone, because

16 Interview, Lai Kyi, 15 September 2016.

she believed that it was caused by the village witch's power. Lai Kyi explained that when her husband goes out at night to drink alcohol his mind becomes more vulnerable to the witch's power. Because of this vulnerability he can easily be possessed by the witch, which makes him malicious and sometimes abusive towards her. Fear of the witch was conveyed to us by several villagers. Many believed that she was the reason for people falling ill or dying. Even discussing the circumstances surrounding the witch was uncomfortable for some of the villagers, as they feared repercussions.

Lai Kyi did not believe that anyone could help her solve the abuse by her husband, because it is, as she believes, caused by a mixture of the malevolent actions of the witch and the bad *karma* caused by her deeds in a past life. Instead of reporting the abuse to the village leader, she wore protective necklaces and bracelets blessed by upper-level spirit mediums.[17] The state judicial system is able to handle domestic violence, but it does not incorporate punishment of witches and witchcraft. However, as people like Lai Kyi believe that witches cause harm, people seek resolution to their suffering through other forums. This, I suggest, by extension undermines the legitimacy of the state.

Reasons for avoiding the state and its legal system

According to Helmke and Levitsky (2004), trust and belief in the capacity of a justice system to deliver desired outcomes are significant when we consider people's preferences for informal and formal institutions. They argue that there may be many reasons for maintaining trust in informal institutions, including the fact that a person's objectives are considered more likely to succeed within the informal system rather than within the formal system. In Hlaing Kone I suggest that this is also the case, but that it is also important to look more closely at both the immediate and the underlying reasons for abstaining from using the formal state system. I would suggest that there are three interconnected reasons for this: firstly, village residents' perceptions of how the state legal system works, which is sustained by a deeper negative narrative of the state, which is informed by the wider historical context; secondly, the discrepancy between state legal norms and local beliefs; and thirdly,

17 Interview, Lai Kyi, 13 September 2016.

the desire to maintain local authority vis-á-vis the state. I will now address these three reasons, making reference to Lai Kyi's case.

Illegitimate costs associated with interactions with the state system, shame and a negative narrative of the state

One of the strongest immediate arguments given by village residents for not using the formal Myanmar institutions was the high financial cost of doing so. The official judiciary was associated with high costs by village residents, including corruption or 'thank you money', which few village residents can afford. When we spoke to other villagers about Lai Kyi's gold theft case, most of the interviewees also highlighted cost as a reason for Lai Kyi's actions. For instance, Thin Kin, the wife of the former village leader, said:

> The woman [Lai Kyi] did not inform the police because if the police were to get involved they would ask for money, and it is very expensive to get them to help solve a case. So everyone always only informs the village leader of a case. The village leader never asks for money, so everyone can go to him.[18]

However, financial cost in itself seemed not to be the only reason. As noted earlier, Lai Kyi spent MMK 300,000 (USD 210) on consultations with spirit mediums and astrologers and on donations to the monastery. In relation to the self-reported average household income of less than MMK 100,000 (USD 70) a month,[19] this is a considerable sum. Not only are costs likely to be higher in the formal system; villagers also have a negative view of the idea of paying money to the state, as they see this as equivalent to corruption. Payments to spirit mediums or for Buddhist rituals are, by contrast, seen as legitimate fees or donations.

Another immediate reason for avoiding the formal system is shame. As described previously, Lai Kyi felt embarrassed about her case, and this restrained her from reporting it to the police. Shame has a restraining effect on people in the village and influences how they think about a dispute and the possible solution to it. In general, it is shameful to take a dispute or crime to a public authority, even to the village leader, but it is seen as even more shameful to take a case to a higher-level authority

18 Interview, Thin Kin, September 13, 2016.

19 Reported in the Everjust household survey on access to justice and security.

outside the village, such as the police (Kyed 2018). Thus, village residents try to keep case resolution at the lowest level possible. This is supported by a shared cultural understanding in Myanmar that conflict escalation should be avoided, captured in the saying: 'Make big cases small and small cases disappear' (Denney et al. 2016). As we saw, Lai Kyi feared to be associated with the shameful behaviour of 'making the case big' by reporting it to the police. While this notion of shame is certainly culturally embedded, the local understanding that shame increases through interactions with the state and that payment to the state is illegitimate are also caused by a deeper negative narrative about the state.

According to Lund (2006), it is important to analyse local narratives about the state, as the state is itself built upon the articulation of such narratives and upon interaction between the population and state institutions. The relative authority of the state is, by extension, dependent upon this narrative about it. In Hlaing Kone the narrative about the Myanmar state legal system is that it is confusing, complicated, unjust and corrupt. Even though village residents have hardly any actual experience with state courts or police, this narrative prevails, and lack of familiarity reinforces non-engagement. The authority of the state in Hlaing Kone is weak precisely because, as Lund (2001, 2006) points out, the authority of a state depends on those interactions with state institutions that deliver services and rights.

This negative narrative about the state is based on a long conflictual relationship with the state, which is historically embedded and does not derive only from recent experiences with the state. As noted earlier, Hlaing Kone village was in a disputed area for many years, and, being Karen, the villagers were, in addition to being affected by armed conflict, also victims of the military government's attempts to suppress and reduce the rights of ethnic minorities. The narrative of suppression by the military state goes deep, and many remember having to flee into the jungle when the Tatmadaw (the Burmese/Myanmar military) passed through the village. This has contributed to the creation of a Karen national identity among residents in Hlaing Kone, who perceive themselves as not being a part of a standard Myanmar identity or as attached to the institutions of the central state (Harriden 2002). In the many interviews we held in the village, people described the police as the 'Myanmar police' and the state as the 'Myanmar state' (*Myanmar asoe ya*), as a way of separating themselves from the centre. This separation is ingrained within the village's identity, something which was apparent when the village leader and residents expressed pride in their ability to handle local issues without the help of the state, e.g. building the local school and renovating roads after floods.[20]

Our informants were mainly older people, as a large proportion of the younger generation emigrated to Thailand. While members of the older generation share knowledge and memories of suppressive rule, the younger generation is geographically detached from Myanmar and has few points of contact with it. This makes it difficult to change the negative narrative about the state, which is exacerbated by the failure of the current Myanmar state to deliver basic rights, such as access to justice. This failure also helps to explain the state's lack of local authority and the continued significance of alternative informal institutions. It is because these informal institutions succeed in offering some level of justice, grounded in traditional animist and Buddhist beliefs, that they enjoy, I would suggest, more legitimacy than the Myanmar judicial system.

Buddhist and animist beliefs

As is evident in Lay Kyi's case, the village residents in Hlaing Kone are guided by Buddhist notions of *karma* as well as by animist beliefs in witchcraft and spirits, which the state legal system does not consider. These beliefs regulate behaviour and provide alternative resolutions, and they also provide explanations for misfortune, including what in state law are defined as crimes (such as theft). Like Lay Kyi, several other village residents explained that it is not a good idea to resolve a theft through formal institutions, as this would reverse the better *karma* that comes with having paid off past life misdeeds, and someone who does this would have to face the risk of dying or having some other misfortune happen to them.[21]

In line with these Buddhist beliefs, many informants explained that they do not want to do anything if they face a dispute or a crime, because they believe that they are themselves responsible for the dispute or

20 Interview, village leader, 12 September 2016 & interview, Thin Kin, 13 September 2016.

21 Interview, U Nyunt Tin, 13 September 2016; interview, Lai Kyi, 15 September 2016.

crime, because of deeds in their past lives.[22] This understanding nonetheless co-exists with a desire to, for example, retrieve stolen goods, as we saw in Lai Kyi's case, through the help of informal institutions – the village leader and spirit mediums. When villagers report cases to the village leader, the purpose of doing this is not to punish the thief but to get compensation and an apology from the perpetrator. When this fails or the perpetrator is not identified, as happened in Lai Kyi's case, the villagers turn to astrologers or spirit mediums. Lai Kyi turned to black magic, in order to harm the thief, make him or her sick, or kill him or her if the gold was not returned. This does signal a desire for punishment of the perpetrator and for justice beyond improving one's *karma*, something which is available within the domain of animist beliefs, where suffering is not only associated with the individual (the victim) but also with evil forces. What is sought here is not the kind of secular punishment that the state system would provide (i.e. imprisonment), but reparation and restitution through the agency of spirits.

The use of informal institutions reflects the existence of other norms and notions of justice than those encapsulated by the state legal system (see also the Introduction to this volume). This illustrates the prevalence of legal pluralism (Merry 1988). Buddhist and animist beliefs offer a substitute for a perceived lack of access to formal or secular justice. When the perpetrator is not identified and stolen goods are not retrieved, as in Lai Kyi's case, informal institutions offer explanations for the misfortune victims face, which provides relief and comfort in the absence of secular justice. Thus the use and legitimacy of informal institutions in Hlaing Kone is reinforced by the lack of legitimate authority on the part of formal institutions. This is, in part, caused by the weak presence of the state and its perceived incapacity to deliver justice (Helmke and Levitsky 2004), and in part by the discrepancy between state legal principles and local norms and beliefs. The negative narrative about the state that villagers have in their minds is important to take into account in understanding these discrepancies, but equally important is the need to consider how this negative narrative benefits the informal institutions' sustenance of local authority, as I address next.

22 Interview, Lai Kyi, 15 September 2016; Interview, Thin Kin, 13 September 2016; Interview, Mu Hee Tar, 13 September 2016.

Shopping forums and maintenance of local authority

Keebet von Benda-Beckmann (1981) introduced the concept of 'forum shopping' to describe situations where disputing parties switch between different dispute resolution forums in pursuit of the most favourable outcome (see also Thang Sorn and Kyed, Chapter 1, this volume). She refers to these forums as 'shopping forums' (von Benda-Beckmann 1981: 117). As noted by Lund (2001, 2016), shopping between these forums influences the relative authority of the forums, as people's use of them is part of what sustains their authority. When villagers in Hlaing Kone use informal institutions, this helps to sustain their legitimate authority (see also Lue Htar et al, Chapter 3, this volume). Tamanaha (2018) argues, in a similar vein, that legal pluralism gives way to competing claims to authority, based on different normative orders, and that this challenges state law as the sole ruler of a social field. Because authority is at stake in who resolves disputes, it is common, according to von Benda-Beckmann (1981), for forums too to shop – for clients.

In Hlaing Kone, this concept of shopping forums is relevant because it captures the way in which informal institutions support their own importance and legitimacy by perpetuating a narrative that discourages people from reporting cases to the state. Such institutions do not overtly engage in competition with formal institutions, but they do engage in diverting cases away from the state, which are, as noted earlier, supported by the local norms and beliefs that the informal institutions represent. The shame associated with approaching higher level authorities, and the belief that the formal judicial system would annul the positive benefits of experiencing misfortune in order to benefit one's future *karma*, create an environment that favours informal rather than formal institutions. I would therefore suggest that the drive to maintain local authority is also part of the explanation for avoidance of the state, which is conveyed as a corrupt force that has disenfranchised the local population.

The village leader in Hlaing Kone holds an important role, and his perception of various matters plays into the general perception of them on the part of other villagers. He is himself a spirit medium, practising upper-level healing, and therefore has an interest in promoting this informal forum.[23] During an interview, he explained that he would himself not make any complaint if he were to be a victim of theft, be-

23 Interview, village leader, 13 September 2016.

cause this would be perceived as shameful and could lead to a loss of dignity, as theft occurs because of one's own mistakes in the past. The former village leader also spoke about the state system as confusing and said that he believed that interacting with it was a burden for the village residents. In general, village residents follow the advice of village leaders, to whom they report cases initially, and leaders will not normally recommend that they go to the state with their cases but encourage them to seek local solutions (see also Thang Sorn and Kyed, Chapter 1, this volume).[24] Spirit mediums and astrologers also support their own authority by providing explanations of and resolutions to disputes, which undermines any desire to seek formal justice.

While it is apparent that local leaders and spiritual actors maintain authority by handling disputes within the village, it is difficult to fully determine whether this hinders the penetration of formal institutions into Hlaing Kone. Also, it cannot be assumed *a priori* that the absence of formal institutions is what determines the continuing presence of informal institutions or whether the presence of the one is completely independent from the absence of the other. Based on the findings presented in this chapter, I would suggest, in line with Marc Galanter (1981), that there is a symbiosis between the authority of informal and formal institutions. Informal institutions regulate behaviour and substitute for state judicial justice, which pushes the official state and its control mechanisms further away (Galanter 1981). At the same time, informal institutions represent norms and forms of justice that are independent from the state. Spiritual actors in Hlaing Kone offer access to a form of justice that is different from that which is offered within most formal, secular judicial institutions. Against this backdrop, the expansion of formal institutions in the village would not necessarily represent a threat to the authority of informal institutions, as they follow different sets of norms. Instead, one could imagine a situation where formal and informal institutions co-exist and complement each other in handling different types of disputes, depending on what form of justice is desired in each case, leaving village residents with the choice of using either option. This would, however, require that the state be capable and willing to provide justice and rights and to recognise local systems of justice.

---

24 Interview, Mu Sar Phaung, 14 September 2016; Interview, Daw La Khon, 13 September 2016.

Conclusion

Myanmar is undergoing a political transition and the NLD government has officially committed itself to establishing lasting peace, building the state and moving towards becoming a democratic country, after more than 60 years of conflict. However, there are many obstacles to achieving these goals, as is evident in the continued fighting in border areas and in the discrimination that still persists against ethnic minorities. This chapter has focused on a rural Karen village that is now enjoying peace after many years of conflict and Myanmar government control. Seen from the perspective of this village and analysed through the lens of dispute resolution and justice provision, I have highlighted the way in which the institutions of the state continue to lack locally attributed legitimate authority. Residents of the village abstain from engaging with the formal justice system, choosing instead informal institutions, which enjoy local buy-in and which act as substitutes for the lack of justice in the formal judicial system. I have argued that there are several interconnected reasons for state avoidance, related to a mixture of negative narratives about the state, a lack of rights provided by the state and the prevalence of local norms and beliefs that differ significantly from what state law and legal practice offer.

As I have demonstrated in this chapter, local dispute resolution is guided primarily by customary culture and beliefs, which associate involvement with state institutions with shame, and which afford explanations for crimes and misfortunes that relate to beliefs in *karma* and to the actions of spirits. Local justice preferences are not guided by a desire for secular punishment, but by beliefs in spiritual remedies and relief. These beliefs are sustained by the village leader, who is also a spirit medium, and who, despite being recognised by the state, does not feel affiliated to that state. He does not transfer cases to the formal judicial system nor does he recommend that village residents engage with that system, and this further contributes to a sense of alienation from the state within the village.

These local dynamics play out in a context where the central state has not managed to provide sufficient rights, and therefore there is little incentive for the residents of Hlaing Kone to engage with the formal system. The lack of legitimacy of this system reflects a lack of state authority. As Lund (2016) argues, authority is dependent upon the ability of an institution to provide rights. The failure of the formal justice system to deliver rights in villages like Hlaing Kone can therefore be seen as hampering the efforts of the state to establish authority. This situation is reinforced by a negative narrative of the state shared by village residents, with the state being see as corrupt, confusing, and unjust – a narrative rooted in a long history of conflict and state repression. The state is not absent; but its position continues through this negative narrative, which is part of affirming the identity of the village and its residents through negating the state.

The insights of this chapter raise important questions about the future of state-building in Myanmar, including how the state should relate to informal justice mechanisms and how it can and should embrace the ethnic diversity of the country together with the traditions that mark their sense of identity on the part of different ethnic groups, as well as local ideas about justice and aspirations in terms of accessing this through the state. In what follows I will touch upon some of the potential downfalls of seeking to reform access to justice by focusing solely on either formal or informal institutions of justice.

As noted by Tanja Chopra and Deborah Isser (2011), two dominant and often conflicting approaches to developing justice systems in post-conflict states prevail: one adopts a state-centric approach and supports the transformation of formal justice institutions, while the other views informal justice systems as the focal point for achieving equitable access to justice. Although this dichotomy is very simplified, it helps us to understand the basis for programmes to transform justice systems, as these are primarily based either on one or the other of these approaches. However, both approaches have a poor record in terms of leading to demonstrable, sustainable and legitimate institutional transformation. By focusing solely on either formal or informal institutions as the primary key to sustainable institutional reform, both approaches fail to take into consideration the cultural, socio-economic and political contexts in which these institutions exist and have developed (ibid.: 24–26).

The lack of concrete tools to allow engagement with what are complex informal systems means that many development programmes continue to focus primarily on supporting state institutions (see also McConnachie, Chapter 10, this volume). Despite this lack of tools, it is imperative to engage informal judicial systems in development policy, as engaging solely with the formal system has proven empirically inefficient in terms of transforming formal justice institutions to meet internationally-recognised standards of rule of law (Chopra and Isser 2011: 23–24). Informal judicial systems are often more accessible to the population and reflect local norms to a larger degree than do formal judicial systems in post-conflict or fragile states.

It needs to be understood that the presence of formal institutions does not necessarily exclude the possibility that structural inequalities within society, such as between men and women, will continue to persist in the context of justice provision. Although the written laws of the judicial systems might *de jure* comply with international rule of law standards, village residents and justice personnel may well handle cases based on social codes that do not comply with these standards (ibid.: 25–26). In the case of Hlaing Kone, expanding formal courts and providing police stations closer to the village would not necessarily mean that cases would be handled formally or according to the rule of law. The domestic violence in Lay Kyi's case would, in the context of local culture and beliefs, undoubtedly still have been believed to have been caused by the witch – and would, in any case, have been a personal matter. The theft she suffered would, similarly, still have been perceived to have been the result of bad *karma*. Also, forcing formal judicial change onto a population without considering customary and spiritual practices risks enforcement without local legitimacy. This relates to Lund's (2016) argument that institutional legitimacy is, in part, built up in the context of interaction with citizens. It is therefore challenging for formal institutions to build legitimacy without handling conflict resolution effectively. At the same time, as Lund (2001, 2016) argues, the *de facto* legitimate authority of institutions is never a constant but is continuously changing, and is renegotiated over time – and it is built up in the context of interaction with it and investment in it on the part of the local population and of the state itself. Given that Hlaing Kone has for a number of years been experiencing a big outflux of youth going abroad for work, investment in and interaction with the informal judicial institutions is in decline, and its legitimacy presumably likewise. This leaves a space for renegotiating legitimate authority on the part of other judicial institutions, including for formal institutions to gain legitimacy.

As discussed in this chapter, to report a case is associated with great shame, and to encourage Lai Kyi to take her theft case to the state system would have had the potential to impact on her social status in the village, as well as reducing her karmic status. Also, Lai Kyi, and people in general, told us that she did not wish to punish the thief, and thus incarceration of the perpetrator would have been an unwanted consequence of engaging with the formal justice system.

As mentioned above, many donor programmes engage with reforming informal institutions to avoid some of the limitations highlighted here. These programmes often seek to eliminate negative aspects of customary laws and norms that can be discriminatory or in other ways non-compliant with international standards. A widespread strategy in trying to achieve this has been 'codification' of customary law with the aim of standardising and harmonising informal justice practices and eliminating discrimination. But there is no guarantee that the process of codifying set laws will remove power from dominant groups or that it will successfully eliminate discriminatory practices from customary law. There is no empirical evidence that written non-discriminatory laws will have any impact on underlying social norms (Chopra and Isser 2011: 30–32). Also, codification does not address those social norms in Hlaing Kone that dictate non-confrontational case resolution. There is a range of other strategies that pursue informal justice sector reform. For most of these there is weak empirical evidence of sustainable and significant impact.

I would suggest that the most sustainable way to improve access to justice is to accept the basic premise that legal pluralism exists and that seeking to eliminate it is impossible, as well as counter-productive in terms of securing access to justice (Tamanaha 2008; Chopra and Isser 2011: 34–35). It is clearly imperative to establish the rule of law, because this is fundamental for lasting peace and security in Myanmar, and this means that a justice system must be developed to replace existing formal institutions, which are unjust. However, this will not be achieved by undermining or suppressing informal systems. Instead, formalised laws should deliver and guarantee basic civil rights, including access to justice. This would motivate, but not force, citizens to engage with formal institutions. It would carry the advantage that people would not be forced to choose an institutional setup that does not fit their specific needs or desired outcomes. Securing access to basic human rights, which is central to establishing legitimacy (Lund 2016), is best achieved through opening up options, not through closing them down. Allowing people access to whichever institution best fits their needs in specific circumstances means providing for rights more effectively. This would also reduce competition between formal and informal institutions. In Myanmar, engaging with a mix of both formal and informal institutions would appear to be the best approach in the pursuit of *de facto* access to justice.

References

Chopra, T. & Isser, D.

2011. 'Women's access to justice, legal pluralism and fragile states.' In P. Albrecht et al. (eds), *Perspectives on Involving Non-State and Customary Actors in Justice and Security Reform,* pp. 23–38. Rome: International Development Law Organization.

Denney, L., Bennet, W. & San, K.T.

2016. *Making Big Cases Small and Small Cases Disappear: Experiences of Local Justice in Myanmar.* London: British Council, Overseas Development Institute and Saferworld.

Galanter, M.

1981. 'Justice in many rooms: Courts, private ordering, and indigenous law.' *Journal of Legal Pluralism and Unofficial Law* 13(19): 1–47.

Harriden, J.

2002. '"Making a name for themselves": Karen identity and the politicization of ethnicity in Burma.' *Journal of Burma Studies* 7(1): 84–144.

Helmke, G. & Levitsky, S.

2004. 'Informal institutions and comparative politics: A research agenda.' *Perspectives on Politics,* 2(4): 725–740.

Human Rights Watch

2016. *'The Farmer Becomes the Criminal': Land Confiscation in Burma's Karen State.* www.hrw.org/report/2016/11/03/farmer-becomes-criminal/human-rights-and-land-confiscation-karen-state.

Kyed, H.M.

2018. *Community-Based Dispute Resolution: Exploring Everyday Justice Provision in Southeast Myanmar.* s.l.: US Agency for International Development, International Rescue Committee and Danish Institute for International Studies.

Kyed, H.M., Harrisson, A.P. & McCarthy, G.

2016. *Local Democracy in Myanmar: Reflections on Ward and Village Tract Elections in 2016.* Copenhagen: Danish Institute for International Studies.

Kyed, H.M. and The Thitsar, M.

2018. 'State-making and dispute resolution in Karen frontier areas.' *Independent Journal of Burmese Scholarship* 1(2): 29–55.

Lund, C.

2001. 'Precarious democratization and local dynamics in Niger: Micro-politics in Zinder.' *Development and Change* 32(5): 845–869.

2006. 'Twilight institutions: Public authority and local politics in Africa.' *Development and Change* 37(04): 685–705.

2016. 'Rule and rupture: State formation through the production of property and citizenship.' *Development and Change* 47(6): 1199–1228.

McCartan, B. & Jolliffe, K.

2016. *Ethnic Armed Actors and Justice Provision in Myanmar*. San Francisco: The Asia Foundation.

Merry, S.E.

1988. 'Legal pluralism.' *Law & Society Review* 22(5): 869–896.

Podder, S.

2014. 'State building and the non-state: Debating key dilemmas.' *Third World Quarterly* 35(9): 1615–1635.

Saferworld

2018. *Justice Provision in South East Myanmar: Experiences from Conflict-Affected Areas with Multiple Governing Authorities*, s.l.: Saferworld.

2019. *Security, Justice and Governance in South East Myanmar*, s.l.: Saferworld and Karen Peace Support Network.

South, A. et al.

2018. *Between Ceasefires and Federalism: Exploring Interim Arrangements in the Myanmar Peace Process*. Yangon: Covenant Consultancy Co. Ltd.

Spiro, M.E.

1996. *Burmese Supernaturalism*. Expanded edition. Piscataway, New Jersey, USA: Transaction Publishers.

Tamanaha, B.Z.

2008. 'Understanding legal pluralism: Past to present, local to global.' *Sydney Law Review* 30(3): 375–411.

von Benda-Beckmann, K.

1981. 'Forum shopping and shopping forums: Dispute processing in a Minangkabau village in West Sumatra.' *Journal of Legal Pluralism and Unofficial Law* 13(19): 117–159.

Walton, M.J.

2016. *Buddhism, Politics, and Political Thought in Myanmar*. Cambridge: Cambridge University Press.

5 Dispute resolution and perceptions of security among urban Karen: The role of religious and ethnic identity

Lwin Lwin Mon

Introduction

This chapter explores everyday dispute resolution and perceptions of (in)security among urban Baptist Sgaw Karen residents of Kasekho, a pseudonym for a village situated in Insein Township in Yangon. The findings are based on ethnographic fieldwork carried out between 2016 and 2019.[1] A core argument of the chapter is that Christian religious norms and a shared ethnic Karen identity strongly influence village residents' perceptions of (in)security and how they prefer to deal with social disputes and crimes. At the same time, the dominant practice of keeping dispute resolution within the Karen community forms part of continuous identity formation, that is, of producing and maintaining a Karen ethnic identity. My chapter shows that identity, coupled with religious norms and activities, is an important factor in understanding legal pluralism in Kasekho.

Kasekho is situated within a Myanmar state-administered area and falls under a ward that is headed by a Bamar ward administrator, and thus Myanmar law and institutions officially apply to the area. Nevertheless, the Baptist Karen try as much as possible to avoid reporting disputes and crimes to the state. They prefer to find resolutions within their own religious and ethnic community and inside the physical place of the village (*ywa* in Burmese).[2] Either they deal with problems inside the family or the church community, or they report cases to the village and

1 I conducted 150 qualitative interviews and did participant observation in the village. This included interviews with the Kasekho Baptist minister, the 100-household leaders, local government staff, NGO workers, taxi drivers, overseas workers, traditional dress sellers, Sunday school teachers and students.

2 I use the word 'village' (*ywa* in Burmese) here as this is still the word used by the residents of Kasekho, although officially the area is now part of a ward, as it is now within the urban area of Yangon.

religious leaders, who are also Karen Baptists. This preference for local solutions is, I suggest, not due to a conflictual relationship with the Bamar as another ethnic group or because the Baptist Karen are hostile towards the state *per se*. Rather, the preference for resolving disputes inside the Karen community is linked to a preference for religious over legal norms and to efforts to nurture an image of the Baptist Karen as peaceful, honest and harmonious people, and a shared identity grounded in this image. While religion is understood to control behaviour and to produce 'good persons' (*lu kaung* in Burmese), their shared Karen identity is also given by the village residents as an explanation for the fact that Kasekho village is a secure and peaceful area. Thus, many residents told me that 'there is peace and security in the village because we are Karen and because we live together as Karen'. They believe that there is a strong connection between shared ethnic identity and security or peace. This has implications not only in terms of how the Baptist Karen produce an internal shared identity, but also in terms of how they think of and speak about outsiders or non-members.

As Barth (1969) has argued, ethnic identity formation does not happen in isolation and is not defined by cultural content, but through interactions with and production of boundaries with 'others', which involves a 'continuing dichotomisation between members and outsiders' (ibid.: 14). This certainly applies in Kasekho, where self-identification by Baptist Karen as peaceful people co-exists with a shared understanding that thieves are outsiders, namely non-Karen and non-Baptists. Insecurity comes from the outside, and this leads to a notion that Karen in Kasekho must look inwards and preserve their areas as purely Karen. The formation of a distinct Karen ethnic identity has been nurtured by a long history of Karen nationalism and by efforts to unite the Karen, which have been influenced by colonial ethnic classifications and later by the formation of Karen political organisations and insurgent groups which have fought for Karen self-determination and recognition within Myanmar. However, in Kasekho the residents engage in Karen identity-formation not through armed insurgency, as has occurred in other parts of the country, but through 'quiet' practices. They thus form part of the category of Karen that Thawnghmung (2008) has referred to as the 'quiet Karen'.

In Kasekho, the 'quiet' practices of identity formation are principally organised around religious actors and communal church activities. The Sunday school and pre-school play an important role not only in teaching good behaviour, but also in nurturing Karen identity through Karen language and history teaching. Donations and mutual support through the church also contribute to a shared identity. Religious actors are important in secular dispute resolution. Sometimes residents take marriage disputes, including ones relating to domestic violence, to the Baptist minister. Baptist norms, for instance against divorce, also influence the dispute resolutions methods that are used by the minister and village leaders. In this chapter I address these various practices, after a brief discussion of the theories I draw upon and some historical background to the Karen in Myanmar in general and Kasekho in particular. I also discuss how Baptist Karen in Kasekho relate to the surrounding society and other ethnic groups as well as to the state. In the concluding discussion I turn to the question of what the consequences are of the fact that the Baptist Karen face inwards and focus on internal dispute resolution.

Linking legal pluralism with religion and identity

Theoretically, my chapter contributes to a discussion of the role of ethnic identity and religious norms in contexts of legal pluralism. Following Wang Qiliang (2009), I approach legal pluralism as a situation where more than one legal system or institution coexist with respect to dealing with disputes and social order. Qiliang (2009: 2–3) particularly addresses how religion can be part of forming the local legal order. This is because:

> Religion, with its functions in cognition and interpretation, is able to provide its followers some appropriate attitudes to facing nature, society and the other, which generates the correct and just style of living and behavior. In other words, religion defines what are the sacred/mundane, correct/wrong, legitimate/illegal, just/unjust, etc. Given that a legal culture can be regarded as a kind of tendency for human beings, in the course of arranging a social order, to ponder over what should be correct and just, religion then acts as a decisive factor in the formation of this tendency. Religion, hence, could be a basic element in forming local legal culture (ibid.: 3).

In Kasekho village, I suggest that the Baptist Church plays this role of forming the local legal culture. It is not merely a guide to beliefs; the church and its authority figures are also local social regulators who set the boundaries for correct behaviour and who engage in dispute resolution. Kasekho Karen Baptist people choose to avoid state law in dispute resolution and instead follow religious norms. They also prefer reconciliation and social harmony in dispute resolution. As Laura Nader (1990: 87–88) points out, this preference for reconciliation and harmony differs from justice provision by the state, which is focused on confrontation, punishments and identifying a winner and a loser in a case. According to an ideology of harmony, 'a bad agreement is better than a good fight'. Winning a case is less important than preserving good relations in the community. Compensation is valued over vengeance. Nader (1990) argues that the focus on harmony in dispute resolution is part of a strategy of avoiding the formal state and thus of preserving some autonomy from the state.

Kasekho village is a good example of alternative forms of dispute resolution and practices inside Myanmar that take place alongside but distinct from Myanmar state law. This reflects legal pluralism at the broader level of Insein Township. In Kasekho people adhere to their own local legal culture and try to avoid external law. Only in very few cases do they go to court, and this is only when local dispute resolution has failed, and when non-Karen are involved.

In the context of Kasekho, avoidance of the state and local dispute resolution is also, I suggest, closely linked to ethnic identity formation. Anthony Cohen argues that '... ethnicity has come to be regarded as a mode of action and of representation: it refers to a decision people make to depict themselves or others symbolically as the bearers of a certain cultural identity' (Cohen 1994: 119). According to Keyes (1979: 4), '... cultural expressions such as myth, religious belief, ritual, folk history, folklore, and art ... these symbolic formulations of ethnic identity provide individuals with meanings that make relationship between ethnic groups meaningful'. While these symbolic aspects of identity are important in self-representation, I follow Fredrik Barth's (1969) understanding that ethnic identity is always an aspect of a relationship, rather than a fixed property of a person or group. The existence of an ethnic group must be affirmed socially and ideologically through general recognition on the part of its members and outsiders. Following Hummell (2014) and Wimmer (2013), I would contend that ethnicity is therefore the product of specific kinds of inter-group relations. An ethnic group cannot exist in isolation. Its formation and continuation are dependent upon interaction with 'others', as Barth (1969) has argued. This means that ethnic groups are maintained through a continuing dichotomisation between members and outsiders. That ethnicity is not defined by culture does not downgrade the importance of cultural forms, their vitality and their variation, or the way in which culture and ethnicity mutually stimulate identities and actions. In Kasekho village, the articulation of the ethnic identity of the Baptist Karen in local dispute resolution and in relation to understandings of community security is likewise formed in relation to specific images of outsiders. Keeping local dispute resolution within the Karen community is also part of nurturing an image of the Karen as peaceful and pure.[2] In these ways, the linkages between harmony, shared identity, and religious norms are key to the dynamics of legal pluralism in the village.

A brief history of Karen struggles and identity formation

The Karen do not constitute a homogenous group; but the long history of tension between Karen and Burmese, as well as various efforts to produce a common Karen identity, have been influential in generating a sense of Karen identity. Far from all Karen took part in explicit opposition and insurgency against the Burmese government. Many lived peacefully among the Burmese. However, even for this latter group, which includes my study area, shared Karen identity and language have remained important.

The Karen ethnic group encompasses about 20 subgroups of Karen-speaking people with different religions, culture, and geographic backgrounds. They live across various regions of Myanmar (including in Yangon, in the Delta region, in the Central Bago Yoma mountain range as far as the eastern hills along the Thai border area, in Karen State and in Tanintharyi division). They are the second-largest minority group in Myanmar, with a population estimated at 5 million. There are two main Karen groups accounting for 80–85 per cent of Karen (Myanmar Census 2014): the Sgaw Karen, who are mainly Christians or animists, and the Pwo Karen, who are mainly lowland Buddhists (Thawnghmung 2008).

The Karen have had a long history of tensions with the majority Burmese group, the Bamar, which, according to Marshall (1927), began in pre-colonial times when individual Burman kings tried to force

2 On how this image of a pure and peaceful Karen people has been nurtured over a long historical period, including by the Karen National Union (KNU), see Gravers (1996: 255).

Karen hill tribes to adopt Burmese religious beliefs, cultural practices, and agricultural methods (ibid.: 22; Mark 1978: 55). During colonisation, the British took advantage of these tensions, which began during the Anglo-Burman wars in 1853 and 1885 and continued through the colonial divide-and-rule policies, which separated the governance of different areas and ethnicities in Burma (Cady 1958: 42–43, 137–141; Smith 1999: 43). This contributed to a solidification of ethnic identity in general, which also led to further separations of the Karen (and other minorities) from the Burmese. During colonial rule many Karen were also influenced by American missionaries, leading to conversions to Christianity and to the adoption of Western-style education and writing, rather than an orientation towards Burmese and Buddhism. The colonial solidification of ethnicity also informed the earliest efforts of Karen leaders to unite the Karen people across Burma, around a pan-Karen nationalism and a shared (mostly Sgaw) Karen language. These were spread to diverse Karen villages, previously not tied together in a political organisation, through missionary-sponsored Karen schools and churches and through newspapers in the vernacular (Gravers 1996). One Karen leader, Doctor San C. Po, also announced a 'Karen State' and advocated for the creation of an autonomous Karen nation under the aegis of a loosely federated 'United States of Burma' (Po 1928: 81). During the negotiations for independence from the British in the 1940s, Karen leaders hoped for an independent Karen State, but this did not materialise, as the British chose instead to make an agreement with the Burmese nationalists. They denied the Karen their secessionist wishes. The Karen leaders were disappointed, because they had expected to be rewarded by the British for having assisted them in fighting the Japanese army that invaded Burma during the Second World War. During the war, many Karen were victims of violence committed by Burmese nationalist forces because of resentment of the privileged status of the Karen and their association with the British. This heightened the tensions between Karen nationalist organisations and the Burmese. In 1947 the Karen National Union (KNU) was formed, which brought together different Karen organisations in their joint quest for a separate Karen State after independence. An armed wing of the KNU was also formed, known as the KNDO (Karen National Defence Organisation), which later became the KNLA (Karen National Liberation Army) (Gravers 1996). However, the new Burmese government did not meet the KNU's demands for secession. Instead, after independence in 1948, the Karen were guaranteed 'minority rights' in the form of 22 reserved legislative seats in the Chamber of Deputies as well as a Karen minister who would have control of all administrative, educational, and cultural affairs relating to the Karen (Smith 1999: 82). Dissatisfaction remained within the KNU and there were various internal splits among Karen leaders, who had differing views as to whether they should be part of the Burmese nation or not. In early 1949, the Burmese government demanded that the KNDO and other Karen veterans surrender their arms (Cady 1958: 589–594). This move, combined with long-held grievances against the Burmese and a strong collective pan-Karen identity, led the KNU to initiate an armed insurgence in late January of 1949. This insurgency lasted six decades, until a ceasefire was signed in 2012. The insurgency began with the seizure of several towns, including Taungoo, Prome and some parts of Bassein, by Karen troops (Smith Dun 1980: 62), which was followed by battles between Burmese forces and the Karen insurgents in Insein Township in Rangoon (now Yangon). The war in Insein lasted for more than three months, and afterwards the KNU/KNDO had to surrender and retreat to the areas around present-day Karen State. The armed struggle continued there (Thawnghmung 2008). After the takeover by the military government in 1962, the armed struggle intensified, as did efforts by the military government to restrict ethnic minority culture and language. The military government discouraged the use of minority languages in areas outside Karen State by making Burmese the official language of instruction. In minority areas, the use of minority languages was permitted only until the fourth grade in government schools. In response, Karen organisations – including organisations as diverse as Buddhist monasteries, the Karen Literature and Cultural Association, and the Karen Baptist churches – and private Karen citizens tried to preserve Karen identity by offering training in the Karen language (Thawnghmung 2008). During the many years of armed struggle, some Karen joined the insurgency, but a sizeable number of Karen did not, and continued to live within areas controlled by the Burmese government. Whereas some rejected the principles and methods of the KNU, others thought the risk of joining the armed resistance was too great or they were simply politically passive. Thawnghmung (2011) in her book *The Other Karen in Myanmar*, refers to the Karen who remained outside the resistance as the 'quiet Karen'. These include prominent figures, both Buddhists and Christians, who lived alongside the Burmese and who nevertheless commanded a great deal of respect within the Burmese community. While there are many Karen in Insein Township who have remained loyal to the KNU and who have had multiple links with the insurgents, the vast majority of my informants in Kasekho can be placed in the category of 'quiet Karen'. Nonetheless, a shared Karen identity and language have remained important to them.

Figure 5.1 A view of the village from the Baptist church. *Colour image, p. 361.*

The 'quiet Karen' Baptists of Kasekho

Kasekho is part of a larger ward in Insein Township and contains approximately 200 households, with a majority of them Sgaw Karen Baptist Christians. Only 16 households are not Karen, but are Bamar Buddhists or belong to the Wa or Chin ethnic groups. The surrounding wards also have a majority of Karen Baptist Christians, but in some wards they are mixed with Bamar Buddhists. The village has been divided into three parts since 1991–92. Each part has a 100-household leader. These leaders are local residents, but they work under the ward administration, which is headed by a Bamar. The three 100-household leaders work with a five-member committee, which deals with community development matters and dispute resolution.

At the top of the hill in the village is the main Baptist church, which most of the residents attend. Here, the main Baptist minister is Saw Ba Do, and there are three assistant ministers. There is also a Jehovah's Witness church and a Gawrakha church, but these are mainly attended by outsiders. There is also a Myanmar government school in the village and the Insein High School No-1 is nearby. Most residents have lived in Kasekho their whole lives, as their grandparents settled there. There are very few recent newcomers. The Karen residents of Kasekho have a moderately good economic situation, bringing in enough to enable them to survive on a day-to-day basis. The majority have jobs as government staff, NGO workers, factory workers or taxi-drivers. A smaller number have small shops or are skilled workers, and there is a larger group of people who work in overseas shipping companies or are migrant workers in Thailand, Malaysia or Singapore. As in other Karen communities, remittances from migrants are important to the family economy in Kasekho.

Figure 5.2 The weekly service at the local Baptist church in the village. *Colour image, p. 362.*

I did the fieldwork for my master's degree in Kasekho in 1995. Returning in 2015, I sensed that their Karen identity and community remained strong. Despite some material and physical developments, such as improved housing and the use of mobile phones, I found the same level of strong devotion to religious beliefs and practices. People maintained their Sgaw Karen language and literature through the Kasekho Baptist church, and on every special occasion and festival they would wear their traditional Karen dress. There was still a strong sense of community and care for each other, including when people fell ill, for instance with HIV/AIDS. The area felt peaceful, and it was quiet and clean. The residents of Kasekho expressed their own sense of this difference between their area and surrounding neighbourhoods where, they said, people did not want to accept HIV/AIDS and tried to avoid those who had the disease. This differentiation between themselves and outsiders is part of a wider narrative of self-identification through which Karen present themselves as more caring and peaceful than others.

Disputes and security: Keeping problems within the Karen Community

Of all the 21 wards in Insein Township, Kasekho is spoken about – by both insiders and outsiders – as the most peaceful and the most secure. This view was echoed by the ward administrator, a Bamar, who said that the Baptist Karen are the most peaceful of the people he administers.

There is a strong sense that the village is safe and free from crime. As one 54-year-old Karen Baptist resident said: 'Even though I put our bicycle in front of the house on the road, it has never been stolen'.[3] There is a strong belief that security and peace prevail because of shared ethnic and religious identity, which, it is believed, supports mutual community care. The church-based community is regarded as playing an important role in disciplining and socialising the villagers in order to protect their property and well-being. Individual prayer and prayer at the church constitute the main ways to deal with challenges and problems. In general, people try first to resolve family matters by themselves by keeping it within the family and by dealing with it through prayer. If they cannot resolve a matter themselves or if more serious disputes occur, they seek advice and help from other church members, and sometimes from the 100-household leader and his wife, who are also Karen Baptists, and from the Baptist minister. There is a strong preference for keeping problems inside the Karen community and within the physical space of the Kasekho village. Security is strongly associated with sticking together as Karen and keeping the village Karen. My informants told me that Karen residents prefer to sell land and rent out houses to other Karen people. This may help explain why there are very few residents who are non-Karen in the village, and why very few non-Karen newcomers settle in the village. This attitude may be regarded as a kind of 'security strategy' rooted in the notion that security is obtained by keeping the community Karen. People in the village believe very strongly that it is outsiders who pose a potential threat to security.

Next, I want to address how disputes are resolved internally in the village by the Karen, firstly by looking at the role of prayers and the family and then by exploring third party solutions achieved through local leaders and the Baptist minister. I will then return to the issue of avoiding outsiders, including the state.

Prayer and family solutions

Daily life is very much structured around prayer and the church, which constitutes the primary locus for addressing problems. Every morning between 5 and 6 am, Baptist residents engage in 'dawn prayer'. When

3 Interview with 54-year-old Karen resident, Kasekho village, Insein Township, Yangon, 12 February 2016.

the church bell rings, families go to church, where the minister recites a verse from the Bible and explains its meaning for about fifteen minutes. After that, members of the church community share their concerns and views and the minister asks them: 'Does anyone have a prayer to submit?' People can then come forward and share their difficulties relating to work, married life, health and other matters. Everyone listens, and the minister then prays for those who have shared their difficulties, asking God to grant that they should escape from these. In the evening, around 8 pm, some families also pray within their own family. They say that this helps them to cope with difficulties they are facing.

While the church community is central to addressing problems, Baptist Karen in Kasekho first try to keep their difficulties within their family, or they pray to God directly as individuals. For instance, the father of one family told me that when he faced a problem in his job he did not tell his family, because he did not want them to worry about him. He prayed on his own to God. When the problem continued, he went to discuss the matter with the minister. In the inheritance and family disputes that I encountered, Baptist Karen in the village also tried first of all to negotiate a solution within the family. In most situations this works. For example, one of my informants has six brothers and sisters. The youngest sister, who lived with their parents until they died, had the right to inherit the family land and house. None of the other siblings complained at first, but when the eldest brother retired as a government officer he asked his sister to allow him to rent the family house, because he was about to lose his government housing. He never forcefully requested the land or any money but was able to negotiate with his siblings without involving any outside authorities.

On other occasions, family misfortune and lack of family support is dealt with through prayer and belief in the power of God. This was evident in the case of Naw Mu Mu, a 65-year-old Baptist Karen woman, who was a merchant, then worked in a clinic, and was finally a voluntary missionary. Naw Mu Mu has five daughters. When her husband died, about 25 years ago, she expected to get help from her brothers and sisters, who are very rich, but they did not come forward to help her. She felt very upset but she did not contact them. She faced many difficulties. One year after her husband's death, she started to hear God's voice, telling her that she could rely on God wherever she went. After she had heard God's voice, she forgave her siblings and began visiting them again. God told her to engage in religious work after her husband's death, so she quit her job at the clinic. She had a debt of 3 lakh at that time. She started work as a missionary, although she did not have a preaching certificate. She prayed for relatives and on special days, and this gave her enough in donations to pay back her debt. She also prayed for her daughter, whom she had had to give up for adoption because she had not been able to afford to keep her. The child's adoptive parents had not wanted to give her daughter back to her when she had requested this. She prayed hard to God and 10 years later she got her daughter back. Now her daughter is happily married in Taungoo. The minister also helped her, giving her money when she needed it. In 2011 and 2013, she fell twice and broke her leg, and she saw this as a sign from God to help her to know how to overcome her troubles. Later, she met a man who was able to cure her broken leg for a fair price. At that time, she heard God's voice again, and she was able to overcome all of her troubles by praying to and believing in God. Now her life is peaceful, and she travels with other Kasekho missionary women to other cities. She has also been able to use the money she has received in donations to buy a garden in Taungoo, a mobile phone and a gold chain. She told me that she feels that it is safe for her and her daughter in Kasekho, because the Kasekho area is 'clean and pure', and its people have good characters.

As is evident in this case, belief in God is central to concepts of trouble and how to resolve it among the Karen of Kasekho. There is also a notion that the Karen community is 'clean and pure'. When situations arise where this purity and peace is challenged, and religious means are insufficient, the villagers seek advice and help from the minister and from village leaders from within the Baptist Karen community.

Solutions arrived at with the help of local Karen leaders and the Baptist minister

The 100-household leaders, who are Karen themselves, are the key people in dispute resolution and in ensuring that the village is orderly and clean. The most common cases that the 100-household leaders deal with in Kasekho are those relating to drinking and fighting among young people, land disputes over ownership and over the fencing of household plots, quarrels over money lending and wastewater, divorce, verbal abuse, and, on rarer occasions, cases of theft. Serious crimes such as murder, rape and robbery hardly ever occur in the village. If they do they are not resolved by the 100-household leaders. The 100-household leaders are connected to the ward administration, and therefore to the official Myanmar state, and they regularly perform duties such as registration of population and other matters for the administration. However, most of their work pertains to dealing with matters internally in Kasekho, and there is a strong emphasis on not taking disputes outside the village. The 100-household leaders are also the main providers of village security. They perform regular patrols early in the morning around 4 am. Only if there are situations and strangers that they cannot control do they telephone the official police. These patrols also check for fires in the summertime and control the use of electricity. If people use electricity outside of the designated hours (04:00 to 10:00 am and 4:00 to 8:00 pm), the 100-household leaders issue a warning and require the trespasser to sign a 'promise letter' (*kahn won*) in which he or she agrees not to commit the offence again. Similarly, if a resident burns leaves at his/her house or throws rubbish in the drain, there is also a warning and a *kahn won*. The 100-household leaders also gather volunteers to keep the village clean, for example sweeping the roads. They also deal with the maintenance of the main road to Kasekho.

During my fieldwork I spoke many times with the 100-household leader of Kasekho Part 2, whose name is U Lon Htein. He is a Kawkareik Karen native but has lived in Kasekho for 30 years. He has been 100-household leader since 1988. His wife helps him with his duties. They are both Baptists and closely connected to the Baptist church community. While his position is connected to the Bamar ward administrator, he tries as much as possible to keep the resolution of disputes within the Karen community. He also collaborates with the Baptist minister, especially where there are marriage disputes. The minister told me that he only wants to get involved in religious affairs, but sometimes he also gets involved in social affairs, because the village residents want him to. During my fieldwork, I encountered two such cases. They both involved domestic violence and could in principle have been forwarded to the police and courts. However, they were resolved internally, with a strong emphasis on keeping the matter within the Karen community. A key concern was to restore the marriage according to the Karen-Baptist religious norm that prohibits divorce.

In the first case, a Baptist Karen woman called Naw Se Se made a complaint to the 100-household leader because her husband drank alcohol and beat her. She wanted to divorce her husband. However, her parents went to the church and requested the minister to negotiate with the couple, because the parents did not want their daughter to divorce. In their view, their religion does not allow divorce. A couple must live together until they die. The case was negotiated with the help of the minister as well as that of the 100-household leader who lives in Kasekho Part 1. This 100-household leader is said by many to be the person whom most of the villagers consult in relation to cases that concern them. The conclusion was that the couple stayed together.[4]

In the other case, a young Baptist Karen man called Saw Eldo drank and fought with his wife, Naw Elle. The woman's parents were very angry with her husband, so they made a complaint to the 100-household leader. They wanted their daughter to divorce. The 100-household leader negotiated with them and calmed down the parties, and they agreed not to divorce. In this case, the husband's parents discussed the case with the minister, who advised them not to get divorced. The wife also knew that she should follow the religious norm and she saw this as a way to keep the Karen community a pure and peaceful place to live. The 100-household leader consulted the wife and according to him and other villagers, the woman did not feel oppressed by her husband. She said that she simply wanted her husband to stop drinking alcohol and quarrelling with her when he was drunk. In this case the couple reconciled and later they had a child. According to the 100-household leader, they 'lived happily' thereafter, and the husband stopped beating the wife.

These cases show that there is a strong emphasis on following the Baptist religious norm about keeping families together, even if domestic violence occurs. Had the parties taken the case to the ward administration or further up in the system, the wife might have been able to get a divorce, and the husband might have been punished. However, the local solutions which were used in these cases demonstrate a preference for keeping problems within the Karen community and for maintaining an appearance of harmony, rather than seeking punishments and confrontations. This preference is expressed in the way in which the 100-household leaders resolve disputes using negotiation, mediation and reconciliation. It should also be noted that in both of these cases

4 Unfortunately, I did not get the chance to interview the Karen woman in this case, as she did not want to talk to a researcher because she felt ashamed of what had happened.

the aggrieved women submitted themselves to the advice and norms of local justice providers, who emphasise harmony at the expense of women's individual rights. This reflects, as Lauren Nader (1990) has also shown for Mexican villagers, a preference for social harmony over punishment and public confrontation, which is coupled with a respect for local leaders. The aggrieved women chose harmony over having their husbands punished as this accorded both with their parents' preferences and with the advice of religious and village leaders. Moreover, they would also have felt shame if they had gone to the official court to pursue their cases, as this would have meant losing face in public.

With fighting and money lending disputes, there is also a strong emphasis on resolving cases inside the village and avoiding confrontation. Another 100-household leader, Saw El Htoo, who has held the post since 2011, told me that he has resolved five money-lending disputes, of which only one went to court. He tries as much as possible to negotiate with the parties and to make the borrower pay back the loan over a period, so that the case does not escalate and end with the police. In cases where young people have physical fights, for instance due to the drinking of alcohol, they also do not report to the police, but to the 100-household leaders who will intervene to reconcile the parties, together with the families of the young people Here there is a preference for restoring peace rather than punishing the perpetrators. My informants told me that this way of dealing with fights accords with Karen customs and ways, which strive to create a peaceful way of living together as Karen. As in other smaller face-to-face societies, the focus on peace and harmony may be influenced by the fact that many Kasekho residents have blood ties with each other and know each other well (Nader 1969: 90). I would suggest that the way in which residents talk about dispute resolution also plays into efforts to project an image of the Karen as peaceful people who do not want conflict with other people. This image is part of the formation and maintenance of a shared Karen identity, which I address next. This is supported by church activities and a moral Christian education.

Nurturing Karen-ness through Baptist church schools

The Karen National Union (KNU) and an increasing number of Karen political parties are (and the KNU has for a long time been) engaged in nurturing and seeking official recognition of a united Karen identity. In

Kasekho village, the KNU and the Karen political parties do not have any daily presence or direct influence on Karen identity formation, but only appear around the joint celebration of Karen New Year Festival. Instead, it is the Karen Baptist organisations which have the most influential impact in the village in terms of nurturing Karenness. This makes identity formation something that is nurtured more in the context of religious activities than that of politics.

Most Christian Baptists in Kasekho attend Sunday school and Karen language teaching sessions in summertime. There is also a pre-school and various other church activities that bring together the Baptist Karen community. Church teachings are focused not only on the Bible but also on nurturing and preserving Karen identity and language. This includes a strong focus on discipline and on creating 'good Karen citizens'. The teachers and the Karen Baptist Association want to support a strong Karen identity by teaching the Bible in the Karen language and by practising their spoken and written Karen language. The teachers also tell traditional Karen stories to children and provide lessons for Karen young people about drugs, HIV/AIDS, human trafficking, child labour and premarital sex. By doing this, they believe they can reduce crime in their community and live in a more peaceful way. Moreover, the younger generation will, they believe, become more moral and maintain Karen traditions.

Every Sunday morning between 8–10 am, about 150 children (between the ages of 5 and 17) attend Sunday School, where they are taught Karen and other languages. During Sunday School, the children sing songs in both Bamar and Karen. The teacher also teaches the Bible in the Karen language, and children try to learn to read and write in Karen. Teachers try to teach mainly in Karen, but not all of the children understand Karen well, so they also teach some subjects in Bamar. The teachers also focus on teaching Karen literature, and they tell Karen traditional stories. They also teach the children how to maintain Karen traditions and customs. Every June there are also volunteer teachers from the Sgaw Karen Bible School who come to teach the Sunday School and there is also a Karen Language class in Kasekho Church in the summertime. The Sunday school also aims to educate the young people in good discipline. Sometimes the teachers follow up with young people whose behaviour is not exemplary, explaining to them how their behaviour needs to change and giving them special attention. Teachers have close connections with their pupils' families. Sometimes Sunday school children invite the teachers and the other children to their homes, where they all pray together for the host family's well-being. Karen young people also attend the Youth Development Association. Here they share their experiences and difficulties with each other. Kasekho Church also has a pre-school, which is open from 8:30 am to 3 pm for children between two and five years old whose mothers are working. It is led by the wife of the Baptist minister, Reverend Saw Ba Do, who works with four other teachers. All the students and teachers are from Kasekho village. Their parents pay MMK 10,000 (USD 7) per month in school fees and the teachers get a salary of about MMK 60,000 (USD 40) per month. Other expenses are covered by the Church Association fund. The school teaches biblical stories, short biblical texts, and songs in three languages: Karen, Bamar, and English. Most of the songs are about loving Karen national identity and language and are aimed at promoting Karen patriotism. There is also a Karen Language class during the summer, in April. This began around 50 years ago. The aim was to rectify the fact that many Karen children speak more Bamar than Karen, as they learn Bamar in the Myanmar state's public schools and because the surrounding society speaks Bamar.

Every second week of the month, a festival called *pwe-taw-min-ga-lar* ('Christ's last supper') is held at the Church. It starts at 11 am and includes prayers and readings from the Bible, read by the minister. The youth association and women's groups sing songs in Karen and pray to God. After that, communion is held, sharing bread and wine. Donations are also collected for the benefit of those in need. On the last Sunday of each month, the volunteer teachers celebrate the birthday of those children born during that month at the Kasekho church. One of the teachers, Saya Saw Sue Se, taught the children about happy birthday songs in Sgaw Karen language and English language, playing the guitar, and the children learned the song in both Karen and Bamar. Children are given birthday presents, paid using church funds deriving from donations. Each week, through the Sunday school, nearly MMK 16,000 (USD 12) is collected, and the praying association collects about MMK 36,000 (USD 26). Church funds are also used to pay for prizes for the children at the end of the year. The youth association and the women's association have their own funds and use them for social events. The Baptist *a-thin-daw* (Burmese for 'association') contributes towards the cost of funerals from its funds and Sunday school family members also donate money towards the cost of funerals. Church members also provide support to anyone who is ill and needs to go to hospital. When a child passes the high school entrance exam, he or she gets a prize, paid for using Sunday school funds. Mother's Day, Father's Day, and Children's Day are all celebrated, with the cost of this covered by the funds of the Baptist *a-thin-daw*. There is also a celebratory annual meeting each February, at which presents are given to members as reward for their hard work.

All these donations and mutual support linked to the Baptist church illustrate the efforts towards establishing unity within the Karen community. It is apparent that, besides sharing religious beliefs at the church, Karen Baptists and their organisations are strongly focused on nurturing Karen identity right from childhood. At the same time, the children also attend the Myanmar state's public schools. Thus, while they are part of the wider Myanmar society, which surrounds them, they also look inwards and preserve Karen culture and identity. How does this affect relations with the non-Karen and the non-Christians in the area, and how does it affect relations with the state? How do the Karen live within a wider Buddhist society while also preserving Karen identity? I address these questions next.

Dealings with outsiders and avoiding the state

As in other contexts within Myanmar, including among the Bamar majority (Kyed 2018; Denney et al. 2016), Kasekho residents are afraid of court processes and try to avoid the police. They share with the Bamar the perception that it is best that cases should remain small, disappear and be resolved locally (i.e. the saying in Burmese: *Kyi te amu nge aung, nge te amu pa pyauk aung*, meaning 'make the big cases smaller and make the small cases disappear'). In fact, according to one of the 100-household leaders, only two cases from Kasekho have gone to court in the last 20 years. These were disputes about household fencing and land ownership, and they only went to court because the 100-household leader committee at ward level gave up on negotiating with the two parties. In these cases, one of the parties was non-Karen and the other parties were Karen. This mixture of ethnicities was partly the reason why the 100-household leader could not resolve the case internally in the Karen community, and therefore he went to the ward administration. However, in most cases, even when there is a non-Karen involved in the case, they will try not to go beyond the ward level administration if at all possible. As shown in research for other areas too, going to the state with cases is seen as a last resort and something to avoid for Karen as well as for other groups, including the Bamar (Kyed 2018; Mon 2018; see also the other chapters in this volume). Taking cases to public places is associated with shame and conflict escalation. As is evident in the other chapters of this book, the Kasekho Baptist Karen also find the formality of the courts intimidating and cumbersome, and they prefer forgiveness over seeking a remedy. What is interesting about Kasekho is the additional role played by shared Karen identity. When compared to other places, it is noteworthy that the residents also try as much as possible to avoid even going to the ward administrator. They prefer to go to their Karen 100-household leader. Is that because the ward administrator is Bamar and not Karen or Baptist? When I posed this question to the village residents, they told me clearly that it is not because the ward administrator is Bamar, but because they simply prefer resolution within their own community. The avoidance of the ward administrator and the state is therefore not because they are hostile towards or in tension with the Bamar as a different ethnic group, but because they want to keep problems within their community in order to project an image of unity and peace within that community to people outside the community.

However, this image of the peaceful Karen is co-produced through a counter-image of outsiders, using processes of othering whereby an ethnic Karen identity is produced through generating a social boundary with those outsiders. This is a process that Hummell (2014) has pointed to as occurring in this type of context, based on Barth's theory of ethnicity. It is common in Kasekho to hear people say that insecurity is caused by 'outsiders'. This feeds into efforts to preserve their identity on the part of Kasekho Karen. The informal rule that Karen should not sell or rent houses to non-Karen is a clear illustration of this. Some villagers also expressed a feeling that the security situation was changing due to the increased influence of outsiders. A 60-year-old Baptist Karen woman said to me: 'In the past I used to leave my house without locking it and nothing was stolen. But nowadays we lock our fences and our houses to prevent theft. However, most of the thieves are outsiders and not our villagers'. I was also told that nowadays some newcomers, who are not Karen, fight each other over the fences between house plots, something which the 100-household leaders then have to deal with. Kasekho villagers also say that they have heard about an increase in cases of theft, for instance theft of mobile phones, in the nearby ward. Recently, a thief was caught and went to prison. He was a 15-year-old Bamar boy. This kind of case supports the notion in Kasekho that there are more thieves among the Bamar and that cases of theft are more frequent in Bamar populated areas. While my informants never said directly that they dislike the Bamar or other ethnic groups, the notion of outsiders as security threats informs an avoidance of outsiders and efforts to preserve an enclosed Karen community. This does not lead to a conflictual relationship with others, however. On the contrary, Baptist Karen try to maintain a peaceful co-existence with Karen Buddhists, Bamar and other non-Karen groups in the surrounding area. They do this by participating in Buddhist festivals and making donations to the monks. For instance, Baptist Karen support the *kahtein pa-de-sa pang (kahtein* means offering of yellow robes to the monks, *pa-de-sa* means plenty in Pali, *pang* means tree in Burmese*)* during special religious days. These are donations for the monks on wooden triangular structures, hung with things like sets of yellow robes and other articles such as Buddha images, alms bowls, umbrellas, towers, napkins, cups and things such as utensils, soaps, various kinds of medicine, books, pencils, pens, slippers, mats, a kyat note, a handkerchief, a cake of soap. They also participate in making offerings of food to the monks during the three-month annual retreat of Buddhist lent every year. The two Baptist ministers also collaborate with Karen Buddhist household leaders in shared activities. Every year they make a *pa-de-sa pang (pa-de-sa* means plenty in Pali and *pang* means tree in Burmese) in the village and collect money from both Buddhist and Baptist Karen. The 100-household leaders also make signboards carrying the message that donations may be made by people from any religion and any ethnic group. Every year they collect around MMK 400,000 (USD 290), which is given to the Buddhist monastery. Buddhist Karen and Bamar also donate to the Christians for their religious activities, such as at Christmas, and to the costs of other social activities such as weddings and funerals. These joint activities help to maintain a good relationship between the different religious and ethnic groups in the area, while also preserving the differences between the groups.

As Hylland Eriksen points out, although ethnicity relies on interactions with and identification of differences with the 'other', it does not always entail conflict or lead to overt tensions. Ethnicity may be 'expressed in quite undramatic ways through everyday definitions of situations, impression management, in religious cults and other peaceful phenomena' (Hylland Eriksen 2001: 262). In Kasekho this is certainly the case, and, as I have shown, it is also expressed through practices and preferences relating to dispute resolution within the Karen community.

Concluding discussion

This chapter has described everyday case resolution among urban Karen. My core argument has been that the Karen Baptists of Kasekho prefer to have their social disputes and crimes resolved within their own ethnic and religious community, and that they also believe that security is very good in their area because they have a shared ethnic and religious group identity. Having a specific identity, based on religion and ethnicity, thus plays an important role in the village dispute resolution system and forms part of the wider context of legal pluralism in Yangon. While Kasekho is within the Myanmar state and must officially use state law, village residents predominantly draw on local Karen leaders, secular and religious, as well as on non-state religious and local norms, to tackle problems and disputes relating to such things as health, jobs, theft, marriage, fences, and money lending. They prefer prayer, sharing problems in the church, and mediation, negotiation and reconciliation to state-legal processes and punishment. Religious norms and activities around the church influence the local legal order and play an important role in the socialisation of children and young people, and therefore in social regulation as well as in identity formation.

In this conclusion I wish to discuss the implications of the ways in which Kasekho Karen resolve disputes internally and what this means in the context of their relationship with the wider society. Firstly, as I have shown in this chapter, when resolving problems and disputes inside the village the Karen community relies on projecting an image of a united and peaceful Baptist Karen community, which is, for them, in contrast to non-Karen communities. This does not reflect a dislike of or a conflictual relationship with other ethnic or religious groups, such as Bamar Buddhists, but it does have the effect of consolidating ethnic boundaries, with the significant 'other', that is, outsiders, being associated with threat and disorder (Barth 1969). As I have shown, insecurity is associated with outsiders by Kasekho Baptist Karen, and this supports their strategy of preventing outsiders from living in the village. When newcomers arrive, there are also efforts to convert them to the Baptist church, in order to incorporate them into the Karen community. While religious conversion is not compulsory, it is easier to become part of the community if they convert. I observed this in one case where a newcomer Buddhist Karen wanted his children to become Baptists, as he thought this was the best way to integrate into the village. It was his own decision, but the Karen Baptists immediately welcomed his idea, as they prefer people with the same religion living in the area. It is difficult to live in the village if you are not Baptist and Karen, in other words. One consequence of keeping matters internal and of understanding insecurity as something produced by outsiders is therefore that the Baptist Karen are not very open to including outsiders and non-Karen in their community. However, conflicts based on ethnic and religious identity differences are avoided because the Karen Baptists do things that make their co-existence with the surrounding Buddhist society peaceful, such as making donations to and participating in Buddhist activities. Nonetheless, this is an example of the ways in which ethnic boundaries are generated, boundaries that involve significant forms of inclusion and exclusion within Myanmar society.

Secondly, I suggest, in line with Nader (1990), that the focus on community harmony and on keeping dispute resolution within the Karen community can be seen as a way of avoiding state interference and thus of preserving some autonomy from the state. On the one hand, avoidance of the state is a practical way to avoid what are perceived to be the negative and harmful aspects of formal justice, including corruption, slow, difficult procedures, and unfair decisions. On the other hand, state avoidance also creates a distance between the Karen community and the Myanmar state based on ethnic identity construction. Most Kasekho Baptist Karen think that if they mind their own business, they will also be able to keep control of their own village and of their young people, and in this way they will be able to preserve their religious norms and their identity. Autonomy from the state becomes one way of nurturing this form of local control and identity preservation. In the current period of transition to democracy, these strategies of state avoidance and ethnic boundary-making are two of the major challenges that Myanmar and its citizens face. They reflect the fact that there is still widespread mistrust of the state, and there are also wide divisions within society – even though in some areas, such as Yangon, such divisions remain relatively peaceful. The Karen Baptists in Kasekho village know that civil war associated with ethnic differences is still going on in some areas of Myanmar, and that Karen armed organisations are still engaging in negotiations for peace and federalism. Although Kasekho Karen Baptists are not directly involved in these higher-level ethnic politics, they – as quiet Karen (Thawnghmung 2008) – feel themselves to be affiliated to other Karen in the areas partly or fully controlled by the KNU. This is shown in their concern for the Karen as a people and in their strong desire to preserve their ethnic identity. Although they have engaged with state institutions more extensively than their counterparts in peripheral areas, they are very well aware of the negative consequences of civil war, and they therefore try to live their own urban life in Yangon peacefully, among people with other ethnicities. At the same time they also contribute to reproducing ethnic boundaries, as a strategy to maintain peace and security within their own community. At a deeper level of analysis this shows how wider divisions in society are being reproduced even within very peaceful and harmonious contexts. In this chapter I have tried to show how this plays out through the lens of everyday justice and dispute resolution.

References

Barth, F.

1969. *Ethnic Groups and Boundaries: The Social Organization of Culture Difference.* Bergen and London: Universitetsforlaget Press and Allen and Unwin.

Cady, J.F.

1958. *A History of Modern Burma.* Ithaca and London: Cornell University Press.

Cohen, A.P.

1994. *Self Consciousness: An Alternative Anthropology of Identity.* London: Routledge.

Denney, L., Bennett, W. & San K.T.

2016. *Understandings of Justice in Myanmar.* Policy Brief, November 2016., s.l.: MyJustice and Saferworld., November 2016.

Gravers, M.

1996. 'The making of a Karen nation.' In Antlöv, Hans and Stein Tönnesson (eds), *Asian Forms of the Nation*, pp. 237–270. London: Curzon Press.

Hylland Eriksen, T.

2001. *Small Places, Larger Issues. An Introduction to Social and Cultural Anthropology.* London and Virginia: Pluto Press. 2nd edition.

Hummell, Eloise

2014. 'Standing the test of time – Barth and ethnicity.' *Coolabah* 13: 46–60.

Keyes, Charles F.

1979. *Ethnic Adaptation and Identity: The Karen on the Thai Frontier with Burma*. Institute for the Study of Human Issues, Wiley Online Library.

Kyed, Helene M.

2018. 'State-Making and dispute resolution in Karen 'frontier' areas.' *Independent Journal of Burmese Scholarship* 1(2): 29–55.

Mark, T.A.

1978. 'The Karen revolt in Burma.' *Issues and Studies* 14(22): 48–84.

Marshall, Harry

1927. 'The Karens: An element in the melting pot of Burma.' *The Southern Workman* 56: 26–33.

Mon, Lwin Lwin

2018. 'Legal hybridity in everyday justice provision in a Mon village.' *Independent Journal of Burmese Scholarship* 1(2): 121–149.

Myanmar Census, MIMU

2014. *Census Atlas Myanmar: The 2014 Myanmar Population and Housing Census.* The Republic of the Union of Myanmar. themimu.info/sites/themimu.info/files/documents/Census_Atlas_Myanmar_the_2014_Myanmar_Population_and_Housing_Census.pdf.

Nader, Laura

1969. *Law in Culture and Society*. Chicago: Aldine Publishing Company.

1990. *Harmony Ideology: Justice and Control in a Zapotec Mountain Village.* California: Stanford University Press.

Po, San C.

1928. *Burma and the Karen*. London: Elliot Stock.

Qiliang, Wang

2009. 'Religion, legal pluralism and order in a multiethnic society: A legal-anthropological study in contemporary China.' *Journal of Legal Pluralism and Unofficial Law* 41(59): 1–27.

Smith, Martin

1999. *Burma: Insurgency and the Politics of Ethnicity*. London: Zed Books.

Thawnghmung, A.M.

2008. *The Karen Revolution in Burma: Diverse Voices, Uncertain Ends*. Washington: The East–West Center; Singapore: ISEAS Publishing.

2011. *The "other" Karen in Myanmar: ethnic minorities and the struggle without arms*. Lexington Books.

Wimmer, A.

2013. *Ethnic Boundary Making: Institutions, Power, Networks*. New York: Oxford University Press.

6 Are we so different? Interreligious collaboration in a rural Karen-Muslim village in Hpa-An township

Than Pale

Introduction

'Identity politics' plays a significant role in both violent and non-violent conflicts, and the roles of ethnicity and religion in both self-identity and othering are important. However, in much of the literature identity construction is increasingly understood as fluid (Butler 1990), which means that identity is multi-layered and can shift according to context and time. Recent communal violence in Myanmar has been framed primarily as ethnic and/or religious conflict (Cheesman 2017). This assumes the primacy of ethnic and religious aspects of identity, a point that this chapter modifies. Instead, I show how in a mixed Karen-Buddhist and Muslim village in Karen State, self-identity is derived more from a sense of shared place (being born and living in the same village) than from ethnic or religious differences. Shared place here provides a common communal identity.

This chapter is based on ethnographic research on local dispute resolution and community security between 2016 and 2019[1] in a mixed Karen-Muslim village in Hpa-An township (Karen/Kayin State).[2] My findings reveal that there are no ethno-religious conflicts or forms of

1 I carried out qualitative interviews and participant observation. The data was obtained during six field visits in 2016–2019, each lasting 10 days. In January 2019, a follow-up field visit was conducted. Village elders and respected persons were interviewed to find out how they had solved problems in the past and how they were solving them in the present. 35 Karen men, 17 Karen women, 20 Muslim men and 15 Muslim women were interviewed.

2 The current situation regarding Muslims in Myanmar is a very sensitive issue. As I am Buddhist, I worried that I would not be trusted by the Muslims. First, I tried to cultivate close relationships with them and approached the Muslim elders through informal conversations and help from a local assistant. In the next trip, I visited the Muslims' houses to learn about their daily life and the relationship between the Karen and Muslims in the community. I was invited to participate in the funfair on

discrimination between the Karen Buddhists and the Muslims inside the village. This is despite the conflicts between Buddhists and Muslims that have occurred in other parts of Myanmar, especially since 2012 (Roos 2013; Davis, Atkinson and Sollom 2013; Cheesman 2017), the recent conflict in Rakhine State (2016–17) targeting Muslims, and the ongoing discrimination against Muslims on the part of state authorities in Karen State, in terms of limiting their access to citizenship rights and land ownership (Karen Human Rights Group 2017: 247). I argue that the absence of conflict between the two religious communities in my study area is due to a shared communal identity which itself is based on a long history of shared place. This is enacted through collaboration between Buddhists and Muslims in everyday dispute resolution as well as in the context of social affairs and development activities. The village leaders from the two ethno-religious communities resolve crimes and disputes through mutual collaboration, and this allows them to live peacefully together and to avoid larger conflicts. In addition, I argue that the absence of tensions between Buddhists and Muslims is due to the ability of village residents and leaders to avoid external interference in resolving village affairs on the part of official state authorities and religious leaders, who have elsewhere participated in nurturing religious tensions based on an anti-Muslim narrative (Schissler et al. 2017). We therefore see a combination of internal and external factors that reduce the likelihood of identity-based conflicts in the village.

There are three significant factors reducing identity-based conflict within the village. The first is internal to the village, and is shared identity. This has been nurtured by approximately one hundred years of co-habitation, including some intermarriages. This is evident in shared language and dress, and through participation in each other's social activities and ceremonies, such as weddings and New Year celebrations. While one Muslim elder said: 'The original place of our great grandfathers is foreign countries like India or Bangladesh', Muslim residents told me that they felt that they were integrated into the Karen village and that they had more in common with their fellow Karen villagers than they do with Muslims outside the village. They speak mainly Karen, and some Bamar, but no other languages (such as, for instance, Hindi). The Muslims and the Buddhists in the village do practise their own customs,

Independence Day by the Muslim women. I tried to develop mutual understanding while I was collecting the data.

for instance when resolving internal marriage disputes, but they assist each other in resolving matters that go beyond these customs.

The second significant factor is external to the village. Muslim and Buddhist residents and their village leaders both try, as much as possible, to avoid engaging with the official Myanmar state. This is evident in a shared preference for resolving disputes internally within the village, and for avoiding cases being forwarded to the Myanmar justice system and the police at higher levels. They share a mistrust of the Myanmar state, which also serves to strengthen their inward-facing shared identity within the village. Karen Buddhists in the village know that there is increased discrimination against Muslims on the part of the Myanmar state. However, this does not mean that they feel inclined to discriminate against the Muslims living in their village. Indeed, they themselves feel alienated from the state and from the official courts, which they find complicated and costly. They believe that they too will be discriminated against in the courts, as they, like the Muslims, are poor villagers. When cases cannot be resolved inside the village, both Muslim and Buddhist villagers prefer to get help from individual Karen members of ethnic armed groups with whom they have personal connections. This includes known members of the Border Guard Force (BGF)[3] and of the Karen Peace Council (KPC),[4] which are splinter groups of the Karen National Union (KNU), the most influential ethnic armed organisation in Karen State. A core reason for turning to these actors is that the villagers know them, because they grew up in the area. They have a shared identity grounded in place – which means that the armed actors do not discriminate against Muslims based on their religious identity.

The third significant factor is also external to the village. It is that neither Muslim nor Buddhist religious leaders from outside the village become involved in village level dispute resolution nor do they try to ignite tensions or to create discrimination based on religious differenc-

3 The BGF comprises soldiers who used to be part of the Karen National Union (KNU), but who had been part of an internal split in the KNU in 1994–5 that led to the formation of the Democratic Karen Buddhist Army (DKBA). In 2009–10 several factions of the DKBA were converted to BGFs, bringing them under the command of the Myanmar military (see Keenan 2013).

4 The KPC emerged in 2007 as a splinter group led by the long-time commander of KNU Brigade 7, and signed a government ceasefire, which was renewed in 2012 (UNHCR 2014). Rank-and-file KPC members can be found in some Karen villages. They provide a supporting role in making the village safe and peaceful.

es. Although Muslim religious leaders from the town and from a nearby village have visited the village, for example to discipline and educate Muslim young people, they have not interfered in the resolution of disputes. The main Buddhist monk in the area has not involved himself in secular village affairs either, and he has had a positive attitude towards the Muslims in the village. There has been no sign of any attempt to influence matters within the village on the part of the monks of the Ma Ba Tha organisation or from other monks in Karen State who are known to be anti-Muslim, and who have spread negative narratives about Muslims and defended Buddhists in cases involving Muslims (See Chapter 7, this volume; Schissler et. al. 2017; Htar 2018).[5] This absence of the Ma Ba Tha in the village did not mean that the villagers were not aware of religious tensions outside the village, as was evident during the height of the Rakhine crisis in 2017 when many thousands of Muslims were forced to flee to Bangladesh. During that period the Karen State authorities initiated restrictions on the movements of Muslims and tried to prevent Muslims from entering the villages in the area. Facebook and media reporting that have ignited tensions and hatred between Buddhists and Muslims also spread in the village, but according to my informants this did not undermine or threaten the shared identity of the villagers. The Muslims in the village said that they identified more with their fellow Karen villagers than with Muslims elsewhere in the country. They were not in favour of allowing Muslims from outside to enter the village, as they feared that this would create a bad situation for them in relation to their fellow Buddhist villagers. Therefore the Muslim villagers participated in the patrols to keep out strangers. These shared activities confirmed to me that identity based on place is more significant to the villagers than religious identity.

In this chapter I explore shared identity construction through the lens of everyday dispute resolution and community security. Overall, I suggest that everyday collaboration in dispute resolution offers a hope-

5 Ma Ba Tha (known in English as the 'organisation for the protection of race and religion') is an organisation mainly comprising nationalist Buddhist monks with branches all over Myanmar. It was formally established in 2014. It is mainly known for its anti-Muslim campaigns and for drafting four controversial laws that were approved by parliament in 2015, which are designed to regulate religious conversion and interfaith marriage and enforce monogamy and population-control measures. In July 2017 Ma Ba Tha was banned by the State Sangha but continued under a new name (see Gravers and Jørgensen, Chapter 7, this volume).

ful paradigm for legal pluralism, where belonging is defined by shared place rather than by ethnic and religious differences. Theoretically, the chapter contributes to the debate about legal pluralism (Pospisil 1971; Griffiths 1986; Moore 1986: 870) by focusing particularly on the influence of identity. I link theories of identity related to ethnicity, religion, and community to the debate about legal pluralism.

The chapter has three sections. The first section introduces theoretical concepts. This is followed by a second section providing a background to the research area and to the situation of people from the two religious groups. The third section explores the ways in which disputes and crimes are resolved in the village, with a focus on how Muslims and Buddhists collaborate, and on what they do when cases cannot be resolved inside the village. I explore both the internal and external factors that influence how conflicts are avoided in this village.

Linking legal pluralism, identity and community

I draw on a broad literature on legal pluralism (Pospisil 1971; Griffiths 1986; Moore 1986; Hooker 1975), and use a basic definition that holds that legal pluralism describes situations where social actors identify more than one source of law within a social arena (Tamanaha 2008) and where two or more legal systems coexist in the same social field (Griffiths 1986). As evidenced by recent studies, these forms of legal pluralism exist in both rural and urban areas of Myanmar (Kyed 2018). Lue Htar (2018), for instance, shows how plural authorities and different rules of land ownership co-exist in the resolution of land disputes in Karen State. Customs, religious beliefs, culture, and state law all influence legal pluralism in different ways, across different contexts (Tamanaha 2008). Merry (1988) describes the way in which religion in India inevitably generates legal pluralism, and Lwin Lwin Mon (2018) has shown how religious beliefs and practices influence local dispute resolution and understandings of problems in Mon State, Myanmar. Although I do not deny that religious beliefs, Buddhist or Muslim, influence how people perceive problems and injustices, I would argue that religious identity does not dominate how disputes are dealt with in my study area. Instead, I show that despite religious differences, the Buddhists and Muslims share, in the main, the same ways of dealing with everyday disputes and crimes, and that they often resolve these together. An exception is internal marriage disputes, which each group resolves according to their own customs; but when it comes to other social disputes and to crimes, they resolve these in similar ways, by using village leaders or the village tract administrator, and, on rarer occasions, the local police. They also share a preference to avoid resolving cases in the official system, and they do not involve their religious leaders. What is most important in local dispute resolution in this village is shared place rather than religious identity differences. This is within a wider context in which ethnic and religious identity are significant forms of differentiation, including in relation to access to justice. As noted by the Karen Human Rights Group (KHRG), ethnic minorities in Karen State face discrimination when they report cases to the Myanmar police and local authorities, and are often exposed to threats. It is their perception that their cases are not taken seriously due to their ethnicity (Karen Human Rights Group 2017: 246).

These findings have led me to follow a social constructivist understanding of identity (Waters 1990; Butler 1990; Barth 1969; McBeth 1989), rather than an essentialist approach that views identity as fixed and given beforehand. As Waters (1990: 389) argues, ethnic identity is a product of personal choice and is a social category that individuals actively decide to adopt or stress. However, an individual's self-identification is often combined with outsider ethnic designations (Barth 1969), as it is in Karen State and in Myanmar as a whole. McBeth (1989) too highlights the fact that identities are constructed by both the individual and the group, and points out that this is important both in relation to othering and to self-identity. Importantly, ethnic identity has also been closely related to identity politics, which Ross (1982) identifies as a significant aspect of contemporary politics. Identity politics has played a significant role in violent ethnic conflict (Mežnarić 1993) as well as in nationalism more generally (Ålund 1995). Gravers (2007) has shown how identity politics related to ethnicity has been extremely prominent in Myanmar in both colonial and post-colonial times. It has infused the long-standing civil war between the Myanmar military and the many ethnic armed groups as well as being prominent in recent incidents of communal violence and the exodus of Muslims from Rakhine State. Mikael Gravers (2007) writes about ethno-nationalism as an integral part of politics in Myanmar. One example is the list of 135 *taing-yin tha* (national races) published by General Ne Win in the *Workers' Daily* newspaper in 1990 (Gravers 2007: 4). This list became important in military identity politics and remains very important in identifying who belongs and who does not belong as a citizen of Myanmar, although it has many errors and is not complete. In the list Chinese, Hindus and Muslims became non-indigenous people. In present-day Myanmar this continues to be a challenge for Muslims in terms of getting identity cards and access to rights and public services (see Gravers and Jørgensen, Chapter 7, this volume). While ethnic and religious identities are very important to self-identification, othering and politics in Karen State (and in Myanmar more broadly), my chapter also suggests that communal identity, in particular localities, is more significant than ethnic and religious identity. Therefore, I also draw on theoretical understandings of community and communal identity.

Following Cohen (1985), I approach communities as symbolically constructed social places that provide an important setting in which individuals can articulate themselves through the integrative element of social interaction (see also Wilkinson 1986). Gurr (1993: 294) argues that people have many possible bases for communal identity related to sharing historical experiences, language, religious beliefs, region of residence and/or customs. In addition, notions of community 'feeling' or 'spirit' frequently involve interrelationships between people living in the same location or place, which engender a sense of shared identity (Lee et al. 1990). Stedman (2002) argues that place is central to the social world. Places consist of spaces that include not only the physical setting, but also the range of human activity and social/psychological processes that are carried out there (Stedman 2002: 902). In my study area, I found notions of community spirit and place to be significant to local identity on the part of both of the two religious groups. A sense of sharing the same place promotes collaboration in dealing with community affairs such as village security, village development and everyday dispute resolution. Social interaction also adds to the formation of shared identity (Cornell 1988; McBeth 1989; Nagel 1994: 155).

A peaceful village in a complex and contested Karen State

Since shortly after independence in 1948 and until 2012, many parts of Karen State were marred by armed conflict between the military and ethnic armed organisations (EAOs). Karen State has also experienced significant military discrimination and atrocities against civilian Karen (Buddhists as well as Christians) and other non-Bamar minority people living throughout the state (Karen Human Rights Group 2017). Ethnic and religious minorities in Karen State therefore share a long history of oppression by the central military state and of exclusion from access to state protection and rights. Since 2012, when the Karen National Union (KNU) signed a ceasefire with the new semi-civilian government, there have been reduced levels of armed conflict in Karen State, with only small pockets of fighting between small splinter groups, the military and one of the KNU brigades (Saferworld 2018). Despite significant improvements, however, research by Saferworld (2018) and the Karen Human Rights Group (2017) shows that ethnic minority peoples in Karen State continue to face insecurity and to experience abuse from the authorities. A high level of mistrust in the state also prevails due to the long legacy of conflict and discrimination. Although insecurity is highest in the areas of recent ceasefire, mistrust in the state is shared by the majority of people across Karen State.

Discrimination against Muslims in Karen State also seems to be on the rise. The World Report from 2016 on Myanmar argues that discrimination against the minority Muslim community in southeast Myanmar (which includes Karen State) has been present for 25 years, including restrictions on their right to citizenship, to owning land and to running local businesses. This is largely in line with a discriminatory and divisive trend in Myanmar as a whole, where anti-Muslim sentiment has spiked in recent years. Most recently, discrimination against Muslim residents in southeast Myanmar, including Karen State, is reported as coming not from armed groups but from the Myanmar government, local Myanmar government officials, extremist monk organisations – including Ma Ba Tha and the 969 movement – and some local residents (Karen Human Rights Group 2017: 247; Gravers 2018). Mikael Gravers (2018) has, for instance, written about the long-time Karen monk, U Thuzana, who, until his death in 2018, tried to promote a united Karen Buddhism by directly attempting to reduce Christian and Muslim influence.

My study shows that external forms of divisive identity politics may be tempered and prevented by internal collaboration and shared identity across ethno-religious groups. This is the case, at least, in my study area, Kaw Pyan village, where peace and lack of discrimination between Buddhists and Muslims prevailed during my fieldwork. The wider context is, however, beginning to have a certain impact on the villagers, especially the Muslims, although it has not led to any significant tensions within the village. I will now address, firstly, the ways in which shared community identity is nurtured in the village; and secondly, how the wider context is shaping attitudes on the part of the villagers of Kaw Pyan.

Shared communal identity inside the village

Kaw Pyan village is situated not far from Hpa-An town, the capital of Karen State.[6] Despite armed conflict in other areas, the area around this village has been relatively peaceful for 20 years, according to the villagers. After the KNU signed the ceasefire in 2012, the situation improved even further, as it allowed the villagers to move freely between the village and other places. Nevertheless, the significance of the armed groups is still felt in the village, and the KNU, the Border Guard Force (BGF), and the Karen Peace Council (KPC) still have a presence near the village. While the presence of the KNU in the village is mainly in relation to regulation of fishing restrictions, I also found that the BGF and the KPC are sometimes consulted in relation to dispute resolution within the village.

The village has 155 households, with 58 Muslim households and 97 Karen households. The two religious groups live in two separate wards of the village but share the same livelihood activities (rice farming, chicken raising and fishing) and engage in numerous joint activities. The two groups have a long history of cohabitation and a strong communal identity around shared place, while they are also aware of their religious differences. A 50-year-old Karen Buddhist villager explained to me:

> The Muslims have lived in this Karen village for a long time. I have never heard of any dispute between Karen and Muslims in this village. If Karen celebrate a wedding, they invite the Muslims. They usually serve the Muslims rice and chicken curry (neither halal nor pork). They [the Muslims] eat rice and curry, but they avoid pork and they also avoid food that has been cooked in the same pot as pork. Karen know that Muslims do not eat that food [pork] because

6 All original names, both that of the village and those of people, are anonymised in this chapter.

> of their religion. Similarly, if a wedding ceremony is celebrated in the Muslim ward, Karen go and eat at the Muslim house. We help each other in social activities without discriminating against each other.[7]

According to local elders from both religious groups whom I interviewed, the Muslims have lived in the village for nearly one hundred years, and the Muslim population has grown recently as some Muslims have moved there from a neighbouring village because they married people in the village. While older Muslim villagers said that their great-grandfathers were from India, all the Muslims in the village today are natives and were born there.[8] 'Although we have a different religion, we are Karen-Muslim,' I was told by several Muslims. While some are purely of Muslim origin, they see themselves as Karen-Muslim, because they live in a Karen area. Others have mixed origins, with a Karen parent or grandparent. This means that many of the Muslims see themselves as being of mixed blood, due to mixed marriages in the past. There is a sense of strong ties between the two groups. This may be owing to the fact that the Muslims have adapted to Karen ways, assimilating culturally. The Muslims speak Pwo Karen as their everyday language and wear Karen *longyi* (women) and *paso* (men). The Muslim women I spoke to said: 'We are Karen speaking Muslims'. U Har Du, a 10-household leader in the Muslim ward, said something similar to me: 'We are Karen-speaking Muslims because we live with Karen people and we speak the Karen language'. He said that nobody can speak the 'Muslim' language in the village.

This sense of shared communal identity is also evident in and is strengthened through joint engagement in various social and development activities. The two groups engage in joint school development and road repairs, pooling funds and labour. During my fieldwork, I observed a meeting of the leaders on the two sides to discuss how to get electricity to the village. That same day, I saw a Karen midwife sharing out mosquito nets among Muslim and Karen women in front of

7 Interview, Karen woman,15 October 2017.

8 During British colonial rule, there was a steady migration of Indians to the Burmese province, beginning in the mid-nineteenth century (Egreteau 2011: 34). In 1921 there were one million Indians in Myanmar, half of whom were Muslims. According to the 2014 census, 4.6 per cent of the population in Myanmar is Muslim, and Muslims constitute a similar minority in Karen State (Ministry of Labour, Immigration and Population 2016).

the Karen 100-household leader's house. The Muslims also participate actively in the Karen New Year festival, which is held at the village tract level. Although, according to externally ascribed notions, this should be a 'Karen cultural tradition', the Muslim villagers participate in the same way as do the Karen, for instance in terms of planning the event and sharing the food. One 76-year-old Muslim man said: 'We participate in the Karen New Year ceremony because we live in Karen State, and we live with Karen people. So this ceremony is our concern too. It is a responsibility, and we have to pay respect to this traditional Karen festival'.[9] Before the ceremony, Karen and Muslim leaders held a meeting to plan the food, and they each collected money from their own community for the celebrations. The Muslims are not forced to pay, and the poor do not need to donate, but those Muslims who can afford to make donations do so because, as one Muslim told me: 'The Muslims value and respect the culture of the Karen'. As noted in the quote above, the Karen also participate in Muslim wedding ceremonies.

These joint activities illustrate and help nurture a good relationship between the two groups, despite the differences between them in terms of religious and ethnic identity. Both of the groups placed emphasis on the sharing of everyday life within the village. I often heard villagers saying things like: 'We attended school together. We played together at school, and we speak Karen. Our daily activities are the same – we all farm, we wear the same clothes, we speak the Karen language. The only difference is our religion'.

When I asked the Muslim villagers if they felt discriminated against within the village, the answer was no – not socially, economically, or in terms of religion. I did not find that there was any economic competition with or discrimination against Muslims when it came to land ownership either, something that the Karen Human Rights Group (2017) has reported as taking place in other villages. Two thirds of the Muslims in the village own land, which has been passed down to them from their grandparents, or which they have bought from the Karen. They have informal contracts of sale for land, which are signed in front of the 100-household leaders and the village tract leader. Few of the Muslims, however, have proper land titles (known as 'Form Seven Land Papers') from the government, which probably relates to the wider restrictions on land ownership on the part of Muslims. Nevertheless, I found no evidence of land disputes in the village or of efforts by the Karen to minimise access to land on the part of Muslims (for a contrasting example, see Gravers and Jørgensen, Chapter 7, this volume). On the contrary, both Muslims and Karen allow each other to freely use any land that is left vacant, without payment – for instance land belonging to families who have migrated to Thailand for work. Anyone who wants to use such land simply needs to inform the owner.[10] It was clear from my observations and from interviews with Muslim and Karen villagers that Muslims also engage freely in minor business activities such as brick making, sale of goods and large-scale chicken raising. When it came to religious activities and other cultural and social activities specific to one or other group, I never observed nor did I ever hear about any negative interference of one community or its religious leaders in the affairs of the other.

Figure 6.1 Celebration of Karen New Year ceremony in the village attended by Muslims and Buddhists. *Colour image, p. 362*

There is no mosque in the village, but there is a small mosque in a neighbouring village just five minutes' walk away. According to a 76-year-old Muslim elder, the mosque was built in 1962 with funds from wealthy Muslims. The Muslim religious leader from this village, and sometimes the leader from Hpa-An town, do visit the village, but they do not become involved in village affairs. The Muslim village leaders have on occasion asked the members of the Muslim religious organisation to help educate and discipline Muslim young people who have been using drugs, consumed excessive alcohol, or spoken rudely to other villagers. The purpose, I was told by a 56-year-old Muslim man, was to ensure that Muslim young people behaved well, so that there would be no problems for the Muslims in the village, but the Muslim religious association does not get involved in village dispute resolution. The same applied to the Buddhist monks who live at the monastery in the neighbouring village. When I spoke to a monk at this monastery, he was very clear that monks do not get involved in village affairs such as dispute resolution. When I asked him if the Ma Ba Tha organisation was active

10 Interview with Pa-O woman who is married to a Muslim man, 20 October 2018.

in the area, he denied having any knowledge of it. I got the clear impression that the monk was not a supporter of the Ma Ba Tha and their anti-Muslim approach. One of the Karen villagers also told me that the Ma Ba Tha was not active in the village.

Figure 6.2 Competition among Muslim and Buddhist village children on Independence Day. *Colour image, p. 363.*

Figure 6.3 Competition among village residents on Independence Day. *Colour image, p. 363.*

My findings therefore indicate that in my study village there have been no active efforts by religious leaders to ignite tensions or forms of discrimination based on different religious identities (as noted in other areas by Gravers 2018; Karen Human Rights Group 2017; Gravers and Jørgensen, Chapter 7 this volume). Changes in the wider political context, including the recent Rakhine crisis and the spreading of information on Facebook regarding ethno-religious tensions, have, however, had a certain impact in the village, as I discuss next. This includes in relation to how Muslims are referred to and in relation to restrictions within Karen State to their access to ID and to their movements outside the village, especially during the Rakhine crisis.

The challenge of external influences

It has been common for the Karen villagers to call the Muslims Kalar. In Burma, the Indian communities have long been referred to as Kalar, which originally described any individual coming from the outside world and maritime routes, from across the sea as a *'ku-la'* (from *ku*, meaning crossing a maritime space, and *la* meaning to come) (Egreteau

2011). However, this is now changing, because Kalar is increasingly seen as a derogatory term, and the Muslims have noted this by following postings on Facebook.[11] One of the Muslim teachers told me that after she read about it on Facebook she did not want to be called Kalar. She said: 'We [Muslims in the village] did not come to this village from a foreign country. We were born here in the Karen village and attended school in this village. We grew up in this village, so we are not Kalar. We are Muslim.'[12] Therefore, she told me, teachers as well as Karen in general are now taking more care not to use the word Kalar, especially for young Muslim people. Muslim young people disliked being called Kalar or Kalar *lay* at school, according to one schoolteacher.[13] However, while Muslim elders and middle-aged villagers to whom I spoke preferred to be called Muslim, rather than Kalar, they had no big issue with the term. One elder even told me that Muslim and Kalar are the same. The Karen villagers told me that they used Kalar not in a negative sense but because it was easier to pronounce than their Muslim names (meaning their personal names).

The growing restrictions on citizenship for Muslims in Karen State (and beyond) (Karen Human Rights Group 2017) are also beginning to be felt in the village, particularly among young people, for whom it is more difficult to get ID cards than it was for their parents in the past (see also Chapter 7, this volume). According to local Muslims whom I interviewed, some Muslims have old ID cards, but it takes a very long time to get a new ID card. One of the Muslim women said: 'I have an old ID card. I tried again and again to get a new ID card from the government office but so far I have not received it. I feel discrimnated against in relation to this.'[14] Thus, while she and the other Muslim villagers to whom I spoke did not feel discriminated against inside the village, the current lack of access to ID cards from the state is raising concerns about external discrimination, which the local leaders cannot do much about. Similar concerns have emerged since the Rakhine crisis with regard to freedom of movement outside the village.

---

11 On the notion of Kalar see also Gravers and Jørgensen, Chapter 7, this volume.

12 Interview, 15 October 2018.

13 *Lay* means child or youth in Myanmar language. It is common to use the terms *thar lay* (male children) and *tha mee lay* (female children) in schools, for instance.

14 Interview with 50-year-old Muslim woman, 3 January 2019.

On September 26, 2017, the Karen State government, as a result of the Rakhine crisis, restricted the movement of Muslims in Karen State and ordered Muslim residents to report their travel plans to their local administrative offices. To the media, one government official said: 'It [the travel restriction] is for their [the Muslims'] own protection and not because of religious discrimination. It is normal for everyone to be required to carry an identity card or other personal document when they travel. This is part of security measures to avoid unnecessary conflicts that may arise, such as that in Rakhine State'.[15] When I asked the local Muslim women if they felt discriminated against when they went outside the village, they said that there had never been any problems in the past, but that they had been afraid to leave the village since the Rakhine crisis. They felt that people from outside would not speak to them and they said that being outside was different from being in the village. This idea reinforces my argument of 'shared locality' – villagers clearly feel more comfortable among people whom they know. But in relation to this issue I felt that they did not want to speak openly about their feelings. It was clearly sensitive.

Muslims usually travel with their ID card or a letter of recommendation from the VTA in their area, to avoid arrest or interrogation by the police or local immigration authorities. However, some Muslims have travelled without taking a letter of recommendation from the VTA, and they were able to do this because they speak Karen, and could therefore draw on their identity related to place, i.e. their Karen village. For instance, one 45-year-old Muslim man said: 'I travelled to Myawaddy without taking a [letter of] recommendation from the VTA. At the gate going into Myawaddy, I was checked by the police. I explained that I am from Karen State and that I grew up in a Karen village. I spoke fluently in Karen and this was very effective. So the police didn't ask any other questions and I got home safely'.[16] His identity related to place (the village) rather than to religion had been important in avoiding restrictions, and knowing how to speak Karen was significant in this context.

During the Rakhine crisis the Karen State government ordered the villagers to be vigilant and to patrol the villages to ensure that no Muslim strangers entered. This was supported by rumours within the

15 coconuts.co/yangon/news/muslims-can-no-longer-travel-freely-kayin-state (26 September 2017).

16 Interview with Muslim man, 2 January 2019.

village as well as from neighbouring villages that 'stranger' Muslims from the conflict-affected areas in Rakhine State would try to enter Karen State and cause trouble. The rumour reached both Karen and Muslim villagers in Kaw Pyan. One female Muslim villager said to me: 'I heard a rumour from my Muslim friends that the village would be set on fire and poisonous things would be put into our well, and other things, by the stranger Muslims.' She said that these rumours had reached both Karen and Muslim villagers. They kept an eye out for each other during that period. Both Karen and Muslim villagers participated in the security patrols, following the instructions of the local village leader. Nothing happened in the community.[17]

In this context, the Muslim villagers participated, together with their fellow Karen villagers, in the government-organised patrols to prevent 'outsider' Muslims from entering. Following the instructions from the township administration, the Karen patrolled the Karen ward and the Muslims patrolled the Muslim ward. The police and the village tract leader also came to oversee the village at night and to check if the villagers were carrying out their security duties. Some of the Karen members of the Karen Peace Council also participated in the patrolling. The patrols continued for just one month, and there were no security problems during that time. Thus government actions related to the Rakhine crisis and the negative rumours about Muslims on Facebook did affect the villagers, but they tried as far as possible to maintain their communal identity based on shared place. What this points to, overall, is that the maintenance of shared communal identity depended not only on internal collaboration, shared history of co-habitation, and joint activities, but also on avoiding the potential negative effects of external influences. I now turn to village dispute resolution to further illustrate this point.

Interreligious collaboration in dispute resolution

More serious crimes such as murder and robberies do not occur in the village, but more minor cases such as marriage disputes, chicken theft, public disturbances related to alcohol and disputes related to fishing re-

17 Interview with 23-year-old married Muslim woman, 3 January 2019.

strictions do arise.[18] When there are marital problems, cases are resolved internally within the two groups – Muslims and Karen – according to their customary practices. Muslims resolve internal marriage problems such as divorce cases through the Muslim religious association and the Karen settle such cases through their Karen 100-household leader and sometimes with the involvement of the Karen village tract administrator (VTA). In other types of cases, the Karen and Muslim village leaders and respected elders get together to find resolutions. When these leaders face difficulties in settling a case inside the village, they call the village tract administrator (on the Myanmar Government side) or members of Karen armed groups with whom Muslim and Karen villagers have personal connections.

There is a strong emphasis on avoiding conflict escalation, and part of this avoidance is related to shared efforts to avoid cases being brought to the Myanmar state system at higher levels. The VTA also supports these efforts. I begin with cases which Karen and Muslim village leaders resolved internally within the village, and then move on to those where they had to involve external support.

Resolving cases inside the village

Case 1 – Chicken-raising dispute and conflict avoidance

A group of Karen villagers complained to the Karen village leader that chicken farming on the part of the Muslim villagers was producing bad smells and leading to the presence of many flies, which are bad for health. The village leader informed the village tract administrator (VTA), who asked the Muslim village leader to discuss the case. The village leaders from the two sides sat together with the Karen complainants and the Muslim chicken farmers and found a solution. During the meeting, the Muslim leader explained that the chicken farmers had invested a lot of money in raising chickens. If their business were to be stopped, they would be in financial trouble. They suggested that the farmers could use a spray that would reduce

18 Regarding fishing restrictions, I found that both the KNU and the government have enforced rules that prohibit fishing during certain periods of the year. I also encountered one case where the village leaders reprimanded villagers who did not respect these restrictions and referred them to the KNU.

the bad smell and the flies. The Karen villagers agreed to this solution and the Muslim farmers got assistance from a vet in Hpa-An to reduce the smell.

A 56-year-old Karen woman confirmed that the smell and the flies were disturbing the village, but she also said that she found the solution good, because: 'The Karen people do not want to affect the other people's [Muslims'] economy. It is their main economy. They have spent a lot of money investing in it. Neither the Karen nor the Muslims who do not raise chickens want to disturb other people's economic activities'. She said to me: 'This [solution] shows that the Karen villagers do not discriminate against the Muslim villagers and that we avoid bigger conflicts between the communities'.[19] One of the Muslim chicken farmers, who has 500 chickens and is 60 years old, told me that he was satisfied with the solution. Even though he has had to spend some money on the vet and the spray, he was satisfied that a conflict has been avoided.[20]

I also interviewed the VTA about the case, and he confirmed that it had been resolved successfully because the village shared a common concern for each other's economic well-being. He also emphasised that it was best to resolve such a case inside the village and avoid interference from the outside. He said that if the Karen village had made a complaint to the police, and the problem had been resolved in the official way, the villagers would have had to spend a lot of time and money on reaching a solution. There was also the risk that the police might have prohibited the Muslims from raising many chickens, and then the Muslims would have faced big problems.[21] This case clearly shows how Karen and Muslim villagers and local leaders try to avoid the escalation of conflict through collaboration and a shared understanding of the challenges that face each side.

Case 2 – Chicken theft and the Muslim Karen community

A Muslim elder told me about a case that he had helped to resolve among Karen villagers.[22] One night, a local Karen man stole a chicken from a Karen house. He was an alcoholic and he had no job. The thief

19 Interview, Karen woman, 24 Oct 2017.

20 Interview, Muslim man, 24 October 2017.

21 Interview, VTA, 24 October 2017.

22 Interview, Muslim elder, 6 January 2018.

was caught by the victim, who informed the Karen village leader of what had happened. The village leader wanted to punish the thief, but he could not make the decision to do so on his own without the advice of various locally respected persons in the village. So he called together respected persons and village leaders from both the Karen and the Muslim side. At a hearing with the victim and the accused present, the accused admitted guilt. Together, the Karen and Muslim leaders decided that the thief should pay compensation to the victim. Through this, they hoped that such a case would not occur again in the village. The thief also had to write an informal promis letter (*kahn won*), in which he promised not to repeat the office. The resolution was effective, as the thief paid the victim.

This case shows how Karen villagers consider Muslim elders to be important persons in case resolution processes inside the village, even when both sides of the case are Karen. I was told that all village cases, except internal marriages, are the concern of both Karen and Muslims. I suggest that this mutual concern reflects and contributes to a sense of shared communal identity based on place. This collaboration between Muslims and Karen Buddhists in dispute resolution as well as the importance of shared place are also evident in the next cases I will discuss, which involve external actors. Here, efforts to avoid involving the higher levels of the Myanmar state system are particularly evident.

Involving external actors and avoiding the higher levels of the state

Case 3 – Public disturbance and armed group authority

In 2015, a group of young Muslim men aged between 15 and 18 were accused of creating a public disturbance by riding motorbikes at night without exhaust pipes. A 68-year-old Muslim elder told me about the case. The boys were making a lot of noise, so much that sick and elderly people in the village (Karen as well as Muslims) were being woken up. The Karen villagers complained to the Karen 100-household leader, who immediately informed the Muslim village leader. The Muslim leader called the young men and warned them, saying they should not do it again. The young men promised to listen to him, but a few days later they again made noise. The Karen 100-household leader informed the VTA, who advised the Muslim village leader to ask for help from the Muslim religious association in Hpa-An. A member of this association came to reprimand the young men, telling them to behave better. This time the boys again promised that they would stop making noise, but a few weeks later they did it again.

The Muslim and Karen village leaders discussed the case and decided to inform the VTA again. Initially the VTA suggested reporting the problem to the police officer at the tract level, but the Muslim leaders did not like this idea, as they did not want to resolve the case using official channels. They feared that the young men would be punished by the police and that the process would take a very long time in the official system. The Karen village leaders agreed, and instead they got permission from the VTA to seek help from an armed member of the BGF, who is Karen and born in the village. Both village leaders know him very well and they were convinced that he could control the young men. The VTA gave them permission, and the BGF member came to the village to speak to the young Muslims. During the meeting the two village leaders were present, and the VTA and the tract-level police also attended. The armed group member did not speak to the boys in an angry tone, but said: 'You are young and I understand that you can make mistakes in life. However, you have to stay in the village without disturbing the local people'. He told them that if they did it again, he would take action against them. The village leader told me that the BGF member would not really take action – it was just a warning. However, the young Muslims knew that the BGF member had power, so they were afraid of disobeying him. The Muslim leader thanked the BGF member for having resolved the problem peacefully. Both the Karen and Muslim village leaders have a high level of trust in the BGF member, and they also like him because he donates money for village school development and is respectful towards the elders in the village. They told me that he has a powerful mind, and that therefore the villagers, like the young people, respect him.

This case clearly illustrates the strong collaboration that exists across the ethno-religious divide within the village, and it also shows that the VTA, despite being part of the Myanmar state administration, accepts the idea of using alternative external actors to resolve village disputes rather than sending cases to higher levels of the state. The external actor brought in was Karen and from the area. Even the local police officer seemed to accept the use of the BGF. What was most important here was not, however, the authority of an armed organisation, but the connection to a particular individual member of the armed group who is native to the village. For both the VTA and the BGF member, identity based on place is therefore important, and for the villagers it is also important that the case does not leave this sphere of local relationships and does not become an official matter at higher state levels. The next case reflects the way in which reliance on Karen armed actors is also related to the power of these groups to issue immediate punishments and resolutions, which contrasts with the slower process of official state justice.

Case 4 – Turkey theft and knife threats

In the past, around 20 years ago, the village leaders could use village punishments in cases of theft. Thieves were punished by the village head using the *htat tone* or *chauk pauk* (a kind of pillory or foot lock with six holes). The parents of a thief also had to apologise for their child's mistakes and get a pardon from the village head. They had to guarantee that their child would not commit the offence again. Nowadays, village leaders cannot punish using the *htat tone*, which has gradually disappeared as a punishment tradition in the region. However, it is still used by the Karen Peace Council (KPC), the armed splinter group from the KNU, which has a sub-division camp close to Kaw Pyan village. When cases have got too complicated, the villagers and village leaders have turned to this group for assistance. The KPC also has a rule that the thief has to give MMK 15,000 (USD 10) to the KPC to be placed in the *htat tone* and another MMK 15,000 to be released from it. The 52-year-old Karen village leader told me about a turkey theft case that was resolved in this way in November 2017.

The perpetrator is from a neighbouring village and he is Karen. He very often used to visit a relative of his in Kaw Pyan village. He is over 20 years old and he has no job. The victim was a Karen woman. One night, she lost a turkey. She suspected the perpetrator, because he was a stranger who used to visit her neighbour. The next day, the man concerned returned to his own village. He visited the village again several times, but the woman did not mention her lost turkey. However, when she lost another turkey, she could not remain calm and went to the stranger to ask him directly if he had taken the turkey. He denied this, at first, but finally he admitted to having taken it and said that he had already cooked the turkey. He promised to compensate the woman for the turkey with money, but he never did. He said to her: 'I cannot pay – you may inform anyone you wish [about the case]'.

The Karen woman then complained to the village leader. He declared that a turkey is expensive. A turkey is worth over MMK 30,000 (USD 20). Because of this, the village leader saw this as a big case. The village leader therefore informed the village tract administrator (VTA), who informed the VTA in the thief's village, who informed the thief's parents. The next day, the thief drank a lot of alcohol and went to the Karen victim's house. He threatened her with a knife. She immediately informed the village leader that he had done this.

The village leader told the woman: 'If I do not punish him, he will commit the crime again. If I resolve this problem the official way [forward it to the state system], it will take time. So I have told the VTA that I would like to inform the Karen Peace Council organisation'. The VTA agreed. After informing the Karen Peace Council by phone, three people from the KPC, together with the village leader, went to the perpetrator's house and arrested him. He was taken to the headquarters of the KPC. The thief was put in the *htat tone* for one night. In accordance with the rules, the thief also paid MMK 30,000 before he was released. In addition, he had to pay the value of the turkey to the victim. The thief said at the time that two of his friends were also involved in stealing turkeys. So his friends shared the cost of the turkey. At the KPC, the thief signed an promise letter *(kahn won)*, in which he promised that he would not repeat the offence.

When I talked about this case with the village leader, he said that this informal way of dealing with theft is preferred to going to the police because with the Myanmar police the process takes a long time. This view is shared by both Karen and Muslim villagers – as we saw in the case about the motorbike noise. The village leader said: 'This informal solution is more effective. Also, young Karen men are afraid of the Karen Peace Council'.[23] So there is a strong preference for resolving cases outside the official state system, whether you are Muslim or Karen Buddhist. Turning to members of the armed group is never, however, the first option. The village leaders always try to resolve cases together first, and if they cannot do this they go to the VTA in the nearby village.

23 Interview 5 January 2019

If the VTA cannot resolve a case, the option is not then to go higher up in the state system, but to use close-by members of the Karen armed groups, who are more trusted than the Myanmar state. This is not only due to the preference for informal and rapid resolution, but also because the villagers share a sense of shared place with the Karen armed actors, as well as a mutual understanding about the need for flexibility in justice provision. Karen and Muslim villagers whom I interviewed told me that they do not understand the Myanmar court system, it is very lengthy, and it is very stressful to use the courts.

Concluding discussion

Since colonial times, violent conflict and discrimination in Myanmar have largely centred on differences in ethno-religious identity, and tensions and violent clashes between Muslims and Buddhists have been pronounced since 2012 (Gravers 2018). This chapter provides an example of a village in Karen State where such tensions are absent, and where disputes are not caused by identity differences. By exploring everyday dispute resolution and justice provision from a village-level perspective, this chapter contributes insights into how and why residents of the same village with different ethnic and religious identities manage to avoid bigger conflicts and tensions. It shows how the Muslim and Buddhist residents of the Karen village that I studied share everyday lives and social activities as well as collaborating with each other in resolving disputes. This kind of collaboration promotes a sense of mutual understanding and familiarity and helps to avoid the escalation of conflict. Collaboration at the same time reflects and further strengthens a shared communal identity that goes beyond ethnic and religious differences – which is, I suggest, centred on shared place.

With regard to 'community place making', Cohen (1982) and Gupta and Ferguson (1997) emphasise not only a community's physical boundaries but also the symbolic meaning of place. Place is not only embodied within a physical locale, but is also replete with symbolic meanings, emotional attachments, and feelings that individuals hold about a given setting (see also Brandenburg and Carroll 1995; Cuba and Hummon 1993; Dominy 2001; Greider and Garkovich 1994; Marsden et al. 2003; Stedman 2002). This is not to deny differences, since community includes 'simultaneously both similarity and difference'

(Cohen 1982: 12). In this Karen village we can also identify differences in religion and ethnicity, but daily life, language, social activities and place of birth are the same. Here, community place-making is nurtured through a shared desire for village peace and development. This was, for instance, evident in the motorbike disturbance case, where, although the perpetrators were Muslim men, leaders on both sides saw it as a common village problem that needed to be resolved together. Similarly, in the chicken theft case Karen leaders called in Muslim elders to help resolve a case where the perpetrators were Karen Buddhists, because they viewed it as a shared village problem. Roberts (2016: 5) argues that 'place is where identity can appear, where differences must be confronted as people gather in a particular location and make sense of each other'. In this Karen village the residents' psychological feelings are the same when it comes to resolving disputes and crimes, and there is a mutual understanding and respect for each other's livelihoods, as is reflected in the dispute about chicken raising. The Karen people did not want to undermine the Muslims' livelihoods, and the Muslims found a solution that was accepted by the Karen.

The question is whether shared place is the only reason for the avoidance of ethno-religious tensions in this Karen village? I have suggested that sharing of place is very significant, but avoidance of interference of external actors in village affairs is another important factor. As is evident in other towns and villages in Myanmar, violent clashes can occur between Buddhists and Muslims who have lived in the same place for many years, as happened in Meikhtila in 2013 (Davis, Atkinson and Sollom 2013). As Gravers (2018) and Wade (2017) suggest, these clashes do not reflect deep-seated animosities between the ethno-religious groups as such, but are brought about because of external influences, in particular identity politics whereby the manipulation of identities by ruling elites, including some monk organisations, has laid the foundations for violence. Although the residents of Kaw Pyan village are aware of the conflict in Rakhine State and have followed the negative messages that are spreading on Facebook, their shared communal identity has not been damaged by such external influences. Shared place is more important than religious identity, as was evident during the patrols that the state government initiated to keep out stranger Muslims during the height of the Rakhine crisis in 2017. At the same time, I have argued that the preservation of shared communal identity may also be due to the fact that neither Muslim nor Buddhist religious leaders interfere in village affairs or in dispute resolution,[24] and that there is a common interest in resolving matters locally, rather than engaging the Myanmar state system at higher levels. By avoiding the state system at higher levels, the villagers not only avoid high costs and slow court processes, but also potential discrimination based on ethnic or religious minority status, which could harm their communal identity. As Gravers (2018) notes, the politics of identity also runs deep within the Myanmar bureaucratic system, including in the courts and the administration, in terms not only of identity documents but also of the way in which people are treated.

In fact, crucial to escaping conflict escalation in everyday justice provision is avoidance of the Myanmar state at levels above the village tract. The village leaders do this by keeping dispute resolution within the village, and, if that fails, by then turning to the village tract administrator, who, although he is part of the state administrative system, is also a local Karen villager. Eventually, if necessary, the village leaders may get help from Karen ethnic armed actors, with whom both Muslim and Karen villagers are familiar and whom they trust. Although the local armed group member of the BGF is a Buddhist Karen, he takes care of his native villagers without discriminating against the Muslims in the village, because he shares an identity grounded in place with them. Armed actors like him are also able to provide quick resolutions at a low cost. This preference for informal and local resolutions is supported by the village tract administrator and even by the local police, because they too share an identity based on place.

At a deeper level of analysis my findings confirm the fact that ethno-religious conflict is politically constructed from the outside, rather than being the result of identity differences in everyday life, where Muslims and Buddhists share more similarities than differences. My chapter also provides a promising paradigm for legal pluralism and

24 This can be contrasted to Harrisson's (2018) work on a Muslim–Buddhist ward in Mawlamyine, where she found that many Muslims have taken on a strategy of 'local subjugation' that prevents conflicts from escalating, but means that they get unequal access to local justice. Part of the reason for this could be that, unlike in Kaw Pyan village, Buddhist religious leaders, or monks, take an active role in dispute resolution and are biased in favour of the justice needs of the Buddhists. This kind of interference was absent in Kaw Pyan, where Muslim and Buddhist leaders resolved matters together, and where religious leaders were absent from dispute resolution.

community-based dispute resolution, demonstrating how shared identity based on place can work to reduce conflict escalation and tensions. However, the wider contextual conditions for this kind of identity construction are also crucial, and an analysis of the extent to which the nurturing of intercommunal relationships between minority groups is easier than between a minority and the majority population remains a topic for future research.

References

Barth, F.

1969. *Ethnic Groups and Boundaries*. Boston: Little, Brown and Co.

Brandenburg, A.M. and M.S.Carroll

1995. 'Your place or mine? The effect of place creation on environmental values and landscape meanings.' *Society and Natural Resources* 8(5): 381–398.

Butler, J.

1990. *Gender Trouble: Feminism and the Subversion of Identity*. New York: Routledge.

Cheesman, N.

2017. 'Introduction: Interpreting communal violence in Myanmar.' *Journal of Contemporary Asia* 47(3): 335–352.

Cohen, A.P.

1982. 'Belonging: The experience of culture.' In A.P. Cohen (ed.), *Belonging: Identity and Social Organization in British Rural Cultures*. Manchester: Manchester University Press. Pp. 1–18.

1985. *The Symbolic Construction of Community*. London and New York: Routledge.

Cornell, S.

1988. *The Return of the Native: American Indian Political Resurgence*. Oxford: Oxford University Press.

Cuba, L. & Hummon, D.M.

1993. 'A place to call home: Identification with dwelling, community, and region.' *The Sociological Quarterly* 34(1): 111–131.

Davis, B., H.G. Atkinson, and R. Sollom.

2013. 'Massacre in Central Burma: Muslim Students Terrorized and Killed in Meiktila.' Physicians for Human Rights Report. May.

Dominy, M.D.

2001. *Calling the Station Home: Place and identity in New Zealand's High Country.* Lanham, MD: Rowman and Littlefield.

Egreteau, R.

2011. 'Burmese Indians in contemporary Burma: Heritage, influence and perceptions since 1988.' *Asian Ethnicity* 12(1): 33–54.

Gravers, M.

2007. *Exploring Ethnic Diversity in Burma*. Copenhagen: Nordic Institute of Asian Studies Press.

2018. 'A saint in command? Spiritual protection, justice and religious tensions in Karen State.' *Independent Journal of Burmese Scholarship* 1(2): 87–119.

Greider, T. & Garkovich, L.

1994. 'Landscapes: The social construction of nature and the environment.' *Rural Sociology* 9(1): 1–24.

Griffiths, J.

1986. 'What is legal pluralism?' *Journal of legal Pluralism and Unofficial Law* 18(24): 1–55.

Gupta, A. and Ferguson, J.

1997. 'Beyond "culture": Space, identity, and the politics of difference.' In A. Gupta and J. Ferguson (eds), *Culture, Power, Place: Exploration in Critical Anthropology*. Durham, North Carolina: Duke University Press. Pp. 33–51.

Gurr, T.R.

1993. *Minorities at Risk.* Washington, DC: United States Institute of Peace.

Harrisson, A.P.

2018. 'Everyday justice for Muslims in Mawlamyine: Subjugation and skilful navigation.' *Independent Journal of Burmese Scholarship* 1(2): 57–85.

Hooker, M.B.

1975. *Legal Pluralism: An Introduction to Colonial and Neo-Colonial Laws.* Oxford: Clarendon Press.

Htar, L.

2018. 'Everyday justice and plural authorities: Insights from Karen State about land disputes.' *Independent Journal of Burmese Scholarship* 1(2): 181–210.

Karen Human Rights Group (KHRG)

2017. *Foundation of Fear: 25 years of Villagers' Voices from Southeast Myanmar.* khrg.org/2017/12/foundation-fear-25-years-villagers-voices-southeast-myanmar.

Keenan, P.
2013. *The Border Guard Force. The Need to Reassess the Policy.* Briefing Paper No. 15, July 2013. Chiang Mai: Burma Centre for Ethnic Studies.

Kyed, H.M.
2018. 'Introduction to the special issue on everyday justice.' *Independent Journal of Burmese Scholarship* 1(2): i–xxii.

Lee, R.G., Field, D.R. & Burch, W.R.
1990. 'Forestry, community and sociology of natural resources.' In R.G. Lee, D.R. Field and W.R. Burch (eds), *Community and Forestry: Continuities in the Sociology of Natural Resources.* Colorado: Westview Press. Pp. 3–14.

Marsden, T., Milbourne, P., Kitchen, L. & Bishop, K.
2003. 'Communities in nature: The construction and understanding of forest natures.' *Sociologia Ruralis* 43(3): 238–256.

McBeth, S.
1989. *Layered Identity Systems in Western Oklahoma Indian Communities in Western Oklahoma Indian Communities.* Paper presented at the annual meeting of the American Anthropological Association, November 17, Washington, DC.

Merry, S.E.
1988. 'Legal pluralism.' *Law and Society Review* 22: 869–896.

Mežnarić, S.
1993. The rapists' progress: ethnicity, gender and violence. *Revija za sociologiju, 24*(3–4), 119–129.

Ministry of Labour, Immigration and Population
2016. *The Union Report: The 2014 Myanmar Population and Housing Census. Census Report, Volume 2.*

Mon, L.L.
2018. 'Legal hybridity in everyday justice provision in a Mon village.' *Independent Journal of Burmese Scholarship* 1(2): 121–149.

Moore, S.F.
1986. *Social Facts and Fabrications: Customary Law on Kilimanjaro, 1880–1980.* Cambridge: Cambridge University Press.

Nagel, J.
1994. 'Constructing ethnicity: Creating and recreating ethnic identity and culture.' *Oxford Journal* 41(1): 152–176.

Pospisil, L.

1971. *The Anthropology of Law: Comparative Theory of Law*. New York: Harper and Row.

Roberts, J.L.

2016. *Mapping Chinese Rangoon. Place and Nation among the Sino-Burmese*. Seattle: University of Washington Press.

Roos, J.

2013. *Conflict Assessment in Rakhine State*. Danish Refugee Council report. February/March.

Ross, J.A.

1982. "Urban development and the politics of ethnicity: A conceptual approach." *Ethnic and Racial Studies* 5 (4): 440–456.

Saferworld

2018. *Security, Justice and Governance in South East Myanmar: A Knowledge, Attitudes and Practices Survey in Karen Ceasefire Areas*. Yangon: Saferworld and Karen Peace Support Network.

Schissler, M., Walton, M.J. & Thi, P.P.

2017. 'Reconciling contradictions: Buddhist–Muslim violence, narrative-making and memory in Myanmar.' *Journal of Contemporary Asia* 47(3): 376–395.

Stedman, R.C.

2002. 'Toward a social psychology of place: Predictive behavior from place-based cognitions, attitudes, and identity.' *Environment and Behavior* 34(5): 561–581.

Tamanaha, B.Z.

2008. 'Understanding legal pluralism: Past to present, local to global.' *Sydney Law Review* 29: 386–450.

UNHCR

2014. *Kayin State Profile*, pp. 1–13.

Waters, M.

1990. *Ethnic Options: Choosing Identities in America*. California: University of California Press.

Wilkinson, K.P.

1986. 'In search of the community in the changing countryside.' *Rural Sociology* 51(1): 1–17.

Wade, F.

2017. *Myanmar's enemy within: Buddhist violence and the making of a Muslim 'other'*. Zed Books Ltd.

Ålund, A.

1995. Alterity in modernity. *Acta sociologica*, 38(4), 311–322.

7 Being excluded – Muslim and Hindu communities in Karen State

Mikael Gravers and Anders Baltzer Jørgensen

Introduction

This chapter analyses the discrimination of Muslim and Hindu communities in Karen State. Discrimination affects access to justice on the part of these communities. After the nation-wide anti-Muslim riots in 2012–13, Muslims and Hindus in Karen State encountered increasing discrimination from the authorities, from nationalist monks, and also within some Christian communities. This was through exclusion from citizenship and civil rights, negative ethnic categorisation, and having to make exorbitant payments to officials. After decades of cooperation with their Buddhist neighbours, Muslims and Hindus are encountering negative ethnic categorisation from nationalist monks in the Association for Protection of Race and Religion (Ma Ba Tha). These monks create tension with Muslims, Hindus and Christians. Ma Ba Tha and its ideology are strong in Hpa-An and around Ein Du town, as well as in areas dominated by followers of U Thuzana, the late monk who was patron of the Democratic Karen Buddhist Army (DKBA).

Muslims and Hindus are categorised as Kalar, 'foreigners from India', in daily discourse.[1] We argue that discrimination against Muslims and Hindus is part of current identity politics and of a historical process of ethnic/racial identification in Myanmar. After the nationwide ceasefire was signed by Karen armed groups and the army (Tatmadaw) in 2015 and during the ongoing negotiations about the creation of a federation based on ethnicity, identity registration and papers have become very

1 The word *Kalar* probably derives from a combination of *kula* (caste), 'tribe' in Sanskrit, and *gola* in Mon, meaning 'inhabitant of Bengal/Indian' (Shorto 1971: 74). However, it has the connotation of 'black' (*kali*). Pwo Karen speakers have adopted the word and pronounce it *khola*. They use the term *khola seung* to refer to people of Indian origin. It means 'black *khola*'. The British were described as *khola Engelai* or *khola wa* ('white *khola*'). A bogeyman in Burmese is a *kalar gyi* – a 'big *kalar*'.

important. Moreover, the Myanmar authorities have gained more influence in parts of the frontier areas formerly controlled by the KNU and the DKBA, and ID cards are thus crucial for personal security and justice. However, most Muslims and Hindus in Karen State, who are the subject of this chapter, cannot obtain citizenship.

We begin this chapter with a brief discussion of citizenship and exclusion, followed by an outline of nationalist ideas of ethnic identification and bureaucratic power in Myanmar. The next section analyses the role of Ma Ba Tha monks and their spiritual power. The effects of bureaucratic and religious discrimination are highlighted in cases from two neighbouring Karen Muslim and Karen Buddhist villages and two Hindu communities. We focus on the problems of obtaining ID cards and on perceptions of exclusion. Finally, we discuss the consequences of this exclusion in the current unstable transition.

Citizenship – a constitutional right?

In his topical discussion of what he describes as an 'antimonic relationship' between modern citizenship and democracy, Etienne Balibar (2015) focuses on the tendency in contemporary politics to limit universal civil rights, not just through inequalities but also through social exclusion. This seems to be a global trend and may be related to the issue of migration, as has, for example, come to the fore in the political situation in Europe. However, the history and traditions of nations vary a good deal. The antimony Balibar refers to (2015: 3) appears, he argues, when *constituent power* is replaced by *constituted power*. In Myanmar this has occurred through a bureaucratic mechanism based on ethnic, race and religious categorisation, which is supported by a nationalist ideology, as discussed in the following section. The main antimony has been between the definition of a Myanmar citizen in chapter viii of the 2008 constitution and that in the citizenship law of 1982. The Myanmar constitution states: 'The union shall not discriminate against any citizen of the Republic of the Union of Myanmar based on race, birth, religion, official position, status, culture, sex or wealth'. Section 34 provides for freedom of religion, and Section 362 includes Christianity, Islam, Hinduism, and Animism as religions, with Buddhism having 'a special position'. Moreover, Section 364 states that the abuse of religion in politics is forbidden. However, the 1982 citizenship law overrules the guarantee of equal rights in the constitution. It does not equalise all who are born and live in the country. It conflates race, ethnicity, and religion, as shown below.

In Myanmar, citizenship depends on a political hierarchy of ethnic groups or 'races' that was introduced during colonial rule. This hierarchy persisted during military rule and is still present and in function. National citizenship is defined by constitutional power and implemented through bureaucratic powers. These powers are institutionally embedded and culturally defined, a fact making them difficult to dispute or contradict. In Myanmar, ethnic categorisation is the main instrument of inclusion/exclusion (cf. Jenkins 2008). The imaginary of an ethnic hierarchy originating before colonial conquest has been used to emphasize 'national ('racial') unity and sovereignty' during military rule and is still a forceful imaginary. To challenge this can mean being categorised as a traitor.

Ethnicity and nationalism: The power of categorisation and limited citizenship

There is no space here for a long genealogical history of ethnicity and religion. Both were inscribed into personal identification and ID cards during military rule, following the 1982 citizenship law. The current ethnic categories originated in British census ethnography and the division it set up between 'indigenous races' (Burman and minorities) and 'Indian races'. These categories were used in the 1931 census, which also included classification by religion.

The main categories in the 1982 law excluded those who did not belong to the 'eight national races' – Bamar, Karen, Shan, Kachin, Rakhine, Mon, Chin, Kayah, and the 135 *taing-yin-tha* – the ethnic groups originating in precolonial Burma.[2] The origin of the list of

2 See the detailed discussion of citizenship in South and Lall (2018). The terms *luo myo* ('race/ethnicity'), *amyo* ('race') and *amyotha* ('nationality'), which all have biological connotations, often seem to overlap. The 2014 census (Republic of the Union of Myanmar 2015) used the *taing-yin-tha* list of 'races'/ethnic groups considered to be native, which is flawed. Ethnic groups are listed under the eight main 'national races' in each state, in other words many groups are not listed separately. For example, Wa, Pa-o, and Lahu are listed under Shan (see Callahan 2017, who gives a critical assessment of the census and racial categorisation). Karen organisations objected to the category 'Kayin' and demanded that the term 'Karen' be used. Before the 1973

135, published in the newspaper *Workers' Daily* in 1990, is obscure, as Cheesman (2017) and Tonkin (2018: 235–236) have shown. The 1982 citizenship law treats the list as a fixed ethnic hierarchy, and it excludes Muslims and Hindus from India and people of Chinese origin, as these are defined as non-indigenous races. These categories of people could still obtain two types of citizenship intended for residents who arrived before 1948: associate citizenship ('guest' citizenship); and naturalised citizenship, which was for those who had strong supporting evidence of residence before 1948. These two groups of *legal citizens* were allowed to apply for full citizenship later.[3] Only people belonging to the groups listed as *taing-yin-tha* (see footnote 2) could become *native citizens*. However, the citizen list and the practices of today should be understood as embedded in recent Burman nationalism, in particular the military version, and its focus on national unity and integrity encompassing all groups within one Myanmar nation and in a unitary state.

Racial rhetoric flourished during military rule. In 1979, Ne Win warned against people of mixed race in his explanation of the ongoing struggle against insurgency. He said: 'If people of pure blood act this way (disloyal to their race and country) we must carefully watch people of mixed blood' (cited in M. Smith 1999: 37). This rhetoric relating to 'mixed blood' (*thway nar*) and 'mixed race' (*amyo kabya*), which is an indirect reference to descendants of marriage between persons originating in India and Bamar, has been resumed in the recent nationalist rhetoric of Buddhist monks and their lay followers.[4] Mixed race, in nationalist ideology, constitutes a danger to unity and are considered 'immoral flows' (Herzfeld 2001: 200). People of mixed race are viewed as abusing the nation's hospitality (Herzfeld 1992: 171).

Walton (2013) has discussed aspects of Bamar hegemonic cultural identity, which is founded in what he calls a 'primordial nationalism' combining blood ties and territory in the collective memory and iden-

census, the Ministry of Home & Religious Affairs listed 144 *taing-yin-tha*.

3 Applicants for associate citizenship had to appear in person in front of a committee and confirm their allegiance to the State. Persons who had not yet applied for citizenship before 1948 could apply for naturalised citizenship. (Tonkin 2018: 247–254)

4 Recently, the minister for Labour, Immigration, and Housing announced that the list of national races would be updated, and that a new mixed Mon-Karen race would be added (Myanmar Times 2017). The categories used are not based on self-identification. Immigration offices still have a special counter for persons of 'mixed blood'.

tification.[5] The nation becomes sacred land when under a perceived threat from enemies. These primordial nationalist attachments create a 'surplus of affects' in the general population, of either acceptance or silence. However, the negative 'surplus affects' of these attachments can also be used to mobilise popular sentiments against specific ethnic and religious groups.[6] This is part of the nationalist discourse that is dominant nowadays, and produces *symbolic power*, which in turn legitimates *symbolic violence* (cf. Bourdieu 1992: 169). In the current situation, nationalist affects have been exacerbated by the violence in Rakhine State after 2016, when the army violently attacked Rohingya Muslims, who are not considered an indigenous group. The violence sent 800,000 Rohingya fleeing to Bangladesh.[7] In other words, nationalism justifies the use of force, preventive actions, and discrimination in censuses, through surveillance, and in relation to citizenship. The result is a process that not only escalates violence but may also continue to widen the incompatibilities between nationalities or ethnic groups, as occurred during the civil wars across Myamar. This is a process of ethnic and religious *schismogenesis* (Gravers 2015b: 34), and is one that is unfortunately still at work in Karen State.

When ethnicity, nationality, and religion are entered on ID cards, the fact that a person is 'mixed race' is also entered. After an anti-Muslim campaign in 2001, we were told by informants in Karen State that it became increasingly difficult to obtain identity papers. Muslims and Hindus were denied citizenship and could not even get a Foreign Registration Card (Karen Human Rights Group 2002: 5), which states that they are foreigners with permission to stay in Myanmar. During military rule, ethnic and religious identification as a non-Buddhist and non-*taing-yin-tha* (see footnote 2) could mean that a person was regarded as a potential traitor or an enemy of the Union of Myanmar. Ethnicity and religion increasingly became decisive in official categori-

5 See Shils (1995) for a discussion of primordial attachments, the 'givens' (blood ties, language, culture, and territory) of national identity.

6 Harrisson, chapter 8 in this volume, defines affects as the more instinctive and unconscious sentiments in individuals when they, in her case, try to avoid state control.

7 Appadurai (2000: 132) argues that this kind of strong nationalist attachment has its roots in forms of violence, for example ethnic cleansing. In the worst cases it may result not only in the denationalisation but also in the dehumanisation of specific groups (Árendt 1976).

sation (Jenkins 2008: 75), as a qualification for citizenship and in daily processes of inclusion/exclusion. The origin of ethnic/racial categorisation is colonial rule, but it persists as the core of Burman imaginations of their nation.[8]

Daw Aung San Suu Kyi has provided an interesting explanation of Burmese nationalism. She argues that it was founded in Burma's cultural homogeneity and that it was a fundamental part of the Burmese ethos (Aung San Suu Kyi 1991: 103–14). Thus it is, she argues, perceived as being the natural, primordial core of being Burmese – or rather, perhaps, of ethnic *Burman* culture and moral orientation. Buddhism constitutes a fundamental part of Burman culture and cosmological orientation, and is crucial to understanding the concept of *taing-yin-tha* (see footnote 2). Aung San Suu Kyi added, 'In a strange way the Burmese seemed to value their cultural integrity more than their ethnic identity' (ibid.: 104).[9] In his critical assessment, Walton (2013: 2) emphasises the fact that Burman-ness is regarded as superior, and that this inhibits inter-ethnic unity. Furthermore, this unity is regarded as a *moral notion* related to the Buddhist concept of harmony in the form of *samagga* (association), which is a marker of unity and consensus (Walton 2015; Houtman 1999: 65). Thus, Burman nationalism focuses on cultural and moral integrity. The arguments of Ma Ba Tha monks clearly demonstrate this, as discussed below. First, a brief outline of bureaucratic power.

Bureaucratic exclusion

The power/authority (*ana* in Burmese) to define citizenship rests in bureaucracy and offices.[10] The army used to control the General

8 On post-colonial imaginings of the nation, see Chatterjee (1993). On cultural nationalism, see Hutchinson and Smith (1994: 123 ff); on cultural nationalism in Burma, see Boshier (2018) and Gravers (1999).

9 At the International Court of Justice, Aung San Suu Kyi defended her country as the sovereign Myanmar nation, not the military and its human rights violations, against accusations of ethnic cleansing and genocide in Rakhine (Kyaw Phyo Tha in *The Irrawaddy* 19 December 2019).

10 In Pwo Karen this power is termed *a khó a na'* ('head, force'), in powerful institutions such as the army, or on the part of individual persons. An official in Pwo is a 'big person' (*hoe dó*). Authority is thus power vested in both persons and offices; see Arendt (1970: 45). However, Karen often use Burmese terms.

Administrative Department (GAD, previously under the Home Affairs Ministry). In 2018, despite protests from the military, the NLD (National League for Democracy) government placed GAD under the Office of the Union Government. However, the minister is still an army officer, as are other leading officials. GAD supervises and coordinates the administration, the police, internal security, and immigration, including the key areas of household registration and administration of citizenship and immigration. Voter lists are based on household lists. GAD thus controls local elections. This administrative control has increased in Karen State. According to Jolliffe (2015: 30), GAD has expanded its influence into townships in Karen State since 2012 (the year of the bilateral ceasefire agreement between the KNU and the central government), and Village Tract Administrators (VTAs) are under the GAD.

The discriminatory practices of the GAD in relation to citizenship on the part of Muslims and Hindus can, we suggest, be understood as a form of *bureaucratic indifference*, as defined by Herzfeld (1992). This indifference implies a denial of both official identification and self-representation on the part of these two groups, who cannot use their own ethnonyms as official identification. Herzfeld explains that in classic nationalism, blood ties and the idea of mixed race are depicted as being a problem to national sovereignty (ibid. 22–25). This is the dominant Myanmar discourse on *taing-yin-tha* (see footnote 2), which is rooted in race and ethnicity. Herzfeld, in his discussion of Western bureaucracy, argues that the roots of official intolerance and indifference, which are characteristics of nationalism, lie in popular attitudes (ibid.: 49). Without widespread popular acceptance, it would be impossible for radical nationalists to openly identify Muslims as 'enemy no 1' and as a 'black tsunami' (Wade 2017: 101; Cheesman 2015: 114 ff.). The recent anti-Muslim movement and its actions thrive on this structural and culturally based hyper-anxiety and 'surplus affect' of the primordial nationalist attachments. Nevertheless, this is not a primordial hatred embedded in Burman culture and identity – but a politically generated, while strong, resentment, based on nationalist ideology as a moral fact and collective representation (cf. Herzfeld 1992: 35).

Citizenship in Myanmar is therefore not a common and universalised form of social citizenship, but is divided into an ethnic/race hierarchy that excludes some inhabitants from 'constituted right to rights' (Balibar 2015: 65–66). They are even excluded from fighting for their civil rights and deprived of constitutional protection. The citizenship law and bureaucratic power reflect a deeper structural discrimination based on ethnic categorisation. Nationalist monks support bureaucratic measures by using their spiritual power, as discussed in the following section.

The spiritual power of monks

Parallel to power wielded by the bureaucracy is the *spiritual power* or 'influence' (Burmese: *awza*, as compared to *ana*, 'power/authority') of monks, who are often consulted by civilians in secular matters. Spiritual power is charismatic and depends on the status and knowledge of a monk.[11] However, in Pwo Karen religious power is *phya sa' nae aung*, (directly translated: 'trust in the monastery and in the *sasana*' ['the dispensations of the Buddha']). It means that people trust in the authority of Buddhist institutions and its leaders when they engage in secular life. When monks support the premises of ethnicity as a racial hierarchy, as described above – something they often do – their lay followers listen and agree – or at least do not contradict.

There is one Buddhist association that has been particularly active in anti-Muslim nationalism: the lay movement Ma Ba Tha, founded in 2014. The Ma Ba Tha is not a formal part of the Myanmar Buddhist monastic order (*sangha*) but it includes a significant number of monks. Ma Ba Tha monks have used, and sometimes abused, the authority derived from their monastic position. They have used negative ethnic categorisations of Muslims and Hindus and published extra-judicial rules excluding them, as described below.[12] The following is an outline of the dominant nationalist ideology of the Ma Ba Tha monks and their influence in Karen State, which is a Ma Ba Tha stronghold.

---

11 See Kawanami (2009: 223) and Gravers 2012 on Buddhist concepts of power. One is *kan-hpón*, 'karmic power'. Supra-normal power based on meditation is *abbiñña*, 'higher knowledge'; supernatural power is *dagó*.

12 Do we misunderstand the monks' role, as Walton (2017) argues we do? Their engaged Buddhism is a combination of charity among lay followers, promotion of Buddhism, and defence of nation, race, and Buddhism. These are intertwined. Some monks are supporters of the Union Solidarity Development Party (USDP), which is linked to the military; others are NLD supporters, but emphasise that they are not part of the political system. However, some monks have been used politically by USDP, and the recent 'communal violence' was exploited by the USDP, according to Zin (2015). Monks are not allowed to vote or to join political parties.

Those monks whom we interviewed who were not Ma Ba Tha agreed with the central ideology of the Ma Ba Tha, and with its fear of Islam, but disagreed with Ma Ba Tha's actions and rhetoric, as described below. Historically, it has always been problematic for monks to become involved in secular matters (*lokuttara*). This was evident during the demonstrations in 2007 (Gravers 2012).

In 2017, we interviewed the chairperson of Ma Ba Tha in Insein, the learned and highly respected Sayadaw U Tiloka Bhivamsa, Ywarma Sayadaw.[13] He emphasised his view that the protection of race and nation implies the protection of Buddhism 'because Myanmar is threatened by a Muslim invasion in Rakhine', he said. He explained that the 'Bengalis' (Rohingya) were guests in Myanmar and that they were displacing their host. 'When guests become immoral and do not respect their host's moral rules (*sila*) it is legitimate to defend race, nation, and religion. Muslims bribe authorities and are criminals who exploit the freedom under the NLD government. They are recruiting aggressively and are influenced by Western media', he said. Thus, Muslims threaten the morality and unity of Myanmar, in his view. He did not condone violence, however, stating: 'Those who use violence are not Buddhist – they do not understand Buddhism … We have to save the race and religion and avoid becoming like Afghanistan … We must attack them with *dhamma* (the Buddhist doctrine) and we must support our lay followers,' U Tiloka concluded.

The guest and host metaphor is important, because it defines access to the national territory and to citizenship, symbolically, as a question of hospitality and reciprocity. These are framed as the moral obligations of an outsider. If there is no reciprocity or proper deference, outsiders become a problem for the sovereignty of the perceived integrity of a homogeneous culture (Herzfeld 1992: 171, 175).[14] In Myanmar, a threat to the nation is a threat to 'race' and to Buddhism as well. In Ma Ba Tha logic, this situation demands defence and special bureaucratic control of the Muslim population.[15]

---

13 U Tiloka Bhivamsa was jailed in 1990 for his protests against the military dictatorship. We would like to express our gratitude to Htet Min Lwin, who introduced us to the monk and translated our conversation.

14 U Tiloka mentioned that some Muslim students did not pay respect to Myanmar's flag in schools.

15 This has been a constant theme in Myanmar's history. It was expressed in a nationalist song used during the anti-Indian riots in 1938: 'Exploiting our economic

All Ma Ba Tha monks we interviewed mentioned conversion from Buddhism to other religions as a threat to Buddhism, as well as to race and nation. This is because renouncing Buddhism also means changing one's national, cultural, and ethnic identity – as explained in the quote from Aung San Suu Kyi above. It becomes an attack on national unity and is thus a disloyal action and a moral failure.

One Ma Ba Tha monk in Mawlamyine, who also mentioned the demographic problem, explained that some Muslims are good, but '[people of] mixed race' (*amyo kabya*) are impolite and bad Muslims – 'not real Muslims'. This is another reason for arguing against mixed marriages. Those who insult Ma Ba Tha and aim to repeal the four 'race protection' laws and those who want to change the constitution are classified as enemies.[16]

In Hpa-An, the leading Ma Ba Tha monk at Zwe Kabin Mountain, Sayadaw U Kawidaza, a Bamar, is Ma Ba Tha vice-chairman and has been head of the Hpa-An Sangha Council. He became Sayadaw in 1995, when the Democratic Karen Buddhist Army (DKBA) and the army gained control over the district.[17] He is known to have a close relationship with the former military leader Than Shwe and his wife. U Kawidaza explained that in his view: 'Muslims are extremists and have a plan to rule the world in the 21st century. That is why they use the numbers 786 on their halal shops. This is a numerological conspiracy, because 7+8+6 is 21,' he said. 'Muslims almost rule Thailand,' he claimed, adding: 'The Thai PM (General Phrayut) is a Muslim – and Muslims also want to control Myanmar. They have five wives and 15 children. They bully and rape minority women. That is why Ma Ba Tha monks here have put up the signboards urging people not to trade with Kalar or sell houses or land to them'.[18]

---

resources, seizing our women, we are in danger of racial extinction' (cited in Yi 1988: 96; see also D.E. Smith 1965 and Mendelson 1975 on the 1938 riots).

16 The four 'race protection' laws are: 1) the monogamy law; 2) the Buddhist special marriage act (official approval for interfaith marriages); 3) the religious conversion act (application to township conversion board); and 4) the population control law, which urges people to limit the number of children they have. The laws have support in the population – in particular among women (Walton et al. 2016).

17 DKBA was formed in 1994 by the monk U Thuzana and with the help of the Burmese army. See Gravers (2018).

18 The category Kalar includes Hindus, although we were told they used to be termed *Galae*, perhaps derived from Mon *gola*, cf. footnote no 3. Hindus are not mentioned

Figure 7.1 Pagoda constructed by the late monk U Thuzana at the entrance of a Muslim mosque in a town near Hpa-An in 2017. *Colour image,p. 364.*

He explained how the Muslims and Hindus have taken over the market in Hpa-An, from the Clock Tower to the Hlaing Bwe road junction. This perception of Muslims being aggressive in their economic expansion is sometimes voiced among Karen who feel they cannot compete with skilled Muslim traders. He said that Muslims favour their relatives and other Muslims, expand their communities, and squeeze Karen out. Karen from other denominations seem to share this perception. For example, a Christian Pwo Karen village on the road to Mawlamyine has banned Muslim, Hindu, and Chinese from settling in the village. The Pwo Karen pastor said that if they settle, they soon dominate life and trade in the village: 'They use their money to take our girls, control business, and overwhelm us' (*ma noêng ma na* in Pwo). Other Christian informants gave more examples of anti-Kalar attitudes among Christian Karen.

Many lay people are involved with Ma Ba Tha. We interviewed members of the committee of Ma Ba Tha (Karen State), all of whom were Bamar businessmen. They emphasised, that 'they help and defend the Karen nationality' vigorously in charity work. For instance, they said, they run a clinic at Mae Baung Monastery, and they insisted it was open to everyone, including Kalar. They help Karen IDPs in Myaing Gyi Ngu with food, and they confirmed that the Border Guard Force (BGF) supports the association.[19] They were proud of an alleged donation of 2000 lakh MMK to the military border fence in Northern Rakhine State, which they claimed was set up to defend the nation against a Muslim invasion.[20]

as enemies, perhaps because their temples have Buddha statues and are often visited by Buddhists.

19 Myaing Gyi Ngu is the centre of the late monk U Thuzana and the former headquarter of the DKBA. BGF was formed in 2010 by units from DKBA, the Democratic Karen Buddhist Army. The army (Tatmadaw) controls BGF.

20 One lakh is MMK 100,000, circa USD 65. 2000 lakh MMK is USD 130,000.

Although we did not hear monks in Karen State condone violence, their rhetoric of defence implies their support of potentially violent actions. A violent rhetoric was evident in October 2017 during the Rakhine crisis, when the Sitagu Sayadaw gave an important sermon in a Tatmadaw camp in Karen State.[21] He is one of Myanmar's most influential monks. He used to support the party in power, the National League for Democracy (NLD), but is now connected to Ma Ba Tha. In his speech, he drew on the 5th century Sinhalese Mahavamsa chronicle about King Dhuttegamani, who drove out an army of Tamils and killed 'millions'. The king felt remorse and consulted eight monks, who explained that non-Buddhists were not to be considered any higher than beasts and half-humans. Thus, what he had done was not an action bringing negative *karma*. Therefore, Burmese soldiers need not worry when they follow orders and engage in fighting, as they do in Rakhine, against the Arakan Rohingya Salvation Army. The military (the Tatmadaw) is needed to protect Buddhism, as the monks are needed to promote the Buddhist doctrine. The Sitagu Sayadaw thus condoned what Balibar (2015: 85) terms 'preventative counter violence' in the name of protecting Buddhism and the nation. The Sitagu Sayadaw legitimised the Tatmadaw's use of force, its political position, and indirectly the exclusion of non-Buddhists.[22] This alliance of an influential monk known for his secular engagement in charity and the army underlines the climate of fear among many ordinary people of all denominations in Karen State rooted in the interfaith tensions present in the state and the uncertain ceasefire situation. Widespread access to social media since 2010 has meant that sermons by monks are instantly shared, as are rumours of a Muslim invasion and other fake news. The following two sections describe how the discrimination against Muslim and Hindu communities occurs and what effects it has.

Karen Muslim communities: Between harmony and religious tensions

Muslims first came to the area near the Thanlwin River before 1900. Scott O'Connor, who travelled along the river around 1900, reported

21 See Paul Fuller (2017) for a translation of the sermon.

22 The concept of no-harm, no-violence – *ahimsa* – is part of the 8-fold path of Buddhist ethics. Direct intentional harm produces negative merit. See Jerryson (2018) for an important discussion of Buddhism and violence.

that the polers who operated his boat were Muslims, and that the small district town of Papun had a wooden mosque and a few shops belonging to Chittagongians, i.e. Muslims from Chittagong (O'Connor 1904: 310, 316).[23] Muslim and Hindu traders and farmers settled in and around Hpa-an and Shwe Gon.

The ancestors of the Karen Muslims we interviewed, who are mainly peasants, came to the area around 1900, from Bengal. They were probably from the poorest segment of Sunni Muslims. Most of the migrants were men, who married Karen women and settled in Buddhist Pwo Karen villages. They identify as Phloung (Pwo) Muslim, speak mainly Pwo Karen, and grow paddy and raise animals, as do their Buddhist neighbours. The houses are not very different from the solid teak houses of Buddhist Pwo. We did not encounter any Muslim Karen families where a man had more than one wife. The Village Tract Administrator confirmed that there are none. It is crucial for these people to identify as Karen Muslims in order to signify that they are integrated into the local communities.

During the Rakhine crisis in August 2017, villagers in the Pwo Karen Muslim village and the neighbouring Buddhist Pwo Karen village south of Hpa-An formed vigilante units to patrol their area together. Rumours on social media had warned against Rohingya spies and a Muslim invasion. Authorities urged villages to patrol the outskirts and report on strangers (see also Chapter 6, this volume). At night, the roads were silent for two weeks. Then the villagers decided to stop patrolling – nothing had happened. However, in this way Karen Muslims and Buddhist Karen had confirmed their wish to cooperate and preserve harmony – a harmony contradicting the sad tales of 'communal violence' in Rakhine State – 'which are not of our concern', the Karen Muslim village administrator (VA) emphasised.[24] While Karen

23 On the immigration of Muslims from India and to the present, see Bennison (1931) on the British Census, Yegar (1972), Taylor (1981), Egreteau (2011), Berlie (2008). On the Rohingya crisis, see Wade (2017). On Hindu migration, see Binns (1935), Tin Gyi (1931), Adas (1974), and Harvey (1972).

24 Interview in November 2018. This chapter is based on fieldwork in 2017 and 2018. We are grateful for the excellent assistance of three Karen researchers, Saw Say Wah, Saw Eh Dah and Nan Tin Nilar Win, who provided contacts and helped in interviews and analysis of data. We do not disclose the names or location of the villages in order to protect the identity of vulnerable informants. We conducted intensive interviews with more than 50 persons, both male and female, including village administrators

Muslims emphasised a strong sense of belonging to their mixed communities, some Buddhist Karen villagers regarded them with suspicion; however, Karen Muslims were not threatened during this episode. As of 2019, there have been no incidents of communal violence.

Than Pale (Chapter 6, this volume) gives a detailed description of how villagers in another mixed community have tried to avoid or defuse conflicts in order to preserve harmony. However, this harmony is not found in all parts of Karen State. The situation for Muslims became more precarious after the DKBA was founded. The DKBA and its patron U Thuzana evicted Muslims from Myaing Gyi Ngu and Kamamaung in 1995. U Thuzana's idea was to revitalise what he believed to be an old Buddhist civilisation and unite all Karen groups. Thus, Christians and Muslims were excluded from his domain.[25] In 2001, nation-wide anti-Muslim riots hit Karen State. In 2006, there were 30,000 Muslim refugees in camps in Thailand, and even more Muslims were living as migrants outside the camps.[26]

In 2017 and 2018, we conducted fieldwork in two Pwo Karen Muslim villages, which both have an adjacent neighbouring village that is inhabited by Buddhist Pwo Karen. The first Pwo Karen Muslim village and its neighbouring Pwo Karen Buddhist village are situated south of Ein Du town, where Ma Ba Tha has a stronghold.[27] The second pair of villages is situated south of Hpa-An, with less direct Ma Ba Tha influence.

Relations between Karen Muslims and Karen Buddhists

The first Karen Muslim village and its neighbouring Karen Buddhist village used to be one village and was called 'Peaceful Land' in Pwo Karen. According to the Village Tract Administrator (VTA) it is also still registered as 'the same territory' (i.e. as one village) by the Land Registration

in two Muslim villages, two Hindu communities and Pwo Buddhist villages, NGO leaders, Karen, Hindu, and Muslim leaders, Interfaith and Ma Ba Tha leaders and Buddhist monks. We are most grateful for the friendly reception we received and for the conversations with all our informants.

25 On the DKBA and its patron, U Thuzana, the Myaing Gyi Ngu Sayadaw, see Gravers 2015a and 2018.

26 See Karen Human Rights Group (2002) and Blair and Zaw (2006). We have not found any recent figures for Muslim refugees and migrants.

27 In Ein Du, a Ma Ba Tha stronghold, Muslims are not permitted to live in the town, but they can still own shops.

Department. However, in reality, the village is now perceived as split into two villages or sections: the Muslim and the Buddhist villages. The Pwo Karen Muslim village has 45 households, and the neighbouring Buddhist Pwo Karen village has 35 households. The Karen Muslims grow only one rice crop per year and have no other important crops. They raise cows, goats and ducks for sale, and their economic status is generally equal to that of their Buddhist Karen neighbours. They told us stories of Muslim men converting to Buddhism or Christianity in the past and following the religion of their Pwo Karen wife in accordance with Karen custom.

We interviewed a former Karen Buddhist VTA who said that Muslims had lived in the area for more than 100 years, and no major conflicts had occurred. Karen Muslim villagers confirmed this and said that the Buddhists and Muslims used to participate in each other's religious festivals and other events, as Than Pale (Chapter 6) describes, although the two groups no longer pray or pay respect to each other's religious buildings. A Ma Ba Tha monk from a neighbouring monastery stopped the sale of houses to Muslims, and the local monk applies one of the Ma Ba Tha rules – that Karen Muslims cannot buy land from Buddhist Karen – although he is not against trading with Muslims and Hindus. He also advises against intermarriage or conversion to Islam. However, the VTA emphasised that Muslims do come and seek his advice. At the same time, a Ma Ba Tha monk from a neighbouring monastery stopped sale of houses to Muslims.

In this area, monks have put up their four rules in front of houses owned by the Pwo Karen Buddhists: 'Do not buy from Muslims; do not sell to Muslims; Muslims cannot own land; Muslims cannot own houses.' In 2017, monks and police put up a red signboard at the road leading to another Buddhist Karen village saying: 'Drugs and Kalar of other religions no entrance.' In 2018, a new signboard saying 'All Kalar no entrance' was put up. The reason for setting up the first signboard, we were told, was that the daughter of the Buddhist Village Administrator (VA) had married a Muslim man. The couple was evicted from the village after intervention of local Ma Ba Tha monks, and the VA had to step down.

In 2017, The Maha Nayaka Sangha Council, the governing body of state monastic order, stated that Ma Ba Tha was not an organisation recognised within the sangha and its nine sects, according to section 4 in the Sangha rules. The council later banned the name Ma Ba Tha and its signboards and activities, but the leading monk in Hpa-An refused to remove the signboards. In 2018, we saw the signboards in Hpa-An and in villages. One signboard that had been put up for a meeting in Hpa-An in 2017 was still in place in November 2018. The BGF, and a small unit of DKBA that remains loyal to U Thuzana support the Ma Ba Tha in Karen State. These armed groups sometimes appear at the monasteries 'providing security' and giving donations (Hintharnee 2017). Anti-Muslim inhabitants in Karen State thought this alliance was a force strong enough to control the Muslims.

Figure 7.2 Signboard at the entrance to a Buddhist Karen village. It reads "Drugs & Kalar of other religions no entrance". *Colour image, p. 365.*

During our fieldwork it became apparent that the two villages had an increasingly tense relationship. A conflict arose when a Muslim man began constructing a house on what he claimed was his own land. The place of construction was situated near the Buddhist village section, and subsequently the two female village administrators (VAs) of the Buddhist village, who led actions against Muslims, claimed that the place was inside their part of the village. The Muslim man stopped the construction, and the Buddhist section demarcated their part with boundary poles in order to separate the two communities, even though the VTA said that the two villages were one. The Muslim man can still grow rice on 'his' land, but the conflict escalated and involved both villages. When the Buddhist villagers demanded that the Muslims repaired the road near the disputed land, the Muslims replied, 'But you say the road is in your village'. They only repaired their part of the road. However, the Karen Muslims emphasised that they tried to avoid conflicts, as they know they would lose any dispute or conflict with the Karen Buddhists. In case of accidents or conflicts, they always have to pay more in compensation, they told us. An important challenge for the Muslims is their lack of official documentation.

Few Karen Muslims in this village have citizenship cards, and those who applied never got a reply from the immigration authorities. Some have the new green ethnic verification card, but even that is difficult to obtain. Without this, a person cannot travel, get a driver's licence, or borrow money. The ID card problems are elaborated below, but these people obviously feel discriminated against, and they clearly have very limited access to justice. They do not have title deed on their land – only tax receipts – and own less land than their Buddhist Pwo Karen neighbours. If they do not use their land, it comes under the new land act, the Vacant, Fallow, and Virgin Land Management Law, of 2012 and could be confiscated unless a person has a title deed. This is a common problem in Karen State and elsewhere. However, Karen Muslims here have the green farming book, an official document, which allows them to borrow money for farming.

In 2017, we visited their new mosque. Karen Muslim informants explained that it was completed just before the four 'race and religion protection laws' were approved by the parliament in 2015 (see note 16). The construction would not have been possible after that time when authorities generally began to reject permissions to build mosques. We did not hear about polygamy, and women generally do not wear a scarf, only in the Koran School. We saw young women return from the Koran school with a scarf and remove it at home. As most villages in Karen State, young people migrate to Thailand and Malaysia. However, without ID cards they have to pay a smuggler at least 6–7 lakh MMK (USD 4–500) and stay as illegals. Some are able to send remittances and help their family.

The Pwo Buddhist VTA emphasised that despite these challenges for the Karen Muslims – in addition to the Ma Ba Tha interventions – interactions between the two communities were in general amicable. However, the Karen Muslims feared that tensions with their Karen Buddhist neighbours could escalate due to Ma Ba Tha influence. Concerning ID cards, the old three-folded green card, as we were shown, secures 'naturalised citizenship' for persons whose parents lived in Myanmar before Independence in 1948 but did not register at that time.[28] We have not seen the blue card for 'associate ('guest') citizenship'. The two cards are probably not re-issued any more. These two cards were supposed to qualify for a full citizenship with a pink card in due time. The recent green plastic card is a national/ethnic

28 In a population of 1.5 million in Karen State, the 2014 census lists 656,024 as holding full citizenship, 624 people with 'associate' citizenship, 7,521 who are naturalised and 17,639 who hold the green national/ethnic registration card with limited rights. However, many in KNU-controlled areas were not counted.

verification card, asking the holder to apply for citizenship. Muslims mentioned a new brown national registration card, which we did not see.[29] In 2015, Thein Sein's government issued the white card for foreigners to Karen Muslims. It would have enabled them to vote but it was quickly withdrawn before elections because the Union Solidarity Development Party (USDP), the military's party, sensed the general, historically founded Burman resentment towards Muslims as 'foreign immigrants'. While the area around Ein Du is under strong Ma Ba Tha influence, there are pockets less influenced by the Ma Ba Tha north of the town as described below.

The second Karen Muslim village

The other Karen Muslim village we studied has 57 households, and its twin Buddhist Karen village has 98 households. Whereas the first pair of villages seem to have been one administrative unit before tensions arose, the second pair of villages are separate administrative units with a Karen Muslim village administrator in the Muslim village and a Buddhist Karen in the other. However, Karen Muslims and Buddhists both emphasised that they considered the two villages 'to be one community'.

A third neighbouring village, which is mixed Karen Muslim and Karen Buddhist, has three monasteries and a mosque, which also serve the two villages discussed here. There are fields belonging to Karen Muslims situated near this village.[30] Most households in the Muslim village have land of their own; only two or three households do not possess land and rent from neighbours. The living standard in these villages is that of an average lowland Karen village. All the people we met emphasised the fact that there is a harmonious relationship between the two communities. They give donations to each other's festivals but do not join in. Muslims do not take food from Buddhists, which could contain pork. Muslims grow paddy on irrigated land. They can grow two crops every year – 'winter rice' (*ba dah*) and 'summer rice' (*dawae*).

In the Karen Muslim village, we enquired about their citizenship and ID cards, and many informants came to us with their stories, while we sat in houses or shops. At least half of the households have members who are migrants in Thailand and Malaysia. However, it is increasingly

29 Perhaps this is the new citizenship scrutiny card mentioned in KHRG 2017.

30 These three villages may have been administered as one village in the past.

difficult to migrate now. Without pink ID cards, it is impossible to obtain a passport. Migration is a crucial part of the economy in Karen State, and half of the younger population is absent.[31] Most remit some money to parents and grandparents, who look after their children. If they migrate without a passport, they have to be smuggled out of Myanmar. They pay at least 12 lakh MMK (approximately USD 780) to get to Thailand, and even more to get to Malaysia. Sometimes they take a loan from a loan shark; if they do this, they pay ten per cent interest per month to borrow one lakh MMK.

It was difficult to get a clear picture of how many people in this Muslim village have full citizenship. However, an estimate by an older man was that fewer than 20 households (of 57) do, and it is mostly older persons who still have the pink card. If they lose their cards, they cannot obtain new ones. Those who have pink cards had Buddhist Pwo Karen parents. When there is a mixed marriage, it is much more difficult to obtain citizenship, because people of 'mixed race' are not considered to be 'pure' (in other words, they are not considered to be *taing-yin-tha* – see footnote 2), as explained above. One old man showed us his pink card. It categorised him as *Bangala Kayin Islam* (Bengali Karen Muslim). He had obtained it many years ago. His son only has a folded green card, as a 'naturalised citizen'. He will have to apply for a pink card and pay at least four lakh MMK for it. The old man's grandmother was a Karen and was, interestingly, a sister of the Kyaung Ga Lae Sayadaw, an influential monk nearby who is a member of Ma Ba Tha. The old man's son studied in a Muslim Seminary in Uthar Pradesh, India to become a Mulawi – a Koran teacher in a local Koran School. This is now one of the few career paths open to the younger generation of Muslims, who cannot get citizenship. He had a daughter who stopped going to school after grade 11 without obtaining a certificate. She has only a green verification card and can never enter university. The old man said: 'We were born here, and we have grown up here, we have Karen parents or grandparents. Why can we not obtain citizenship? We are unhappy – disillusioned (in Pwo Karen *mau ae*')'.

31 The 2014 Census of Myanmar (Republic of the Union of Myanmar 2015: 142, 145) listed 304,980 migrants from Karen State in Thailand of a total of 1,418,472 Myanmar migrants. The population of Karen State was listed as 1,574,079 people, but many were not enumerated.

A married couple told us that he had a pink card and she had a three-folded green card obtained thirty years earlier. All five of their children have pink cards – and the wife said that she had paid 10 lakh MMK for four cards in 2017, for four of the children, and her husband had paid two lakh MMK for the fifth. She said that she had not paid for a pink card for herself, as she does not travel. 'Only Muslims have to pay that much', she explained (she described what they had to pay, in Pwo, as *being thjông pado* – 'big money'). How did they get the pink cards? Her husband is from Hpa-An and has 'good connections' (*a say a shwe* in Burmese), she explained. They did not disclose their 'connections' – this could well be with a member of USDP (see Harrisson 2018, on the relationship between Muslims and the USDP in Mon State).

In the past, informants said, people did not worry about ID cards. During the civil war, which is described as the 'rebellion era' (*tabôn khé),* authorities were not always within reach. In 2001, after the nationwide anti-Muslim riots (Karen Human Rights Group 2002) it became increasingly difficult to obtain ID cards, informants explained. Some were told directly that immigration authorities had stopped issuing cards to Muslims. Those who are not registered and have a youth card have to take an oath in the local court when they turn 18. They must promise to be loyal citizens and they have to renounce their Muslim heritage. They must do this before applying. They also have to make informal payments to the court. They have to make one to the court secretary of MMK 5,000, one of MMK 10,000 to the 'legal supervisor' and finally one of MMK 15,000 to the judge. The NGO representative in Hpa-An who explained this to us said that the amounts were unofficial payments to achieve 'mutual understanding' and are what is referred to as 'tea-money'. Unofficial payments like these are considered normal, and a necessary reciprocity for a service. There are a number of terms which relate to these payments in both Pwo Karen and in Burmese, including the term being *thjông phado* ('big money') mentioned above, *aung being thjông* in Pwo Karen ('to eat money'), and *lat be-lat yu* in Burmese ('money service'). However, when these payments are regarded as unjustified or do not lead to a result, Karen resent them.

One story from this Karen Muslim village illustrates many of the problems of bureaucratic indifference and structural discrimination encountered by Muslims. The person who told us the story is an older

Karen Muslim with a family of seven children. One daughter and two sons work in Thailand. Three daughters live in the village (there was no mention of their spouses). The informant was afraid to speak but decided to do so after we guaranteed not to disclose our informant's identity. Hence, the wording in the following is somewhat awkward. The informant holds a pink card with the categorisation *Kayin Bouda Batha* (Karen Buddhist). This was obtained 30 years ago, when the immigration authorities came to the informant's village and issued cards, and the informant paid a fee of MMK 300 for it. One of the informant's grandmothers was Karen, and one grandfather was Muslim. The informant's mother was Karen, and the informant's father was of 'mixed race'. One of the informant's sons holds a three-folded green card categorising him as *Bangala Kayin Islam* (Bengali Karen Muslim). This son's passport was about to expire while he was in Thailand, and he needed a new ID card in order to renew his passport. He thought MMK 50,000 would be sufficient to cover this. He needed a letter from the immigration office, but the immigration officers were not allowed to issue the letter before he had his ID card. Therefore, the family contacted a broker who demanded 10 lakh MMK. Our informant went to the immigration office with the broker, who remained outside the office. The broker did not help our informant, who had to negotiate alone with the official. It took a year to sort out, and at every meeting, the official asked our informant for shrimps from the village. He got the shrimps, and the broker saw this and posted the fact that these had been given to the official on Facebook, saying: 'My client gave shrimps – got no ID card'. He did this ostensibly because he wanted to expose the official. The broker ridiculed his client for not following his advice. The official became angry and refused to deal with our informant. A new broker was hired, who asked for four lakh MMK. This time our informant had again to go in alone to negotiate with the official. Another year passed. Our informant paid for fingerprints, documents from school, from the police, and from a VTA, but nothing happened, and the informant complained to the VTA. This made the broker angry. The son of our informant then declared that his parent talked too much, and he preferred to return from Thailand – after three years had gone by and a lot of money had been spent.[32] Our informant was ashamed, and did not

32 'To talk too much' (*khlaing ah*) in Pwo Karen means to be too visible, to boast, to be annoying, and not to be respectful. The broker was probably angry that he too

want to be seen. The official who handled the case is a Christian. The staff at the office always referred to our informant as 'that Kalar' and talked down to our informant. Despite the ID card categorising our informant as Karen Buddhist, our informant did not hide the identity as a Muslim at the office. Our informant sometimes had to wait outside the office until eight in the evening. Every time our informant went to the office, the informant left 'tea money' under the papers. The officials asked for documents relating to the informant's grandparents. However, these documents do not exist. Meanwhile, our informant saw that Buddhist Karen would get their papers in five days, after paying MMK 50,000. A green card only allows one month of travel and the holder may face two years in jail if he or she exceeds this, our informant learned. Three of our informant's children have a green card, and for the son's card the informant paid 2,5 lakh MMK five years ago, but our informant could not get the pink card at that time. It is obvious that our informant did not have 'connections'. Our informant's brokers were all Muslims but they could not really help. Because their client, our informant, insisted on trying, our informant ended up paying 'big money'.

Every year, immigration officials come to the schools to hand out cards for children's examinations, but cards are not issued to Muslims. They must go to the office in Hpa-An and see if they can get one. Buddhist Karen children who do well in school sometimes get three lakh as a prize from the Buddhist *sangha*. Muslim children are not given prizes. Informants said that this is because of instructions given by the leading Ma Ba Tha monk, the Zwe Kabin Sayadaw. Since they cannot get a high school certificate, many Karen Muslim children drop out of school and enter the Koran school. Without a certificate, they cannot enter university. As their parents do not want to pay for school uniform, books and 'donations' to teachers, Muslim children often leave school before the 10th or 11th grade. The 'donation' referred to here is *cetana* – a 'goodwill' gift from the parents. Unless this payment is made, children risk bad treatment in school.

Another problem here, and in Buddhist Pwo villages as well, is the household list. A person must be on the list in order to obtain an ID card. We heard examples of parents who were travelling when the

---

was drawn into the conflict. The informant's son thought that our informant did not know the proper tactics and behaviour. See Harrisson's (2018) analysis of the navigation skills of Muslims in similar situations.

officials came to register children. In some cases, parents even forgot to mention the name of one child. If a person is not on the household list, he/she is left without identity papers, pinned to the place where they live and without any rights: They become virtual non-persons. It is generally impossible to get one's name on to the list once one is an adult, we were told. This situation creates major justice and security problems for persons who are not on the list. They cannot travel safely and are barred from jobs in state institutions.

Yet there are also paradoxes. These two Karen Muslim and Karen Buddhist communities enjoy the protection of Bo Mu Thu, an influential Buddhist Karen BGF commander, who is from the Karen Buddhist village. He often comes and urges the two groups to live in harmony. Recently, he was appointed special patron (*nayaga*) of the Interfaith Dialogue Group (IDG), which normally has patrons from the major religious denominations. The event when he was appointed patron was supported by a donation of 50 lakh MMK to the IDG from a hotel owner and crony, who had made the proposal to appoint Bo Mu Thu. While this type of contact with armed groups such as the BGF does not change the fact that there is general suppression of Muslims, it may provide some protection.

Losing influence and living subdued – Hindu communities

In 2017–2018, we held a number of interviews with Hindus in Hpa-An town. We visited one Hindu hamlet several times and interviewed a Hindu 10-household leader from a nearby community. Most Hindus, urban as well as rural, explained that their great-grandfathers had come from South India, but that their grandparents were born in Burma. Like the Muslims, none of the Hindus we spoke to could or would say from which specific location in India his or her ancestors had come. We had the clear impression that Hindu communities had actively terminated their connections with India a long time previously. Especially the rural Hindus would speak Pwo as their first language. They all said that they still have the freedom to practise their religion. Hinduism is considered very close to Buddhism, and many Buddhists attend ceremonies in Hindu temples. Buddha images were also in prominent positions in all Hindu temples we visited. In the large temple in Hpa-An there are also pictures of the prominent monks U Thuzana and the Thamanya Sayadaw.

Hindu leaders explained that in the past, they had had access to leading Buddhists and officials, and these connections have been part of their authority and influence. However, during the last 20 years their communities have been under pressure and have been subject to various limitations in their access to the state and to the authorities in general. They have been subject to land grabbing; their land has been expropriated for roads, for military camps, and for development projects. They have received very little compensation, if any. For example, the Tatmadaw confiscated land belonging to the main Hindu temple in Hpa-An in order to expand a nearby camp. Hindu leaders said they had repeatedly found that going to the courts did not work. They would spend large sums of money and still lose the case, because they are Hindus. Formerly, Hindu leaders could find a way out of the situation in such cases.

As with Muslims, the main concern that Hindus have is the difficulties they experience in renewing and obtaining ID cards. They said that previously they had been able to get ID cards, often with the help of local Hindu leaders and brokers. People whose parents had had ID cards had been able to acquire them too. Recently, however, it has become an extremely tedious process to obtain ID cards. In fact, each time we talked to Hindu leaders we found that the difficulties had increased. Eventually, they told us that many of their leaders had not even been able to obtain ID cards. In recent years, they have tried many times, using various approaches, to obtain them, but always with negative results.

They explained that rural as well as urban Hindus now need 21 signatures on an application for citizenship: six at township level, eight at state level, and finally seven at national level. Those at national level are required because the applicants are considered foreigners and are not one of the 135 *taing-yin-tha* (see footnote 2) in Myanmar. Each time they need a signature they have to pay an official. Very few people – especially among Hindu villagers, as explained below, but also among less influential townspeople – are able to get all these signatures together on their own, so they have to rely on a broker or an influential Hindu.

Hindus we met in Hpa-An town said that only 100 Hindus in Hpa-An district had pink ID cards, while 3,000 have green ethnic verification cards. They said that altogether more than 600 Hindus in Hpa-An township have applied for ID cards, and are waiting for them. None of them has received a response as yet. They are now realising that this could become a permanent situation. They fear that there will be no future for their children, who will not even be able to receive examination certificates. Moreover, with no ID cards they cannot get government loans or an official position. Without proper ID, their income possibilities have also narrowed.[33]

Figure 7.3 The Buddha is placed in a prominent position among the Hindu gods signifying the closeness between Hinduism and Buddhism. Behind the Buddha is a photo of the Karen monk U Thuzana. *Colour image, p. 365.*

As in Muslim communities, this gradual exclusion has had a huge impact on the social lives of Hindus. Due to their degraded status and lack of ID cards, they face problems if they enter into a dispute, or if someone takes part of their land. They are now deprived their rights in court cases and in administrative matters. Even in everyday situations such as traffic accidents, they face problems and have to pay even if they are the injured party. Leading Hindus explained that they had requested a meeting with the chief minister, and they had still been able to arrange this. The chief minister had said that she would do her best to help them. However, this has led to nothing so far. One of the leaders of the Hindu community told us that after he had been waiting for many months for a new ID card, he wanted to shorten the long process and had paid five lakh MMK to the immigration officer, without receiving a receipt. When he later came to enquire about the case, the officer just asked, 'Who are you?' The Hindu leader told us that he had become furious with the officer and had scolded him, using strong words. He was clearly frustrated by the fact that he had got nothing back in return for the payments he had made. This experience of negative reciprocity is not uncommon, as discussed below. After this happened, he realised that there was no point proceeding any further along these lines. He reported the officer to the chief minister. Again, nothing came out of this. Therefore, the Hindu leaders said, they have concluded that strategies of paying bribes, engaging authorities, hiring brokers, and even bringing cases to the chief minister do not work for them any longer.

33 A group interview in the Hindu hamlet painted a similar bleak picture.

There was no room for tactical manoeuvre anymore. They were being met by total bureaucratic indifference (cf. Herzfeld 1992).

Challenges for rural Hindus

Hindus in the countryside live in small hamlets that are parts of larger villages, in which there are also Buddhist Karen and Pa-O. Houses in the village visited are of a reasonable standard, mainly due to remittances from labour migration to Malaysia. From the small hamlet's 30 households, 2 women and 18 men are in Malaysia. Only a few households have irrigated rice. All households have cattle, poultry, and ducks. They grow vegetables and sell these in neighbouring Buddhist villages or work in the neighbouring villages as unskilled agricultural and construction labourers.

In the village cluster, several 10-household leaders are Hindus. Even though there are more than 100 Hindu households in the village tract, they have not been allowed to elect a 100-household leader or a VA (Village Administrator). A VTA from another village tract told us that Buddhist villagers in the village tract would not allow a Hindu to become a VA. He told us that Kalar are not allowed to wield this authority, because of the strong influence of Ma Ba Tha in the village tract.

As in the urban context, there are many uncertainties with ID cards. During the civil war, the villagers did not worry about having ID cards, but now they are essential, as the Myanmar state is taking more control. However, only a few people have ID cards and passports. The villagers explained that immigration officers came to the village in 2010 and issued ID cards to everyone over 16 years of age. They were given green cards, i.e. national or ethnic verification cards carrying the right to apply for citizenship. We saw one woman's green card that stated that she is Tamil Buddhist. Thus, Hindus are at times classified as Buddhists. Only very few people have a pink card now and are able to obtain passports. Of the 20 people who are in Malaysia, only three have passports. The other 17 travel illegally, with all the dangers this involves. Some have tried to obtain a passport through a broker, but they have not succeeded. As in Muslim communities, Hindus in this village believe that the difficulty in obtaining ID cards is due to an order from the national level. During interviews in the hamlet, they told us that 20 per cent have green cards while 80 per cent have nothing. It is the same for women and men. They also informed us that two or three old people have the old green folded card (naturalised citizenship). They also told us that 20–30 people from the hamlet had gone to Hpa-An to apply for pink cards. They had paid 6–7 lakh MMK each to a broker. However, the broker had disappeared after he had received the money.

We asked the villagers what they hope for in the future. They said that they want to be normal respected taxpaying citizens with ID cards, to be able to do business, to work like other people, and to be able to travel legally to Malaysia. These humble requests are, however, impossible to realise in the present situation. Hindu leaders cannot do much to help them. In fact, Hindu leaders explained that they feared losing their own status and authority. They feel that they are unable to serve their ethnic constituencies and say that they cannot act as intermediaries because they are denied real access to the state and its authorities. They are excluded because of bureaucratic indifference and have lost any possibility of navigating Buddhist Burmese society.

While possibilities for tactical manoeuvring are restricted in the social domain, there are still some possibilities for Hindus in the religious domain. However, these also seem to be narrowing. They said that at present there is only one influential religious individual whom the Hindu leaders could approach to help them in important cases. This is Ashin Pyinyathami, the Taunggalay Sayadaw, who resides north of Hpa-An.[34] We interviewed the Sayadaw, and he said that he would only involve himself in important cases, not petty cases. He also told us that in the cases he took on, he focused on recreating harmony and did not insist on justice. In all the cases in which he had become involved, the Hindus had been determined to be guilty, but fines had been of a reasonable size, and anger from the involved Buddhists had been effectively defused. Hindus to whom we spoke were convinced that the Sayadaw had to make such decisions, even if they were unjust; otherwise the cases could not have been closed, and there would have been tensions in the community. It was a strategy to defuse conflicts and not one intended to achieve justice (cf. Harrisson 2018).

One village monk near the first Karen Muslim village, who is a Ma Ba Tha sympathiser, explained the purpose of gradual exclusion. He

34 This Pa-o-Karen Monk has connections to Than Shwe's (previous military general and head of state) wife and is very influential. He has been involved in a major land grab case (see Gravers forthcoming).

believes that the Kalar are attempting to become powerful. When we pointed out that the Hindu villagers are particularly weak and powerless, he replied that they (and the Muslims) should be excluded in order to keep them weak. 'They are only weak because they are subdued,' he emphasised. If they had the chance, he said, they would inevitably show their true aggressive face. He said that 'the Hindus are also Kalar, so they have the same nature'. It can be argued that he and other monks are exponents of Balibar's 'preventative repression' (2015: 85) and of symbolic violence. However, we also learned that Buddhist Karen ignore the Ma Ba Tha ban to trade with Hindu vendors who sell vegetables and fish in Karen Buddhist villages. These vendors are regarded as providing fair credit to their Karen Buddhist customers.

Concluding discussion: The effects of exclusion

Discrimination against Karen Muslims and Hindus has three main elements: 1) legal, bureaucratic discrimination against them as minority ethnic groups; 2) discrimination against them from a religious, spiritual and moral perspective, which is connected to the bureaucratic and ethnic discrimination that they experience; 3) social exclusion, in that they have limited rights and limited space to manoeuvre, including exclusion from the right to vote. The powers and influences used against these two groups produce a combination of structural, cultural and symbolic violence, and ultimately a denial of justice. Following Herzfeld (1992), we would argue that the bureaucratic indifference which they experience is a denial of identity and a rejection of their legal existence in Myanmar. This discrimination creates internal boundaries between them and other groups, and deprives these two groups of 'the right to fight for their rights' (Balibar 2015: 66, 69).

As demonstrated in this chapter, the space of exclusion in which Hindus and Muslims exist is characterised by limited access to ID cards, limited right to travel and limited access to health and education. Their ownership rights are also limited, and their personal rights of contact and intermarriage seem to be more and more reduced. Finally, they have to pay higher formal and informal payments to the authorities, both to avoid conflicts and if there are, for example, accidents or disputes over land – but even so they do not obtain the outcome for which they believe they have paid. The output of bribes is mostly a negative reciprocity. All ethnic groups encounter unfair payments. However, a reasonable level of payment for the settlement of a dispute or offence is regarded as acceptable in a moral sense, and is considered 'fair', especially if the payment is not too excessive. Payment is a way of 'getting things done' and of reducing problems (see Enlightened Myanmar Research 2014: 20). However, when Muslims and Hindus pay bribes to get things done, not only are the bribes they pay excessive but the officials whom they have bribed do not do what they have been 'paid' to do. Informants thus had a perception of a general negative reciprocity in all encounters with authorities.

Neither Muslims nor Hindus can be elected as village tract administrators (VTAs) in the town Shwe Gon on the Thanlwin River. This town has been on the influence of the Karen monk U Thuzana. The same is the case in the first Karen Muslim village we analysed in this chapter. In the Hindu village we studied, a Hindu cannot even become a recognised village leader (VA). This exclusion from recognised local leadership seems to be applied as a 'rule' in Karen State. Moreover, as most Muslims and Hindus cannot vote at national elections, they are now totally disenfranchised. They may also be a target of discrimination during the 2020 elections, especially if the main opposition party, the USDP, cooperates with Ma Ba Tha and uses nationalism and defence of religion as a political strategy to defeat the NLD. Since 2012, Muslims have not been allowed to construct new mosques. Before that, the BGF and the Tatmadaw used to demolish mosques (Karen Human Rights Group 2017: 246–267) and they also confiscated religious and agricultural land for camps or plantations (ibid.: 250).

Finally, the effects of primordial nationalism mean both an actual and a symbolic exclusion of the 4–6 per cent of the population who are Muslim and the 0.5 per cent who are Hindu from the legal population of Myanmar. A globalised fear of immigration and of international terror, as well as media-borne rumours and 'fake news', seem to exacerbate xenophobia. In our view the nationalism of the Ma Ba Tha monks is founded in a strong, generalised, Myanmar nationalism among military personnel and Buddhist lay followers, rather than being grounded in Buddhism and its doctrine. The monks' nationalism and their negative rhetoric against 'foreigners' is a justification for using symbolic violence; it is also a justification for defending Buddhist morality, as a kind of modern theodicy. This theodicy reflects a religious, sacred justification of special sanctions against non-believers that is expressed in bureaucratic rules and national laws. Thus, religious selfhood has merged with national selfhood.[35] The spiritual power of monks, backed by the armed power of the BGF and the Tatmadaw, has made any protest or disagreement almost impossible. Who among lay people or monks wants to be exposed as an unpatriotic traitor and accused of insulting religion, according to Section 295 in the penal code? Who dares to oppose the spiritual power of senior monks? Thus, the fear bordering on paranoia which is felt by many Buddhists vis-à-vis Muslims and Hindus is an ontological and anthropological reality we have to understand.[36] It dominates the cosmological orientation of the majority of the population, an orientation that is composed of religious, ethnic/racial, bureaucratic, and political-ideological elements in the current identity politics. Furthermore, it influences justice and security during the ceasefire; and it may generate more violence in Karen State, as indeed it may elsewhere in Myanmar.

Many ordinary citizens, in particular those belonging to ethnic minorities, fail to gain justice in the official justice system. However, Muslims and Hindus face even more serious discrimination and denials of justice. While other minorities may compensate by seeking alternative solutions from respected elders, Muslims and Hindus rarely have this opportunity because their leaders have limited power or authority outside their communities.

The long process of exclusion has been facilitated by the powers of the still *de facto* Tatmadaw-controlled GAD and by the Ma Ba Tha. Constituent power is enforced by acts of constituted bureaucratic indifference and by what Balibar (2015: 85) terms 'preventative repression', which refers to the symbolic violence of exclusion in 'defence of race, nation, and religion'. This constitutes the fulcrum of a process of gradual dehumanisation (Arendt 1976: 437–459) of those belonging to the category Kalar.

There have been various steps in this process of dehumanisation. Firstly, the 'judicial person' of individual Muslims and Hindus has been drastically reduced, almost eliminated, and their political rights have

35 On modern normative and political use of religion, see Asad (1992); Juergensmeyer (2010).

36 Monks interviewed in Mae Sot by Mikael Gravers who were involved in the 2007 demonstrations explained that Ma Ba Tha monks had little formal education and lacked knowledge of international politics. This may well be true of some monks, but primordial nationalism is shared by a broader section of society.

been removed. Secondly, in recent years their moral identity has been reduced or eliminated through their negative categorisation, by nationalists, as 'foreign and immoral guests' or 'enemies'. Finally, their personal access to justice and security has been endangered or eliminated. The next step could well be 'preventative counter violence' against them, in the name of the protection of nation, race and state.

We can only hope that this will never happen. However, the present situation is that the integrated, peaceful Karen Muslims and Hindus in Karen State have been turned into subjugated, humiliated, and stateless non-persons. This is a major backward step in relation to the transition to democracy. When Muslim leaders visit, or young Mulawis return from foreign Koran schools, they may well urge a more conservative Islam and the creation of a distance between Muslims and those belonging to other religions. Although we did not observe signs of radicalisation, the current exclusion and negative categorisation of Muslims (and indeed Hindus) could foster radical ideas and attract foreign intervention.

The communitarian strategy of the Ma Ba Tha, of members of the GAD and of the Tatmadaw, using ethnic-religious hierarchy as a political instrument, reduces civil and political rights on the part of Muslims and Hindus considerably. This situation inhibits the transition to democracy and the rule of law – as demonstrated by Cheesman (2015) and South and Lall (2018). Ethnic boundary-making and exclusion also inhibit any prospects of a federal constitution (Kyed and Gravers 2018). The lack of justice and security for the Hindu and Muslim population inhibits democratisation and the nation-wide unity so often proclaimed by nationalists.

References

Adas, M.

1974. 'Immigrant Asians and the economic impact of European imperialism: The role of the south Indian Chettiars in British Burma.' *Journal of Asian Studies* 33(3): 385–401.

Appadurai, A.

2000. 'The ground of the nation-state. Identity, violence and territory.' In K. Goldmann et al. (eds), *Nationalism and Internationalism in the Post-Cold War Era*, pp. 129–142. London, Routledge.

Arendt, Hannah

1970. *On Violence*. Orlando: Harvest Books.

1976. *The Origins of Totalitarianism*. San Diego, New York: Harvest Books.

Asad, T.

1992. 'Religion and politics: An introduction.' *Social Research* 59(1): 3–16.

Aung San Suu Kyi

1991. *Freedom from Fear and Other Writings*. London: Penguin Books.

Balibar, E.

2015. *Citizenship*. Cambridge: Polity Press.

Bennison, J.

1931. *British Census of India of 1931*. Rangoon: Government Press.

Berlie, J.

2008. *The Burmanization of Myanmar's Muslims*. Bangkok: Lotus.

Bourdieu, P.

1992. *Language and Symbolic Power*. Oxford: Polity Press.

Binns, B.O.

1935. *Burma Gazetteer, Amherst District. Volume A*. Rangoon: Supdt. Govt. Printing and Stationery, Burma.

Blair, E. & Aung, Z.

2006. 'Burma's Muslims: Looking for a deal.' *The Irrawaddy* 14(1): 20–23.

Boshier, C.A.

2018. *Mapping Cultural Nationalism. The Scholars of the Burma Research Society, 1910–1935*. Copenhagen: NIAS Press.

Callahan, M.P.

2017. 'Distorted, dangerous data? Lumyo in the 2014 Myanmar population and housing census.' *Sojourn: Journal of Social Issues in Southeast Asia* 32(2): 452–478.

Chatterjee, P.

1993. *The Nation and Its Fragments. Colonial and Postcolonial Histories*. New Jersey: Princeton University Press.

Cheesman, N.

2015. *Opposing the Rule of Law. How Myanmar's Courts Make Law and Order*. Cambridge: Cambridge University Press.

2017. 'How in Myanmar "national races" came to surpass citizenship and exclude Rohingya.' *Journal of Contemporary Asia* 42(2): 1–23.

Egreteau, R.

2011. 'Burmese Indians in contemporary Burma: Heritage, influence, and perceptions since 1988.' *Asian Ethnicity* 12(1): 33–54.

Enlightened Myanmar Research (EMR)

2014. *Between Fear and Hope. Challenges and Opportunities for Strengthening Rule of Law and Access to Justice in Myanmar.* Yangon: The Pyoe Pin Programme.

Fuller, P.

2017. *Sitagu Sayaaw's Mahavamsa Sermon.* paulfullerbuddhiststudies.wordpress.com/page/2/.

Gravers, M.

1999. *Nationalism as Political Paranoia in Burma. An Essay on the Historical Practice of Power.* London: Curzon.

2012. 'Monks, morality and military. The struggle for moral power in Burma – and Buddhism's uneasy relation with lay power.' *Contemporary Buddhism* 13(1): 1–33.

2015a. 'Religious imaginary as an alternative social and moral order – Karen Buddhism across the Thai–Burma Border.' In A. Horstmann and J-H. Jung (eds), *Building Noah's Ark for Migrants, Refugees, and Religious Communities*, pp. 45–76. New York: Palgrave Macmillan.

2015b. 'Disorder and order: The ethno-nationalist struggle of the Karen in Burma/Myanmar. A discussion of the dynamics of an ethicized civil war and its historical roots.' *Journal of Burma Studies* 15(1): 27–78.

2018. 'A saint in command. Spiritual protection, justice, and religious tension in the Karen State.' *Journal of Independent Burmese Scholarship* 1(2): 87–119.

forthcoming. *Dynamite, Military and Monks – The Powers Governing Karen State Frontier Land.* Paper given at the Warwick workshop on *Border Governance: Everyday Life in Transition at Myanmar's Margins* (2018). In preparation for publication in *Modern Asia Studies* 2021.

Harrisson, A.P.

2018. 'Everyday justice for Muslims in Mawlamyine: Subjugation and skilful navigation.' *Independent Journal of Burmese Scholarship* 1(2): 57–85.

Harvey, G.E.

1972 (1946). *British Rule in Burma 1824–1942.* London: Faber and Faber.

Herzfeld, M.

1992. *The Social Production of Indifference. Exploring the Symbolic Roots of Western Bureaucracy.* Chicago: University of Chicago Press.

2001. *Anthropology. Theoretical Practice in Culture and Society.* Oxford: Wiley-Blackwell Publishing.

Hintharnee'

2017. 'Karen Ma Ba Tha Chapter Refuses to Remove Signboards.' *The Irrawaddy* 27 July 2017. www. the irrawaddy org/

Houtman, G.

1999. *Mental Culture in Burmese Crisis Politics. Aung San Suu Kyi and the National League for Democracy*. Tokyo: Tokyo University of Foreign Studies, Institute for the Study of Languages and Cultures of Asia and Africa.

Hutchinson, J. and A. Smith (eds)

1994. *Nationalism*. Oxford, New York: Oxford University Press.

Jenkins, R.

2008. *Rethinking Ethnicity. Arguments and Explorations*. Second Edition. Los Angeles: Sage Publications.

Jerryson, M.

2018. *If You Meet Buddha on the Road: Buddhism, Politics and Violence*. s.l.: Oxford Scholarship Online, www.oxfordscholarship.com/view/10.1093/oso/9780190683566.001.0001/oso-9780190683566.

Jolliffe, K.

2015. *Ethnic Armed Conflict and Territorial Administration in Myanmar*. Report. Yangon: The Asia Foundation.

Juergensmeyer, M.

2010. 'The global rise of religious nationalism.' *Australian Journal of International Affairs* 64(3): 262–273.

Karen Human Rights Group (KHGR)

2002. *Easy Target: The Persecution of Muslims in Burma*. s.l.: KHGR.

2017. *Foundation of Fear: 25 years of Villagers' Voices from Southeast Myanmar*. s.l.: KHGR.

2018. *Development without us: Village Agency and Land Confiscations in Southeast Myanmar*. s.l.: KHGR.

Kawanami, H.

2009. 'Charisma, power(s), and the Arahant ideal in Burmese-Myanmar Buddhism.' *Asian Ethnology* 68(2): 211–237.

Khin Yi

1988. *The Do Bama Movement in Burma (1930–38)*. Ithaca: Cornell University.

Kyaw Phyo Tha

2019.' Legal team defended Myanmar to'best of their ability' Daw Aung San Suu Kyi says'. *The Irrawaddy* 19 December 2019. www.irrawaddy. org/

Kyed, H.M. & Gravers, M.

2018. 'Representation and citizenship in the future integration of ethnic armed actors in Myanmar/Burma.' In A. South and M. Lall (eds), *Citizenship in Myanmar. Ways of Being in and from Burma*, pp. 59–86. Singapore: Chiang Mai University Press and ISEAS.

Mendelson, M.

1975. *Sangha and the State in Burma. A Study of Monastic Sectarianism and Leadership.* Ithaca: Cornell University Press.

Min Zin

2015. 'Anti-Muslim violence in Burma: Why now?' *Social Research* 82(2): 375–397.

Myanmar.

2008. The Constitution of The Republic of the Union of Myanmar. Naypyidaw, Ministry of Information (also available online).

Myanmar. Republic of the Union of Myanmar

2015. *The 2014 Myanmar Population and Housing Census Vol. 2.* Nay Pyi Taw.

Myanmar Times

2017. 'Mixed Mon, Karen races to be on new ethnic race list.' 15 December 2017, www.mmtimes.com/news/mixed-mon-karen-races-be-new-ethnic-race-list.html.

Nyi Nyi Kyaw

2016. 'Alienation, discrimination, and securitization: Legal personhood and cultural personhood of Muslims in Myanmar.' *Review of Faith & International Affairs* 13(4): 50–59.

O'Connor, V.C.S.

1904. *The Silken East. A Record of Life and Travel in Burma.* Hong Kong: Kiscadale.

Shils, E.

1995. 'Nation, nationality and civil society.' *Nations and Nationalism* 1(1): 93–118.

Shorto, H.L.

1971. *A Dictionary of the Mon Inscriptions from the Six to the Sixteenth Centuries.* London: Oxford University Press.

Smith, D.E.

1965. *Religion and Politics in Burma.* Princeton: Princeton University Press.

Smith, M.

1999. *Burma: Insurgency and the Politics of Ethnicity*. London: Zed Books.

South, A. & Lall, M. (eds)

2018. *Citizenship in Myanmar. Ways of Being in and From Burma*. Singapore: ISEAS Publishing and Chiang Mai University Press.

Taylor, R.H.

1981. 'Party, class, and power in British Burma.' *Journal of Commonwealth & Comparative Politics* 19(1): 44–61.

Tin Gyi, U.

1931. *Burma Gazetteer, Thaton District, Volume A*. Rangoon: Supdt. Govt. Printing and Stationery, Burma.

Tonkin, D.

2018. 'Exploring the issue of citizenship in Rakhine State.' In A. South and M. Lall (eds), *Citizenship in Burma*, pp. 1–43. Singapore: ISEAS Publishing.

Transnational Institute

2018. *Implementation of Burma's Vacant, Fallow and Virgin Land Management Law: At odds with the Nationwide Ceasefire Agreement and Peace Negotiations. A commentary by Jason Gelbort.* www.tni.org.

Wade, F.

2017. *Myanmar's Enemy Within*. London: Zed Books.

Walton, M.J.

2013. 'The wages of Burman-ness: Ethnicity and Burman privilege in Burmese politics.' *Journal of Contemporary Asia* 43(1): 1–27.

2015. 'The disciplining discourse of unity in Burmese politics.' *The Journal of Burmese Studies* 19(1): 1–26.2017. 'Misunderstanding Ma Ba Tha.' *Asia Times*, 9 June 2017.

Walton, M.J., McKay, M. & Khin, M.M.

2016. 'Women and Myanmar's "religious protection laws".' *Review of Faith & International Relations* 13(4): 36–49.

Yegar, M.

1972. *The Muslims of Burma*. Wiesbaden: Otto Harrassowitz.

8 Everyday trepidation: State affects and mental absconding in a marginal neighbourhood in Mawlamyine

Annika Pohl Harrisson

Introduction

'You have to live carefully' a driver once told me after speeding away from a scene of an accident just outside of Mawlamyine, involving a motorcyclist whom we left behind bleeding in the road. The driver was not to blame for the accident. Still, he did not want to help the victim because he wanted to stay away from the authorities. When I discussed this with friends later on, they told me such behaviour was not unusual. They had often observed that people would just drive by a traffic accident. People are afraid to get involved. As one of my friends told me:

> When the police come, you have to give your name and maybe even show your ID card because then you are a witness. Being a witness can cost money and time and causes you problems, because maybe they will even call you to the court. Also, you could risk being blamed for something by the police. No, it is better to stay away from the problem.[1]

In this chapter, I explore how poor urban people experience the state in a developing democracy, following 50 years of military dictatorship. How do state–society relations play out and how do they affect everyday life? A starting point is to explore how people solve their problems and disputes, in a country where distrust of the government and its institutions is prevalent and the police and the courts are considered inefficient and corrupt (Cheesman, Skidmore and Wilson 2010; Cheesman 2015). The driver's behaviour at the scene of the motorcycle accident reflects this distrust but also opens up a broader enquiry into how this everyday trepidation is related to people's relations with and care for others.

This chapter builds on political anthropological literature (Trouillot 2001; Hansen and Stepputat 2001; Linke 2006; Laszczkowski and

1 Conversation 8 February 2017

Reeves 2015; Navaro-Yashin 2012) about state affect and the state on its margins, which emphasises the state's imaginative and discursive construction and goes beyond a focus on governmental and national institutions. I argue that people evade the state because of mistrust of the state system and because making contact with the state can create problems. The state is perceived as being not caring but exploitative. This has deeper implications for social relations between ordinary people, and I will argue that this is a state affect.

The ethnographic setting is the poor ward of Yatkwet Thit on the outskirts of Mawlamyine.[2] Yatkwet Thit is divided into an upper and a lower part, and is home to some 5,500 adults, who form a diverse group in terms of both ethnicity and religions, as there are Hindus, Muslims of Indian and Malay origin, Karen, Mon, Pashu and Myanmar Buddhists. On this poor 'urban margin' (Goldstein 2012) there is a general lack of state infrastructure and of official justice provision, and there is a scarcity of employment, all of which gives a sense of abandonment to the neighbourhood. Studies of Yangon's informal settlements illustrate a similar situation for people living at the urban margins in Myanmar's largest city, where there is a lack of protection, no social cohesion, and mistrust of neighbours (Kyed 2019; Forbes 2019).

The main argument put forward in this chapter is that, despite the seeming absence of the state, the state is omnipresent qua its affects. I will show how the lack of state care and its disrespect for human life translates from state policy into human sociality and subjectivities at the urban margin. Distrust of the state leaks into social relations in the form of suspicion and distrust between neighbours. The lack of state care is also imbued in geographical features; the landscape stimulates an affect and undermines any sense of feeling 'at home'. I assert that people want to evade the state. Instead of fleeing into geographically remote areas, their practice is to turn away from physical instantiations and places where the state could possibly be. However, the power of the modern state cannot be evaded, because the state is already omnipresent in that very decision that makes people turn away. Even mental absconding is therefore an affect of the state. This is a novel argument related to James Scott's (2009) theory on state evasion.

The neighbourhood of Yatkwet Thit is at the margins of the state on many levels – in terms of geography, economic integration, and infra-

2 All person and place names are anonymised due to the sensitive nature of this text.

structural development. In line with Das and Poole (2004), I find the fundamental importance of the state in everyday life to be most clearly visible at its margins. Following this, I demonstrate that the boundary between state and people is elusive, leaving the state entrenched in everyday lives, actions, and thoughts (Mitchell 1999). I show how ideas of the state are asserted within everyday life, and how the state is made real and present through everyday forms of imagination even in the absence of state care and services. To be sure, some assertions of the state are physical and visible, but many others are immaterial and elusive. I argue that the state – which is associated with 50 years of military rule – although apparently absent, shapes everyday decision-making and affects relations between citizens and their life trajectories in Yatkwet Thit. Anthropological studies have explored the state at its margins (Das 2004; Goldstein 2012; Scott 2009) and a recent body of literature focusses on affective forms of state power, exploring the state as the object of emotional investment and as the site of fear, paranoia, mutual suspicion and recognition (Laszczkowski and Reeves 2015; Pinker and Harvey 2015; Navaro-Yashin 2012; Bozzini 2015; Trouillot 2001). Combining insights from these two bodies of literature, I show how the state manifests itself as a force that carries trepidation. I contend that residents engage in strategies of state avoidance even in its seeming absence, as it is imagined everywhere – and in a particular way, namely as the military state. I will call the potential omnipresence of a state that is relatively absent a state affect: in the absence of state care, there is nevertheless a state presence, which affects social life and relations. I define affect as those instinctive forces – not to be confused with conscious knowing and emotions – that can serve to drive us toward movement, thought and actions (Gregg and Seigworth 2010: 1). This I will look at through exploring dispute resolution and everyday life in Yatkwet Thit, which make apparent state affects related to illegibility, evasion, and lack of social cohesion.

In the first part of the chapter, I introduce the two bodies of scholarship from within political anthropology that I combine here, on state margins and on state affect. I then present a case study, which I have chosen to focus upon in this chapter because it is representative of many other life histories in Yatkwet Thit. Following the presentation of this case, I introduce the context, the Myanmar State, from a historical perspective. I argue that the image of the military state is conflated, as far as my interlocutors are concerned, with the state today. Thus the state today is not, for them, the newly elected NLD (National League for Democracy) government; it is, rather, the intrusive state institutions of administration, police and military that were in the past and that remain under the Burmese armed forces, the Tatmadaw, that dominate imaginings of the state. These imaginings have a powerful effect on daily behaviour, even in the relative absence of state institutions, as I will show in the subsequent sections, by returning to the main case and other related cases. I conclude the chapter by further reflecting on how a place as peripheral and marginal as Yatkwet Thit nevertheless has a strong 'presence in absence of the state'.

Affective authoritarianism in state margins

Michel Trouillot suggests that the state needs to be conceptualised at more than one level and is best analysed as a set of practices, processes and effects (Trouillot 2001: 127). The effect of the state, besides being reproduced by bureaucratic practice, infrastructural development, and brute force, is reproduced through the '… affective engagements of ordinary citizens and non-citizens in relation to state agents and state-like activities: their feelings, their emotions, their embodied responses as they navigate state bureaucracy or anticipate state violence' (Navaro-Yashin 2009: 9). According to Yael Navaro-Yashin (ibid: 8–9), those affective engagements need to be studied against the background of historical contingency and political specificity. In Yatkwet Thit ward, the subject of study is a forcefully relocated community at the social margins, in the context of a transitional process following 50 years of rule by a strict military regime. These circumstances are formative of today's imaginings and of relations between people and the state. It is a known trait of authoritarian regimes to generate unstable and fragile patterns of cognition and thus to generate 'states of fearful anticipation' (Bozzini 2015: 44). Whether those threats are real or imagined, the force of the affect is the same. I follow an understanding of 'affect' as an intensity or force that moves people, but which is not equivalent to emotion (Gregg and Seigworth 2010; Massumi 1995; Laszczkowski and Reeves 2015). While an emotion is always semiotically mediated and the quality of an experience is owned and recognised, affect is rather what can be said to lay the ground for expressions of emotions (Massumi 1995: 88).

Affect is more like a sense, something unformulated and undefined that moves people towards a behaviour.

For an understanding of social life on the margins of the state, I turn to Veena Das and Deborah Poole (2004) and Daniel Goldstein (2012). An anthropology of the margins allows us to perceive margins as '… a necessary entailment of the state, much as the exception is a necessary component of the rule' (Das and Poole 2004: 4). Thus, margins are constitutive of the centre; they constitute the otherness, the exception that is fundamental for statehood. Margins can simultaneously be spaces of exclusion and inclusion. Margins should not be understood as merely territorial; they can also be political, economic, symbolic or bodily. This chapter will discuss social life in Yatkwet Thit neighbourhood, which has a population of poor Muslims, Hindus and Buddhists who are on the margins of society in multiple ways. They live in a peri-urban ward, a territorial margin, but they are marginal in other ways, too: economically, culturally, and politically. Nonetheless, this population is subject to the effects of state making, in fact their very marginalisation is arguably such an effect. Their specific experiences of the state also inform how they deal with strategies of control and the ways in which they try to claim justice or a better life. Through these strategies and claims the boundaries of the state are extended and remade.

In his influential book *The Art of Not Being Governed*, James Scott (2009) describes how people in Southeast Asia have sought historically to escape the reach of the state and to avoid its effects. Scott's focus is on people living in the Southeast Asian mainland massif, an area for which Scott adopts the term 'Zomia', coined by Willem van Schendel in 2002. Zomia is '… the largest remaining region of the world whose people have not yet been fully incorporated into nation-states' (Scott 2009: 13). Zomia is not only a region of resistance but also one of refuge, and it is where people have retreated to escape predatory behaviours by states. In Scott's own words, these regions of refuge constitute a state effect, as they are an effect of state-making and state expansion (ibid.: 326). In Zomia, people have experienced relative safety and freedom from forced labour, taxes, conscription, epidemics, war and crop failures. Thus, people residing in this mountainous and inaccessible region are not simply backward hill-people or remnants from pre-state periods, but are people who have consciously chosen to live outside the gaze of the state. That 'Zomians' were not irrational but instead continuously chose and skilfully managed to live outside the confines of nation-states is Scott's key argument. Albeit Scott is apprehensive about the usefulness of his argument in the context of globalisation after 1945 (ibid.: xii), I contend that it is also relevant in present-day Myanmar. For my interlocutors, there is of course no physical Zomia in which they can seek refuge away from state rule. In Yatkwet Thit state evasion is not about a retreat into physically hilly and treacherous areas. Evasion instead takes the form of practical distancing and avoidance of all material manifestations and physical instantiations of the state, such as the police, local administrations and checkpoints – as well as any circumstances that may potentially lead to contact with the state. The causes of this flight or evasion are to a large extent the same as those that have been identified by Scott (taxation, repression, impositions from state officials, political dissent and poverty), but the flight is enacted differently, since present-day conditions are different. Whereas Scott writes about a historically observable 'exceptional proclivity of villagers to migrate whenever they were dissatisfied with conditions or perceived opportunities in a new direction' (ibid.: 142), I find that people in Yatkwet Thit do not have the resources or the communal solidarity for this kind of endeavour. Besides, Zomia is no longer a 'region of asylum', as Myanmar state control is pervasive. The exception may be the pockets that are controlled by some of the ethnic armed groups, but these areas are not freely accessible to ethnicities other than those who belong to that associated with a particular ethnic armed group (see Harrisson 2020).

Scott's analysis also allows for an interpretation of state evasion as a process that is not bound to physical movement. In his contribution to the book *Burmese Lives: Ordinary Life Stories under the Burmese Regime* (Scott 2014), he explores the life story of his informant Dr. U Tin Win, whom he calls an 'escape artist', as he absconds into the world of American popular music and films. This 'internal migration' is embarked upon in an attempt to 'block out the steady privations and pressure of plodding military dictatorship' (ibid.: 4).

This chapter adds to the above literature on state margins and state affects, as an exploration of the latter on agency, decision-making processes and social relations, operating in indirect and circumstantial ways. Thus, moving away from a focus on emotions directed towards the state or directly emanating from it, I investigate the affects that state practices and policies provoke in individuals and in social relations, through everyday experiences and imaginaries. State practices and policies produce state *effects* that should not be understood as deliberate and calculated actions of a state as an actor; but they result in state *affects* in the sense of the state as something imagined and experienced in everyday life. In this way, the state is installed in the imagination and not (merely) experienced through institutions and policies. Let me now turn to the main case dealt with in this chapter.

Legal precariousness: Disappeared by the state

Daw Shwe's life experiences represented one of the most forceful expressions of state affect that I encountered in Yatkwet Thit. The first time I met her was on my first visit to Yatkwet Thit in early 2015. Daw Shwe had heard of my visit and had made her way to the doctor's practice where I was based. She was one of eight women I met who all had stories to tell about alcoholic and violent husbands, debt cycles, unresolved conflicts, and concerns about living in an area that was flooded during the rainy season. Daw Shwe was a widow, a Hindu woman in her sixties, her black hair turned almost entirely white. Daw Shwe had been born in Mawlamyine and so had her parents and grandparents. She remembered how her grandfather had mastered the English language well and had worked for the British colonisers. Daw Shwe only spoke the Bamar language and had only ever held temporary jobs in construction or as a house cleaner. In the course of her life, she had given birth to seven children. Two of her children had died of disease when they were still small and two of them as adults, one of AIDS and the other due to alcohol abuse. Now her only daughter and one son were living with her. The son, a construction worker, provided the main income for the household. Daw Shwe was weeping while she was recounting a confusing story of what had happened to her other son, Ko Min, who had disappeared while in state custody. One day in November 2008, a close neighbour and friend confronted Daw Shwe with the claim that her then 22-year-old son Ko Min had raped the neighbour's 4-year-old daughter. The neighbour asked Daw Shwe for money to go to the hospital, as she claimed that the girl had sustained injuries from the assault. The woman said that she did not want to file a report with the police because of the daughter's honour. Daw Shwe never clearly told me whether she believed, at this point, that her son had actually committed the assault. Regardless of the truth, she took a loan at a high rate of interest from the ward administrator and paid the money to the girl's mother. The following day she saw that the 4-year-old girl was playing in a carefree manner outside with other children, so when the female neighbour came back to ask for more money for another hospital visit, Daw Shwe started to suspect that the story of the rape was a lie and that it was a ruse to extract money from her. She brought in the ward administrator, asking him to hold a negotiation meeting about the case, but this prompted the neighbour to go directly to the police and to file a case of rape against Ko Min. The following day the police caught Ko Min on his way home from work and placed him in the detention cell at the local police station. When Daw Shwe wanted to visit her son, she was asked to pay MMK 250,000 (approx. USD 200) to be allowed to see him. She told the prison authorities that she would pay after seeing him and was allowed in. She described how Ko Min was crying and scared, pleading his innocence. She promised Ko Min that she would help him, a promise that still haunts her, as she feels that she has deserted him. Because she never managed to come up with the money that she was supposed to pay the police, Ko Min was held in local custody, and his case was not forwarded to the court for several months. When the case finally went to court, Daw Shwe felt powerless. She was excluded from meetings with jurors. She had no financial resources to pay the court officials, and Ko Min had no viable defence. The case ended with a sentence of five years in prison with hard labour for attempted rape. When Daw Shwe asked why the indictment had been changed from rape to attempted rape, she was told to keep quiet by the prosecutor. Ko Min was sent to prison. She took food to him there, but on day 15 of his imprisonment she was told that he was now missing. The government had drafted 300 prisoners for the army.[3] She was told that he had been taken for the Hpa-An army in Karen State, but when she went to ask for him there, they said he was not there. She contacted the state court and was told that they did not know of any order that her son had been called to work for the Tatmadaw (the Burmese army). Nobody knew where he had gone, and by the time I met her several years had gone by. Daw Shwe was still having a hard time accepting the loss of her son.

3 The Myanmar army engages in offensive operations against armed ethnic groups, and it is not unusual to send prisoners to military service camps and use them as porters at the front line. See also AAPP 2002.

Daw Shwe blamed the police, the prison, and the Tatmadaw for making her son disappear. She had no proof or evidence of his death and kept trying out different strategies aimed at locating him. She also felt betrayed by the state's inability to protect her son from what she saw as a false accusation. She even suspected complicity between her neighbour and the state, as the state seemed to have used the conviction to conscript Ko Min into the army. She tried consulting a *bedin hsaya* (astrologer), who advised her to plant a coconut tree and place five glasses of water on the ground next to it and then call out Ko Min's name. However, this did not work. As a poor and marginalised woman, she knew that she could not get clarification or accountability from the state. She said to me: 'People like me are not important. We can live or die, nobody will care'.[4] I promised to come back and hear more of her story.

Based on this and other similar stories, I contend that there is a 'legal precariousness' (Reeves 2015) at play in Yatkwet Thit, particularly for those who have fewer resources or who are members of a religious or ethnic group that is not considered to be a proper part of 'Myanmar identity'. Daw Shwe is Hindu and also very poor. Another case which illustrates this is that of a Muslim shop-owner called Ebrahim. When he became involved in a conflict, Ebrahim did not dare to contest allegations against him, out of fear that this might have wider repercussions and might challenge his right to be a citizen in the ward, because of his religion.[5] Then there is the case of impoverished Daw Aye, who had a disabled son who was not allowed to go to school because of his handicap. He could only move around on his hands and knees. He was frequently bullied and pushed around by the neighbouring kids. One day he was hurt, as an adult had joined in the harassment. Daw Aye was shaken by what had happened to her boy but did not even report the incident to the ward administrator, let alone the police. Referring to their precarious situation as a poor and marginalised family, she told me: 'I have to be careful because I am not able to afford a conflict'. She worried both about having to pay the ward administrator for dealing with the case and about the possibility that the other party in the case might be cleverer and more resourceful and thus turn the case against her, making her even worse off. Besides, she did not want to stir up a difficult situation amongst the neighbours. She told me: 'I can't get justice here. I want to move away to

4 Interview 13 February 2016.

5 For an elaboration of this case see Harrisson (2018).

a place where people are friendlier, but we took a loan with our house as security. So we can't move. Sometimes I want to die.'

These examples show how neighbours in Yatkwet Thit are adversaries rather than people who lend each other mutual support. This general tendency in the ward is, I argue, ultimately an affect of state policies and practices, which established the ward in the first place as a forced resettlement area. Both disrespect for the people on the part of the state, at a macro level, and distrust of state institutions on the part of individuals, at a micro level, leak into social relations in this marginal neighbourhood.

The nested military state: Encompassed by the Tatmadaw

In order to understand these individual experiences of the state of Myanmar in Yatkwet Thit, the connections between people there and the governing apparatus with which they are entangled, and the ways in which these relations affect sociality and subjectivity, one must also understand the relations that people had with the state prior to the current ongoing transition towards a more democratic and open system. I contend that experiences and memories from 50 years of authoritarian military rule have been formative of present-day experiences, and that the effects of these are still ingrained in people in Yatkwet Thit. In fact, I argue that the military state is what is still the prevalent imaginary of the state in Yatkwet Thit and that it is this imaginary that is at the root of present-day state affects. This is, in part, because memories of the past shape ideas of the state in the present, and in part it is because the police and the administration, which are key in people's encounters with the state in the everyday, remain under the control of the military. The state administration that operates in Yatkwet Thit continues to be the same as under the military. Let me briefly outline the main characteristics of the military state from 1962 to 2010, and then turn to how it looks today.

After several years of ethnic-based conflicts, which followed Myanmar's independence from Britain in 1948, the military under General Ne Win seized power in 1962 through a coup. Ne Win embarked on 'The Burmese Road to Socialism'. This involved a number of initiatives aimed at securing total control: all political opposition was declared illegal, the military took over management of educational and cultural institutions and nationalised the majority of the economy, and the courts lost their independence (Taylor 2009: 293–295, 339). Meanwhile, armed conflict between ethnic armed organisations and the military continued. During the many years of military rule, the country experienced consistent and systematic violations of human rights, strict surveillance, and suppression of civil society. In 1988, nationwide pro-democracy demonstrations, headed by students and driven by the economic crisis caused by the mismanagement and self-interest of the Generals, challenged their dominion. The rebellion was halted by brute force and promises of multi-party election (Taylor 2009: 375ff). Elections were held in 1990 under martial law conditions, with political leaders of the opposition restrained under house arrest. When the National League for Democracy (NLD) headed by Aung San Suu Kyi won a landslide victory, this came as a shock to the military leadership, which ultimately decided not to transfer power to the NLD. Aung San Suu Kyi and other political leaders, as well as newly elected candidates, were kept under house arrest (Taylor 2009: 412).

Monique Skidmore (2004) and Christina Fink (2009) describe existential conditions under military rule in Myanmar, and how the Burmese managed their lives for years on end living with a sense of vulnerability and fear. According to Skidmore, the military employed two techniques to maintain fear and uphold an atmosphere of emergency amongst the population. One was generating a fear of the 'Other' (which could be a neo-colonial presence, a foreigner, an internal traitor, or simply change and difference). The military warned the Burmese to stay alert and be cautious of 'Others'. The threat of 'Others' was projected as associated with a potential loss of independence, as had happened under colonialisation. The other technique that was employed by the military state was to emphasize that only the military could provide security, stability and progress for the country (Skidmore 2004: 37). Fink describes how the military, through this climate of insecurity and fear and the use of violence, successfully infused fear and political passivity amongst the population (Fink 2009).

From 2010 onwards, Myanmar has seen a gradual move towards democratisation. Spurred by economic isolation, civil unrest during the so-called Saffron Revolution in 2007 and international scrutiny following the devastating effects of cyclone Nargis in 2008, a new constitution was passed.[6] This initiated a transition aimed at moving away from state

6 The constitution that came into effect in 2008 had taken almost 20 years to draft; see Crouch 2019.

authoritarianism and international isolation towards a more open political system. In 2011, the military junta was officially dissolved, after parliamentary elections in 2010, and a nominal civilian government was installed. Thein Sein, a former General, was made president. Since then a number of reforms have been launched with the aim of leading the country towards liberal democracy and reconciliation (Lidauer 2014). This, along with the release of Aung San Suu Kyi and political prisoners, has somewhat improved the country's human rights situation and foreign relations and has led to the easing of trade and other economic sanctions. At the democratic elections held in 2015, the NLD won an absolute majority of seats (Thawnghmung 2016). U Htin Kyaw became the first non-military president of the country since the 1962 military coup. Aung San Suu Kyi, who has been constitutionally barred from the presidency, was named State Counsellor. Despite these changes, the country still experiences violent conflicts. The Tatmadaw has repeatedly engaged in attacks on ethnic armed groups in Kachin and Shan States, as well as in the ongoing violent persecution and expulsion of the Rohingya in Rakhine State. A decisive factor in the situation of present-day Myanmar is that the Tatmadaw remains an independent force and is not subject to the democratically elected government. In fact, key areas of governance and control are still under the military. Under the constitution, the Tatmadaw is guaranteed 25 per cent of the seats in the national and regional legislatures and controls three of the most influential ministries: Home Affairs, Defence and Border Security. Their control of the Ministry of Home Affairs, under which the General Administrative Department (GAD) falls, has been particularly significant, as it gives the Tatmadaw authority over state administration. The influence of the Tatmadaw (still) penetrates deep into society and reaches all the way down to household level.[7] In Myanmar, for approximately every 10 households a 10-household leader reports to the ward or village administrator.[8] The latter constitutes the lowest level of

7 In January 2019, after completion of fieldwork and completion of this chapter, the GAD was moved to the civilian Department of the Ministry of the Office of the Union Government. However, Gravers and Jørgensen (Chapter 7, this volume) argue that the GAD is still *de facto* controlled by the military.

8 The ward administrator is not considered government staff, but he is still regarded as the lowest level of Myanmar's bureaucracy. He is paid a small stipend to cover office expenses. The ward administrator has diverse functions: he prepares recommendation letters (these are required in order to apply for a household certificate,

Myanmar's state bureaucracy, which falls under the GAD. Apart from representing ward and village-tract communities and communicating their needs and priorities upwards in the system, local administrators must carry out instructions from and report back to the administration at township level, which currently does not have elected councils or representatives. As such, the local leaders are embedded in a wider system of governance where the higher levels they respond to are not democratised, but ultimately fall under the military (Kyed, Harrisson, and McCarthy 2016).

Surveillance and micro-management all the way down to household level has historically inhibited an active civil society in Myanmar. Alongside strict censorship, propaganda, trained official spies and civil informants living inside communities, they led, during the military regime, to mutual suspicion and the breakdown of interpersonal trust in local civil society (Fink 2009; Skidmore 2004). Having neighbours snitching on each other allowed the state to intrude into personal relations. It also allowed neighbours to blackmail each other and use the state to manipulate relations. Informers – and the state surveillance which derives from having informers – were at the same time hidden and revealed; potential and actual; and presumed and real (Bozzini 2015: 39). The continuing military presence in civilian areas blended 'public' and 'private'. There were also, of course, instances of solidarity and of diligent civil society organisations (South 2008; Fink 2009); but in a general sense interpersonal trust was hampered for decades. I contend that this history still shapes Burmese subjectivities and socialities in places like Yatkwet Thit, and that its effect is even more acute in communities such as this, because of the fact that it was established as a site of forced relocation. The continuing control of the military over local administration in Myanmar communities underlines the continuity between past and present.

Life on the margins: Yatkwet Thit

Yatkwet Thit was established in 2003 when people were ordered by the then military government to relocate there from three other wards,

for a driver's licence, for jobs etc.) and contracts for the sale of land or other property. He also mediates in local disputes and assures law and order in his area (Kyed, Harrisson and McCarthy 2016).

because of the construction of a railway bridge. The land on which Yatkwet Thit was built used to be a paddy field and at the time of the relocation it was divided into numerous small plots. People were only given one month's notice before their relocation and received limited compensation to enable them to build new houses. Forced displacement is condemned under international law; nonetheless, relocation due to 'development projects' is a well-known phenomenon in Myanmar (Human Rights Watch 2005). As well as moving people from their original neighbourhoods and networks, which were closer to the city centre, the relocation has led to a division between Muslim and Buddhist residents, who now live in distinct areas (Harrisson 2018). The infrastructure of the ward is underdeveloped. Only a few of the streets are paved, there is no sewage system, there are too few wells and there are very few generators, which means that people constantly face water shortages and power cuts. In the rainy season, large areas in the lower part of Yatkwet Thit are flooded, and waste floats around. Consequently, many of the wooden houses are constructed on piles. Lack of vegetation worsens the problems when there is heavy rainfall during the monsoon season, as there is nothing to absorb the large quantities of water. During the hot months, when the heat is stifling, life is also difficult; there is no relief in nature, no natural vegetation or old trees tall enough to provide shade. A sense of remoteness and abandonment characterises the area. It is on the outskirts of the city, and is surrounded by vacant lots and fields, and a couple of 'beer stations' that double as brothels.

Where fear is a fundamental part of governing processes, emotions related to the state continually shape subjectivities and interpersonal relations, as David Bozzini found in Eritrea (Bozzini 2015) and as is also the case in Yatkwet Thit. As Bozzini (ibid.: 33) points out, 'state terror is a rather diffuse and complex social phenomenon that questions the limits of the concept of governance as an intentionally planned and institutionally bounded kind of process'. My own argument is built along the same lines. I do not claim that the military government's practices were intentionally directed (though neither do I claim that they were not) at influencing subjectivity, sociality, emotions and decision-making in Yatkwet Thit. What I do claim is that state practices have resulted in a range of affects. These affects, in Yatkwet Thit, include a lack of social cohesion, alienation, distrust and the fact that a serious crime like rape can take place without there being consequences and punishments. State terror here is a state affect, an imaginary of the state, and a threat that may or may not be actual and real. Despite the changes in the national government, it is the effects of decades of authoritarian military rule – the continuous ghostly presence of the military state in the developing democracy – that creates these state affects. What sets my field site apart and inhibits the development of 'instances of solidarity' is the fact that the ward is the result of a forced relocation by the then military state. Forbes (2019) describes a similar situation in another relocation site in Yangon, which is a growing slum and where there was, Forbes found, a lack of social cohesion that he did not find in some of the older neighbourhoods in the city, where there was community unity and mutual support (ibid.). Next, I show how state evasion and state affects are interlinked in local conflict resolution in Yatkwet Thit.

Figure 8.1 In the rainy season the neighbourhood is prone to flooding. *Colour image, p. 366.*

State evasion

The strategy of state evasion is evident in local conflict resolution processes, which involve the evasion of authorities such as the police and of the courts. Recent research demonstrates that the majority of disputes in Myanmar are dealt with through a variety of non-state, traditional, customary, religious and informal dispute resolution systems, instead of through official formal justice institutions such as the police or state courts. Another insight derived from recent research is that a significant number of cases are never even reported to any forum, not even to local institutions (Denney, Bennet and Khin Thet San 2016; Harrisson 2018; Kyed 2019; see also the Introduction to this volume). My research in Yatkwet Thit confirms these findings.

The lack of access to official justice, which is to a large extent fostered by distrust of state institutions, means that there is a risk that conflicts remain unresolved, and that people cannot obtain protection and compensation. This is the effect of corrupt and unreliable state practices. Added to this is the effect on life that legal precariousness produces: in Yatkwet Thit one can never be sure what to expect if one has contact with the authorities. Citizenship and the right of residence may be at stake for the poor or for religious minorities, as may their livelihoods, through blackmail or the extraction of bribes. Daw Shwe's experience with the police and prison feeds into imaginaries of the state as predatory and as worsening an already bad situation. It is once she is exposed to the state system that her son goes missing, and here legal precariousness is not just an affective state but a reality. I will return to this later in the chapter – to how this state affect influenced her decision making the next time she was confronted with a difficult situation.

Understanding the way people live in Yatkwet Thit is important in understanding state affects and state avoidance. Many people in Yatkwet Thit rent their homes. Homes are impermanent. This sense of impermanence translates into how houses are decorated. People do make themselves at home, but even that does not seem to bind them to the place. In part, this comes down to the fact that poor residents have very few belongings; but there is also a general sense of temporality, in that only a few artefacts connect residents to their homes. Such artefacts might be Buddhist or Hindu shrines, or small altars at which the spirits of ancestors and house *nat* (spirits) receive occasional offerings; the nationalist Buddhist 969 stickers; or a poster of Mecca, with Arabic script, on the wall in a central position in the house. A line-up of family portraits may be positioned on one of the horizontal beams. This is often a photograph with a beautiful image – a lake, a forest, a sunset. However, all of these items can move with the people. There are no permanent fixtures and no large investments. Structures are impermanent, anonymous and inconspicuous. They are easy to leave behind, as if people are always prepared for an escape. Scott (2009) shows how there is a complex 'art' to avoiding the state, including particular farming practices, forms of social organisation, ways of relating to locality, oral cultures and ideologies; the type of homemaking we see in Yatkwet Thit demonstrates another aspect of this 'art', expressed in the impermanence with which these houses are imbued – what we might call an 'escape architecture'.

Yael Navaro-Yashin (2012) is concerned with how landscapes stimulate affect in people living in them, as conflicts, past experiences and memories are inscribed in them. She describes feelings of melancholia and an inability to feel at home in the houses that have been abandoned by Greek Cypriots who fled to the other part of the island when the civil war broke out on Cyprus (Navaro-Yashin 2012). The landscape and infrastructure around Yatkwet Thit have a similar atmosphere, which can be said to be rooted in the fact that they are imbued with a lack of state care, a lack which seeps into inhabitants and into the landscape and buildings. Lack of state care undermines a sense of feeling at home. The impermanence and temporary nature of this ward are affects of the effect of the state-making project of the Myanmar state: the forced relocation of people away from the centre to the outskirts, away from solid buildings, tarmacked roads, and state buildings. Thus, here, at the urban margins, the Myanmar state and its influence can paradoxically be clearly identified, in what seems to be an absent omnipresence of the state. This absent omnipresence is reflected in the lack of care by the state, which extends to a sense of how bodies are treated by the state as replaceable.

Figure 8.2 A few goats on the outskirts of the area. *Colour image, p. 366.*

Absence of state care

For an exemplification of state avoidance and of the affect related to lack of state care, let me continue with the story of Daw Shwe, who lost track of her son while he was in prison. She lived in the lower part of Yatkwet Thit in a small house that was constructed of wood and patches of leaves. The roof was made of a tin sheet and a wooden walkway over a garbage-filled ditch connected the house to the street. When I visited her, Daw Shwe would invite me inside to take a seat next to her on the floor. It was dark inside, and there was a strong smell of fish paste, betel nut, and caustic soda, which felt suffocating. Daw Shwe's teeth were black from chewing betel, and sometimes it was difficult for me to understand what she was saying. Throughout our conversations, she would repeatedly spit red saliva (from chewing betelnut) through a hole in the floor. Her daughter also lived there, with her husband. She did not like her daughter's husband, Daw Shwe told me. They had married after he had raped her. This had happened one evening when her daughter was washing herself at a well in a slightly remote location. The daughter was ashamed because of the rape, and Daw Shwe did not want to report it, in part because of the further embarrassment it would cause her family, as they were already stigmatised because of the attempted child rape of which her son had been convicted. Above all, she did not feel there was anywhere she could turn, as she was afraid to go to the police or to court and potentially to lose control of the situation. The rapist was already married and had five children but he wanted to take Daw Shwe's daughter as a second wife. Thus, Daw Shwe chose the lesser of two evils and agreed to the marriage, since the man had taken her daughter's virginity. He built a small annex to Daw Shwe's house, which was their bedroom. This was only separated from the main house by a piece of wooden chipboard. Daw Shwe felt very sad about what had happened to her daughter. At night, she could hear them on the other side of the screen; she could hear how he spoke rudely to her daughter, and how they quarrelled. Daw Shwe found comfort in the fact that her daughter goes regularly to a local woman and gets injections to make sure that she cannot have any children. The tragic irony of Daw Shwe's situation was almost unbearable: she believed that her son had been falsely accused of rape only to be abducted by the state into the military, while she had no state recourse against the rapist of her daughter and had to accept living with him. I suggest that this is how "state trepidation", by which I mean fear of contact with the state, comes to corrode social relations, breeding a form of social inauthenticity that turns neighbour against neighbour.

There are no reliable figures of the exact extent of rape in the country, but sexual violence towards women in Myanmar is clearly an underrepresented problem that needs far more attention. A number of reports and commentaries warn that only the top of the iceberg is visible in statistics, and that widespread domestic violence and sexual violence, including rape, is a problem of huge proportions. A particular worry is that gender-based violence is socially legitimised, accompanied by a culture of silence and impunity and exacerbated by a weak legal system (UN 2008). Gendered violence and difficulties with getting vindication or justice via the law is not a new phenomenon. Jonathan Saha (2013) writes about British colonial state practices in Burma, and about how in those days Burmese women, in cases of sexual violence and exploitation (especially where government employees were the culprits), were suppressed and undermined. In fact, he argues that state formation processes on the part of the British placed women in inferior positions: 'state power was invested solely in men, and preferably those who performed an assertively masculine role of being dominant over women' (Saha 2013: 114). To this day, marital rape is not considered a criminal act, and cases where pre-marital rape is used as the justification for marriage to the perpetrator were documented by a study in 2014 (Gender Equality Network 2014). Victim blaming, where female victims of sexual violence are treated as being responsible for violations of their 'honour' – which is related to the family's honour and respectability – is prevalent. There is also a tendency for parents to pretend that nothing has happened because of fear of both the local community's reactions and of the judiciary (Enlightened Myanmar Research 2014). In a short online blog post, Aye Thiri Kyaw (2017) connects the problem of lack of reporting to state practice:

> The years under the military regime corrupted Myanmar's pillar of justice: the judiciary. The lack of an independent judiciary under military rule has bred a culture of impunity for many years. Rape survivors and their families express distrust towards judges and the wider system because they face long proceedings in court cases and corruption in the judicial system.

Daw Shwe decided that the better choice for her daughter was to marry her rapist instead of reporting him. However, this choice, which was made in an attempt to avoid the state, was already an affect of the state. The imaginary of the state was already inherent in this decision and avoidance was not possible. Daw Shwe's entire situation can be ascribed to the effects of lack of state care, spanning from losing some of her children because of poor health care, through forced relocation, to losing her son to the military. The affect that comes with those state effects is that a man rapes a young girl and gets to marry her. It was her past experience of a lack of state care that informed Daw Shwe's decision not to report the rape of her daughter to the police. She wanted to avoid any direct contact with the state. The lack of community support and social cohesion that prevail in the particular site of Yatkwet Thit made the situation even more difficult. These are rooted in the community history of forced relocation and marginalisation, and thus are also affects of the effects of state policies and practices. I want to turn now to a final case from Yatkwet Thit, one that provides insights into how the residents deal with a state that they distrust and expect to be deceptive. This illustrates the illegibility of state power and its materiality.

The deceptive state: Inherently inauthentic authority

One afternoon in late March we were at Ma Phyu's place. She is a short, stout, entrepreneurial woman and was my host in Yatkwet Thit. Her cousin Myint Soe Aung and a couple of family members had gathered to discuss problems relating to a plot of land. They have a land certificate; Myint Soe Aung's father had bought the plot. He had bought it with remittances that Soe Aung sent back when he was working in Thailand. The former ward administrator, U Than Lwin, facilitated the deal and did the paperwork. The seller of the plot was U Thin Thein, an army general, whose signature and address are in the contract. On the contract, the plot is plot number 76. We used my map from the ward administrator's office to look for it, but it did not exist. They contacted the ward administrator, and he said that the plot of land in question is in public ownership; it is part of a street and cannot be privately owned. The contract and land certificate might, he said, be fake. Myint Soe Aung got upset. They then went to the address of the general, but nobody there knew of him. The former ward administrator had fled the country a few years before, because he was wanted by the police. Myint Soe Aung then went to the Government's General Administration Department (GAD) at the township level. He was told that the certificate was not fake. The stamp, paper and signatures are real; but the contract is not valid because the land is not a plot on which a house can be built. The former ward administrator and the general had tricked them. Ma Phyu was not surprised at all, she told me. It is typical of ward administrators that they only think of themselves, she added. The NLD representative then said: 'The old ward administrator did work for the ward, but he sold everything in the ward for him to eat' (*A lough-lough de yan sade, a lough lough bu doung sade*).[9]

This story shows how a document can be official but may nevertheless not be authentic, meaning that it cannot be used. A document may easily be worthless even when a state official stamps it. Even so, people engage

9 Interview, 31 January 2017. The term 'to eat' is used in Burmese in this context to refer to using a resource in a general sense, with the implication of exploitation.

with and try to use these bureaucratic artefacts and documents, which carry some form of power, even if this power and what it can do for you is uncertain. Something similar can be seen in Indonesia, where Nils Bubandt (2015) argues that there is not necessarily an opposition between authority and uncertainty – or what he refers to as inauthenticity. The trust placed in the state's power is ambivalent because there is a general sense that bureaucratic artefacts and signatures are inauthentic, in the sense that they may be deceptive and unreliable. Nevertheless, people still seek and try to engage with state power, and herein lies an element of the state's authority. The above example of the fake land certificate that nevertheless carried an official state stamp is an illustration of the way in which authority and uncertainty are intertwined, setting up a continuing distrust of the state, but in a way that nevertheless reproduces imaginaries about its power to act and produce some kind of result.

The perpetual insecurity of dealing with state authorities is also expressed in the widespread practice in Yatkwet Thit (and in Myanmar in general) of turning to a mediator, a *pweza*, when someone needs to acquire an official document or permit (see also Chapter 9, this volume). A *pweza* will have an established network and a knowledge of how to speak to, deal with, and bribe state officials efficiently. In other words, a *pweza* helps ordinary people in their contacts with an illegible state, dealing with rules and regulations and 'state signatures' that are always potentially fake (Das 2004). Their service is not free, of course, and on top of paying the 'fee' to the state official for the desired document – for example an ID card, a construction permit, a land certificate, or a business licence – the *pweza* must be remunerated for his or her assistance. The *pweza* relieves ordinary citizens of the necessity of dealing with a corrupt and frightening bureaucracy and bridges the gap between 'us' (*tho*) and 'them' (*thu to*) (de la Perrière 2014: 7, 9). Albeit considered a convenient or sometimes *the* only method to use, the use of *pweza* further removes from the poorest the opportunity to obtain any of those documents. Embarking on the process of dealing with state authorities without the assistance of a *pweza* often lengthens and complicates the processing time. The power vested in the state is ambiguous, because bureaucratic artefacts and signatures are always potentially inauthentic, and in many instances, their validity is zero. Ma Phyu's comment about not being surprised that the document was useless reveals to us that she expected not to be able to trust the state. Nonetheless, this inauthenticity still gives rise to feelings of indignation. There appears, therefore, to be a sense in which they expect the state to be trustworthy and resent the fact that it is not, and the implication of this is that they accept the power of the state. Thus I would suggest that while people in Yatkwet Thit are upset that they are forced to deal with an inauthentic state and do not trust it, and that this is what leads them to evade the state, they do not inherently reject the power of the state altogether. State institutions and the material manifestations of the state can and have to be used, but are never trusted. As exemplified in the case of Daw Shwe, court processes and paperwork also render the state illegible. What happens in court is incomprehensible. The words of state officials and state paperwork made Daw Shwe's son disappear. These characteristics bestow an almost magic quality on the workings of the state (Das 2004; Das and Poole 2004).

Figure 8.3 Children waiting for their evening meal. *Colour image, p. 367.*

Conclusion

Through an exploration of life in the urban margins this chapter has sought to contribute to the study of people in Southeast Asia who are trying to abscond from the state. I have found that people in the margins of the Mon State's capital city live in a situation of simultaneous absence of supportive state institutions as well as in an omnipresence of state affect. There is no state care; however, there is plenty of surveillance, which transcends into mutual surveillance, distrust, and fear, and which installs itself as an affect in people's subjectivity and in their social relations. Daniel Goldstein makes a similar observation in relation to people living on the outskirts of a Bolivian city, where people feel that there is no working state or law: they are left to fend for themselves in any crisis or official encounter and '... inevitably get screwed in the process.' (Goldstein 2012: 82). State absence is not, however, the same as state non-presence. The state is present through the law, which imposes certain requirements and restrictions on citizens, encourages certain behaviours, and punishes others. But by not consistently enforcing these laws, protecting rights, and securing justice there is an absence of the state: it becomes a spectral entity, both there and not there, burdening and abandoning people who are simultaneously oppressed and ignored. Thus, the state makes people less and not more secure (Goldstein 2012: 83). In Yatkwet Thit ward, I found people in a similar situation, but whereas Goldstein found the state to be in an oppositional absence, I found that the state's affects are omnipresent and unavoidable.

According to Scott (2009), there is a long historical practice in Southeast Asia of evading the state, and he highlights ways in which people have done this through physical flight to regions which are beyond the reach of the state. In Yatkwet Thit, where flight is impossible, there is a strategy of avoidance vis-à-vis the state. This is a state affect. However, in present-day societies such as the one I studied in Yatkwet Thit, state evasion is in practice impossible, because the state as an imaginary is already inherent in its own juxtaposition and in its margins. In urban state margins like Yatkwet Thit, which is itself the product of past state policies, the state is already ingrained in the social fabric, transgressing into relations between people, affecting socialities and subjectivities. Here the state has affects even in its seeming absence – in terms of care, protection and rights. This presence-absence has been formed by a history of oppression and forced relocation, during which state effects were characterised by oppression, coercion and injustices. Following Das and Poole, I claim that it is sometimes in its absence that the state becomes most present. What seems to be outside turns out to be on the inside. Margins, in that sense, constitute a necessary condition for the existence of the state. The fundamental importance of the modern state in everyday life is more clearly visible in the margins than in the centre. Poor livelihoods, lack of proper infrastructure, corruption and a malfunctioning legal system are all effects of the state and they affect sociality and subjectivities.

I have argued that social forms of care and trust are hard to come by in a place like Yatkwet Thit. A long life under authoritarian rule leaves its mark on communities. I am not claiming that the situation in Yatkwet Thit reflects the way life is lived by people all over Myanmar, but I do claim that in urban margins like Yatkwet Thit human life seems to be valued less. People can cheat each other, rape, live and die, all without the state taking care of them – with the state experienced as a force to be feared, to be encountered with trepidation. This lack of care is reproduced internally in relations between neighbours and even family members. This is, I claim, an affect of the effect of the ways in which people living in a place like Yatkwet Thit have been treated by the state, not only in the past but in the present too.

References

AAPP

2002. *Assistance Association for Political Prisoners Report on Forced Labor.* aappb.org/2002/05/report-on-forced-labor-may-2002/

Aye, T.K.

2017. *Breaking the Devil's Silence: Sexual Violence in Myanmar.* 16 August 2017. teacircleoxford.com/2017/08/16/breaking-the-devils-silence-sexual-violence-in-myanmar/

Bozzini, D.

2015. 'The fines and the spies: Fears of state surveillance in Eritrea and in the diaspora.' *Social Analysis* 59(4): 32–49.

Bubandt, N.

2015. 'Trust in an age of inauthenticity: Power and Indonesian modernity.' In S. Liisberg, E.O. Pedersen and A.L. Dalsgård (eds), *Anthropology & Philosophy: Dialogues on Trust and Hope,* pp. 141–157. New York: Berghahn Books.

Cheesman, N.

2015. *Opposing the Rule of Law. How Myanmar's Courts make Law and Order.* Cambridge Studies in Law and Society. Cambridge: Cambridge University Press.

Cheesman, N., Skidmore, M. & Wilson, T.

2010. *Ruling Myanmar: From Cyclone Nargis to National Elections.* Singapore: Institute of Southeast Asian Studies.

Crouch, M.

2019. *The Constitution of Myanmar. A Contextual Analysis.* Oxford: Hart.

Das, V.

2004. 'The signature of the state: The paradox of illegibility.' In D. Poole and V. Das (eds), *Anthropology in the Margins of the State,* pp. 225–252. Santa Fe, N.M.: School of American Research Press.

Das, V. & Poole, D.

2004. *Anthropology in the Margins of the State*. Oxford: James Currey (Publishers) Ltd.

de la Perrière, B.B.

2014. 'A woman of mediation.' In W.-C. Chang and E. Tagliacozzo (eds), *Burmese Lives: Ordinary Life Stories under the Burmese Regime*, pp. 71–83. Oxford: Oxford University Press.

Denney, L., Bennet, W. & San, K.T.

2016. *Making Big Cases Small and Small Cases Disappear: Experiences of Local Justice in Myanmar*. London: British Council, Overseas Development Institute and Saferworld.

Enlightened Myanmar Research (EMR)

2014. *Between Fear and Hope: Challenges and Opportunities for Strengthening Rule of Law & Access to Justice in Myanmar*. Enlightened Myanmar Research, September 2014. emref.org/sites/emref.org/files/publication-docs/between_fear_and_hope_eng_version.pdf.

Fink, F.

2009. *Living Silence in Burma: Surviving Under Military Rule*. Chiang Mai: Silkworm Books.

Forbes, E.

2019. 'Migration, informal settlement, and government response: The cases of four townships in Yangon, Myanmar.' *Moussons* 33(1): 95–117.

Gender Equality Network

2014. *Behind the Silence. Violence Against Women and their Resilience, Myanmar*. Briefing Paper, October 2014, www.burmalibrary.org/docs20/GEN-2014-11-Behind_the_Silence-en-ocr-tpo.pdf.

Goldstein, D.M.

2012. *Outlawed: Between Security and Rights in a Bolivian City*. Durham and London: Duke University Press.

Gregg, M. & Seigworth, G.J.

2010. *The Affect Theory Reader*. Durham, N.C.: Duke University Press.

Hansen, T.B. & Stepputat, F.

2001. *States of Imagination: Ethnographic Explorations of the Postcolonial State (Politics, History and Culture)*. Durham, NC: Duke University Press.

Harrisson, A.P.

2018. 'Everyday justice for Muslims in Mawlamyine: Subjugation and skilful navigation.' *Independent Journal of Burmese Scholarship* 1(2): 57–85.

2020. 'Fish caught in clear water: Encompassed state-making in Southeast Myanmar.' *Territory, Politics, Governance.* doi.org/10.1080/21622671.2020.1743200

Human Rights Watch

2005. *They Came and Destroyed our Village again. The Plight of Internally Displaced Persons in Karen State.* Report. Vol. 17(4) (C). www.hrw.org/reports/2005/burma0605/

Kyed, H.M.

2019. 'Informal settlements and migrant challenges in Yangon.' *Moussons* 33(1): 65–94.

Kyed, H.M., Harrisson, A.P. & McCarthy, G.

2016. *Local Democracy in Myanmar: Reflections on Ward and Village Tract Elections in 2016.* Copenhagen: Dansk Institut for Internationale Studier, DIIS.

Laszczkowski, M. & Reeves, M.

2015. 'Introduction. Affective states – entanglements, suspensions, suspicions.' *Social Analysis* 59(4): 1–14.

Lidauer, M.

2014. 'Towards a new state in Myanmar.' In M. Gravers and F. Ytzen (eds), *Burma/Myanmar – Where Now?* pp. 72–86. Copenhagen: NIAS Press.

Linke, U.

2006. 'Contact zones: Rethinking the sensual life of the state.' *Anthropological Theory* 6(2): 205–225.

Massumi, B.

1995. 'The autonomy of affect.' *Cultural Critique* 31: 83–109.

Mitchell, T.

1999. 'Society, economy and the state effect.' In G. Steinmetz (ed.), *State/Culture: State-Formation after the Cultural Turn*, pp. 76–97. Ithaca: Cornell University Press.

Navaro-Yashin, Y.

2009. 'Affective spaces, melancholic objects: Ruination and the production of anthropological knowledge.' *Journal of the Royal Anthropological Institute* 15(1): 1–18.

2012. *The Make-Believe Space: Affective Geography in a Postwar Polity.* Durham, NC: Duke University Press.

Pinker, A. & Harvey, P.

2015. 'Negotiating uncertainty: Neo-liberal statecraft in contemporary Peru.' *Social Analysis* 59(4): 15–31.

Reeves, M.

2015. 'Living from the nerves: Deportability, indeterminacy, and the "feel of law" in migrant Moscow.' *Social Analysis* 59(4): 119–136.

Saha, J.

2013. *Law, Disorder and the Colonial State: Corruption in Burma c.1900.* Houndmills, Basingstoke and Hampshire: Palgrave Macmillan.

Scott, J.C.

2009. *The Art of Not Being Governed: An Anarchist History of Upland Southeast Asia.* Newhaven, Conneticut: Yale University Press.

2014. 'Dr. U Tin Win, escape artist 1.' In W.-C. Chang and E. Tagliacozzo (eds), *Burmese Lives: Ordinary Life Stories under the Burmese Regime.* Pp. 132–146. Oxford: Oxford University Press.

Skidmore, M.

2004. *Karaoke Fascism: Burma and the Politics of Fear (The Ethnography of Political Violence).* Philadelphia: University of Pennsylvania Press.

South, A.

2008. *Civil Society in Burma: The Development of Democracy amidst Conflict.* Washington: East-West Centre. Policy Studies No. 51.

Taylor, R.H.

2009. *The State in Myanmar.* Singapore: NUS Press.

Thawnghmung, A.

2016. 'The Myanmar elections 2015: Why the national league for democracy won a landslide victory.' *Critical Asian Studies* 48(1): 132–142.

Trouillot, M.-R.

2001. 'The anthropology of the state in the age of globalization: Close encounters of the deceptive kind.' *Current Anthropology* 42(1): 125–138.

UN

2008. *Concluding observations of the Committee on the Elimination of Discrimination against Women, Myanmar.* Report submitted by UN Committee on the Elimination of Discrimination against Women. Forty-second session, 20 October – 7 November 2008.

9 Informal (justice) brokers: Buying, selling, and disputing property in Yangon

Elizabeth Rhoads

Introduction

Myanmar is often conceptualised as a 'law-of-status' society (Maung Maung Gyi 1983: 170–171), one without a concept of equal treatment before the law. In a 'law of status' society individuals are treated primarily according to their position in a social hierarchy.[1] Where status is the most important variable in a legal dispute there is likely to be little faith in the official legal system, as its main promise of 'equal treatment before the law' is superseded by social hierarchy, where people are by definition not equals. In Myanmar, this is compounded by an exceptionally hierarchical justice system that has long lacked an independent and impartial judiciary (Cheesman 2011, 2015). In the context of Myanmar, as described in this volume's other contributions, there is a high degree of avoidance of the formal justice system, in which there is no guarantee of equal treatment. As a result, people use localised, socially-mediated, informal forms of dispute resolution (e.g. see Prasse-Freeman 2015; Thang Sorn Poine 2018; see also Introduction to this volume).

While many high-profile or high-value property cases end up in Myanmar courts, a considerable number of cases do not go through the formal legal system, even in government-controlled areas where the Myanmar state seems unavoidable, such as Yangon.[2] Ordinary Yangon residents rely on localised versions of dispute resolution, particularly in everyday property transactions, which frequently employ mutually

1 For more on social hierarchy in Burma, see Keeler (2017). For a legal historical description of a 'law of status' society, see MacNeill's (1923) description of ancient Irish Law.

2 The government reported that 442,000 court cases were filed across the country in 2017, showing a significant increase over 2016 when a reported 417,000 cases were filed (Htoo Thant 2018). This number represents all filed cases reported, not only property-related cases.

agreed arbiters to represent the transacting parties. In some cases, these mediators are lawyers, but more often than not they are *eain pweza* (property brokers), individuals well-known in the neighbourhood or acquaintances of all the parties involved, who facilitate legal and extra-legal property transfers and other transactions in exchange for a commission.

This chapter explores avenues of informal justice in relation to property cases in urban Yangon, with a specific focus on the role of brokers known as *eain pweza* (in Burmese). These are actors who are part real estate agents, part fixers, and part mediators. I argue that the involvement of *eain pweza* in dispute resolution is both a strategic choice and a practical necessity, as the specific contours of property disputes may prohibit access to formal justice procedures. *Eain pweza* use their roles as information and relationship brokers to secure housing transactions, in many cases serving as a primary arbiter in housing-related dispute settlement. As most property transfers in Yangon are informal, as this paper shows, contemporary attempts at regulating the sector may lead to a closure of avenues for property-related disputes, weakening access to justice for the majority of Myanmar's urban residents.

Urban property is an important entry point to understanding informal or local justice, as property involves vertical state–society power relations, as well as horizontal power relations such as those between landlord and tenant or between neighbours. In both vertical and horizontal power relations involving property, a sense of justice and belonging are embodied. In reshaping property relations during times of transition, it is these local understandings of justice and belonging that are disrupted. Central to all of Myanmar's political and economic transitions, since the British occupation, have been changes in property legislation and practices, disrupting prior understandings of justice and norms of property distribution (Rhoads 2019). Collective memories of who owns what, who confiscated what, and who was dispossessed remain strong in the present. Contemporary property relations are built on these previous categories, events and identities (cf. Peñalver 2011). This chapter takes a socio-legal approach to understanding property transactions and disputes in Yangon. Research for this chapter was conducted in central Yangon over a total of 15 months between 2014–2020. Semi-structured and unstructured interviews were conducted with property brokers, property developers, lawyers involved in property cases, and homeowners. Fieldwork was complemented by a review of case law and of newspaper and media articles, and by archival research in the Myanmar National Archives, the India Office Records of the British Library, and the United Kingdom National Archives at Kew.

In order to examine the role of *pweza* in everyday property cases in Yangon, the chapter begins with a short description of *pweza* and the literature on brokerage, followed by an overview of the evolution of Myanmar's legal system, placing informal justice brokers in context. This legal history is important, as approximately one-third of Yangon's downtown core was built prior to the Second World War.[3] Myanmar's immovable property has been governed and greatly affected not only by the current legal context but also by previous contexts dating back to the British colonial period. Next, the chapter will address the types of transactions in which brokers are used and why, followed by a discussion of the Myanmar government's moves towards increased regulation of property transfers as well as of brokers (*pweza*) and what this regulation may mean for everyday dispute resolution and justice provision.

Brokers and Brokerage

In formal and informal property transactions, *pweza* charge a fee for their role in brokering the transaction, usually one month's rent on a 12-month lease from both the lessee and the lessor, or 2 per cent of the property price on a sale.[4] This is a hefty fee for bringing the parties together, contracting the sale, making sure the title is clean (where possible), and that the relevant fees and taxes are paid for formal transactions – not unlike formal real estate agents in other jurisdictions. But the fee does not only cover bringing the two parties together and brokering the lease or sale, but essentially buys the *pweza*'s time for the duration of the lease, or the duration of ownership in the case of a sale. As Boutry et al. (2016) have noted, the function of the broker is to provide a kind of guarantee on the transaction in an unregulated market. This guarantee

3 I would like to thank Yangon Heritage Trust for this insight on the ages of buildings in contemporary downtown Yangon.

4 Rather than a deposit, Yangon rentals usually require rent paid in cash in full at the start of a lease. 12-month leases are often paid at the time of signing or paid in two 6-month installments. This adds to the importance of the *pweza*'s role, as even renting is a considerable investment and leaves the tenant in a precarious position if there is a dispute (i.e leaking roof, etc.) with the landlord as they cannot withhold rent. In some low-income properties such as hostels, rent is paid month-to-month in advance.

may prevent the sale of the same property to different parties, though it may not be able to guarantee that the property is secure from state intervention (Boutry et al. 2016: 41).

Eain pweza play a role long after property has changed hands, or the lease signed, bearing responsibility not only for brokering the transaction, but oftentimes mediating, and settling, any disputes that may arise. While involved in formal and informal transactions, the role of the *eain pweza* is all the more important in informal transactions, as there is no recourse to the courts in the case of a dispute. In many property cases, a *pweza*'s social connections and diplomatic skills may be the only route to dispute resolution (see Di Certo 2013).

Scholars have pointed to the moral uncertainty or ambiguity of the broker (James 2011), who often seems to be looking out for themselves first and foremost when assisting others in accessing housing, land, visas, markets, etc. Lund (1999) argues that brokerage encourages the perpetuation of disputes, to the benefit of brokers. Lund's (1999) description of Burkina Faso and James' (2011) findings in South Africa are not so dissimilar to the Myanmar context but there are important differences. In practice, the expectation for *pweza* to actively mediate and settle any disputes that arise is not always met, leading to the reputation of *pweza* as unscrupulous actors who after receiving their commission are nowhere to be found (Brac de la Perrière 2014: 77).

However, James (2011) and Lund (1999) portray brokers as needing to be understood in the context of patron-client relationships, in that brokers have clients and patrons of their own and can facilitate a range of work for themselves as intermediaries between their patrons and their clients. By contrast, in Yangon, while brokers do rely on their networks and social standing, for the most part they do not have any particular patrons or a set of clients or followers. Like brokers in other contexts, a successful *pweza's* trade is in their social relations and negotiation skills. As Brac de la Perrière (2014) notes, their utility is in their good relationships with those in their field of business. In property, this may be other *pweza*, developers, landowners, local authorities, and others. While *pweza* may be known as a 'bloodsucker class' and are often seen as taking advantage of clients, taking their commission and leaving, ultimately their continued success rests on their reputation (Ibid.: 77). Their ability to retain clients and attract clients in the future is due to perceptions of trustworthiness and their capacity to lend their social connections to guarantee or provide further security for a transaction (Ibid.).

Pweza are involved in property transactions much as realtors are involved in property transactions in other contexts, except that in Myanmar there is no regulation of realtors and the majority of property transactions are extra-legal. This chapter highlights how the more reliable and responsible *eain pweza* actually provide services not easily obtainable through legal actors or procedures. The role of a Myanmar property broker extends far beyond that of a typical real estate agent, to that of an informal justice broker.

Myanmar's legal system

Pre-colonial Burma had an indigenous legal system that was arguably the most advanced in Southeast Asia (Huxley 1997), and unique in the Buddhist world (Lammerts 2018). Pre-colonial Burmese Buddhist law was complete with law texts (*dhammasattha* "treatise on law") (Lammerts 2018), judges, and lawyers (*she-ne*) (Huxley 1998; Lammerts 2018). Scholars have argued that pre-colonial Burma's legal culture was similar to British legal culture and rather dissimilar to Asian legal cultures (Huxley 1998; Stanton 2014). A key substantive difference between the pre-colonial Burmese legal system and the British legal system was that Burmese law focused on achieving a harmonious solution for the disputing parties, while British law sought punitive justice, usually in the form of a winner and a loser of a case or dispute (Furnivall 2014 [1948]: 131; Huxley 1998; Stanton 2014: 14). However, as the British conquest of Burma and piecemeal annexation progressed during the 19th century, rather than using the existing Burmese legal system and legal culture the British colonial administration modelled the legal system in Burma on British India. This consisted of transplanting colonial legal codes and precedents from British India, based on Benthamite ideas of law and economic growth (Bentham 1843; Trubek and Santos 2006: 1). This effectively truncated the Burmese legal system, giving it no opportunity to evolve (Stanton 2014). As Andrew Huxley (1998) has argued, the British 'deliberately destroyed a literate and professional legal culture'.

However, Burmese laws and practices relating to religion, marriage and succession were to remain, to 'persuade the Burmese that they, as well as the colonisers, had a stake in the colonial legal system' (Huxley

1998). What is important to keep in mind in relation to these changes is that the resultant legal system is generally adversarial, with winners and losers. However, personal law (often referred to as family law in other contexts) is regulated by Burmese customary law or by codified personal law based on the religious affiliation of the individuals involved. This includes important property issues such as marital property, religious endowments, inheritance and succession. Thus, unlike contract or criminal law, property cases related to marriage, religious endowments or inheritance are dealt with in a more hybrid and localised way, combining elements of British Indian legislation and case law, Burmese customary law, and religious law (Crouch 2014b, 2016). While 'Western ideas of individual property in land were substituted for the Burmese custom of family possession' (Furnivall 1948: 135) in cases involving personal law, adjudication frequently brought the religious and ethnic identity of the parties to the fore, in order to determine which customary law or personal law should apply.

At Independence, Burma inherited a common law tradition from the British colonial authorities, Indian legal codes, precedents from all over the British Empire (but mainly from India), and anglicised, codified religious and personal laws (Crouch 2014b). For the first ten years, the judicial branch of the Union of Burma was very active and independent, frequently issuing rulings defending the 'rights of citizens against the excesses of the state' (Cheesman 2011: 804). However, following Ne Win's 1962 *coup d'état*, the judiciary was undermined by a 'radical legal decolonisation' (Huxley 1998) which joined the judiciary, legislative and executive branches together in a one-party state driving towards the ultimate goal of a socialist economy (Cheesman 2011; Huxley 1998). From 1962 to 2011, individuals had no ability to challenge the government in court (Crouch 2014a: 2). In 1972, judges were replaced by lay people, to establish a 'system of people's justice' (Huxley 1998; Cheesman 2011), which did not use precedent or foreign rulings (Myint Zan 2004: 422).

While the professional judiciary returned to the bench following the formation of the State Law and Order Restoration Council (SLORC) in 1988, it seems that the damage to the use of precedent may have already been done. Myint Zan's 2004 study comparing Burma's 1948 and 1998 law reports found that the cases reported in the High Courts and Supreme Court in the 1948 Burma Law Reports contained an average of 4.61 cases per reported ruling, while the 1998 Myanmar Law Reports, reporting Myanmar Supreme Court cases, contained 1.27 cases per ruling, showing a decrease in the use of precedent in court rulings (Myint Zan 2004: 422). While foreign investors consider Myanmar's common law status and British legal history to be advantageous to business, this legacy is complicated by decades of authoritarian rule and rule by decree (Cheesman 2011, 2015; Crouch 2014a). Recent studies by donors and policymakers reveal uncertainty surrounding precedents due to unreported cases (Crouch 2014a), and judges ability to select favourable precedents and ignore contrary rulings, if the courts rely on precedential decisions at all (cf. UN Women 2016: 39–40).

This is the legal context within which past and current decisions regarding property have been made and are being made. During some periods precedent was used and there was heavier reliance on colonial law. During other periods rule was by decree. As Huxley, contemplating what might succeed authoritarian rule in Burma, wrote, 'Since law has undergone so many changes over the last fifty years, there is no single *status quo ante* to which a democratic Burma could return' (Huxley 1998). The frequent changes to the legal system, coupled with the use of personal law in property cases regarding inheritance, marital property and religious endowments, created a patchwork of legal rulings and little perception of legal certainty. The only way the general public is able to predict the outcome of a property case is based on the social status of the plaintiff and the defendant (Rhoads 2019). As others have noted there is an oft-repeated sentiment in Myanmar that "it does not matter what a contract, or the law, actually says, because power is more important than law" (Briggs and Burrows 2017:2). For much of the last 30 years, courts have been focused on enforcing the State Law and Order Restoration Council (SLORC) and later the State Peace and Development Council (SPDC) policies, so they are likely to have ruled in favour of the government or of those aligned closely with the government (Cheesman 2015), making court an unlikely place to voluntarily bring a case, particularly those involving only private parties or involving an uneven power dynamic between parties.

State institutions: Avoidance and exclusion

The Myanmar public's wariness of state institutions extends far beyond the judiciary (e.g. Turnell et al. 2008). Anthropologist Bénédicte Brac de la Perrière (2014: 79) writes about the role of *pweza* as brokers, or rather as go-betweens between ordinary people and the state, occupying 'a shifting space between officials and civilians. They provided a social space for negotiating the moving frontiers between "them" and "us"'. Brac de la Perrière focuses on the role of brokers in what she calls 'intermediation' or negotiations between ordinary Burmese and the state. She notes how brokers were:

> [...] found in any endeavor: buying a car, helping people connect to the power network, getting identity cards and residence certificates or passports to go abroad. Pweza were mainly stand-ins between civilians and officials who took on administrative transactions in a corrupt and frightening bureaucracy. (Brac de la Perrière 2014: 76)

Avoidance of the state and reliance on go-betweens leads to the exclusion of many property actors from the formal legal system even before a dispute begins. Valid property transfers require at least six procedures (World Bank 2020), involving four separate government entities,[5] and scrutiny of various aspects of the buyer's and the seller's everyday lives, from source of income to ancestry. While this is the case in many systems, as mortgage lenders require proof of income and jurisdictions may restrict ownership of immovable property to their own citizens, in Myanmar there is neither an active formal lending sector (Turnell et al. 2008; Turnell 2014) nor transparency on how the bureaucracy of the Myanmar state handles the relationship between ancestry,[6] citizenship and property (Rhoads 2019 & 2020). Some procedures and requirements for a legal transfer of property are detailed in the next section to give the reader an understanding of what property actors are avoiding by using informal transfers and why informal brokers are engaged.

---

5 Government entities involved in urban property transfers in Yangon include: the Inland Revenue Department of the Ministry of Finance, the Office of Registration of Deeds under the Ministry of Home Affairs, the Criminal Investigation Department of the Myanmar Police Force and the City Planning and Land Administration Department of the Yangon City Development Committee (YCDC) (or the Department of Human Settlement and Housing Development – DHSHD of the Ministry of Construction, depending on the location) (MBF 2016: 2).

6 Since Myanmar's independence, citizenship has been defined by ethnicity and/or length of settlement of oneself or one's ancestors in the country. However, the 1982 Citizenship Law repealed previous legislation and created a tiered system of citizenship based primarily on ethnicity and secondarily on settlement in the country prior to Independence, either by oneself or one's ancestors.

Legal procedures in transferring property

A valid transfer requires both the buyer and the seller to pay taxes prior to registering the transfer. Since 2015, the seller of the property pays capital gains tax at a flat rate of 10 per cent on all property transfers (Section 27b, Union Tax Law, No. 17/2015) and 10 per cent on total rental income (Section 19(b)). But Myanmar also uses formal property transfers as a way to capture unpaid taxes. The buyer of a property is liable to pay income tax if the buyer's source of income is not able to be verified and has previously escaped tax assessment. If this is the case, as it frequently is in a cash-based economy with very low tax compliance, then there is a graduated tax (15–30 per cent)[7] based on the property sale price, levied on the buyer. If the buyer can show the source of all income used in purchasing the property, then no income tax is levied on the buyer. If none of the income used has been assessed and is without a verified source, it will be taxed at 30 per cent. If only part of the income used in purchasing the property is accounted for, then the remaining income will be taxed based on the graduated rate (Section 24, Union Tax Law No. 22/2016). This creates a significant income and capital gains tax burden at the point of sale, requiring large amounts of cash to complete and legally register any transfer.

Even without income tax liability, a property transfer (sale, lease, gift, etc.) cannot be registered and legally completed until the buyer pays the applicable stamp duty. Rates range from 0.5 per cent of the entire amount payable under the lease, for leases of less than one year, to 6 per cent of the sale price for Yangon property transfers.[8] If the name of the current

7 The graduated tax rate currently starts at 15 per cent for unassessed income up to approximately USD 20,000 (MMK 30,000,000), 20 per cent for MMK 30,000,001 to 100,000,000 (about USD 65,000), and 30 per cent for anything above approximately USD 65,000 (MMK 100,000,000). In the 2019–2020 tax year there is a tax amnesty provision, lowering the rates to start at 3 per cent of unassessed income up to MMK 100,000,000, 5 per cent from MMK 100,000,001 to 300,000,000, 10 per cent for MMK 300,000,001 to 1,000,000,000, 15 per cent for MMK 1,000,000,001 to 3,000,000,000 and 30 per cent for anything over MMK 3,000,000,001 used to purchase or construct property or buy, expand or establish a business (Union Tax Law 2019). A similar tax amnesty was last granted in 2015, but the rates of taxation were considerably higher than the 2019 tax amnesty. For more on previous tax amnesties and the use of the tax on unassessed income to 'whiten' illicitly derived income, see Bo Bo Nge (2020).

8 Since the formation of the Rangoon Development Trust in 1921 an additional two percent stamp duty is levied on transfers of immovable property in Rangoon

owner is not on the deed, a lease on immovable property cannot be registered. However, to have the current owner's name on the deed and registered, all previous transfers must be registered as well (MBF 2016: 9). The owners of properties that have a long chain of unregistered transfers may not be able to establish themselves as the current titleholders or may incur high penalty fees and tax liabilities. The statutory penalty for not paying stamp duty (proof of which must be shown to register the transfer of property) is up to three times the applicable stamp duty on the property (Law Amending the Myanmar Stamp Act, 2019).

In formal property transactions, brokers (*pweza*) may be used to locate the former official owner (the person whose name is on the last registered deed of sale) and broker an agreement under which they formally transfer the property, for a fee (e.g. Zay Yar Lin 2016a). This is complicated, as property valuations are now set by the Internal Revenue Department, and the official owner whose name is on the registered deed is liable for capital gains tax on the sale. A large fee is often charged by the former official owner at this stage to cover the transaction costs, and the person now in possession of the property, who may have purchased it from the official owner long ago but never registered it, now has to pay stamp duty based on the current property valuation. There may be income tax liabilities as well, further complicating the transfer, as technically the 'buyer' will have to show where they got the funds to purchase the property, in which they may already have been living for decades following an informally brokered sale. Furthermore, transfers under the 1882 Transfer of Property Act can only be between living persons (Section 5; see also Eggar 1931: 5). If the person whose name is on the deed is deceased, only the legitimate heir or legal representative can transfer the deed to their name in accordance with the inheritance practices of their religious community (MBF 2017: 4; Eggar 1931: 19).

The above regulations entail lengthy and repeated interactions with government institutions and considerable scrutiny of both buyer and seller. The World Bank's report *Doing Business in Myanmar* (2020) put

(Rangoon Development Trust Act 1921 Section 63(1); Pearn 1939: 281). The 2014 Law Amending the Myanmar Stamp Act revoked the surcharge applied in the Rangoon Development Trust Act. In 2017 this was amended again, reinstating the surcharge in the Act. Since 2013, the stamp duty on immovable property sales in Yangon has moved from 7 per cent in 2013 to 4 per cent in 2014 to 6 per cent in 2017 (Lincoln Legal Services 2017; Luther 2017; Law Amending the Myanmar Stamp Act 2014; Law Amending the Myanmar Stamp Act 2017).

the median length of time required to transfer a property in Yangon at 65 days. This is assuming that the property has no occupants, is not mortgaged, is fully owned by the seller, is peri-urban but within the official limits of a municipality, and has no title disputes. Due to all of the above restrictions, plus tax liabilities, and other complications, in 2018 there were only 2,894 official property transfers made in Yangon, exceedingly few transfers for a city of more than 5 million people (World Bank 2020: 27). The vast majority of property transfers occurred between parties outside of the formal system, as will be discussed in the following sections.

Informal property transfers

Informal transactions in Myanmar frequently occur, not only of property but also in relation to lending, remittances or money transfers, and trade. Informal transactions can be attractive because of the legal status of the individuals involved, the legality of the transaction, the legality of the goods or services being transferred or performed, the weakness or inaccessibility of formal institutions, or simply because of the parties' lack of familiarity with formal mechanisms or institutions (Turnell et al. 2008). While Myanmar's financial services remain weak (Turnell 2014), the growing use of technology in banking and financial services[9] contrasts with the continued use of informal transactions, particularly in property.

Transfers of property frequently occur without registration of the deed of sale, the lease, or other instrument that is required to legally complete the transaction. In the media and according to government representatives, the lack of registration is portrayed as due to a culture of property speculation and tax avoidance amongst the general population.[10] But there are multiple other reasons why Yangon residents would not be able or would not choose to transfer property legally by officially registering the transfer.

9 Only about 19 per cent of Myanmar's population had a bank account in 2015 (Schellhase and Sun 2017: 6), but data from 2017 shows that about 30 per cent of adults 25 and older had an account with a financial institution or mobile-money service provider (World Bank 2017). Reforms to the banking sector have been made to allow for the use of ATM machines, meaning that banks can now issue debit cards (Turnell 2014).

10 For relevant media descriptions and portrayals of the culture of tax avoidance, see: Myat Nyein Aye 2014, 2016a, 2016b; Myat Nyein Aye and Ko Ko Aung 2015; Kyaw Hsu Mon 2014; Zay Yar Lin 2016a and 2016b.

Many property buyers and sellers in downtown Yangon may have no understanding of the legal requirement to register property, such as those buying the right to occupancy of an apartment where the landowner did not change in the transaction. For many residents contracting informal property transfers whom I interviewed in Yangon, the sales contract is considered a legal document, even without registration. If transacting parties use a lawyer to draw up the contract and a realtor to broker the deal, the property transfer is regarded as legal and formal by those contracting it, even if it is not regarded as such in the eyes of the state. Furthermore, Section 53a of the 1882 Transfer of Property Act allows for part execution of a contract involving immovable property if the buyer or transferee is in possession of the property, even if the instrument is not yet registered. This allows residents to possess property based on an unregistered sales contract without fear that they will be dispossessed by the transferor (The Nation 1964), providing fairly strong security of tenure for most practical purposes.

There are multiple reasons why property may go unregistered. Owners may have bought or sold occupancy rights or other rights that were not legally transferrable at the time (Boutry et al. 2017), such as individual apartment units. The buyer's or the seller's citizenship status may have prevented many property owners from transferring property through official channels (Rhoads 2019). Changes regarding who was eligible for Myanmar citizenship with the passing of the 1982 Citizenship Law, and changes limiting property transfers to citizens in the 1947 and 1987 Transfer of Immovable Property (Restriction) Acts limited the pool of people who could legally transfer property (Rhoads 2020). Both in cases of the sale of rights which were not legally transferrable, and where property is transferred between parties classified post-1948 or post-1982 as 'foreigners', there are large incentives to stay under the radar of the state so as to avoid the risk not merely of tax liabilities, but also of property confiscation.

But the efforts of Yangon residents to avoid interactions with state institutions and their unfamiliarity with regulations are not the only reasons why the sale of property goes unregistered. Outside of issues relating to state institutions like the cost of registration, or the difficulties in proving citizenship, inheritance disputes and lost records plague property transfers. Most properties in Yangon do not have a clear chain of ownership, and those that do often have an unregistered chain of ownership documents (MBF 2016: 9). Andrew Scherer (2015) found that informal property transfers in Yangon occur, and property transfers go unregistered, because unclear ownership status precludes the ability to contract a formal property transfer. A legal property transfer cannot be completed using a chain of unregistered sales contracts, even if the current relationship between buyer and seller is documented, as it is unclear if the transferor actually has the legal right to make the transfer. Thus, for many Yangon properties, the only option for transferring property may be informal, and even if buyers would like to register their ownership, they may be unable to, due to the property's past.

Mutual understanding: Brokering informal property transactions

The use of *pweza* in property transactions does not only reflect an aversion to formality but also highlights both Yangon residents' underlying distrust of the legal system as well as their general exclusion from it. This is particularly clear in property cases because all Myanmar residents are involved in real estate in some way. Everyone has a relationship to property in some form whether as tenants, squatters, occupants, guests, heirs, purchasers, sellers, or owners. Informal transactions between private individuals based on mutual agreement and understandings rather than contracts secured by state institutions remain the primary mode of transferring property.

Most informal transactions involve an element of *nalehmu* between parties. Literally, *nalehmu* refers to an abstract idea of 'an understanding' (as a noun). It can be used to describe a range of informal social, institutional, or business relationships based on mutual understanding. These can include activities as diverse as corruption; sharing space in an apartment; or not interfering with your neighbour's religious practices (Roberts and Rhoads 2018). Thawnghmung (2011: 646) defines *nar-lai-mu* (sic) as 'an informal and tacit agreement struck with authorities, service providers and business partners to overcome constraints, whether natural or institutional, in order to utilise the opportunity to fulfil individual and collective needs'. *Nalehmu* transactions or property access arrangements are based on mutual understanding and trust, often supported by kinship, religious, friendship, neighbourhood, or ethnic networks. *Nalehmu* arrangements may be supported by state law or in contravention of it and serve as a form of *de facto* ownership or locally recognised property rights (Campbell 2019: 8; Rhoads 2019). While the practice of using *nalehmu* in everyday life is widespread in Myanmar, it is a particularly useful concept through which to explore dispute resolution and property transactions. When parties cannot rely on social or geographic proximity to secure a transaction based on *nalehmu*, *pweza* serve as useful intermediaries between them, securing a transaction between people who are outside of each other's personal networks.

Access to formal justice in the informal property market

Historically, not being able to legally transfer property due to lack of documentation meant very little, as property sales occurred under the table throughout the socialist period (1962–1988) and before (e.g. Boutry et al. 2017). People traded properties within their own communities and created informal agreements based on mutual understanding (*nalehmu*) that allowed them to transfer properties without official paperwork and in contravention of regulations (Campbell 2019; Rhoads 2019; Simone 2018: 36). However, problems arise when there are disputes over property or a need to prove ownership, including in requesting building or renovation permits; fights against confiscation through eminent domain or extra-legal seizure; divisions of property in divorce or inheritance; or when there is joint liability for taxation.

As detailed above, immovable property sold or leased in Yangon is subject to payment of stamp duty before a legal transfer of property takes place. The 1899 Stamp Act requires the payment of stamp duty for any contract to be considered valid or admissible as evidence in court (Section 35). This includes contracts for joint ventures, leases, and sales contracts for immovable property. A stamped lease or deed of sale allows both parties to defend themselves in court, if suit was brought against them, but a registered lease is necessary to initiate court proceedings (49(c) Registration Act 1909).[11] This leaves few, if

11 Excepting specific instances under the 1877 Special Relief Act and the 1882 Transfer of Property Act. Interestingly, the Transfer of Property Act (Section 53A) allows for protection of the immovable property of the transferee from the transferor in the case of an unregistered transfer if there is a contract in writing and the transferee has already taken possession of the immovable property.

any, avenues for formal legal recourse if either party does not uphold contractual elements of an unregistered lease or sale.

Pweza interviewed in Yangon and the local media report that buyers and sellers are paying some tax.[12] Prior to changes in property valuation from the Internal Revenue Department in 2013,[13] buyers and sellers made two sets of sales contracts, one with the real price, and one with a lower price, which was used for paying stamp duty (Myat Nyein Aye 2014; Yu Wai 2017). While stamp duty was paid on the sales contract, the name on the registered deed did not change because the deed of sale was never registered. Those who have paid stamp duty on their property can defend themselves in court if they are ever sued for eviction, but they would not be able to sue others for eviction from their property, as, without a registered deed, they cannot initiate a suit. In these types of cases, the role of informal brokers becomes exceedingly important in guaranteeing the informal property market.

The role of informal brokers

Pweza are engaged in all types of property transactions. In formal transactions they may be responsible for processing building permits, assisting property buyers in their dealings with state institutions by registering the deed of sale, or assisting buyers and sellers in creating a power of attorney to transfer property without a deed of sale (and incurring a lower stamp duty) (Myat Nyein Aye 2016a; Waldie n.d.: 13; Zay Yar Lin 2016a, 2016b). Brac de la Perrière (2014: 75) has described the position of broker as 'acting on behalf of ordinary people in formal procedures or in transactions.' Often these brokers are lawyers or real estate agents, but they can also be acquaintances of the property owner who are well-versed in what it takes to interact with government authorities. This could be as simple as someone literate and fluent in

12 This chapter does not address municipal property taxes, as these taxes are not relevant to the transfer of the property, but such taxes would be assessed on properties after purchase or occupation. For more on municipal property taxes, see: McDonald & Arkar Hein (2017).

13 As property buyers were routinely under-reporting the sale price on property transfers when reporting to the Internal Revenue Department to pay stamp duty and income tax, in 2013 the Internal Revenue Department made an assessment list for each of Yangon's neighbourhoods to be used for valuation of property for tax purposes (Myat Nyein Aye 2016b).

Burmese. Particularly in ethnic minority communities, a broker may be someone who has gone through government school and can navigate government offices and authorities on behalf of less integrated community members (Rhoads in press). Such a go-between has a foot in both worlds – able to speak the language of the state as well as that of their local community. Sometimes *pweza* may be a tenant in a building who may help to find new tenants when there are vacancies. In other cases, someone may be a good broker due to their social connections: they may be a former government official or the family member of an official; someone with a well-placed patron; or someone well-known in the neighbourhood.

Pweza can range from established real estate agencies registered as businesses and unregistered real estate agents with semi-formal offices, at the more formal end of the spectrum, to unregulated individuals working infrequently and assisting in transactions using their social networks. In many areas of Yangon, *pweza* do not have formal offices but work from their flats, or, in many cases, a teashop, betel nut stand, or, in the days before widespread cellular phone service, a phone shop. Each neighbourhood, and often, each ward, has an individual or a group of *pweza* who are known to be knowledgeable about available flats for rent or properties for sale, as they frequently act as intermediaries in these transactions. Their real trade is not in housing but in connections and information. With no formal regulation of the real estate services sector, both formal and informal transactions ultimately rely on trust and on information flows between brokers, buyers and sellers (see Zay Yar Lin 2016c).

The most common word used for broker, is *pweza*, which in Burmese is a pejorative word referring to the taking of commissions (Brac de la Perrière 2014: 77)[14] However, due to the pejorative connotation, *eain*

14 Brac de la Perrière (2014: 77) translates *pweza* as 'eater of the plate'. While I am not a linguist, in my research, I found multiple other suggestions as to the etymology of *pweza* including 'someone who eats from a festival' (or 'ceremony'), referring to the role of the *pweza* in bringing people together or making an event happen, and then receiving some sort of financial or in-kind benefit in return; taking a cut of the table (as in gambling); and as *pwe-ka beniq yauk sa ma leh* – a common question asked during a transaction involving multiple *pweza* meaning 'how many people will eat from this portion fee' – or how many will be taking a cut? While the social history of *pweza* and the origin of the term may be a topic for further research, whether referring to eating portions, plates, making events, or otherwise, the general sense amongst both *pweza* and those who use their services is that '*pweza*' refers to someone who does something in return for a commission.

pweza often refer to themselves as *eain a-cho-saung*, which is closer to 'estate agent'. There are multiple words in Burmese, in addition to *pweza*, to describe someone in a government office or someone familiar with government institutions who can help you to get something done (such as *a-thi* and *a-ket*). These actors may broker a deal on the side but have a primary role or occupation that is not commission-based. A variety of these types of connections may be employed both in property transactions and in settling disputes related to property.

Brokers are often involved in transactions that bridge formal and informal property relations. A broker may be used to negotiate with a landowner to accept a new tenant in a building when an apartment is sold, or to obtain permission from neighbouring residents before construction begins (Myat Nyein Aye 2016). In such cases the landowner and the neighbours often request fees for their signatures. My empirical analysis illustrates that *pweza* are not just intermediaries between the state and ordinary people but also perform the role of informal intermediaries and in many cases serve as mediators between private parties.

In some areas, particularly in Yangon's outlying townships, *pweza* involved in land or informal housing transactions may simultaneously serve in government roles (Boutry et al. 2016). It is common for *pweza* in these areas to also play the role of the 10- or 100-household leaders, often with the tacit approval of the ward administrator (Forbes 2016: 219; Kyed 2019: 84; see also Simone 2018). In some cases, *pweza* may be the ward administrator, or the ward administrator may receive a share of the *pweza*'s commission to approve a lease or sale. In other areas ward level political party representatives may be involved as property brokers (see Kyed 2019: 84). Those community members viewed as the most secure and powerful patron able to protect one's property transaction will vary. Even in an informal transaction, the presence of and 'permission' from local government officials or party officials lends an air of formality to the transaction, with the result that those involved in the transaction may perceive it to be legally binding.[15] In lower-income areas, like Yangon's outlying townships, there tend to be more 'brokers' involved in transactions, perhaps because property is more tenuously held and therefore needs more intermediaries to secure it. This has significant repercussions. Every person involved in making

15 For an example, see the recent case in Dagon Seikkan (Win Zar Ni Aung 2019). See also explanations in Boutry et al. (2016).

the social connection between the person who has land or housing and the person who ultimately purchases or rents it requests a cut of the transaction. As the chain of responsibility and social connection is diffuse, if problems occur later it is less likely that any of those involved will assist in resolving disputes.

Unregistered transfers commonly occur with the sale of apartment units (Zay Yar Lin 2016a), which means that there is no way to check if the seller actually has the right to sell any given property (Lincoln 2017). The uncertain and unregulated nature of apartment unit ownership is made less risky by the use of informal intermediaries or brokers who are acquainted with both buyer and seller. In some property transactions, multiple brokers are involved, representing the buyer, the seller, and, in the case of apartments, the landowner. In other transactions there is just one *pweza* as go-between. In vouching for the party they represent, or for both parties in some cases, brokers rely on their social capital (Putnam 1993), generating the trust necessary for an informal transfer to proceed without recourse to formal justice in the case of a breach of contract. This sense of trust brokering is important in the *pweza's* ability to continue their trade (Brac de la Perrière 2014: 77).

The rate charged by *pweza* is high because they are witnessing the transaction and putting their name and reputation on the line if it should fall through. In some cases, *pweza* may be the ultimate arbiter in the event of a dispute between buyer and seller or landlord and tenant. While the sale or lease may be completed, there could be other issues with the property, eviction threats, maintenance and renovations, or a lease could need renegotiating. A long history of unregistered transactions on a property means there may be no reliable way to do a title search, and people may lay claim to property years after a transaction is completed. Furthermore, as Myanmar uses a deed registration system rather than title registration, what is registered is simply the deed of sale, not all the other interests there may be in the property. There may be an existing lease, a mortgage, or a right of way that the seller has not disclosed to the buyer, or of which no records were available to the buyer at the time of purchase. The *pweza* is thus as close as one may come to an insurance policy for disputes involving informal property transactions in Central Yangon, as parties are usually precluded from using the formal justice system, since they lack official documentation of the transaction. This happened in a case that I came across during fieldwork, where a mutual friend had agreed to serve as a *pweza* between two friends enacting a high-end property transaction in Yangon, as described in what follows.

Case of dispute over a property transaction

A *pweza* brokered a transaction between a buyer and a seller for a plot in an expensive area of Yangon, but the original deed was very old. The seller did not disclose to the buyer that there was a government right of way on the property, which did not appear on the deed of sale. After the sale was completed, the buyer began construction on the plot before applying for a building permit and was subsequently fined by the municipality for building without a permit. When she was cited and fined, she was also informed that part of the building site she had purchased was government land, meaning that she was not the legal owner of that part, despite what her sales contract stated. The buyer was understandably angry with the seller, as a portion of the property she had been sold could in fact not be legally used as she wished. Rather than go to court and potentially further implicate herself in building on government land without a permit and perhaps other violations, however, the buyer called the friend who had served as the *pweza* and asked her to intervene. The *pweza* spent a year negotiating between the two parties and they reached a *nalehmu* agreement similar to a settlement out of court, but with the *pweza* rather than a lawyer as the mediator. The seller ultimately agreed to refund part of the purchase price to the buyer to make up for the piece of unusable government land.

This case was a formal property transfer in that the deed of sale contained the new owner's name, the transaction was registered with the relevant authorities, and relevant taxes were paid. But when a problem arose, the *pweza* played the role of an informal mediator or 'justice broker', rather than the parties taking the case to court. Even in formal transactions, using a *pweza* as a mediator may prove to be quicker and more flexible than the formal legal system, which can easily take two to three years in the court of first instance (World Bank 2020: 27) and it allows both parties to avoid the courts. In the above case, even though the buyer did not know that she was building on government land, the fact that she did not apply for the right permit might, if she had filed suit against the seller, have brought government scrutiny upon her, which would have caused her problems. In hoping to avoid further scrutiny and potential fines from state actors, she chose to negotiate a settlement through the *pweza*. In informal property transactions there is no choice between formal and informal; the *pweza* is the only source of dispute resolution available to the parties, as their informal documents do not allow them to initiate proceedings in court.

Another case illustrates what happens when a *pweza* is unwilling to serve as intermediary in a dispute or is unsuccessful and negotiations break down.

Case of dispute concerning property demolition and redevelopment

A landowner in Yangon wanted to tear down their colonial house and replace it with a taller apartment building. There were existing tenants in the building, and they came to an agreement whereby they would receive flats in the new building. The landowner brokered an agreement with a contractor and, after the new apartment was built, all existing tenants claimed their flats in the new building. Usually in an agreement like this the landowner does not sell the land to the contractor nor does he pay for the cost of the new building. The landowner offers the land free of charge to the contractor and the contractor builds a new apartment block. Rather than charge the landowner for the cost of construction, the cost of both the land and the construction are recouped through an agreement between the landowner and the contractor to split the flats in the new building between them to sell or lease, to turn a profit on the new construction. In recent years, contractors have also pre-sold flats to raise money for construction. But without formal documentation of property ownership there is no recourse for flat buyers who are defrauded by contractors who build without a permit or are unable to complete construction (Ei Thandar Tun and Zin Thu Tun 2016). The new building was several storeys larger than the old building and several flats remained empty after the existing tenants were allocated flats. But the contractor and the landowner could not reach a compromise as to how to divide the empty new flats between them. Some 15 years later the dispute is unresolved and the flats are unoccupied and locked, so that neither the landowner nor the contractor can use them. As there is no legislation regulating these informal arrangements between contractors and landowners, and the *pweza* was not successful in mediating between the parties, both formal and informal dispute resolution failed.

Regulation and efforts to formalise the role of *pweza*

In 2019, a draft bill to regulate real estate brokers was submitted to the Union parliament (Htoo Thant 2019). The bill, drafted by the Myanmar Real Estate Association, an industry body established in 2012, was intended not only to regulate the industry but to dictate who can become a broker, through a licensing body and licensing exams in up to eight subjects. The bill includes provisions for setting fees for brokers and for protecting brokers in case their fees are not paid. It allows brokers to act as agents for their clients in securing mortgages from state and private banks. The bill does not contain any consequences for brokers who raise fees or violate their contracts (Yee Ywal Myint 2018). Proponents of the bill claim that due to the lack of regulation of the sector, property transactions must involve trust between buyers, brokers, and sellers, and this leads to weakness and inefficiency (Zay Yar Lin 2016c). They claim that regulating the industry would cap broker fees and require brokers to pay taxes on their income from property transactions. A licensing scheme would help to professionalise the industry while signalling to potential clients which firms or individuals they should trust.

Another industry-sponsored bill, currently under consideration, is the Apartment Law, sponsored by the construction industry. The bill is an effort on the part of the industry to provide more certainty for apartment purchases, in the hope that individual apartments can be registered like land and used as collateral for lenders. A law regularising trade in apartments would allow for legal recourse in the event of a dispute as well as certainty of ownership, as the deed of sale for an apartment could be registered. Most helpful of all for the industry, apartments would be able to be used as collateral with lenders, which would allow for mortgages on individual apartment units and stimulate a sluggish real estate sector (Htet Shine 2018).

Pweza fulfil a vital, yet unregulated and sometimes controversial role in the day to day transactional life of Myanmar residents. However, the lack of regulation allows unscrupulous *pweza* to operate with a level of impunity that is limited only by their network of contacts and reputation rather than any fear of legal sanction. This is generally adequate, perhaps more than adequate, as reputational damage can be seen as more damaging and more likely than swift justice. Regulation of *pweza* will likely narrow the current role of *pweza* as broker, fixer, mediator, and real estate agent to that of real estate agent alone, limiting their ability to be involved in dispute resolution and thus relegating disputes to government offices or the court system. Such regulation and formalisation of the real estate sector will most likely strengthen the landlord's hand in landlord-tenant relationships as they will be more likely to be familiar with formal dispute resolution mechanisms and have the time and money to file cases.

However, for those dependent on the informal market, such formalisation of real estate brokers may further silo the more trustworthy *pweza*, potentially confining them to the formal real estate market. An even more inequitable system of property transactions may develop, with stark divisions between formal and informal transactions and formal and informal justice when disputes arise. While the Apartment Law might provide further clarity for new buildings, purchasing existing apartments with a chain of unregistered deeds of sale would likely continue to be handled informally. This stark division between registered real estate brokers and new build apartment buildings and unregistered brokers conducting informal transfers of apartments in older buildings would contrast with the current situation available to buyers and sellers, where they can mix and combine elements of formal and informal transfers in any transaction. The ability of *pweza* to cultivate diverse social contacts enables them to draw up informal contracts and allows for a guise of formality through sales contracts and informal arbitration, as well as enabling them to shepherd buyers and sellers through formal registrations and transfers.

Conclusion

James (2011: 336) argues that brokers are found 'in a setting where the state intervenes', both as a means of facilitating the market and ameliorating inequities. This chapter shows that brokers in Yangon do not only mediate between the state and the people, but broker mutual agreements between individuals, often leaving state authorities out of the equation entirely. In Yangon, the existence and use of brokers in property transactions reflects continued distrust in formal institutions, which may be neither fair nor easy to navigate, if they can be employed at all. But this avoidance of the state comes with a cost. Those contracting informal property transactions with *pweza* have only the negotiating skills, connections and reputation of the *pweza* to fall back on in the case of a dispute. Without formal property transfers, parties are precluded from accessing the courts to resolve any disputes arising over their property rights. In the context of the general weakness and heterogeneity of the application of the rule of law in Myanmar, informal agreements offer security of tenure and transactions that allow residents to exchange and make productive use of their assets. Increased regulation of *pweza* may only serve the wealthiest and most well-connected property actors, adding to, rather than decreasing the overall precarity of property claims, and further restricting access to property-related dispute resolution for the majority of Yangon residents.

The distinction between formal and informal property claims may be an ineffective way of categorising the diversity of transactions and tenure practices seen in Yangon. Such a distinction of a formal/informal binary immediately makes one inferior, transient, and less relevant – a practice that exists in unregulated spaces rather than deregulated spaces (Roy 2009). Such categorisation erases the possibility of informality as a strategic choice, practical necessity, or response to legal and political change (Rhoads and Wittekind 2018). Rather than grades of formality, an alternative model might be to think in terms of legal pluralism (or living heritage), as do other contributors in this volume. Property transfer practices have evolved over time through layers of law, state practice, and local customs, making *pweza* an integral part of urban property relations and property dispute resolution.

Author's note

Research for this chapter was funded in part by the Dickson Poon Fellowship from the Dickson Poon School of Law, King's College London, and in part by the British Academy grant HDV190226 'Framing Living Heritage as Tool to Prevent Spatial Violence' in partnership with the Development Planning Unit of The Bartlett School, University College London. I would also like to thank Courtney Wittekind, Elliott Prasse-Freeman, David Ney, and the London Burma Studies Reading Group for their comments on drafts of this chapter.

References

Asian Development Bank (ADB)

2019. Financing Affordable Housing in Yangon. Manila: Asian Development Bank.

Bentham, J.

1843. 'Principles of the Civil Code.' In John Bowring (ed.), *The Works of Jeremy Bentham Vol. 1*. Edinburgh: William Tait. www.laits.utexas.edu/poltheory/bentham/pcc/index.html.

Bo Bo Nge

2020. 'Urban real estate and the financial system in Myanmar.' In P. Chachavalpongpun, E. Prasse-Freeman & P. Strefford (eds), *Unraveling Myanmar's Transition: Progress, Retrenchment, and Ambiguity Amidst Liberalization*, pp. 111–135. Singapore: NUS Press.

Boutry, M., Khin Pyae Sone, Sung Chin Par, & Tin Myo Win

2016. *Land Dynamics and Livelihoods in Peri-Urban Yangon: The Case of Htantabin Township*. Yangon: GRET.

Boutry, M., Allaverdian, C., Mellac, M., Huard, S., U San Thein, Tin Myo Win, & and Khin Pyae Sone

2017. *Land Tenure in Rural Lowland Myanmar. From Historical Perspectives to Contemporary Realities in the Dry Zone and the Delta*. Yangon: Gret.

Brac de la Perrière, B.B.

2014. 'A woman of mediation.' In W.-C. Chang & Eric Tagliacozzo (eds), *Burmese Lives: Ordinary Life Stories Under the Burmese Regime*, pp. 71–82. Oxford: Oxford University Press.

Briggs, A. and A. Burrows.

2017. *The Law of Contract in Myanmar*. Oxford: Oxford University Press.

Cheesman, N.

2011. 'How an authoritarian regime in Burma used special courts to defeat judicial independence.' *Law and Society Review* 45(4): 801–830.

2015. *Opposing the Rule of Law: How Myanmar's Courts Make Law and Order*. Cambridge: Cambridge University Press.

Di Certo, B.

2013. 'Signing a lease: What you need to know.' *The Myanmar Times* 20 October. www.mmtimes.com/business/property-news/8512-signing-a-lease-what-you-need-to-know.html.

Campbell, S.

2019. 'Of squatting amid capitalism on Yangon's industrial periphery' *Anthropology Today*, vol. 35(6): 7–10.

Crouch, M.

2014a. *Access to Justice and Administrative Law in Myanmar*. Report for USAID as part of the project 'Promoting the Rule of Law'.

2014b. 'The layers of legal development in Myanmar.' In M. Crouch and T. Lindsey (eds), *Law, Society and Transition in Myanmar*, pp. 33–58. Oxford: Hart Publishing.

2016. 'Personal law and colonial legacy: State–religion relations and Islamic law in Myanmar.' In M. Crouch (ed.), *Islam and the State in Myanmar: Muslim–Buddhist Relations and the Politics of Belonging*, pp. 69–95. Oxford: Oxford University Press.

Eggar, A.

1931. *The Laws of India and Burma: Parts 18–2:1 Landed Property (Transfer)*. Rangoon: Supdt., Govt. Printing and Stationery, Burma. British Library IOR/V/27/130/6.

Ei Thandar Tun & Zin Thu Tun

2016. 'Yangon construction market faces unlicensed contractor menace.' *Myanmar Business Today* 4(9). www.mmbiztoday.com/articles/yangon-construction-market-faces-unlicensed-contractor-menace.

Forbes, E.

2016. 'On the frontier of urbanization: Informal settlements in Yangon, Myanmar.' *Journal of Burmese Scholarship*, vol. 1(1): 197–238.

Furnivall, J.S.

2014 [1948]. *Colonial Policy and Practice: A Comparative Study of Burma and Netherlands India*. Cambridge: Cambridge University Press.

Htoo Thant

2018. 'Most court cases resolved in 2017: official.' *Myanmar Times* 16 May. www.mmtimes.com/news/most-court-cases-resolved-2017-official.html.

2019. 'Real Estate Services Bill submitted to parliament', *Myanmar Times*, 1 February. www.mmtimes.com/news/real-estate-services-bill-submitted-parliament.html.

Huxley, A.

1997. 'The importance of the dhammathats in Burmese law and culture.' *Journal of Burma Studies* 1: 1–18.

1998. 'The last fifty years of Burmese law: E. Maung and Maung Maung.' *LawAsia: Journal of the Law Association of East Asia and the West Pacific* 17: 9–20. www.ibiblio.org/obl/docs/The_last_50_years_of_%20Burmese_law.htm.

James, D.

2011. 'The return of the broker: Consensus, hierarchy and choice in South African land reform.' *Journal of the Royal Anthropological Institute* 17(2): 318–338.

Kyaw Hsu Mon

2014. 'Realtors Predict Rangoon Property Market Slowdown in 2015.' *The Irrawaddy* 30 December. www.irrawaddy.org/business/realtors-predict-rangoon-property-market-slowdown-2015.html.

Keeler, W.

2017. *Traffic in Hierarchy: Masculinity and Its Others in Buddhist Burma.* Honolulu: University of Hawaii Press.

Kyed, H.M.

2019. 'Informal settlements and migrant challenges in Yangon.' *Moussons* 33: 65–94.

Lammerts, D.C.

2018. *Buddhist Law in Burma: A History of Dhammasattha Texts and Jurisprudence, 1250–1850*. Honolulu: University of Hawaii Press.

Lincoln Legal Services (Myanmar) Limited

2017. *Newsletter 27.* www.lincolnmyanmar.com/wp-content/uploads/2017/06/Lincoln-newsletter-27.pdf.

Lund, C.

1999. 'A question of honour: Property disputes and brokerage in Burkina Faso.' *Africa: Journal of the International African Institute* 69(4): 575–594.

Luther

2017. *Myanmar News*. Available at: www.luther-lawfirm.com/fileadmin/user_upload/PDF/Newsletter/Myanmar/NL_Myanmar_November_2017_Stamp_Registration.pdf.

1923. 'Ancient Irish Law: The Law of Status or Franchise,' *Proceedings of the Royal Irish Academy.* Royal Irish Academy (36): 265–316.

Maung Maung Gyi

1983. *Burmese Political Values: The Socio-Political Roots of Authoritarianism.* New York: Praeger.

MBF (Myanmar Business Forum)

2016. *Land Working Group – Issues Matrix*. Union of Myanmar Federation of Chambers of Commerce and Industry, Myanmar Business Forum, Urban Land Working Group.

2017. *Land Working Group – Issues Matrix*. Union of Myanmar Federation of Chambers of Commerce and Industry, Myanmar Business Forum, Urban Land Working Group.

McDonald, L. and Arkar Hein

2017. Managing the Challenges of Rapid Urbanisation: A Review of the Existing Property Tax System in Myanmar. Policy Brief. Yangon: Renaissance Institute.

Myat Nyein Aye

2014. 'Property values raised for taxes.' *The Myanmar Times*, 13 October. www.mmtimes.com/index.php/business/property-news/11930-property-values-raised-for-taxes.html.

2016a. 'Real estate agents pin foreign investment hopes and tax consistency on new policy.' *Myanmar Times*, 26 October. www.mmtimes.com/business/property-news/23244-real-estate-agents-pin-foreign-investment-hopes-and-tax-consistency-on-new-policy.html.

2016b. 'Real estate taxes to jump in coming fiscal year.' *The Myanmar Times*, 29 January. www.mmtimes.com/index.php/business/property-news/18737-real-estate-taxes-to-jump-in-coming-fiscal-year.html.

2016c. 'Contractors association bands together with YCDC grievance.' *Myanmar Times*, 5 September. www.mmtimes.com/business/property-news/22308-contractors-association-bands-together-with-ycdc-grievances.html.

Myat Nyein Aye & Ko Ko Aung

2015. 'New property tax rates can spur demand for real estate market.' *The Myanmar Times*, 24 April. www.mmtimes.com/index.php/business/property-news/14113-new-property-tax-rates-can-spur-demand-for-real-estate-market.html.

Pearn, B.R.

1939. *A History of Rangoon*. Rangoon: American Baptist Press.

Peñalver, E.M.

2011. 'Property's memories.' *Fordham Law Review* 80(3): 1071–1088.

Prasse-Freeman, E.

2015. 'Conceptions of justice and the rule of law.' In D.I. Steinberg (ed.), *Myanmar: The Dynamics of an Evolving Polity*, pp. 89–114. Boulder, Colorado: Lynne Rienner Publishers.

Putnam, R.D.

1993. *Making Democracy Work: Civic Traditions in Modern Italy.* Princeton, NJ: Princeton University Press.

Rhoads, E.

2019. Property in Transition: Uncertainty, Agency and Belonging in Yangon, Myanmar. PhD Dissertation, King's College London.

2020. Manuscript submitted for publication. 'Property, Citizenship, and Invisible Dispossession in Myanmar's Urban Frontier'.

forthcoming. Citizenship and Property: Muslim Experiences of Agency and Exclusion in Yangon, Myanmar. *Muslim Minorities in East Asia: Accommodation and Contestation in the Lived Experience of East Asian Muslims.* Amsterdam: Amsterdam University Press.

Rhoads, E. and C.T. Wittekind.

2018. 'Rethinking Land and Property in a "Transitioning" Myanmar: Representations of Isolation, Neglect, and Natural Decline.' *Journal of Burma Studies* 22 (2): 171–213.

Roberts, J.L. & Rhoads, E.

2018. Nalehmu: Myanmar's Practice of Everyday Politics. Presentation at the International Burma Studies Conference. Bangkok.

Roy, A.

2009. Why India Cannot Plan Its Cities: Informality, Insurgence and the Idiom of Urbanization. *Planning Theory*, 8(1), 76–87.

Schellhase, J. & Sun, L.

2017. *The Banking Sector in Myanmar: An Assessment of Recent Progress.* Milken Institute. assets1c.milkeninstitute.org/assets/Publication/Viewpoint/PDF/083117-MyanmarBanking.pdf.

Scherer, A.

2015. 'Community preservation and heritage conservation in downtown Yangon: Seven lessons for law and policy.' In *Building the Future: The Role of Heritage in the Sustainable Development of Yangon*, pp. 42–50. Report of an International Conference held in Yangon, Myanmar January. New York: World Monuments Fund.

Simone, A.

2018. 'The urban majority and provisional recompositions in Yangon.' *Antipode* 50(1): 23–40.

Stanton, T.

2014. 'Law and economic development: The cautionary tale of colonial Burma.' *Asian Journal of Law and Society*, January, pp. 1–17.

Thang Sorn Poine
2018. 'Gendered aspects of access to justice in southern Mon State.' *Journal of Burmese Scholarship* 1(2): 1–25.

Thawnghmung, A.M.
2011. 'The politics of everyday life in twenty-first century Myanmar.' *The Journal of Asian Studies* 70(3): 641–656.

The Nation
1964. *Doctrine of Part Performance Clarified in TP Act Case*. 15 February. Available at: British Library, General Reference Collection Microform, MFM.MC1199B.

Trubek, D.M. & Santos, A.
2006. 'Introduction: The third moment in law and development theory and the emergence of a new critical practice.' In D.M. Trubek & A. Santos (eds), *The New Law and Economic Development: A Critical Appraisal*, pp. 1–22. Cambridge: Cambridge University Press.

Turnell, S.
2014. 'Banking and financial regulation and reform in Myanmar.' *Journal of Southeast Asian Economies* 31(2): 225–240.

Turnell, S., Vicary, A. & Bradford, W.
2008. 'Migrant-worker remittances and Burma: an economic analysis of survey results.' In M. Skidmore and T. Wilson (eds), *Dictatorship, Disorder and Decline in Myanmar*, pp. 63–86. Canberra: ANU Press.

UN Habitat (United Nations Human Settlements Program)
n.d.. *Guidance Note on Land Issues in Myanmar.* UN Habitat: Yangon. www.burmalibrary.org/docs12/Guidance_Note_on_Land_Issues-Myanmar.pdf.

UN Women
2016. *Voices from the Intersection: Women's Access to Justice in the Plural Legal System in Myanmar*. Bangkok: UN Women.

Win Zar Ni Aung
2019. 'Dagon Seikkan's housing blues.' *Frontier Myanmar*, 23 January. frontiermyanmar.net/en/dagon-seikkans-housing-blues.

Waldie, P.
n.d. *Unlocking the Potential of Residential Buildings in Yangon's Heritage Zone.* Yangon: Pyoe Pyin and YHT.

World Bank
2020. *Ease of Doing Business in Myanmar*. www.doingbusiness.org/data/exploreeconomies/myanmar#registering-property.

2017. World Development Indicators, Myanmar. databank.worldbank.org/source/world-development-indicators#.

Yee Ywal Myint

2018. 'Bill to regulate real estate brokers open to public.' *Myanmar Times* 26 June. www.mmtimes.com/news/bill-regulate-real-estate-brokers-open-public.html.

Yu Wai

2017. 'Homebuyers must be transparent when buying property, say lawyers.' *Myanmar Business Today* 16 May. www.mmbiztoday.com/articles/homebuyers-must-be-transparent-when-buying-property-say-lawyers.

Zan, M.

2004. 'A comparison of the first and fiftieth year of independent Burma's law reports.' *Victoria U. of Wellington L. Review* 35(2): 385.

Zay Yar Lin

2016a. 'Informal contracts risk bite buyers.' *Myanmar Times* 4 January. www.mmtimes.com/business/property-news/18304-informal-contracts-risk-bite-buyers.html.

2016b. 'Property buyers sacrifice ownership papers to avoid tax.' *Myanmar Times* 1 June. www.mmtimes.com/business/property-news/20608-property-buyers-sacrifice-ownership-papers-to-avoid-tax.html.

2016c. 'Real estate law headed to Nay Pyi Taw.' *Myanmar Times* 28 October. www.mmtimes.com/business/property-news/23369-real-estate-law-headed-to-nay-pyi-taw.html.

Legislation

Law Amending the Myanmar Stamp Act, 2014, Pyidaungsu Hluttaw Law No. 15 of 2014, Republic of the Union of Myanmar.

Law Amending the Myanmar Stamp Act, 2017, Pyidaungsu Hluttaw Law No. 19 of 2017, Republic of the Union of Myanmar.

Law Amending the Myanmar Stamp Act, 2019, Pyidaungsu Hluttaw Law No. 32 of 2019, Republic of the Union of Myanmar.

Rangoon Development Trust Act of 1921, Government of Burma.

Registration Act, India Act No. 16 of 1908.

Special Relief Act, India Act No. 1, 1877.

Stamp Act. India Act II of 1899.

Transfer of Property Act. India Act IV of 1882.

Transfer of Immovable Property (Restriction) Act, Burma Act 86 of 1947, Union of Burma.

Transfer of Immovable Property (Restriction) Act, Pyithu Hluttaw Act No. 1 of 1987, Socialist Republic of the Union of Burma.

Union Tax Law, Pyidaungsu Hluttaw Law No. 17 of 2015. Republic of the Union of Myanmar.

Union Tax Law, Pyidaungsu Hluttaw Law No. 22 of 2016. Republic of the Union of Myanmar.

Union Tax Law, Pyidaungsu Hluttaw Law No. 28 of 2019. Republic of the Union of Myanmar.

10 Everyday justice in Karen refugee camps

Kirsten McConnachie

Introduction

In contrast to the other contributions in this collection, this chapter does not consider everyday justice in Myanmar but among Karen refugees living in camps in Thailand.[1] The first camps for refugees from Myanmar in Thailand were created in 1984, and there are now nine camps, housing around 100,000 refugees, who are primarily (though not exclusively) from Karen and Karenni ethnic groups (The Border Consortium 2019). The situation of refugees in camps in Thailand may seem very distant from the experience of ordinary citizens in Myanmar, but there are a number of similarities in the administration of justice, notably a reluctant engagement with the formal justice system and a preference for minimising disputes by 'making big problems small and small problems disappear' (Denney et al 2016; Kyed et al 2018). One important difference between 'everyday justice' in the refugee camps and inside Myanmar has been the influence of international actors. During military rule international access to Myanmar was restricted. A small amount of international aid was delivered cross-border from Thailand, but this was distributed by local actors rather than international staff and had limited reach. By contrast, refugees in camps relied on international aid for food, shelter, and services, and international agencies exerted an important influence on daily life.

Thai authorities historically had little interest in policing the internal activities of these refugee camps unless a Thai citizen or non-refugee was involved. As a result, camp management was informally devolved

1 Thailand is not a party to the 1951 Convention Relating to the Status of Refugees, and the official status of this population is not 'refugees' but 'people fleeing fighting'. Nevertheless, they are recognised as refugees by the UNHCR and have been treated as such by the wider international community (including, for example, as a population entitled to third-country resettlement).

to camp-based and refugee-led systems. For around twenty years, until the early 2000s, this approach was also tacitly accepted by international organisations working with refugees in Thailand. Indeed, a high level of refugee autonomy in governance was actively encouraged by the primary refugee assistance agency in these camps, The Border Consortium, in order to 'maintain traditional culture, minimise the effect of displacement and leave people ready for return' (Thompson 2008: 26). The level of autonomy for refugees in governance began to be questioned in the early 2000s in the context of wider international concerns about transparency in camp management and the presence of non-state armed groups within refugee camps.[2] UNHCR began a project on the administration of justice in 2003, and international efforts in this area increased in 2005, when the International Rescue Committee (IRC) created a Legal Assistance Centre project (LAC). UNHCR's justice work was initially aimed at increasing access to the Thai national justice system, while IRC's LAC project explicitly recognised a continuing role for camp-based dispute resolution. However, the agencies shared a focus on encouraging case referrals to Thai courts and ensuring that camp-based systems were compliant with international human rights standards. Both agencies also considered addressing gender-based violence within the camps to be a priority issue.

This chapter examines the relationship between international agencies and refugees in relation to dispute resolution. I show that the international reform agenda, which was designed by international and Thai staff outside the camps, led to a struggle for ownership of justice, which was ultimately 'won' by international agencies, in the sense that they succeeded in establishing new rules, institutions, and referral systems for the refugee camps. Contrary to the stated objective of these initiatives, which was to strengthen camp justice, these international interventions had a number of negative consequences, leading to conflict and resentment between the refugee population and international agencies; the alienation of potential allies in justice reform (particularly among refugee-led women's organisations); and a loss of confidence and willingness among refugees to work in camp justice.

The findings presented in this chapter are based on research on justice among refugees that I commenced in Thailand in 2008. Over

2 A full explanation of this policy is beyond the scope of the present chapter but is analysed in McConnachie (2012).

the next four years, I conducted more than 150 formal interviews and held many more informal conversations with camp leaders, members of camp committees, camp justice staff, members of women's organisations, members of youth organisations, church pastors, and others. I also conducted interviews with staff of international organisations (including international staff, Thai staff, and camp-based/refugee staff) in Mae La Oon and other refugee camps, and in Mae Sariang, Mae Sot, Mae Hong Son, and Bangkok. Interviews were conducted in English or with the assistance of interpreters. The majority of my camp-based fieldwork was conducted in Mae La Oon between 2008 and 2010. IRC–LAC do not operate in Mae La Oon, so I dedicated my time in that camp to learning about the functioning of camp governance and justice in its broadest sense. I supplemented my research in Mae La Oon with visits to other camps and interviews with international NGO staff in Mae Sariang, Mae Sot, Mae Hong Son, and Bangkok. In 2012, I spent a month traveling around the border area specifically to learn about the effects of UNHCR and IRC's justice work. I conducted interviews in Mae La Oon, Mae Ra Moe, Mae La, and Umpiem Mai (all managed by the Karen Refugee Committee) as well as in Mae Hong Son and Ban Nai Soi in order to conduct interviews with representatives of Karenni refugee organisations. This chapter draws primarily from that set of interviews, underpinned by my earlier research.[3] The conclusion reflects on the conditions that I encountered in Mae La Oon in my most recent visit, May 2018.

The chapter is arranged in four parts. Part I introduces theories of legal pluralism and the distinction between 'weak' and 'strong' legal pluralism. Part II gives an overview of the institutions and mechanisms of 'camp justice' among Karen refugees in Thailand. Part III examines the entry of international agencies into the landscape of camp justice and explains the struggle for institutional authority, autonomy, and ownership of justice that ensued. Finally, Part IV outlines some consequences of this legal centralism and presents suggestions for a different, 'strong' legal pluralism, approach. These suggestions relate to the context of encampment and refugees in Thailand but have wider relevance for access to justice programming in Myanmar and beyond.

3 A full analysis of my findings on camp justice and legal pluralism can be found in McConnachie (2014).

Legal pluralism in international development

As this chapter will explain, the approach to dispute resolution among Karen refugees in Thailand has much in common with everyday justice approaches inside Myanmar. Nevertheless, the context of encampment is obviously important and has influenced governance and dispute resolution in a number of ways. Most obviously, the restrictions placed on camps and their residents are not shared by villagers in Karen State. Refugees in Thailand are not allowed to leave the camps without the express permission of Thai authorities and thousands of people (and in some camps, tens of thousands) have been confined in these small sites for decades. This establishes another important dynamic of encampment, which is cultural alienation. The camps are located in Thailand but they are not incorporated into Thai society. Instead, refugees remain strongly tied to their areas of origin. Among refugees from Myanmar, the closest affiliation is overwhelmingly ethnicity rather than nationality; i.e. refugees identify as Karen or Karenni but not as Burmese. This is reflected in language choices (among other things), with the *lingua franca* in the majority Karen camps being Sgaw Karen rather than Burmese. The separation of refugees from Thai society has implications for access to the national justice system, as Thai courts are both practically and linguistically distant. Finally, justice and dispute resolution in the camps operate within an overarching political and economic precarity, whereby refugees are reliant on the continued tolerance of the Royal Thai Government and dependent on international organisations for food, shelter, and services. This establishes a backdrop of uncertainty, making refugees reluctant to encounter the Thai authorities for fear of undermining the camps' continued existence. At the same time, they are afraid to oppose international agencies that provide essential resources.

While the refugee camps are a distinctive governance environment, they are not wholly exceptional, and the dynamics of international intervention have much in common with other examples of international engagement with non-state justice systems. This includes the central characteristics of programme design and the overall attitude or ideology of international agencies with respect to the role of non-state justice systems (Kyed 2011; Harper 2011a; Isser 2011). Justice reform is now a regular site of international development interventions (UNDP 2018). In its early years, such assistance tended to follow an approach characterised by Golub (2003) as the 'rule of law orthodoxy': implemented by foreign experts, focused on state-level relationships, and concerned with the creation or reconstruction of state-level legal institutions. This began to change (at least rhetorically) from the late 2000s as international agencies acknowledged that in many countries the formal justice system exists alongside a variety of informal or non-justice systems, including 'traditional' or 'customary' justice systems as well as other entities such as religious orders, armed groups, or local leaders.[4]

Acknowledgement of legal pluralism by international donors and development agencies reflects an awareness that in many countries the majority of disputes are solved by non-state legal systems, and that this has practical advantages including strengthening local capacity, deterring criminal activity, and providing a linguistically and culturally accessible forum for victims (Wojkowska 2006). However, working effectively in a context of legal pluralism requires more than mere recognition of non-state justice practitioners, as it speaks to fundamental conceptions of legitimacy in the administration of justice. A recurring debate in the legal pluralism literature addresses the question of whether law is or should be the exclusive preserve of the state. There is a long-standing critique of 'defensive formalism' (Cain 1985) which privileges state orders and a statist form of legal knowledge in its relations with non-state legal orders. Griffiths (1986) distinguished 'weak' and 'strong' legal pluralism, with the former recognising that administration of justice occurs beyond the state but ultimately seeking to bring those non-state processes under state control. 'Strong' legal pluralism, by contrast, can accept a diversity of justice systems and accommodate their differences (see also the Introduction to this volume).

Griffiths' analysis envisaged the transformation of non-state legal processes by a state or colonial power. Today, transformation of non-state justice systems is more likely to be imposed by international organisations promoting 'good governance' and the 'rule of law' (Comaroff and Comaroff 2006: 25). These interventions continue to treat the

4 In this chapter I have used the term 'non-state justice' to describe the dispute resolution approach used in the refugee camps. This seems the most appropriate term for a refugee context in which there was a very clear separation between the approaches used by refugees and the national justice system of Thailand. I have used other terms such as customary, informal, or traditional justice where this reflects the language of the source document.

state as the more legitimate (and indeed the ideal) justice actor and non-state justice practitioners as targets for reform and rationalisation (Lubkemann et al. 2011; Leonardi et al. 2011; Harper 2011a). Several studies of justice intervention in contexts of international development and 'war-torn societies' (Isser 2011) have found international agencies and donors to be rhetorically supportive of non-state justice systems but determined to reform those systems through training and education for justice practitioners as well as through processes leading to codification, standardisation, and regulation of non-state justice institutions. These efforts share a desire to 'fix' non-state justice systems, to impose 'uniformity and standardisation', 'manage diversity', and ultimately 'tame' their autonomy; recognising plurality, yet also seeking to dictate the form that it takes (Kyed 2011: 7–8; Wiuff Moe 2011; Harper 2011b; Lubkemann et al. 2011). As Kyed (2011: 7) explains, 'what is seen here as "negative" and "positive" is based on international criteria of what is "good" justice; not on those notions of justice grounded in local realities and experiences'.

This approach, which seeks to 'reform' non-state justice systems, can have significant consequences. Dictating justice practices in accordance with international preferences undermines the authority of non-state justice practitioners. It also risks alienating potential allies in reform and shutting down the space for the internal debates and negotiations that would otherwise have brought about change in justice practice. This chapter explores these dynamics as they have played out for Karen refugees in Thailand.

Camp justice: Community, consensus, and a 'harmony ideology'

After surveying the administration of justice in thirteen refugee camps, de Costa (2006: 21–22) found that four primary types of justice system typically operated: the national justice system of the host country; refugee dispute resolution mechanisms; the rules and regulations of governments or political groups in exile; and refugee camp management systems. Refugees' decisions to turn to a particular system were influenced by a range of factors including the type of case or dispute, the location of the camp, the attitude of the host government, and individual beliefs. Despite the variety of legal fora, de Costa (2006) found that the overwhelming majority of crimes occurring in refugee camps were resolved by refugee-led processes. This was also the case in Thailand, where, despite the Thai State's jurisdiction over the refugee camps, Thai police would in practice typically only get involved in disputes affecting a Thai citizen or citizens. When refugees asked the Thai authorities to prosecute a crime or resolve a dispute, my interviewees (including camp leaders, section leaders and representatives of women's organisations) described being rebuffed with responses such as: 'Do it yourself. This is your people, not our people' or: 'This is your community, this is your case.' Thus, the Thai authorities effectively devolved sovereignty over the internal affairs of the refugee camps to the refugee community itself.

As mentioned above, the refugee camps in Thailand are sites of pluralistic governance engaging a variety of stakeholders. These stakeholders can be grouped into three broad categories: Thai authorities, international organisations, and refugees and their representatives. Thai authorities with some role in camp management include the Royal Thai Government, the Ministry of Interior, the police, the military, border control authorities, the paramilitary rangers (*Or Sor*), and the forest department. Each camp has a Camp Commander, who is a Thai District Officer (*Palat*).

International agencies include The Border Consortium (the primary international agency involved in refugee assistance in Thailand), UNHCR, and a range of other non-governmental organisations. These organisations are coordinated through the Committee for Coordination of Services to Displaced Persons in Thailand (CCSDPT), which had 13 organisational members in 2019, down from 20 members in 2007.[5]

Importantly, the camps have a structured and organised refugee-led governance system. The Karen Refugee Committee (KRC) has responsibility for all seven 'Karen' camps and has offices in the Thai towns of

5 In 2018, the Committee for Coordination of Services to Displaced Persons in Thailand had 13 organisational members: Agency for Technical Cooperation and Development; Adventist Development and Relief Agency; COERR Foundation; DARE Network; Handicap International; International Rescue Committee; Jesuit Refugee Service; Malteser International; Right to Play; Save the Children; Shanti Volunteer Association; The Border Consortium; and Women's Education for Advancement and Empowerment. CCSDPT members in 2007 also included: Aide Medical International; American Refugee Committee; International Child Support-Asia; Medecins sans Frontières; Norwegian Church Aid; Ruammit Foundation; Solidarités; Taipei Overseas Peace Service; World Education; ZOA Refugee Care.

Mae Sot, Mae Sariang, Kanchanaburi, and Ratchaburi. The KRC is the main liaison between refugees and other stakeholders, including the Thai authorities, UNCHR, and NGOs. Each camp has its own camp committee with responsibility for management and governance. The structure of camp committees varies, but in Mae La Oon it comprised fifteen members including the camp leader and representatives for social welfare, security, health, education, transport, sanitation, food, and office administration. The camps are further divided in a hierarchy of zones (larger camps only), sections and '10-household leaders'. Each section has its own committee consisting of the section leader and individuals dealing with section security and social welfare. Community-based organisations also play an important role in the camps, particularly the Karen Women's Organisation (KWO) and the Karen Youth Organisation (KYO).

The refugee camps are contexts of legal pluralism, where multiple authorities have a role in setting and enforcing norms. They are also contexts of legal hybridity, deriving rules and norms from a variety of sources, including Karen cultural practices, Christian beliefs, KNU law, Burmese law, Thai law, and international human rights law. When I began my research, a set of Karen Refugee committee camp rules had been drafted, which represented an attempt to codify camp norms. However, dispute resolution was in practice characterised by flexibility and individual discretion for section leaders and camp committees. In this process, the camp rules were largely redundant. I asked many interviewees about the KRC camp rules and almost everyone I spoke to about this (including people actively involved in dispute resolution) knew that the rules existed but was unable to give any detail about their contents. Instead, respondents described the existence of a hybrid, place-specific dispute resolution approach:

> As we are people from another place, we cannot use our own law, but we cannot use Thai law. We use a little KRC, a little UNHCR, a little Thai, we use them all to solve problems. We solve each problem as it comes up.[6]

In Mae La Oon and the other camps in which I carried out my research in Thailand, refugees, camp security staff and camp justice staff all enunciated the same philosophy of dispute resolution that Denney et

6 Interview conducted in Mae Ra Moe camp with a member of the camp committee (role not specified to preserve anonymity), April 2012.

al. (2016) found to be prevalent inside Myanmar: '(T)o make big problems small and small problems disappear', i.e. to prioritise the speedy resolution of disputes and where possible to resolve them at the most local level possible rather than escalate them to a higher or more formal level. There was an emphasis on dispute resolution as occurring 'step by step', an ethos that required refugees to observe a dispute resolution hierarchy (typically from section security to section leader to camp social welfare to camp committee and only then to camp justice). A case would be referred 'up' a step only if it could not be resolved at a lower level. Thus, although Mae La Oon had a dedicated camp justice team, the vast majority of disputes and problems in the camps were resolved at section level. At each stage, the dispute resolution process operated with the consent of the participants and by consulting all affected parties and conducting a wide-ranging examination of relevant circumstances. Decisions were reached by consensus based on general values rather than specific rules, amounting to a shared 'common sense' that was explained as a 'Karen way' of living peacefully and prizing social order.

The ethos of resolving disputes step by step is a classic example of 'harmony ideology', emphasising 'conciliation; recognition that resolution of conflict is inherently good and that its reverse – continued conflict or controversy – is bad or dysfunctional, a view of harmonious behaviour as more civilised than disputing behaviour, the belief that consensus is of greater survival value than controversy' (Nader 1990: 2). The 'harmony ideology' prevailing among refugees is not unique to the camps but reflects community structures and cultural practices that are also found in Myanmar, as detailed in other chapters of this volume. In the camps (as inside Karen State) the premium placed on social harmony has consequences for individuals whose disputes are 'made small' or 'made to disappear'. Nevertheless, as a technique for the maintenance of order, the step-by-step approach of camp-based dispute resolution was broadly effective. At the time of my research, more than 15,000 people lived in Mae La Oon. Conditions were overcrowded and impoverished, yet the security climate in the camp was far from one of extreme and random violence, as has been described and documented as existing in other refugee situations. This is not to say that there were no problems. Common disputes related to theft, fighting, unpaid debts/loans, gambling and the use/sale of alcohol (both of which are prohibited in the camps). Domestic violence also occurred and often went unreported; when reported, it tended to be resolved at section level. Similarly, sexual violence was not always reported and though it was impossible to know the true levels of incidence, those that I interviewed consistently said that it was much less frequent than domestic violence. The Karen Women's Organisation (KWO) compiled records of cases in six Karen camps between 2011 and 2013. They identified 289 cases of 'sexual and gender-based violence', the vast majority of which (92 per cent) were cases of domestic violence. Of the total of 289 cases, 47 had not been reported to camp structures or international organisations (Karen Women's Organisation 2013: 7). While sexual violence and domestic violence were not always acknowledged or taken seriously by camp security structures, consensual extramarital sex (whether adultery or premarital sex) was actively policed as a serious offence.

In the process of resolving cases 'step by step', the first response (particularly at section level) was education or instruction, i.e. a discussion with the offender about their actions and the community's expectations. In my interviews, section leaders described the nature of this 'education' as a process of reasoning with the offender and of explaining their position as part of a wider society which had expectations of appropriate behaviour but which was ultimately caring and protective of its members, as one section leader explained to me:

> First, I will say, you have your own section leader, and the section leader will do the right thing for you. Your leader does not want to harm you, only to make you good. [...] Sometimes the guests and the NGOs and the Thai authorities come and ask how the people in the camp behave. At that time, the camp leader always protects the camp people and says, 'Oh, they are good, no problem'. He always defends his children. We [camp security] explain it like this so that the person who has created a problem will think deeply and change their life. So that they will understand the love and care of their leaders. We say: 'If you behave like this, it won't help your life. It will become difficult and bad things will come to you. To say something is easy, but to do as you say is more difficult. Don't say you won't do it again, but just don't do it again.' Just as parents teach their children – we have to be like parents.[7]

7 Interview conducted in Mae Ra Mo camp with a section leader, April 2012.

This type of moral instruction was (perhaps surprisingly) effective in many cases. Again, this might be understood in light of a 'harmony ideology' that privileges community interests above individual preferences. The fear of gossip or public shaming that often underwrites community-based justice systems takes on an even greater salience in the confinement of a refugee camp, where moving away or leaving the environment is all but impossible. Of course, not every case or problem would be resolved through this type of 'education'. Sometimes a more material response would be required, as in cases of theft or unpaid debts (which would typically be resolved by ordering the return of what had been taken). In other cases, the section leader's moral instruction would be ignored and the offence would be repeated. This was frequently the case with domestic violence which in the refugee camps, as in other societies, often persisted even after sanctions had been imposed. For repeat offences or in response to more serious cases, an offender might be detained. The camps did not have a secure detention unit, so offenders were confined to a bamboo hut designated as the camp 'prison'. To prevent escape the offender's legs would be shackled in wooden stocks. In Mae La Oon, only men were detained in this way. A female offender would be ordered to work with the Karen Women's Organisation for a period of time instead, in a form of community service. A typical sentence of detention was between one and three months. At the time of my research, detention could be avoided by paying a fine of THB 1000 (around ‘ 30) per month sentenced.

In my interviews, refugee staff involved in justice and security matters consistently described their work in essentially *moral* terms, as an attempt to 'rehabilitate' offenders by transforming them into good citizens. This analysis was maintained even in relation to the harshest penalty imposed in the camps, which was to send an offender to the justice system of the KNU (Karen National Union), the main ethnic armed organisation in Karen State (Myanmar). There were two main routes to the KNU justice system. The first was where an offender had committed a crime in Karen State and subsequently came to the refugee camps; such an individual would be returned by the camp committee, if this was requested by the KNU.[8] However, the KNU justice system

8 UNHCR was strongly opposed to there being any role for the KNU in the refugee camps, identifying this as a protection threat and stating that '(r)efugees have reported many incidences of abuse and even death at the hands of the KNU and

might also be engaged as a punishment of last resort in cases of persistent repeat offences or of very serious offences (this category was not defined but might include murder, violent rape or suspected spying or informing against the KNU). In cases of repeat offences, the camp leader and the camp justice team would decide on a period of time (perhaps six months or one year) for the person to live with the KNU or its armed wing, the KNLA (Karen National Liberation Army), and provide assistance such as cooking or cleaning. Referrals of this type became rarer and more secretive after vehement criticism by the UNHCR that they constituted 'forced recruitment' of refugees into the KNLA. Nevertheless, they continued to occur, and they continued to enjoy the support of large portions of the camp community. In my discussions and interviews, many (perhaps even most) camp residents viewed referral to the KNU in such circumstances as an appropriate punishment, and as an opportunity for the offender to learn a 'good way' of discipline, hard work, and subordination.[9]

In principle, therefore, camp-based refugees who experienced a dispute or problem had a variety of options: the Thai criminal justice system; the camp justice and dispute resolution system; the KNU justice system; or international agencies. Of these options, the camp systems were vastly preferred. This came through very clearly in my research but was also evident in research conducted by the International Rescue Committee. In 2007, the IRC surveyed more than 2,000 refugees in Mae La camp and in the two Karenni refugee camps in Mae Hong Son province. Across all camps there was an overwhelming preference for camp justice. More than 70 per cent of respondents said that if they had a problem to resolve, they would go to their section leader or to a member of the camp committee, while 0.5 per cent of respondents said they would go to the UNHCR, 0.2 per cent said they would go to NGOs. Just 0.1 per cent said they would report to the Thai Or Sor and

---

KNPP [Karenni National Progressive Party], especially of ethnic minorities or those perceived to have supported opposition groups' (CCSDPT/UNHCR 2006: 24). I did not encounter this level of control by KNU, nor did I hear of any cases of the return of suspected informers to Karen State, though of course any such cases would probably be dealt with secretly. See McConnachie (2012) for more discussion of this.

9 In Mae La Oon, most residents had been displaced from KNU-controlled areas of Karen State, particularly KNU 5th Brigade, which was immediately across the river bordering MLO camp. The levels of support for KNU may be less pronounced in other camps.

a further 0.1 per cent said that they would report to other Thai authorities (International Rescue Committee 2007: 53). These figures might be interpreted as evidence of refugees' exclusion from Thai justice and therefore as underscoring the necessity of international access to justice programming. However, it was clear from my research that the high levels of reliance on camp-based dispute resolution systems in many cases also reflected a genuine preference for those systems.

In my interviews and conversations, refugees justified their preference for camp justice in a variety of ways, but consistently expressed support for the camp system (which was seen as culturally appropriate and familiar) and a strong desire to avoid the Thai justice system (which was seen as risky and threatening). Many of the reasons given in support of camp justice were similar to those identified by Kyed (2018: viii) inside Myanmar, including a desire to resolve disputes at the most local and familiar level possible and a preference to avoid confrontation, in order to 'live peacefully' (see also the other contributions to this volume for similar findings inside Myanmar). These traits were usually explained to me in terms of Karen identity and culture. The Karen identity that prevails in Mae La Oon is predominantly Sgaw-speaking, Christian, and KNU-supporting. Not all ethnic Karen share these linguistic, religious and political affiliations (Thawnghmung 2011). Nevertheless, refugees expressed consensus on issues that they considered to represent core tenets of Karen identity, notably the sanctity of marriage ('one husband, one wife'), which prohibited extramarital sex and prevented divorce in all but the most exceptional circumstances. Communitarianism, respect for elders and leaders and the importance of 'living peacefully' were described as Karen traits, and as reasons why it was not only desirable to solve disputes within the community but also possible to do so:

> As we are descended from people who love the truth, then all will be truth. The way that we speak, the clothes that we wear, all are according to our Karen traditions. For example, adultery … [a] very important thing in our Karen tradition is one husband, one wife. It is very important. Young people must listen to their parents, this is also important.[10]

10 Interview conducted in Mae Ra Moe camp with a member of the camp justice team, 11 April 2012.

> If we bring problems to them [the Thai authorities] we can't speak Thai, we don't understand the legal system, we don't have the same background. People should have their own law.[11]

In Liberia, Lubkemann et al. (2011: 95) found that people's preference for customary justice structures 'do not merely reflect some sort of reflexive and unconsidered "cultural preference" [...] Rather such priorities represent an astute reading of the realities, constraints and possibilities of social survival in the context in which they live'. Similarly, Karen refugees' preference for camp justice was based on a realistic assessment of their environment. My respondents would often justify their support for camp justice by saying 'we are refugees'. This phrase encompassed a number of reasons that together represented a realist, pragmatic assessment of encampment and its consequences. First, people considered that as refugees they had a shared understanding of the challenges, stresses, and privations of living in a camp and this helped them understand reasons for offending as well as appropriate responses to offences. Second, as refugees they had a shared interest in maintaining order within the camp, to protect themselves and others. This explanation was often given in relation to the prohibition of alcohol within the camps, which it was claimed was necessary to prevent other harm, such as squandering family food rations, fighting and violence. Third, refugees had a vital shared interest in protecting the continued *existence* of the camps. It was feared that bringing cases and disputes from the camps to Thai courts would draw attention to the camps as sites of disorder and might lead the Thai Government to close the camps entirely. Fourth, refugees doubted that they would be treated fairly in Thai courts, as they were generally 'looked down on' in Thai society and they feared that they would also be discriminated against in the justice system. Taken together, these different reasons and rationales led many refugees to believe that Thai justice was risky, and that refugees had a responsibility to resolve cases within the camp wherever possible:

> We are not in our own country. We must live quietly.[12]

---

11 Interview conducted in Mae La Oon camp with a member of the camp committee, 15 February 2010.

12 Interview conducted with a member of the Karen Refugee Committee, 9 March 2009.

> Thai laws can't help refugees because they are only used to punish refugees.[13]

A preference for camp justice did not mean that refugees were blind to its limitations. In my interviews, refugees (including some camp staff and representatives of community-based organisations) complained of unfair decisions, that those with money could pay their way out of detention and/or bribe their way out of punishment, and that prominent people within the camp were given preferential treatment. They complained about inappropriately light punishments, about the difficulty of dealing with serious crimes, and about the inability of camp systems to address problems involving non-refugees. They complained that camp 'judges' were not educated, and that security staff were untrained and used violence to arrest and detain people. The Karen Women's Organisation (KWO) consistently raised concerns about ineffectual responses to violence against women, with some section leaders failing to address domestic violence entirely, while others would repeatedly use the response of 'education' rather than referring the case to a higher level (Karen Women's Organisation 2013).[14]

International intervention and a clash of legal cultures

While many refugees criticised individual decisions by camp justice practitioners, and the KWO in particular recognised a systemic gender inequality, this did not negate an overall belief that dispute resolution by refugees was a legitimate and appropriate form of governance. An evaluation across all nine camps in Thailand found that refugee-led structures commanded a high level of legitimacy, that 'there is deep

13 Interview conducted in Mae La Oon camp on 14 February 2010 with a camp resident, who was commenting on a recent case in which a person from Mae La Oon was sentenced to fourteen days in prison for cutting wood outside of the camp.

14 Indeed the KWO (and its counterpart in the Karenni camps, the Karenni Women's Association) had actively sought to improve camp responses to domestic violence and sexual violence for many years, using a diverse range of initiatives: training workshops and educational posters around the camps to explain what domestic and sexual violence are; encouraging victims to report violence (and working with other refugee women's organisations in Thailand to develop a reporting system, known as 'ARM' or Automatic Response Mechanism); operating 'safe houses' for women seeking protection from violent men; and providing personal support and encouragement to women who experienced violence.

potential for self-governance and self-management in refugee communities' and that 'shared values and vision, and mutual trust, form the foundation of effective refugee camp management' (Turcot 2012: xiv).

International justice interventions approached camp justice structures from a very different position. An 'analysis of gaps in refugee protection' conducted by international organisations dismissed the camp systems as inherently ineffective:

> Refugees in the camps do not have access to effective remedies in the law principally due to the influence of camp justice mechanisms which are resorted to more frequently than Thai ones. (CCSDPT/UNHCR 2006: 35)

> The procedures, penalties and remedies that are applied by these systems are often not in accordance with either Thai law or international human rights standards. They also tend to be highly politicised, since they are administered by camp committees and linked directly with the ethnic military and political groups that exercise social and political control over the camps. (CCSDPT/UNHCR 2006: 36)

The UNHCR's intention (CCSDPT/UNHCR 2006: 35) was to work with the government and refugee communities to set up a functioning system, where serious crimes would be dealt with by the Thai justice system and minor offences would be handled by refugee traditional justice mechanisms. To facilitate this outcome, IRC created a Legal Assistance Centre programme (IRC–LAC), which would provide practical assistance and support to refugees seeking to refer cases to Thai courts, including training for camp justice staff as well as outreach activities among the wider refugee population. LAC began working in three camps (the 'Karenni' camps of Site 1 and Site 2, and the 'Karen' camp of Mae La) in 2007 and expanded to Umpiem Mai and Nu Po camps in 2011. LAC offices were not opened in the remaining four 'Karen' camps (including Mae La Oon), which were nevertheless required to implement the changes in rules and policies described in this chapter, though without the accompanying presence of LAC staff and training programmes.

Legal centralism: 'One nation, one law'

The IRC's programme anticipated a continuing role for refugee-led justice systems. However, both the UNHCR and the IRC considered strengthening access to Thai courts as a priority. Indeed, the prevailing view from senior UNHCR staff was that ideally *all* cases would go to Thai courts, making camp justice redundant. Camp justice was perceived as a 'parallel' legal system that challenged the authority of Thai law. One UNHCR senior staff member said to me: 'Why do they need law for the camps when there is a Thai law covering the whole of Thailand?' When I asked what the guiding principles were for UNHCR's work on justice, this respondent emphasised the importance of complying with fundamental principles of Thai sovereignty and territorial jurisdiction.[15] At one level, it is easy to understand why UNHCR staff would have this perception. As the United Nations' refugee agency, UNHCR is a creation of states and its operations in any given territory depend on the permission of whichever state it is working in. Territorial sovereignty is thus at the very heart of the agency's existence and operations. However, the legal principle of territorial sovereignty is a political fiction, as anthropologists have been pointing out for decades. Assuming the primacy of national law and the illegitimacy of refugee-led dispute resolution ignores the political and social context of these systems, and the reasons underlying their continued use.

In 2013, the KWO reported that 242 sexual and gender-based violence cases had been reported across six camps over the preceding two years. Of these cases, 87 per cent had been handled by camp justice and 13 per cent by Thai justice (Karen Women's Organisation 2013: 7). These cases were not being resolved satisfactorily: one of KWO's key findings was that '(i)n most SGBV cases, women received inappropriate, inadequate and inconsistent justice outcomes' (ibid.: 6). Nevertheless, there was a continued reliance on camp justice for a variety of reasons, as outlined above, including cultural familiarity; a belief that Thai authorities did not want to address cases from the refugee camp; a perception of Thai law as alien and threatening; and a fear that sending cases out of the camp would reflect poorly on the Karen refugee community and might even jeopardise the continued existence of the camps.

UNHCR's standpoint of legal centralism did not leave room to acknowledge these practical concerns. Instead, failure to refer cases to Thai courts was interpreted by UNHCR staff as the result of pressure from camp leaders. This was believed to be a particular problem in relation to

15 Interview with UNHCR staff member (place of interview not given to preserve confidentiality), 24 April 2012.

sexual violence, i.e. that cases were not referred to Thai courts because camp leaders were blocking victims from doing so. In part to address this perceived issue, UNHCR and the American Refugee Committee (ARC) began funding SGBV Committees in all seven 'Karen' camps to operate as an independent liaison between refugees and UNHCR. Instead of a referral going 'step by step' through the camp structures and involving consultation with section leaders, camp security, the KWO and camp leaders, SGBV Committees were to refer cases directly to UNHCR.

The SGBV committees were created to provide a confidential avenue for reporting SGBV offences, to educate refugees about sexual and gender-based violence, and to offer victims of sexual violence a choice of case management agencies. However, they were designed to operate in isolation from pre-existing community structures and were managed by Thai and international staff based outside the camps. Appropriating the language that the UNHCR had levelled against camp justice, the KWO objected to the SGBV committees as a 'parallel justice system' that duplicated work already being conducted by KWO staff – and, furthermore, which were unable to function effectively *without* KWO and other camp staff (Karen Women's Organisation 2013: 10):

> In fact, though, when UNHCR and ARC took on a case they did not have the capacity or resources to deal with it. No counselling, no knowledge, no protection, no security, no money, not present in camp, etc. So inevitably the cases were referred back to the camps (Karen Women's Organisation 2013: 10).[16]

Something similar occurred in a different refugee situation – Kakuma camp in Kenya. Analysing responses to 'intimate partner violence (IPV)', Horn (2010) found that the vast majority of cases were dealt with by community structures and that many refugee women preferred this route, even though community responses to IPV cases often failed to protect them from further violence. UNHCR's attempt to improve responses to IPV did not engage effectively with the existing community-level responses or fully understand the decision-making processes

16 This report opens with a disclaimer that 'KWO respects and acknowledges there is only one law in Thailand and is under the jurisdiction of the Royal Thai Government. When we write about justice issues related to our refugee situation, we intend no disrespect to the Kingdom of Thailand' (Karen Women's Organisation 2013: 2).

that victims of IPV were engaging in. Attempts to encourage women to report directly to the UNHCR (bypassing community structures) failed, and set up international agencies in opposition to community structures. The result, Horn concluded (2010: 168), was that protection goals were undermined and an opportunity for constructive engagement to transform understandings of sexual violence was lost.

Similarly, in Thailand, the role of SGBV committees became a key site of struggle between the refugee community (particularly the KWO) and international agencies, which ultimately alienated potential allies in the struggle for gender justice (Olivius 2013). In 2010, Umpiem Mai Camp Committee expelled the SGBV Committee from the camp. A series of emergency meetings between the camp committee, Karen community organisations, and the American Refugee Committee eventually decided that the SGBV Committee should be disbanded, renamed 'community peace teams', and incorporated into the camp reporting structures.

Legal formalism: Codifying camp justice

In contrast to the 'one nation, one law' legal centralism that was uppermost in the minds of UNHCR staff working on access to justice, the International Rescue Committee's (IRC) legal empowerment approach emphasised the importance of working with refugee-led justice systems and fostering change from within the community. However, LAC's primary objective was to harmonise the camp system with Thai domestic law and international human rights standards (Harding and Varadan 2010) and to 'bring justice to Burmese refugees' (International Rescue Committee 2010). IRC sought to achieve this goal partly by encouraging referrals from the camps to Thai courts, but also by codifying camp rules and dispute resolution procedures.

Defining camp rules and procedures sounded straightforward, following the advice of the Norwegian Refugee Council (2008: 262–263): 'Establishing a set of camp rules is a core responsibility of an international organisation serving as Camp Management Agency, with by-laws or codes to be produced in a process that involves all groups of residents'. In reality it proved much more difficult than IRC had anticipated. Codification was intended to improve refugees' experiences of dispute resolution by increasing certainty. However, the core task of codification was to 'fix' an inherently flexible system, and it was therefore a transformative process in itself. Furthermore, codifying camp rules was not 'merely' a matter of formulating a list of permissible and impermissible behaviours, but was also a matter that affected definitions of authority, legitimacy, and leadership. As such, it rapidly exposed fault-lines between the justice preferences of international organisations and those of refugees and became bogged down in intractable disputes. Areas of particular contention included the policing of adultery and premarital sex and the use of detention (including use of leg-stocks and detention of young people). The IRC and the UNHCR were insistent that the definition of offences in camps must be aligned with Thai law, where adultery is not a crime (in contrast to Myanmar, where adultery is a crime under the national penal code). This was interpreted by many refugees as a direct challenge to Karen culture and tradition, as a member of the Camp Committee told me:[17]

> Now, many NGOs work in the camp and the camp committee is in the middle, between the people and the NGOs. Because things that are very serious to our people are nothing to the NGOs. … especially sex among single men and women. They live together without marriage, but they don't want to get married. This is a serious problem for Karen but it is nothing for the NGOs.[18]

Karen tradition is also that a child is someone under 18. But if a child under 18 commits crimes, then you have to do something about it. If you don't arrest and detain them, they won't respect their elders. As a member of camp security said to me:

> If you say, "child rights, child rights", can't do anything. […] We want a place where they can be held at night but during the day they can go to school and continue their education. But we don't have anywhere like that in camp. Only the detention centre. […] When UNHCR come and complain, they say we are not allowed to arrest and detain children. But I explain, the child committed theft again and again. If I can't detain him, then I will hand over to you. Then you, UNHCR, can take responsibility yourself. UNHCR said,

17 My interviews with members of the Karenni Refugee Committee and the Karenni Women's Organisation indicated that very similar dynamics and perceptions prevailed in the two northern camps of Ban Nai Soi and Ban Mae Surin.

18 Interview conducted in Mae Ra Moe camp with a member of the camp committee, 12 April 2012.

> they cannot take the responsibility, but for security to do themselves whatever they can.[19]

The codification process involved representatives from the refugee camps and the Karen Refugee Committee, but the ability of these individuals to shape the content of camp rules was extremely limited. A staff member of the UNHCR described the process as: '(T)here are points on which we [UNHCR] cannot compromise but then we negotiate and come up with a solution', while a staff member of the IRC emphasised the bottom line of compliance with Thai law:

> The age cut-off [for criminal responsibility] in Thai law is under 15, not under 18. But then in drawing up the camp rules, one camp defined a child a someone under 16. I said, 'Where does this come from? It needs to align with Thai law'.[20]

The 'law reform' process sought to define cases that must always be referred to Thai courts (building on a list of 'absolute jurisdiction' offences that had been identified by UNHCR); cases that could be resolved by camp justice; the procedure to be followed; and the sanctions that could be applied. After several years of deadlocked meetings, a draft document was circulated in April 2010. This was an 80-page document of dense legal definitions, reflecting a vision of law directly derived from common law tradition, oriented towards Thai law and international law, and therefore disembodied from the culturally appropriate legal frame that would be understood by refugees (including village-level sovereignty as well as KNU Law or indeed Burmese law). In 2011, the Karen Refugee Committee circulated its own updated set of 'Rules and Regulations for Refugees' (Karen Refugee Committee 2011). These were produced without IRC input but the influence of the ongoing law reform discussions was discernible in the new rules. They identified three types of offence: 'rule', 'civil lawsuit" and 'crime'. All crimes were to be addressed by turning the offender over to the Thai authorities. Adultery was described as an example of 'abuse of social and cultural norms' and categorised as a civil lawsuit rather than a crime (and therefore as something that could be addressed by camp justice). Permitted

19 Interview conducted in Mae Ra Moe camp with a member of camp security, 12 April 2012.

20 Interview with international NGO staff member (name of organisation not given to preserve confidentiality), 23 April 2012.

responses were 'warning', 'compromising' and 'action taken similar to that of action taken by a related society'.

Ironically, a principal cause of delay in the law reform drafting process was opposition from the UNHCR, who objected to it on the basis that it gave too much legitimacy to refugee-led justice processes by creating something that looked like a criminal code. Several rounds of rebranding took place before a nomenclature was found that was acceptable to the UNHCR and the principle of 'one country, one law', as a member of the camp committee told me:

> Initially, it was called 'law reform'. With agreement between community leaders and LAC, the law reform became DMLS – Developing Mediation and Legal Standards – and the name of camp justice was changed to Mediation and Arbitration Team. Now, the process has changed again to become 'Guiding Principles'. This will be a manual for the camp justice team. After almost three and a half years, the process is still not finished. A lot of community leaders are frustrated. And at the end, we can't make our own traditions and laws. We have to follow Thai law.[21]

In December 2012, the Mediation and Dispute Resolution Guidelines were finally circulated. These guidelines confirmed the list of 'absolute jurisdiction' offences, which were to be sent to Thai Courts. This list consists of seven offences: murder; assault causing grievous bodily harm; narcotics; human trafficking; forestry offences;[22] firearms and explosives; offences against children; and non-compoundable rape.[23]

---

21 Interview conducted in Mae La camp with a member of the camp committee, 24 April 2012.

22 Guidance Note #2 of the Mediation and Dispute Resolution Guidelines states that a forestry offence occurs when a camp resident: cuts, saws or interferes with any trees inside or outside the camp without Royal Thai Government authorisation; collects fruit, bamboo shoots, bee hives or honey without Royal Thai Government authorisation; burns any part of the camp; cuts or interferes with teak trees or rubber trees.

23 The definition of non-compoundable rape follows the Thai criminal code (pp. 276–281) and is rape with aggravating circumstances. These include rape with the use of a gun; rape resulting in grievous bodily harm or death; rape committed in public; rape committed against a person aged under 15; rape committed by more than one perpetrator; rape where the perpetrator was in a position of care vis-a-vis the victim, such as being his/her parent, guardian, or teacher; and other sexual offences against minors under the age of 15 (Mediation and Dispute Resolution Guidelines, Guidance Note #2).

Guidance Note #1 emphasises that '(t)he Royal Thai Government has jurisdiction over all matters in the camp and therefore Thai law governs all dispute resolution in the camp. Camp leaders may not take any action that is contrary to Thai law and all dispute resolution outcomes must comply with Thai law'. The other guidance notes outline the procedures to be followed (#3: conflict of interest; #4 alternative dispute resolution; #5 mediation; #6 arbitration) and give specific guidance for particular case types (#7 disputes involving young people; #8 compoundable rape; #9 domestic violence; #10 adultery; #11 marriage and divorce; #12 debt and loans). The Mediation and Dispute Resolution Guidelines were first implemented in the five camps where LAC had an operational presence and later expanded to the other camps along the border, such as Mae La Oon. By this time, however, the prolonged unconstructive discussions had led to disillusionment among the refugee leadership and within the community (particularly among those who had initially been advocates for reform) and had established antagonistic relationships that were hard to heal.

The consequences of legal centralism

Legal culture in these refugee camps had many similarities with the legal culture inside Myanmar, including a preference for local dispute resolution and a focus on the 'harmony ideology' of making 'big problems small and small problems disappear' (Kyed 2018; Denney et al. 2016). This is an important finding, indicating the extent to which 'camp justice' is shaped by pre-camp identities and ethnic, cultural, and religious values. Central characteristics of camp justice included flexibility and responsiveness, and a process of decision-making that was hierarchical ('we must go step by step') but also participatory and consultative. Guiding principles in decision-making included the protection of 'Karen' values (for example in the prohibition of extramarital sex) and the protection of refugees' interests (a goal that was promoted by 'living quietly' and avoiding attracting the attention of Thai authorities). Refugees had a strong preference for resolving cases in camps rather than in the Thai courts, perceiving camp justice to be accessible and culturally familiar while Thai justice was viewed as inaccessible, alien, and risky. Thus, camp justice was not considered second-best to Thai justice but was the preferred approach in most if not all cases.

By contrast, the UNHCR and the IRC's programmes to strengthen refugees' access to justice were rooted in a different legal culture, one that privileged state law, codification and international human rights norms. This shaped their approach to programme design, establishing priorities such as referring cases to Thai courts, bypassing camp reporting structures, codifying camp rules and standardising dispute resolution procedure. These projects were intended to strengthen camp justice but, by seeking to regulate and control it, they undermined the very qualities that permitted these systems to work effectively, including elements of flexibility, consensus, and shared 'common sense'.

Even when international programmes were at their most participatory, they ultimately sought to reduce the autonomy of camp governance and formalise it within the overall structure of Thai law and legal institutions. These projects generated resistance and contestation among refugees with regard to the appropriate role of camp justice, the appropriate role of the Thai justice system, and the appropriate role of international human rights norms. In 2012 I encountered a striking consistency in views across different camps, and indeed among a number of the staff working for international NGOs. All emphasised the importance of confidentiality, so I have avoided identifying any organisations in the excerpts below. These responses encapsulate themes that I heard from multiple sources: sadness that camp justice had been undermined or even dismantled; a recognition that Thai law could never be an effective response for all cases arising from the camps; frustration with the mixed messages from the UNHCR and the IRC; and a loss of confidence in carrying out camp management and justice work:

> Now Thai law influences refugees. All comes from Thai law. It was different in the past. If someone committed a crime they would meet with the Camp Committee, or someone with responsibility to take action. But now, just Thai law, Thai law.[24]
>
> Basically, I think that the UN are very strong about this – the only law is Thai law. And I think that this has sort of been undermining the traditional justice system. Not that there weren't major problems with the traditional system, but instead of trying to improve and work on the traditional system, their mantra is 'Thai law is the only law'. And, for example, they're also against detention in the camps, so they basically say that detention is illegal in the camp. And that

24 Interview conducted in Umpiem Mai camp with a section leader, 27 April 2012.

is problematic when, say, you have domestic violence perpetrators that you want to keep away from a victim for a while. And it's not like the Thai justice system and the Thai police are readily jumping up to fill the justice roles, their justice roles in the camp. So it's kind of like they're directing everyone to go through this justice system that isn't really there.[25]

Camp justice is now not dealing with any cases effectively. The 'absolute jurisdiction' agreement says that camps are not allowed to do anything about serious cases, but IRC–LAC is only functioning effectively in one of seven Karen camps [Mae La]. So how can camps refer? There are no systems. The message from UNHCR and from the Thai Government is that camps can't deal with cases – but no other system is available. And when camps do try to refer, the Thai authorities are not interested in dealing with cases.[26]

Many NGOs explain one policy, then change their mind. For example, in Karenni camps, the NGOs built detention centres and advised the camps on how to use detention more professionally. Then the advice changed: 'No detention is necessary. If it is a serious case, send to the Thai court'. There is no clarity in the message. They have to decide what they want refugees to do. We are not sure what they want us to do.[27]

Part of the problem is that LAC is dominated by lawyers, and dominated by Thai lawyers. They're not committed to a community perspective, they don't understand it. They're committed to state law. There's not enough effort to engage with the community. At the moment, they arrange meetings and don't show up, cancel at the last minute, keep people waiting, don't take time to get to know people. If you want to enhance protection, you have to be someone that people trust to call when there is a situation to be resolved. You need a personal relationship with people.[28]

We are like a very young child, we can't do anything. They [NGOs] don't need us. Also, we are shy and embarrassed in front of our people because we can't help them. [...] We don't want to be the

25 Interview with international NGO staff member (organisation not named to preserve anonymity) 3 May 2012.

26 Interview with KWO central staff member, 10 April 2012.

27 Interview with member of Karenni Refugee Committee, 2 May 2012.

28 Interview with international NGO staff member (organisation not named to preserve anonymity), 4 May 2012.

> Camp Committee anymore if the UN and NGOs don't need us. We are tired of being embarrassed in front of our people. We just want to be simple residents.[29]

Conclusion: Towards a 'strong' legal pluralism

Conditions in the refugee camps in Thailand have changed enormously since 2012, and even more so since my first visit in 2008. In the intervening decade, an international resettlement programme resettled more than 100,000 people from these camps to countries including the United States, Australia, Norway, Denmark, and Japan (International Organisation for Migration 2012). Resettlement was available only to refugees registered in camps prior to 2005. Departures began in 2007 and over the next ten years drained the camps of their longest-standing residents, including camp leaders, teachers and medics as well as key members of civil society organisations such as women's organisations and youth organisations. This created a rupture in leadership and staffing that was a governance crisis in its own right, but which also meant that international interventions in camp management had a more pronounced effect, as they occurred during major internal disruption (Banki and Lang 2007).

More recently, changes in the refugee camps have been driven by politics in Myanmar. The transfer of power to an elected government led by the NLD (National League for Democracy), and a nascent peace process between the Government of Myanmar and ethnic armed organisations, have created a perception among international agencies and donors that there is no longer a need for asylum, and it is time for refugees to 'go home'. Of course, the depth of transformation in Myanmar remains unclear. Three years after the KNU signed the Nationwide Ceasefire Agreement, a survey of more than 2,000 people in Karen State found that they continued to experience insecurity and routinised violence and had little faith that the peace process would succeed (Saferworld and Karen Peace Support Network 2019). Refugees are understandably afraid to return to conditions of conflict and insecurity, but international funding and services have been withdrawn, creating strong pressure

29 Interview conducted in Umpiem Mai Camp with a member of the camp committee, 28 April 2012.

on refugees to return. Several international organisations have stopped working with refugees in Thailand entirely while those that remain are operating with reduced budgets and staff.

By 2018, many programmes in the camps had been closed – in education, health, gender empowerment and administration of justice. The Legal Assistance Centre programme continued to operate in five of the Karen refugee camps, but the American Refugee Committee had closed its operations and support for SGBV committees. The SGBV committee in Mae La Oon had been renamed the 'Community Peace Team' (CPT) and continued to receive funding from UNHCR, but CPT staff were now charged with educating the camp population about voluntary repatriation and staffing the camp's Voluntary Repatriation Centre. The Voluntary Repatriation Centre had been built around two years prior to my visit, staff said, and not one refugee had yet requested repatriation. The KWO continued to operate a camp safe house for abused and vulnerable women and offered emotional and practical support to any women who requested their assistance, but had never resumed its role of assisting in cases referred to Thai courts. There was no evidence of an increase in cases going to Thai courts (I was told that no cases had been referred from Mae La Oon for at least two years before my visit). There was also no improvement in dealing with cases related to gender-based violence. Indeed, in each of these areas the situation appeared markedly worse than during my earlier research. Troublingly, camp-based KWO staff reported that domestic violence and sexual violence were taken less seriously by camp leaders than in the past, and that KWO staff had been marginalised as a voice in camp management and were no longer routinely consulted by the camp committee and section leaders.

I am not suggesting that this outcome is entirely the result of international justice programming. Other extremely important influences on camp governance over the past ten years include the resettlement of experienced camp leaders and women's activists and the withdrawal of international funding, as discussed above. Nevertheless, it is hard to escape the conclusion that elements of the design and implementation of international justice interventions had critical consequences for the camps. Faundez (2012: 178) has warned that it is not enough for international agencies simply to espouse 'legal empowerment': it is also necessary that they understand that non-state justice systems are wholly unlike formal justice systems and require a different form of intervention. Failure to do this is likely to lead to 'the same disappointing results that have plagued most legal and judicial reform projects since their inception', not only failing to strengthen access to justice but actually undermining the limited stability and security that was previously offered. The alternative would require engaging with the political context of non-state justice systems, recognising that work on changing access to justice is explicitly political although it is rarely recognised as such by international development agencies (Isser 2011; Kyed 2011). This approach fits within the new humanitarian aid agenda for 'thinking and working politically' (Laws and Marquette 2018; Teskey 2017). It also relates to Griffiths' conception of strong legal pluralism and the possibility of recognising non-state justice systems as legitimate justice practitioners in their own right, rather than as satellites of a state justice system. For refugees in camps in Thailand, a strong legal pluralism approach would have accepted that a refugee-led justice process was not an existential challenge to Thai sovereignty but could also be a legitimate justice process; that refugees' preferences for camp justice could be a reflection of this legitimacy rather than a sign of oppression; and that there was a value and importance in decision-making taking place by refugees at the local level. This ideological shift away from instinctive deference to state sovereignty would have immediate processual implications for the power dynamics of justice reform, facilitating a genuinely respectful dialogue with refugees about the nature of dispute resolution rather than assuming that the answers must lie with national legal systems and international expertise.

References

Banki, S. & Lang, H.

2007. *Planning for the Future: The Impact of Resettlement on the Remaining Camp Population*. Committee for Coordination of Services to Displaced Persons in Thailand, July 2007.

Cain, M.

1985. 'Beyond informal justice'. *Crime, Law and Social Change* 9(4): 335–73.

CCSDPT/UNHCR

2006. *Analysis of Gaps in Refugee Protection Capacity*. Thailand: UNHCR.

Comaroff, J. & Comaroff, J.

2006. *Law and Disorder in the Postcolony.* Chicago: University of Chicago Press.

de Costa, R.

2006. *The Administration of Justice in Refugee Camps: A Study of Practice.* Geneva, Switzerland: UNHCR.

Denney, L., Bennett, W. & San, K.T.

2016. *Making Big Cases Small and Small Cases Disappear: Experiences of Local Justice in Myanmar.* s.l.: British Council, European Union and MyJustice Myanmar.

Faundez, J.

2012. 'Legal pluralism and international development agencies.' In Brian Tamanaha et al. (eds), *Legal Pluralism and Development: Scholars and Practitioners in Development,* pp. 177–196. Cambridge: Cambridge University Press.

Golub, S.

2003. *Beyond Rule of Law Orthodoxy: The Legal Empowerment Alternative.* Washington: Carnegie Endowment for International Peace.

Griffiths, J.

1986. 'What is legal pluralism?' *Journal of Legal Pluralism and Unofficial Law* 24(1): 1–55.

Harding, J. & Varadan, S.

2010. 'A community-based approach to refugee protection in a protracted refugee situation.' *Humanitarian Exchange Magazine,* Issue 46.

Harper, E.

2011a. *Traditional Justice: Practitioners' Perspectives on Engaging with Customary Justice Systems.* Geneva: IDLO.

2011b. *Customary Justice: From Program Design to Impact Evaluation.* Geneva: IDLO.

Horn, R.

2010. 'Responses to intimate partner violence in Kakuma refugee camp: Refugee interactions with agency systems.' *Social Science & Medicine* 70(1): 160–168.

International Organisation for Migration, IOM

2012. *Resettlement Milestone Reached as 100,000th Refugee Leaves Thai Camps.* UN Migration. www.iom.int/cms/en/sites/iom/home/news-and-views/press-briefing-notes/pbn-2012/pbn-listing/resettlement-milestone-reached-a.html.

International Rescue Committee (IRC)

2007. *Assessment of Protection Issues, with a focus on Access to Justice and the Rule of Law*. s.l.: International Rescue Committee.

2010. *In Thailand, Bringing Justice to Burmese Refugees*. s.l.: International Rescue Committee, reliefweb.int/report/thailand/thailand-bringing-justice-burmese-refugees.

Isser, D.

2011. *Customary Justice and the Rule of Law in War-Torn Societies*. Washington: USIP.

Karen Refugee Committee, KRC

2011. *Rules and Regulations for Refugees (Temporary Asylum Seekers) in the 7 Camps. Revised and Amended by Representatives of the Camps*. s.l.: Karen Refugee Committee, February 2011.

Karen Women's Organisation, KWO

2013. *Salt in the Wound: Justice Outcomes and SGBV Cases in Karen Refugee Camps 2011–2013*. www.burmapartnership.org/wp-content/uploads/2015/11/290995511-Salt-in-the-Wound-Full-Report-English-Version-FINAL-for-Website.pdf.

Kyed, H.M.

2011. 'Legal pluralism and international development interventions.' *Journal of Legal Pluralism* 43(63): 1–24.

2018. 'Introduction to the special issue on everyday justice.' *Independent Journal of Burmese Scholarship* 1(2): ii–xxii.

Laws, E. and Marquette, H.

2018. *Thinking and Working Politically: Reviewing the Evidence on the Integration of Politics into Development Practice over the Past Decade*. TWP Community of Practice. twpcommunity.org/wp-content/uploads/2018/04/Thinking-and-working-politically-reviewing-the-evidence.pdf

Leonardi, C., Isser, D., Moro, L. & Santschi, M.

2011. 'The politics of customary law ascertainment in South Sudan.' *Journal of Legal Pluralism* 43(63): 111–141.

Lubkemann, S., Isser, D. & Chapman, P.

2011. 'Neither state nor custom – just naked power. The consequences of ideals-oriented rule of law policy-making in Liberia.' *Journal of Legal Pluralism* 43(63): 73–110.

McConnachie, K.

2014. *Governing Refugees: Justice, Order and Legal Pluralism*. Abingdon: Routledge.

2012. 'Rethinking the "refugee warrior": The Karen national union and refugee protection on the Thai-Burma Border.' *Journal of Human Rights Practice* 4(1): 30–56.

Nader, L.

1990. *Harmony Ideology: Justice and Control in a Zapotec Mountain Village.* Stanford: Stanford University Press.

Norwegian Refugee Council

2008. *Camp Management Toolkit.* s.l.: Norwegian Refugee Council/Camp Management Project.

Olivius, E.

2013. 'Gender equality and neo-liberal governmentality in refugee camps.' *St. Antony's International Review* 9(1): 53–69.

Saferworld and Karen Peace Support Network

2019. *Security, Justice and Governance in Southeast Myanmar: A Knowledge, Attitudes and Practices Survey in Karen Ceasefire Areas.* www.saferworld.org.uk/resources/publications/1194-security-justice-and-governance-in-south-east-myanmar-a-knowledge-attitudes-and-practices-survey-in-karen-ceasefire-areas.

Teskey, G.

2017. *Thinking and Working Politically: Are we Seeing the Emergence of a Second Orthodoxy?* s.l.: ABT Associates Governance Working Paper Series.

Thawnghmung, A.

2011. *The Other Karen in Myanmar: Ethnic Minorities and the Struggle Without Arms.* Lanham: Lexington Books.

The Border Consortium (TBC)

2019. *Monthly Camp Population Figures.* theborderconsortium.org/.

Thompson, S.

2008. 'Community-based camp management.' *Forced Migration Review* 30: 26–28.

Turcot, P.

2012. *Adaptation, Resilience and Transition: Report of the Formative Evaluation of Camp Management in the Burmese Refugee Camps in Thailand.* Prepared for the Canadian International Development Agency, Australian Agency for International Development and Act for Peace.

UNDP

2018. *Strengthening the Rule of Law and Human Rights for Sustaining Peace and Fostering Development.* UN Development Programme.

Wiuff Moe, L.

2011. 'Hybrid and "everyday" political ordering: Constructing and contesting legitimacy in Somaliland.' *Journal of Legal Pluralism and Unofficial Law* 43(63): 143–178.

Wojkowska, E.

2006. *Doing Justice: How Informal Justice Systems Can Contribute.* Oslo: UNDP.

Index

f=figure (photograph); n=footnote;
bold=extended discussion or key reference

Figure 1.1 Golden sheldrake monument at the entrance to the village. The sheldrake is the symbol of the Mon National Movement, the New Mon State Party (NMSP). Photo by Helene Kyed.

Figure 1.2 Village tract administrator's office where many disputes are heard and settled in the village. Photo by Helene Kyed.

Figure 1.3 Spirit medium performing a ritual. Many villagers go to the spirit medium for consultation, including to hear if they will have luck in successfully resolving a crime or a dispute. Photo by Helene Kyed.

Figure 3.1 Naga New Year celebration in 2018 showing the traditional garments of Naga men. The celebrations bring together the Naga from the different tribes every year and can be seen as part of Naga nation-building. Photo by Myat The Thitsar.

Figure 3.2 Naga New Year celebration in 2018 showing the traditional garments of Naga women. Photo by Myat The Thitsar.

Figure 3.3 View of the rice storage houses in Dah Tri Guy village. Photo by Helene Kyed.

Figure 3.4 Naga Traditional Museum at Township level. Here disputes are resolved by the Naga Literature and Culture Committee and the houses are also used for other traditional activities as well as serving as museums. Photo by Helene Kyed.

Figure 5.1 A view of the village from the Baptist church. Photo by Annika Pohl Harrisson.

Figure 5.2 The weekly service at the local Baptist church in the village. Photo by Annika Pohl Harrisson.

Figure 6.1 Celebration of Karen New Year ceremony in the village attended by Muslims and Buddhists. Photo by Than Pale.

Figure 6.2 Competition among Muslim and Buddhist village children on Independence Day. Photo by Than Pale.

Figure 6.3 Competition among village residents on Independence Day. Photo by Than Pale.

Figure 7.1 Pagoda constructed by the late monk U Thuzana at the entrance of a Muslim mosque in a town near Hpa-An in 2017. Photo by Mikael Gravers.

Figure 7.2 Signboard at the entrance to a Buddhist Karen village. It reads "Drugs & Kalar of other religions no entrance". Photo by Mikael Gravers.

Figure 7.3 The Buddha is placed in a prominent position among the Hindu gods signifying the closeness between Hinduism and Buddhism. Behind the Buddha is a photo of the Karen monk U Thuzana. Photo by Anders Baltzer Jørgensen.

Figure 8.1 In the rainy season the neighbourhood is prone to flooding. Photo by Annika Pohl Harrisson.

Figure 8.2 A few goats on the outskirts of the area. Photo by Annika Pohl Harrisson.

Figure 8.3 Children waiting for their evening meal. Photo by Annika Pohl Harrisson.